THE FEMINIST PACIFIC

Global America

GLOBAL AMERICA
Edited by Jay Sexton and Sarah B. Snyder

Columbia University Press's Global America series pushes the history of U.S. foreign relations in new directions, sharpening and diversifying our understanding of the global dimensions of American history from the colonial era to the twenty-first century. Books in the series explore America's global encounters, including how external forces have shaped the development of the United States and vice versa; why American encounters with the wider world have produced volatility, ruptures, and crises; the shifting contours of U.S. power over time; and the impact of hierarchical attitudes regarding identity in shaping U.S. foreign relations. Taken together, the series analyzes the global history of the United States; its authors employ a diverse range of methodological, chronological, disciplinary, geographical, and ideological perspectives.

Robert B. Rakove, *Days of Opportunity: The United States and Afghanistan Before the Soviet Invasion*

M. Todd Bennett, *Neither Confirm Nor Deny: How the Glomar Mission Shielded the CIA from Transparency*

Dario Fazzi, *Smoke on the Water: Incineration at Sea and the Birth of a Transatlantic Environmental Movement*

The Feminist Pacific

INTERNATIONAL WOMEN'S
NETWORKS IN HAWAIʻI,
1820–1940

Rumi Yasutake

Columbia University Press
New York

Columbia University Press
Publishers Since 1893
New York   Chichester, West Sussex
cup.columbia.edu

Copyright © 2024 Columbia University Press
All rights reserved

Library of Congress Cataloging-in-Publication Data
Names: Yasutake, Rumi, 1958– author.
Title: The feminist Pacific : international women's networks in Hawai'i, 1820–1940 / Rumi Yasutake.
Description: New York : Columbia University Press, [2024] | Series: Global America | Includes bibliographical references and index.
Identifiers: LCCN 2024003380 | ISBN 9780231208529 (hardback) | ISBN 9780231208536 (trade paperback) | ISBN 9780231557474 (ebook)
Subjects: LCSH: Feminism—Hawaii—History. | Feminism—Pacific Area—History. | Feminism—International cooperation.
Classification: LCC HQ1438.H3 Y37 2024 | DDC 305.4209969—dc23/eng/20240124
LC record available at https://lccn.loc.gov/2024003380

Cover design: Milenda Nan Ok Lee
Cover photo: Women on steps of Hulihe'e Palace at its dedication by the Daughters of Hawai'i, June 11, 1928. From the Collection of the Kona Historical Society.

Contents

Introduction 1

1 Women's Separate Sphere and White Settler Colonialism 14

2 The Politics of Woman Suffrage in the U.S. Territory of Hawai'i 43

3 Territorial Motherhood's Double-Edged Sword: Women's Networks and Unequal Sisterhoods 78

4 Elusive Collaboration for Anglophone Hegemony: Maternalists, Liberals, and Internationalists 104

5 Forming the Delegation to the 1928 Pan-Pacific Women's Conference: United States, Hawai'i, Japan, and China 142

6 Pan-Pacific Women's Voices and Global Feminism 177

Epilogue 205

Acknowledgments 209
Abbreviations 213
Notes 217
Selected Bibliography 283
Index 305

THE FEMINIST PACIFIC

Introduction

Men make the roads, but it is women who teach children how to walk.
—FRENCH PROVERB CITED BY JANE ADDAMS[1]

In June 1928, a ceremony dedicated the renovation-in-progress of the Huliheʻe Palace at Kailua-Kona, Island of Hawaiʻi. Built by King Kamehameha I's brother-in-law John Adams Kuakini in 1838, the original palace used native labor and local materials but adopted a plain New England architectural style. In the early nineteenth century, the neighboring Pacific islands were falling under the rule of European imperialists, and the kingdom felt pressed to modernize and "civilize" to fend off foreign powers. Arriving on the islands in 1820, a year after the death of Kamehameha the Great, American missionaries assisted the Hawaiian royalty in this effort, which facilitated Hawaiʻi's integration into globalizing trade and industrial capitalism. In the late nineteenth century, Hawaiʻi saw a thriving sugar industry, an influx of settler labor from around the world, and Hawaiians displaced from their native land. By the end of the century, Native Hawaiians[2] composed only a quarter of the islands' population.[3] The monarchy became increasingly dependent on foreign advisors and systems to sustain domestic unity and to protect Hawaiian sovereignty from foreign threats. After the subsequent fall of Hawaiʻi to U.S. colonial rule, the Huliheʻe Palace, which had symbolized Hawaiʻi's nobility and served as a residence of Hawaiian royalty, faced neglect and oblivion.[4]

At the center of the dedication ceremony was Julie Judd Swanzy (1860–1941), whose family members had been involved, in multiple ways, in the transformation of Hawaiʻi (Figure I.1). Her pioneer American missionary

Figure I.1 Daughters of Hawai'i members and participants gather on the steps of Hulihe'e Palace during the dedication ceremony in June 1928.
Source: From the Collections of Kona Historical Society.

grandmother Laura Fish Judd had supported women rulers of the Kamehameha dynasty. Her mother, Emily C. Cutts Judd, had once served as a lady-in-waiting for Lili'uokalani of the Kalākaua dynasty. Having her parents active in the kingdom's court, Julie's early life evolved in close vicinity to Hawaiian high society. She acquired cultural common ground with Native Hawaiian women chiefs of the highest rank while being a part of a tightly knit circle of the islands' prominent missionary families. After attending the missionary-founded Punahou School and Mills College in California, the first women's college west of the Rockies, Julie spent a few years in Europe. Still, unlike other missionary descendants who intermarried within the circle in Hawai'i or their cohort from the United States, in 1887 Julie married an Irish-born manager of a British enterprise, which campaigned against American settler colonialism in the islands.[5]

The Hulihe'e Palace dedication ceremony occurred two months before the convening of the first Pan-Pacific Women's Conference (PPWC) in 1928. Initiated by Honolulu women leaders, the conference's primary goal was to empower pan-Pacific women collectively to influence local, national, and international policymaking for the education and welfare of the multiracializing and multinationalizing islands' population. Serving as the PPWC's honorary chair, Julie Judd Swanzy symbolically asserted her authority by standing right next to the large *kāhili*, which marked the presence and spiritual protection of an important individual of chiefly rank.[6] It was an appropriation of Hawaiian tradition to assure American settler colonialism. Still, it is a reverse image of Asian and Polynesian rulers in Western costumes asserting their power. Swanzy's action proves the power of Native Hawaiian culture and the people from whom she had to borrow for the conference's success. Furthermore, the scene indicates the hybridization of cultures among women leaders and the daily lives of people in Hawai'i. The dedication ceremony marked efforts to preserve the "Old Hawai'i" legacy that Julie's generation of women in Hawai'i had cherished. A two-day open-to-the-public ceremony began with Christian prayer and ancient Hawaiian chants, followed by Hawaiian songs, dances, and feasts. The final count of attendees exceeded six hundred. Multiracial women's voluntarism enabled the ceremony to take place and possibly raised funds for women's causes.[7] The scene reminds me of Gary Okihiro's advocacy of questioning "normative assumptions about geographies, race, gender, and sexuality" that compose history. The image inspired me to unbound myself from "the binaries" to "reimagine" women's history in Hawai'i and the Pacific.[8]

Two months later, in August 1928, Hawai'i hosted the first PPWC in Honolulu. With Jane Addams as its international chair, it gathered a diverse group of women delegates representing ten Pacific "countries"—Australia, Canada, China, Fiji, Hawai'i, Japan, Korea, New Zealand, the Philippines, Samoa, and the United States—and India. In 1930, the second PPWC, also held in Honolulu, inaugurated the Pan-Pacific Women's Association (PPWA), the first international women's organization with a Pacific focus. The PPWA sought linkage with Atlantic-based feminists' efforts to identify pan-Pacific women's issues and to have them reflected in emerging intergovernmental attempts at peace and justice in Geneva. It convened two more conferences before the eruption of World War II, the third in Honolulu in 1934 and the fourth in Vancouver in 1937.[9]

On the opening day of the first PPWC in 1928, its honorary chair Julie Judd Swanzy extended an "Aloha kakou!," the Hawaiian spirit of "welcome and good will," to the participants.[10] With Native Hawaiian racial generosity, pioneer missionary wives and their women offspring built collaborative relationships with Native Hawaiian women of chiefly rank. These landed

Native Hawaiian daughters, under globalization pressures, often married foreign businessmen to sustain their status. Through close interactions, the two groups of women culturally hybridized, which affected Hawai'i's historical transformation.[11] In postannexation Hawai'i, missionary descendant women joined Native Hawaiian women leaders in demanding women's rights in the newly imposed U.S. system. They also assumed "territorial motherhood" to assure the health and education of the islands' polyglot children and build a common ground among them so that all would become "bona fide" members of the U.S. territory of Hawai'i. To procure cultural mediators, they tapped the transnational women's network pioneered by ancestors from the U.S. Northeast, who had crossed the boundaries of class, race, and nation to engage in women's civilizing mission. A small number of elite bilingual native and settler women, who were essentially missionary clients and protégés at home and abroad, participated in carrying out this territorial motherhood. In the 1920s, multiracial Hawai'i became an "experimental station" for Anglo-Saxon liberal progressives and their collaborator internationalists.[12]

The 1928 PPWC's international chair Jane Addams and her progressive cohort likewise bore "public motherhood"—the authority and responsibility of securing health and education for children of wage-earning migrant and immigrant families at urban industrial centers. Since their arrival at the North American continent, Anglo settler colonialists sought religious, political, and economic liberalism and instituted a republican governing system that accompanied thriving industrial capitalism. Women assumed "republican motherhood"—inculcating republican ideals among children, future citizens of the emerging polity—strictly in the women's home sphere.[13] As the United States expanded westward toward the Pacific, churchwomen activists from the U.S. Northeast pursued their civilizing mission outside of their homes. Missionary wives worked as their husbands' "helpmates" outside the home and established autonomy in the "woman's work for woman and children," cultivating and expanding American civilization outposts.[14] Upholding women's separate sphere, they interacted and networked with native and settler women they encountered on the way to U.S. expansion, while promoting republican ideals and American gender norms.

Addams and her progressive cohort, at the turn of the twentieth century, adopted England-origin settlement work and promoted public education starting in preschools. With their experiences and expertise working with immigrant and migrant wage-earning families, her Hull House "graduates" also pioneered a "female dominion"—a women's autonomous realm of social activism, policymaking, and professions—initially in fields specializing in women and children. Their efforts transformed motherhood from women's private responsibility to evangelical social charity and to public policy and responsibility. Nonetheless, public motherhood was a double-edged sword; its ultimate goal was the assimilation of multiracial and multiethnic children into the expanding white settler republic and U.S. empire. Thus, American women's pursuit of a maternalist mission facilitated the displacement of Indigenous nations and peoples, while mastering, suppressing, or hybridizing each other's cultures along the route of U.S. expansion.[15]

My study borrows the concept of "globalization" as a phenomenon of people's movements and settlements that have recurred since the prehistoric era. To the present day, with its ebbs and flows, globalization has facilitated contact, exchange, hybridization, and convergence.[16] This study examines women's interactions and networking in American missionary–pioneered networks and their relationship to the historical transformation of Hawai'i and northeast Asia in the late modern phase of globalization from 1820 to the 1930s, a time inflicted with colonialism, imperialism, and war.

The resulting historical narrative revisits Amy Kaplan's reinterpretation of the "anarchy of empire," a concept conceived by W. E. B. Du Bois, who challenged the imperialist claim that anarchy abroad caused imperialist intervention.[17] He argued that the "anarchy of empire" shattered national boundaries for racial exploitation on a global scale. By exposing the deceptive distinction between the foreign and domestic, male and female spheres, nation-state and colonies, and so on, Du Bois envisioned a "unity of the world" and "world citizenship" of the exploited people of color that would transcend the colonial dominance and challenge destruction caused by the anarchy of empire.[18] Paying attention to the "confounding of borders" in her study of cultural representations, Kaplan defies Du Bois's global color line and presents the "anarchy of empire" as "a network of power relations that changes over space and time and is riddled with instability, ambiguity, and disorder, rather than as a monolithic system of domination that the very word 'empire' implies." In her view, the term refers to "the destruction and exploitation" of the colonized but also suggests "internal contradictions, ambiguities, and frayed edges" of imperial powers, invalidating any binary divisions.[19]

The arrival of the Protestant West, which followed the Catholic West, ushered the Americas and the Pacific into the modern phase of globalization. Ports were forcefully opened for explorers, traders, diplomats, and missionaries, who settled to exchange goods, ideas, and peoples globally. The competing Western powers' modern technology and military strength awed the locals. Western material comforts and Anglo-Saxon liberalism captivated them. In the nineteenth century, peoples endeavored to adopt modern state systems, generate nationalism, and introduce industrial capitalism. They needed to enrich and strengthen their nations for survival and development. In the process, rural labor moved to international industrial centers for agricultural and industrial production. Premodern, externally restricted exchange or isolation, which had provided stability for feudalistic and self-supporting societies, collapsed, leading to new phases of social and economic upheaval. Those with luck, resources, or ambition emulated modern ways, and many successfully rode the globalization wave. Those who did not became marginalized, displaced, or exploited in the social transformation, and some became migrants, settlers, or refugees. By the end of the nineteenth century, the gap among peoples and countries widened, and inter- and intra-national inequality and injustice expanded, leading to labor radicalism, ideological contention, ethnic/racial nationalism, colonialism/imperialism, and counter–colonialism/imperialism. The Pacific thus became vulnerable to competing and interplaying colonial/imperial ambitions of Europeans, Americans, and Japanese, who were also inflicted with rapid globalization.[20]

A Pacific narrative of late modern globalization could be told as a male story in which Protestant men forged a brotherhood of liberal religious, political, economic, and civic leaders to cope with volatile human relations at the turn of the century.[21] Nonetheless, women and gender issues were at its heart. Recent scholarly works with a Pacific focus adopt gender perspectives in examining and theorizing trans-Pacific movements of peoples and the resulting phenomena.[22] Among them are studies on the PPWCs and the PPWA, which situated the pan-Pacific women's networking and solidarity building in twentieth-century transnational and international contexts. The women's sphere or dominion was never separate or fully independent of the men's sphere or empire. Still, women attempted to build pan-Pacific women's collective power in order to overcome social divides and injustices caused by a rapidly globalizing world while advancing the status of women and children. For example, historian Paul Hooper claimed that the PPWA was "the first women's group anywhere to be founded upon transcultural premises."[23] Historian Angela Woollacott, who compared the PPWA to the London-based British Commonwealth League (BCL), argued that the PPWA, with its modest goals of promoting friendly interactions and exchanges, was less effective in promoting feminist issues but was potentially more progressive and inclusive than the BCL, which pressed a unified feminist agenda.[24] Meanwhile, historian Fiona Paisley, who illuminated the complex interplay of modernity, culture, colonialism, and racism in the politics of PPWCs from 1928 to 1958, cautioned against the progressiveness of the PPWA's "cultural internationalism." According to Paisley, British Commonwealth women, who experienced the "decolonization" process, began criticizing the conditions of indigenous women in settler colonies or under white colonial rule. Nonetheless, because of "impregnable" feminist Orientalism, the PPWA's "central rhetoric" of "cultural internationalism" assured that only white settler women could assume guardianship of "a new world civilization," ensuring that nonwhite women's participation relied on Anglo-Saxon cultural criteria.[25] Furthermore, burgeoning global feminist studies began including the PPWA/PPWCs in their discussion of global-scale feminist movements in the twentieth century. For example, Dorothy Sue Cobble's study of American feminists' global fights for democratic equality examined their interest in the first two PPWCs and their support for international labor legislation.[26] Yet these comprehensive scholarly works abstracted the PPWA from the local sociohistorical contexts of its birthplace, Honolulu, Hawai'i.

Building on those studies, this book encompasses over a century, from 1820 to the 1930s, and traces the origin of the PPWA in ongoing transnational, interracial and interethnic, and intercultural women's interactions in Hawai'i and around the American missionary–pioneered women's network. The network connected treaty port cities, which developed into globalization hubs that served as American civilization outposts and world trade and industrial centers. This study focuses on women's experiences in Hawai'i, especially Honolulu, a conspicuous globalization hub during the days of ocean travel. It also sheds light on the local sociohistorical milieu of the United States, China, and Japan—three of the Hawai'i settlers' homelands that sent delegations to the PPWCs. The historical narrative of this study illuminates "the confounding of borders" between East and West, white and nonwhite, settlers and natives, men and women, colonizers and colonized, and so on. It links the movements labeled "Christian" and those considered secular, which have often been discussed separately.

Furthermore, it crystalizes ambiguity and elusiveness in the labels of conservative, progressive, liberal, feminist, or antifeminist women's movements, which were retrospectively attached to and often based on their national leaders' inclinations.

With the growing U.S. presence in the Pacific at the beginning of the twentieth century, noted American women leaders—such as Jane Addams and Carrie Chapman Catt, along with Hawai'i local Julie Judd Swanzy—gained influence in shaping elite women's interactions and movements based in Hawai'i. Their socially active churchwomen ancestors from the U.S. Northeast pursued a civilizing mission. They had initiated various strands of women's movements—to save the unfortunate, abolish slavery, demand women's rights and equality, and "civilize" societies to be more women-friendly. Some had sought trans-Atlantic collaboration while generating woman suffrage movements in the land that fell under U.S. republican rule.[27] Others had joined home or foreign missionary enterprises and moved westward through the continent or the ocean to circle around the world. The latter had opened women's homes and schools at American civilization outposts and produced a pool of women who emulated American middle-class women's ways. These missionary clients and protégés constituted the backbone of interracial and trans-Pacific women's networks, through which Anglo-Saxon–origin women's movements not only expanded to but also indigenized in countries in the Pacific.[28] Accordingly, it was not surprising, during the interwar-year rise of women's internationalism, that diverse women's movements intersected and converged in Hawai'i, the crossroads of the Pacific. Addams, Catt, and Swanzy each exercised their influence over pan-Pacific women's organizing for motherhood, human equality, social justice, and world peace.

Addams, Catt, and Swanzy crystallized the changing nature of American women's movements in the early twentieth century. They were the first generation of women with a college education. They sought scientific knowledge and pragmatic expertise, instead of religious and moral discourse to mold social, legal, and political systems to achieve their goals. Nonetheless, their movements were elite-white-centric and imperialistic. Carrie Chapman Catt and her cohort, who had led the American woman suffrage movement to victory, promoted voter education and public opinion building. They also sought international cooperation advocating the vote for women that was premised on the installment of electoral systems.[29] Meanwhile, Addams's Hull House residents and graduates witnessed the misery of wage-earning migrant and immigrant families who lived in ethnically segregated U.S. industrial centers.[30] Concurrently, globalizing laissez-faire industrial capitalism also transformed American overseas civilizing outposts into bustling industrial centers with an influx of multinational labor that suffered exploitation and poverty. These women leaders' international and interracial experiences slowly corrected the imperialistic stance and elite white centricity in their movements.

New Woman progressives and missionaries developed a renewed sense of mission to combat injustices caused by the modern state system, patriarchal gender norms, racism, and Western-antecedent industrialization, mechanization, and consumer culture. They willingly transferred their feminist expertise and scientific knowledge to all who needed them. At the same time, they embraced the norms of their clients and protégés through cross-cultural interactions. Consequently, the women's interactions and movements in the Pacific underwent cultural hybridization in their quest for common ground and collective power to advance the status of women and children locally, nationally, and internationally.

After World War I, when intergovernmental organizations—e.g., the League of Nations and the International Labour Organization (ILO)—formed in Geneva, strands of globalizing women's organizations of religious and secular brands sought collective power in pressuring the emerging male-led new world order to reflect women's voices. While European imperial powers diminished in the Pacific, American and British dominion white women, joined by elite, nonwhite, bilingual women, endeavored to find and vocalize pan-Pacific women's causes in the international arena. They participated in forging a Pacific-based women's community to affect feminist globalism radiating from Geneva.[31]

Nonetheless, the PPWA's attempts at building pan-Pacific women's solidarity and collective power to resist and regulate transnational industrial-capitalist ventures, settler colonialism, and imperialism were complicit with male-instituted nation-state systems and their nationalist, colonialist, or imperialist aspirations. Ongoing interactions and solidarity building in the women's networks pioneered by missionaries were contradictory, unstable, and illusive. This book traces how women leaders of differing cultural, racial, and national backgrounds and feminist consciousness, prudently, undauntedly, and persistently pursued transracial, transethnic, and transnational women's collective power in Honolulu, Hawai'i.

The first chapter, "Women's Separate Sphere and White Settler Colonialism," provides a brief gendered history of the Hawaiian Kingdom from 1820 to 1898. It discusses the contradictory nature of American missionaries' altruistic civilizing efforts, which were bounded by white women's "cult of womanhood." Missionary wives assisted Hawaiian women rulers in asserting authority over their subjects and rivals and protecting the kingdom from European imperialism. Nonetheless, their social activism was complicit with their male counterparts' advocacy of liberalism in facilitating "democracy," private land ownership, individualism, and industrial capitalism. Their activism curtailed Native Hawaiian women's genealogy-based political and economic power, leading to the rise of the white male oligarchy in the islands and U.S. seizure of Hawai'i in 1898.

"The Politics of Woman Suffrage in the U.S. Territory of Hawai'i," chapter 2, focuses on Hawai'i's vibrant woman suffrage movement between 1898 and 1922. Although Hawai'i, against the will of Native Hawaiians, fell under a white male oligarchy and U.S. colonial rule, mainland suffragists did not resist the installation of a republican system. Instead, they pursued their civilizing mission of bringing the vote—the best of U.S. "civilization"—to women of the islands. Carrie Chapman Catt visited Hawai'i in 1912 to generate a woman suffrage movement, and local Native Hawaiian women most enthusiastically responded to her call. For them, demanding suffrage was premised on their acceptance of U.S. colonial rule. Nonetheless, suffrage was a "legal" step forward to recover their political and economic rights lost under the U.S. system. Writing and amending the Hawaiian territorial constitution to give women the vote was in the hands of the U.S. Congress. Local Native Hawaiian and white women leaders, who had been divided over the U.S. annexation, came together to maneuver their way through the territorial and federal legislatures for their enfranchisement. This chapter discusses the process of reconciliation, negotiation, and cultural hybridization among Native Hawaiian, local settler, and mainland suffragists in their suffrage movements before, during, and after World War I. Still, it was not until the Nineteenth Amendment was extended to U.S. territories in 1920 that women in Hawai'i secured the right to vote. Women leaders in Hawai'i, who learned a lesson from their fruitless suffrage movements, tapped the networks they built through wartime patriotic efforts to forge transracial women's collective power. They successfully pressed male politicians in Hawai'i and on Capitol Hill to achieve, in 1922, full "suffrage"—the right to vote for *and* be elected to territorial public office.

Chapter 3, "Territorial Motherhood's Double-Edged Sword: Women's Networks and Unequal Sisterhoods," examines Hawai'i's white settler women's leadership in carrying out territorial motherhood between 1894 and the 1920s. By then, the Native Hawaiian population had declined, and Hawai'i's booming sugar industry had become increasingly dependent on settler labor. Born-in-Hawai'i children, especially those of Asian ancestry, surged in number in the early twentieth century. To avoid transethnic labor movements, planters kept workers in ethnically segregated camps where each spoke their mother tongue. Pidgin became the medium of choice for interethnic communications, establishing itself as the primary language of ethnic children. Anglophone progressives in Honolulu led a double-edged territorial motherhood—while securing a liberal preschool education and improved health for these future voters, they aimed to establish Anglophone cultural hegemony and Americanize the islands' multiethnic children and their families. To realize this goal, Honolulu women leaders sought guidance from mainland progressives as well as cultural mediation from Hawai'i's missionary descendants and their bilingual protégés working in local communities or the settlers' homelands. This chapter addresses Honolulu maternalists' struggles with Hawai'i's paternalist planter oligarchs, who supported women's work, but only when it concurred with their own interests. It also takes an American-Japanese case to interrogate women's relationships with trans-Pacific capitalist-imperialist ventures and networks.

The fourth chapter, "Elusive Collaboration for Anglophone Hegemony: Maternalists, Liberals, and Internationalists," considers how Honolulu-based women leaders became inspired to convene an exclusively women's international conference in the 1920s. By then, the aspirations of Hawai'i's white male oligarchs for brotherhood had generated male-led pan-Pacific movements and inaugurated two male-led international organizations—the Pan-Pacific Union (PPU) and the Institute of Pacific Relations (IPR)—in Hawai'i. Pressed for 100 percent Americanism during and after World War I, Honolulu women intensified their efforts to make private, charitable kindergarten work a public responsibility. By assisting the PPU and the IPR in holding international meetings and conferences, Honolulu women reinforced traditional gender roles but bolstered local women's networks for voluntarism. Their collective efforts successfully placed the maternalist causes at the front stage of the pan-Pacific movements. In the process, white women leaders also collaborated with liberal internationalist men from the U.S. mainland and Asian countries. Nonetheless, trans-Pacific and mixed-gender attempts to promote English-medium public kindergarten education ran afoul of plantation worker communities. Parents desired children to command their mother tongue and traditions, and the most vocal opposition came from the Japanese community. Consequently, Honolulu maternalists experienced complex political entanglements that led to Hawai'i's "foreign-language school controversy." This chapter examines how such events inspired Honolulu women leaders and their collaborators to convene the women-only PPWC by gathering women leaders from the settlers' homelands.

Chapter 5, "Forming the Delegation to the 1928 Pan-Pacific Women's Conference: United States, Hawai'i, Japan, and China," examines how Honolulu organizers navigated the waters of the local white oligarchy, the trans-Pacific patriarchy, and the rising tide of Atlantic-based women's internationalism to convene the first PPWC in 1928. By then, PPU and IPR international conferences had already brought internationally active women leaders to Honolulu. National League of Women Voters (NLWV) and National Woman's Party (NWP) members were reluctant to participate in Hawai'i's maternalist-initiated gender-specific PPWC. This chapter examines the sociohistorical contexts of the delegation-forming process in Hawai'i and three of its settler homelands: the U.S. mainland, Japan, and China. It unearths Jane Addams's service as international chair, maternalist women's enthusiasm, and the multilayered intentions of each delegate to participate in the first PPWC, which came about through the PPU's funding and women's voluntarism.

Chapter 6, "Pan-Pacific Women's Voices and Global Feminism," examines women's interactions at the four PPWCs held before World War II. It illuminates how women's exchanges at and off the conference site convinced initially dubious PPWC participants to form a permanent organization, the PPWA, at the second PPWC held in Honolulu in 1930. The purpose of the PPWA was to prepare for future PPWCs and link the pan-Pacific women's community to globalizing Geneva-based women's endeavors to influence intergovernmental policymaking. This chapter then provides an overview of the turbulent 1930s, when women's relations were strained. Hawai'i, under U.S. colonial rule, experienced racial, sexual, and class prejudices over the infamous Massie Affair, a false rape allegation against local men of color by a white woman socialite. Furthermore, when the transnational women's community failed to take decisive action against Japan's military aggression and establishment of a puppet state in China's northeast,

Chinese women internationalists felt antagonized. Although the PPWA did not take any official action regarding the antilynching demonstration held by a group of Black women activists who burst onto the stage of the fourth PPWC in Vancouver, participants were awakened to the intricacies that gender, race/ethnicity, class, and cultural tradition played in forming identity. The event also pressed them to diligently seek common ground among women from diverse backgrounds for solidarity to achieve global justice. A fifth PPWC, under the theme of "Practical Ways and Means of Promoting International Understanding," was scheduled to be held in New Zealand in 1940 but was canceled due to the onset of World War II. Nonetheless, the PPWA continuously lent its ears to multiple and multilayered women's voices to forge pan-Pacific women's collective power to affect intergovernmental policymaking.

The epilogue discusses the PPWA's resilience in sustaining the trans-Pacific women's community for friendly interactions and bonding among women from diverse backgrounds. It lists significant events after World War II, to which trans-Pacific women's collective power-building and globalizing feminist attempts at justice and equality had contributed.

CHAPTER 1

Women's Separate Sphere and White Settler Colonialism

On January 24, 1895, six months after the inauguration of the Republic of Hawai'i, Queen Lili'uokalani, the eighth and last reigning monarch of the Hawaiian Kingdom, officially stepped down from the throne. The kingdom she had reigned over had been in the hands of a small group of white American settler men who engineered a coup d'état to form a provisional government in January 1893. Although the white men's pleadings with the United States to annex the islands had failed, they managed to convene an all-male constitutional convention to write a new constitution for the republic, thereby overriding the kingdom's 1887 constitution. On July 4, 1894, the Republic of Hawai'i was inaugurated despite strong opposition from Native Hawaiians. Sanford Ballard Dole (1844–1926), son of an American missionary couple and cousin of the Hawaiian Pineapple Company founder, assumed the presidency of both the short-lived provisional government and the Republic of Hawai'i.[1]

On January 16, 1895, an aborted counterrevolution placed Queen Lili'uokalani, who was then in exile, under house arrest on suspicion that she had known of the multiracial counterinsurgent attempt. Central to the rebellion was Robert William Wilcox (1855–1903), son of an American father and a Hawaiian mother of chiefly lineage.[2] Among those who joined Wilcox were Native Hawaiian and settler men, including Lili'uokalani's nephew Prince Jonah Kūhiō Kalaniana'ole (Prince Kūhiō, 1871–1922) and

[14]

white missionary son Charles Thomas Gulick (1841–1897).[3] To avoid bloodshed and in exchange for the release of loyal supporters who participated in the counterrevolution, Lili'uokalani officially abdicated and swore allegiance to the Republic of Hawai'i.[4]

To Lili'uokalani's bitter astonishment, her former subjects and retainers, white and Native Hawaiian, were among the all-male executors at her abdication. Compounding her humiliation was enforced compliance with the U.S. practice of coverture, a legal doctrine in which women, upon marriage, had their legal rights and obligations subsumed under their husband's. Lili'uokalani strongly resented being identified by the family name of her late husband, John Owen Dominis (1832–1891). She wrote:

> The Provisional Government nor any other had enacted any change in my name. All my official acts, as well as my private letters, were issued over the signature of Liliuokalani. But when my jailers required me to sign "Liliuokalani Dominis," I did as they commanded. Their motive in this as in other actions was plainly to humiliate me before my people and before the world. . . . There is not, and never was, within the range of my knowledge, any such a person as Liliuokalani Dominis.[5]

Located at the crossroads of the Pacific, Hawai'i in the nineteenth century was a "gender frontier," where the gender system of the islands encountered, competed with, and negotiated with variants of Christian and Confucian cultures.[6] The arrival of British explorer Captain James Cook drew the islands into late eighteenth-century globalization and ensuing settler colonialism by peoples from throughout the world. Following the explorers, traders, and whalers, the first company of American missionaries—seven missionary couples with their children and four young Hawaiians, three of whom were educated at the Foreign Mission School in Connecticut—arrived in Hawai'i in 1820. Engrossed by the evangelical fever of the Second Great Awakening, the American Board of Commissioners for Foreign Missions (hereafter, the American Board or ABCFM) dispatched more than a hundred missionary men and women in twenty companies to work for its "Sandwich Islands" Mission between 1820 and 1848.[7] Among them were missionary wives who advocated the U.S. Northeast's "cult of true womanhood" and moral standards among the multiracializing and ethnicizing peoples of the islands.

Following in the footsteps of these pioneer missionaries were their relatives, friends, and neighbors, seeking an outlet for their evangelical zeal and economic aspirations. With the missionary charge of saving "heathens," they embarked on a grand endeavor of "civilizing" and "uplifting" Hawai'i. Their self-claimed altruism promoted not only their religious, political, and economic systems but also their patriarchal gender ideology and separate sphere strategy, which encouraged women's bondage and enforced women's domesticity and subordination.[8]

The abdication document signed under the name of "Lili'uokalani Dominis" symbolized the fall of the Hawaiian monarchy and the triumph in the islands of the nineteenth-century American systems. The abridgment of Native Hawaiian sovereignty and women's rights went hand in hand with prevailing American political and economic liberalism, which facilitated individual land ownership and settler colonialism. The increasing pressure for modernization and industrialization slowly transferred the authority of high-ranking Native Hawaiian men and women to settler men. In their pursuit of a civilizing mission, American Board missionary wives facilitated this process by promoting their gender ideology and strategy.

The long-complicated process of settler colonialism in Hawai'i, which culminated in Lili'uokalani's abdication in 1895 and the U.S. annexation in 1898, involved gender, race, class, nation, and "civilization." In particular, unlike in nineteenth-century U.S. society, "miscegenation" and cross-racial adoption were openly accepted in Hawai'i, creating blood mixing and cultural hybridization. This chapter examines the intricate relationship between American women's civilizing mission, prevailing political and economic liberalism, and settler colonialism in transforming the Kingdom of Hawai'i into a republic and later a territory of the United States.[9]

Native Hawaiian Women Chiefs and Missionary Wives: Rank Versus Gender

The ascendancy of U.S. missionaries in the Hawaiian Kingdom put enormous pressure on the freedom that women enjoyed in political, economic, social, and sexual activities.[10] Traditionally in Hawai'i, there was a sexual division of labor, but *rank* rather than gender or race was the most important denominator of power and status. Rank was determined by genealogies, which traced ancestries of *ali'i* (the highest rank of rulers determined by genealogy) to the world of male and female deities recorded in *kumulipo* (creation mythology), and by individual relationship to *aliʻi* chiefs.[11] As of 1820, Native Hawaiian women and men participated in political and economic activities and enjoyed freedom in choosing partners and dissolving relationships. Significantly, ruling-rank women were expected to assume religious, political, and economic leadership.[12]

It was 1820, a year after the death of Kamehameha the Great (Kamehameha I), when missionary wives from the Northeast of the United States began arriving in Hawaiʻi, and two of Kamehameha I's wives, Kaʻahumanu (1768–1832) and Keōpūolani (ca. 1778–1823), gained power, creating gender opportunities and crisis. Kaʻahumanu was Kamehameha's favorite wife and considered "the most imposing figure among the native rulers." Keōpūolani was the mother of both Liholiho (Kamehameha II, reigning from 1819–1824) and Kauikeaouli (Kamehameha III, reigning from 1825–1854). After the death of Kamehameha I in 1819, these influential women publicly defied *kapu* (taboos) by symbolically dining with future kings, Kamehameha II and III. Based on the Polynesian dichotomy of male and female qualities, *kapu* defined women as the profane or dangerous sex because of menstruation blood and the life-threatening delivery process. Accordingly, *kapu* worked more oppressively for women than men.[13] For example, *ʻai kapu* (eating taboo) prohibited women from eating certain foods and dining with men. In breaking *ʻai kapu*, Kaʻahumanu and Keōpūolani ultimately liberated themselves and all other women regardless of rank from the gender system, but they also shook the Hawaiian spiritual tradition that assured *aliʻi* chiefs of power, privilege, and authority.[14]

Still, in the early nineteenth century, rank preempted gender distinctions. The appointment of Kaʻahumanu to the office of *kuhina-nui* (regent/premier) confirmed her role during the king's childhood and as co-ruler after his coming of age. When Kamehameha II unexpectedly died on tour in Europe in 1824, his younger brother Kauikeaouli, then only eleven years old, ascended the throne, becoming Kamehameha III. During his reign, Kaʻahumanu, *kuhina-nui* at the time, assumed enormous power in the position until her death in 1832. Elizabeth Kīnaʻu (Kaʻahumanu II, ca. 1805–1839), a daughter born to Kamehameha I and one of Kamehameha II's primary wives, then became *kuhina-nui*.[15]

In contrast, the United States, a white settler republic, had rebelled against the hereditary privileges of monarchs and nobles, and thus gender more than class or rank determined individual behavior and status among white citizens.

White women citizens assumed "republican motherhood," nurturing sons at home to assume their bona fide citizenship in the American republic, but women were excluded from the male sphere of politics and moneymaking. In the U.S. Northeast, the headstream for America's Great Awakenings and subsequent home and foreign missionary movements, a woman was defined as man's helpmate and subordinate. Furthermore, the common law theory of coverture made a married woman legally incapable and her husband's dependent. Thus, wives were denied sexual freedom, suffrage, property ownership, ordination, and even public speaking. Nonetheless, middle-class churchwomen were reluctant to challenge the emerging gender ideology of "true womanhood" that prescribed women to be innately domestic, submissive, pious, and pure. Instead, they made the home women's autonomous sphere. They created a world separate from the male sphere, where women were not only bounded by a "cult of womanhood" but also bonded with each other for solace, friendship, and solidarity.[16] Because only women of economic means could embody this "true womanhood," it became the hallmark of the respectable nineteenth-century American middle class and its "civilized" status.[17]

In the Second Great Awakening, fiery churchwomen used the separate sphere strategy to engage in collective "woman's work for woman and children" outside of their home and community. They crossed the boundaries of class, race, and nation but not gender. American missionary wives reproduced segregated male and female spheres through their work in Hawai'i. At the same time, as historian Patricia Grimshaw points out, they brought with them "the full force of the American's material wealth, skills, undeniable altruism, and forceful personal attributes."[18] Laura Fish Judd (1804–1872), grandmother of Julie Judd Swanzy who would later become a conspicuous mediator between Native Hawaiian and settler societies, arrived in Honolulu in 1828, accompanying her missionary-doctor husband, Gerrit Parmele Judd (1803–1873). Laura Judd won the trust and favor of the regent Ka'ahumanu and her successor Kīna'u. She encouraged them to wear Western attire and use modern tools to awe their subjects and foes, which contributed to stabilizing the rule of the Kamehameha dynasty and protecting the kingdom from foreign imperialism.[19]

Concurrently, having been integrated into the global trade networks, Hawai'i was exposed to foreign germs, liquor, a cash economy, and the threat of foreign imperialism. Hawai'i desperately needed foreign solutions to the foreign problems. American missionaries were enthusiastic in transferring their knowledge and technologies to Hawaiians and "uplifting" and modernizing their society. Hawaiian female and male *aliʻi* chiefs willingly lent them their ears. With their support and enthusiasm, American missionaries developed the Hawaiian alphabet and built a printing press so that the people on the islands could read the Bible in Hawaiian. The missionaries also founded schools, churches, and dispensaries. Hawaiians, regardless of rank, age, or sex, were eager to learn the new means of communication and modern Western knowledge and customs. Consequently, Hawaiʻi quickly emerged as one of the most literate nations in the world and, in turn, embraced patriarchal New England values and standards.[20]

Native Hawaiian *aliʻi* chiefs embraced the cultural and social transformation for their survival and advancement in the early nineteenth century. At their request, the Judds, along with their fellow American Board missionaries, assisted Juliette Montague Cooke (1812–1896) and her husband Amos Starr Cooke (1810–1871) to build and manage the Chiefs' Children's School, which later became the Royal School, an English-language boarding school specifically for *aliʻi* children. Among the sixteen children who attended the school, five later became monarchs of the kingdom, including Queen Liliʻuokalani who came under its instruction at the age of four. Also among the sixteen were Bernice Pauahi, who married New England banker Charles Reed Bishop, and Queen Emma, who married King Kamehameha IV. Juliette Cooke had fought hard to attain higher education for herself and was eager to provide her female students with instruction in more than reading and writing. She added algebra, geography, history, and natural philosophy (physics).[21] At the same time, the Cookes disciplined young *aliʻi* sons and daughters to become "God-fearing," highly cultivated leaders of their own people and to embrace Western high culture and the civility that would meet New England's puritanical standard. Their stern methods often made *aliʻi* children rebellious, later reviving Hawaiian tradition and nationalism during their reigns.[22]

Missionary wives who established close relationships with the women and daughters of Hawaiian royal families contributed to a cultural hybridization between their own children and the children of Hawaiian royalty. Both groups became fluent in English and Hawaiian and developed deeper understandings of the two traditions than their parents' generation. Also, the Hawaiian custom of child adoption, *hānai*, entrusted white settler families to raise Hawaiian *aliʻi* daughters as their adopted children. In the case of Laura Judd, while she refused to have any of her daughters adopted by Hawaiian royals, she accepted Kīna'u as the middle name for one of her daughters.[23] Later, one of her sons, Albert Francis Judd (1838–1900), made a *hānai* arrangement for Irene Ha'alou Kahalelaukoa 'Ī'ī (1869–1922), a daughter of leading Hawaiian educator and politician John Papa 'Ī'ī, to be raised by American Board missionary Reverend Charles McEwen Hyde (1832–1899) and his wife Mary T. Knight Hyde (1840–1917).[24]

American missionary wives, who closely interacted with *ali'i* women, also played a role in creating a strong foothold for the evangelization and Americanization of the islands. Ka'ahumanu and Keōpūolani urgently needed to fulfill the spiritual vacancy that they had created by breaking *kapu*. Consequently, they were susceptible to the new religion and "civilization" promoted by American missionaries. The Great Kamehameha's wives, Ka'ahumanu and Keōpūolani, and his daughter Kīna'u became avid students of reading and writing. They fell under the influence of Christianity and advocated fervently for the missionary women and their codes of behavior. The kingdom's legal system, which emerged in the 1820s and 1830s, imposed Christian monogamy and outlawed incest, polygamy, polyandry, bigamy, extramarital relationships, prostitution, and any other "illicit" intercourse. Sumptuary laws were also introduced to combat "immorality," such as intemperance and gambling. Hawaiian "pagan" customs, including the "obscene" body movements of hula that could accompany chants linking *ali'i* to their divine ancestors, were prohibited.[25] Pioneer missionary wives contributed to reformulating gender mechanisms, which eventually undermined the divine authority of Hawaiian *ali'i* chiefs and their rank-oriented social system.

These women's influence encouraged Hawai'i to adopt not only the religion, morality, science, and lifestyles advocated by American missionaries but also their ideal patriarchal state system.[26] Despite the influence they attained over the Hawaiian monarchy, missionary wives were circumscribed by the U.S. gender ideology and did not take official leadership. When the kingdom government began to recruit American missionaries and other foreigners to fill its offices, it was *men*, not women, who assumed those official positions. The long-standing secretary of the American Board, Rufus Anderson, emphasized evangelization over civilization and disapproved of missionaries engaging in political and economic affairs in their mission fields. Accordingly, some settler missionaries in the islands, including Laura's missionary-doctor husband Gerrit P. Judd, discontinued formal relationships with the American Board to serve in key government positions.[27]

These men became the main promoters of U.S. ideals of "democracy" and "freedom" in Hawai'i.

Once American male missionaries joined the kingdom government, the ideals they advocated set the course for Hawai'i to slowly adopt the U.S. model, in which only white men were full-fledged citizens able to enjoy the privileges of democracy and freedom. It was in this context that in 1839 Kamehameha III was said to have "voluntarily" made significant concessions to his subjects by issuing the so-called first kingdom's constitution, of which the English version proclaimed: "God hath made of one blood all nations of *men*, to dwell on the face of the earth in unity and blessedness." The 1839 constitution also assured the "same protection" of "chiefs and people" under "one and the same law." Protection by law extended to not only life, body, liberty, and labor or work but also "their lands, their building lots, and all their property." The 1839 constitution developed into the detailed constitution of 1840, equipping the monarchy with partially separated executive, judicial, and legislative powers. In addition to the hereditary House of Nobles, it created an elected House of Representatives.[28]

In reality, the promulgation of the 1840 constitution was another step in making the Hawaiian monarchy correspond to the U.S. model of patriarchal statehood.[29] Nonetheless, Hawai'i's gender egalitarianism persisted, including women's official involvement in kingdom politics. In the House of Nobles, the former Council of Chiefs, approximately a third of the members were women.[30] Public school education was also introduced to the kingdom in 1840 but was conducted in Hawaiian,[31] which allowed the sustenance of rank-based Hawaiian culture and traditions. Although the Act of 1842 organized a jury system—by which Hawaiians tried Hawaiians, foreigners tried foreigners, and Hawaiians and foreigners tried each other in a mixed case—women were included in jury duty and judgeships.[32]

Efforts made by white settler men to "democratize" Hawai'i, however, met prevailing New England gender norms, entailing the legal abridgment of high-ranking Hawaiian women's rights and freedom. The declaration of human rights and the introduction of the constitutional monarchy began to disturb traditional Hawaiian communal relationships based on rank and kinship. New individualistic social relationships regulated by laws were based more on gender than rank. The legal status of women in Hawai'i slowly approximated that of early nineteenth-century New England. By 1845, the common law practice of coverture was codified, and *kuhina-nui* (regency) was no longer reserved for influential women. In 1853, the married woman's right to bring a case to court was disabled. In 1860, a married woman was required to adopt her husband's name. Nonetheless, a number of *aliʻi* women never abided by these laws.[33]

Versed in the modern system, white settler men replaced male and female Hawaiian chiefs as the king's counselors and administrators in governing the islands. Hawaiʻi's feudal system of communal land tenure began accommodating itself to the Western concept of private ownership. The Land Commission was created in 1845 and carried out the Great Māhele (land division), in which Kamehameha III agreed to divide all the lands of Hawaiʻi among the monarch, chiefs, and commoners. The monarch's share was further divided into Crown and government lands; the latter would be managed, leased, or sold in accordance with the will of the legislature for the benefit of the Hawaiian government. By the end of 1850, new laws opened up ways for Native Hawaiian commoners and foreigners to purchase land under fee simple ownership.[34]

These changes slowly encroached upon high-ranking Native Hawaiian women's power, while expanding foreign men's rights, regardless of race or nationality. The kingdom's mid-1840s naturalization laws allowed foreigners who pledged allegiance to the king the same status as Native Hawaiian subjects. Furthermore, in 1850, the government agreed to create a new category of "denizenship" to maintain the loyalty of foreigners who rendered important services to the kingdom. Denizens were aliens to whom the king granted "letters patent of denization," entitling them all rights, privileges, and immunities of a Native Hawaiian. Thus, male foreigners "desirable to the kingdom" could enjoy every right granted to Native Hawaiian men, including suffrage and land ownership, without giving up their homeland citizenship.[35]

Despite the prevailing American gender system, "miscegenation" remained widely accepted in Hawaiʻi, allowing white men to marry landed Native Hawaiian women. Under the pressure of rapid commercialization and industrialization, landed Hawaiian families of the ruling rank felt compelled to marry their daughters to foreign merchants or businessmen to maintain their property and status. Increasing cases of intermarriage between landed Native Hawaiian women and foreign settler men—most conspicuously American and European merchants and businessmen—facilitated shifting economic power from Native Hawaiian women to foreign settler men. For a foreign man, marrying a landed Native Hawaiian woman was the most promising way to enhance his status and gain access to land in the

Hawaiian Kingdom. Through these intermarriages, there emerged plantations, ranches, and buildings that were built with foreign capital on lands controlled by Hawaiian chiefs.[36]

The constitution of 1852 issued by Kamehameha III, often referred to as the most "democratic" in the kingdom's history, harbored settler men's intentions to further decrease the power of the Hawaiian monarch and women. It guaranteed universal suffrage for male subjects and denizens and their eligibility to be elected to the House of Representatives but disqualified women from voting and being elected representatives. Furthermore, the hereditary members of the House of Nobles were replaced by lifetime monarchical appointees. The number of women members slowly decreased, and the year 1855 marked the appointment of the last woman to the House of Nobles.[37] The excessive "democracy" was rectified by the 1864 constitution, which instituted property and literacy qualifications for representatives and the electorate but also abolished the traditionally female office of *kuhina-nui*.[38]

In November 1855, *The Folio*, an English newsletter for women in Hawai'i, carried an open letter speaking for the "great cause of poor oppressed womanhood" in Hawai'i. A few settler men and women spoke against the declining status of Native Hawaiian women but not enough to generate a movement to fight for women's rights. The letter warned men of "the volcanic fires of Mauna Loa avenging women" who were being deprived of their rights to property. It encouraged Native Hawaiian women to emulate the leadership assumed by Queens Elizabeth and Victoria of England. The letter even called on "all women" to make the nineteenth century the era of "Women's Emancipation." *The Folio* was originally prepared as a handout for a fair sponsored by the "Ladies of the Protestant Mission," a group of local churchwomen from the U.S. Northeast who assisted their husbands' moral reform and charity efforts. The letter was probably authored by Catherine Whitney, whose husband, a son of a missionary, was the first postmaster and founder of several newspapers in Hawai'i. She was most likely assisted by Julia Damon, whose husband Samuel C. Damon was an American Seamen's Friend Society–appointed chaplain.[39]

Across the U.S. mainland, in Seneca Falls, New York, a small group of churchwomen abolitionists—who had recognized that American gender and race ideologies legitimized and naturalized the denial of human rights of women as well as African Americans—convened a meeting in 1848 to demand women's economic and political rights. Unlike these pioneer

American suffragists who generated an independent women's movement, local white churchwomen in Hawai'i committed themselves to performing women's duties, which they saw as complementing male efforts in civilizing and uplifting the islands. Letter writers Catherine Whitney and Julia Damon were aware that prevailing U.S. economic and gender systems curtailed the rights and freedom of privileged Native Hawaiian women. Nonetheless, they were reluctant to challenge the superiority of the U.S. system and civilization. Accordingly, succeeding newsletter issues were promised but never materialized, and no independent women's movement followed to demand women's rights in Hawai'i.[40]

Women's Civilizing Mission Amid Globalizing Industrial Capitalism

The rising political and economic power of American settler men came at the expense of Hawaiian female chiefs and coincided with the global spread of industrial capitalism and multiracial/national settler colonialism. Soon after the arrival of British explorer James Cook, Chinese ships began calling at the islands, followed by migrants and settlers from various parts of the world. British imperialism was forcefully integrating China into world trading networks, and Chinese businessmen saw an opportunity in Hawai'i. Some settled on the islands and married landed Native Hawaiian women to engage in trade and agriculture. While denizenship became obtainable for foreigners regardless of race, these early Chinese entrepreneurs profited from rice and sugar cultivation and began using Chinese contract labor. For example, Chun Fong (Ah Fong), a pioneer Chinese settler, married a Hawaiian woman chief and became a celebrated businessman in Hawai'i between the 1840s and 1890.[41]

Expanding sugar plantations brought prosperity to these foreign entrepreneurs and land-owning Native Hawaiian chiefs. Typically, white male counselors to the monarch slowly seized considerable influence as Hawai'i needed their mediation to introduce modern Western technology and capital for the kingdom's survival and development. Although the land division opened up ways for Hawaiian commoners and foreigners of any race or nationality to own land, white planters were the ultimate beneficiaries.[42] Most conspicuous among them would be founders of the so-called "Big Five"—the five largest and wealthiest sugar agencies in early twentieth-century Hawai'i, initially owned by American, British, or German men. They assumed responsibility and control over various aspects of the plantation industry, including marketing produce and procuring labor for fieldwork.[43] Among the Big Five were Castle & Cooke and Alexander & Baldwin, the two most influential companies carrying the names of pioneer missionaries.[44]

The thriving sugar industry brought increasing numbers of contract laborers of various nationalities to Hawai'i and drastically changed the islands' demography. The increasing flow of goods and peoples introduced epidemics fatal to Native Hawaiians, and foreign labor replaced Hawaiian commoners who had been cultivating their native land for generations. When the sugar industry established itself as Hawaii's economic backbone in the 1870s, plantation labor predominantly came from Chinese bachelors. As they quickly moved out of rural plantation camps to compete with white traders and entrepreneurs, the kingdom government restricted Chinese immigration in 1882 and looked for other sources of plantation labor.[45] In the process, numerous transnational capitalist ventures formed to introduce low-cost labor from throughout the world. To replace Chinese, Portuguese came from the sugar-producing Azores and Madeira islands. Japanese followed and were succeeded by Filipinos. In an attempt to diversify the nationality of plantation labor, workers were also recruited from neighboring Pacific islands, Korea, Puerto Rico, Spain, Germany, Russia, and Norway. Nonetheless, white planters preferred Asian field laborers. Accordingly, the self-sufficient society of Native Hawaiians, ruled by male and female chiefs, rapidly embraced plantation communities, which were typically composed of Asian field hands at the bottom, Native Hawaiian or Portuguese overseers in the middle, and white planters and managers at the top. As the thriving sugar industry increasingly depended on foreign labor, Asian immigrants soon outnumbered Native Hawaiians.[46]

The arrival of a conspicuous number of foreign laborers, unfamiliar with modern American ways, opened another theater for local white church people to pursue their civilizing mission. By then, the tightly interlocking circle of white settler families had extended their paternalistic and maternalistic influence on the Hawaiian Islands. Missionary family descendants intermarried or attracted additional white settlers from the United States through marriage. During the Civil War, the American Board decided that Hawai'i was sufficiently Christianized and disbanded its Sandwich Islands Mission in 1863. Missionary sons were compelled to seek nonmissionary careers, such as government officials, educators, and businessmen, but a few continued to work as missionaries.⁴⁷ Accordingly, the missionary descendants worked together to gain influence in every aspect of Hawai'i and beyond the islands. In 1852, they had established the Hawaiian Mission Children's Society to support the second generation of missionaries working in Micronesia.⁴⁸ In 1863, the local Hawaiian Evangelical Association (HEA; aka, the Hawaiian Board) took over primary responsibility for evangelizing and civilizing projects from the American Board. Their transnational connections in missionary outposts played a role in procuring laborers for the islands' sugar business. In return, missionary heritage planter families contributed profits to ongoing civilizing endeavors in Hawai'i and elsewhere in the Pacific Northeast.⁴⁹

Their civilizing projects, however, were indifferent to the human rights of those whom they endeavored to "uplift." At the time, pre- and early modern indentured labor existed throughout the world. Ironically, those churchmen and women hailing from the U.S. Northeast, where headstrong movements to abolish slavery had emerged, failed to stop the kingdom government from introducing a penal contract–based, quasi-slavery labor system. The Hawaiian Constitution of 1852 banned slavery, but the 1850 Hawai'i Master Servant Act had allowed employers to "bind" workers for fixed terms of up to ten years. By the act, fines, imprisonment, and doubling the contract's length were imposed on laborers for desertion or absence from work. Like many paternalistic slave owners in the U.S. South, white planters in Hawai'i justified exploiting field hands as an altruistic effort to "save" and "civilize" heathen workers.⁵⁰ Although New Englander men with evangelical impulses, such as Henry Whitney and Samuel C. Damon, became vocal opponents of the contract labor system, the HEA prioritized saving souls and improving the living conditions of contract laborers rather than freeing them immediately.⁵¹ Only after the U.S. annexation of the islands was the penal contract system finally outlawed.⁵²

Local white churchwomen joined male family members in "uplifting" and civilizing the expanding communities of settler and migrant workers in Hawai'i and the Pacific. In 1871, they established an independent women's organization, the Woman's Board of Missions for the Pacific Islands in Honolulu (WBMPI-Honolulu). In fact, their efforts constituted a part of American churchwomen's growing efforts to civilize the inhabitants of their expanding republic. To support the ABCFM's missionary efforts, fellow Congregationalist churchwomen in the United States also founded the Woman's Board of Missions in Boston in January 1868, the Woman's Board of Missions of the Interior in Chicago (WBMI-Chicago) in October 1868, and the Woman's Board of Missions for the Pacific in San Francisco in 1873.[53]

Although the original purpose of WBMPI-Honolulu was to promote "Christian work among women in heathen lands,"[54] the WBMPI-Honolulu, along with the HEA, directed resources to their work in Hawai'i. By doing so, they bolstered the paternalistic and maternalistic influence of white settlers, which further reduced the authority of Native Hawaiian royalty and marginalized their subjects in the kingdom. As increasing numbers of male and female contract laborers from abroad arrived in Hawai'i in the late nineteenth century, the HEA, which had previously been conducting work among Native Hawaiians, began additional work among Chinese in 1882, Japanese in 1885, and Portuguese in 1888. In the case of Japanese, American Board missionary couples who had already been working in immigrant homelands were recruited to initiate work among the respective immigrant community. The couples often brought Christianized native protégés from their host society who worked as assistants in newly assigned work on the islands.[55]

From the viewpoint of white settler missionaries, Native Hawaiians, other Pacific Islanders, Portuguese, Chinese, and Japanese were all non-Protestant "heathens" to be uplifted and civilized. For example, Mary T. Knight Hyde, the WBMPI-Honolulu president, wrote a report in 1892 stating that "herds of Chinese and Japanese laborers, with as darkened minds as any South Sea Islanders, have been brought into this kingdom in such numbers, as with the poor and ignorant Portuguese immigrants, to more than equal the Native Hawaiian population."[56] Missionary wives and their daughters felt compelled to expand their civilizing projects for Polynesians and Micronesians to include immigrant workers in Hawai'i.

American Versus Anglo Settler Colonialism and Native Hawaiian Resistance

Native Hawaiian resistance toward white settler colonialism involved complex gender, race, national, and cultural rivalries. In the face of expanding settler communities and the increasing power of the missionary circle during the reign of Kamehameha III (1825–1854), some Native Hawaiian men and women saw the need to stop, in the words of Lili'uokalani, the prevailing "habits and prejudices of the New England Puritanism."[57] The wives and daughters of the cross-racial couples, who embraced modern Western ways, came to play crucial roles in mounting lawful resistance against the further advance of U.S. settler colonialism. In fact, "discovered" by British explorer James Cook in 1778, Hawai'i embraced the tradition of the British constitutional monarchy that was then under the reign of Queen Victoria. After the death of Kamehameha III, who had occupied the throne for almost three decades, ruling-rank Native Hawaiian women took leadership by evoking British tradition against the power of American settler men who were averse to female monarchs.

Prior to the arrival of American Board missionaries in the eighteenth century, John Young, Isaac Davis, and other British seamen—who offered Kamehameha I military advice about establishing hegemony over the islands—married Native Hawaiian women of the chiefly rank. These mixed-blood and culturally hybrid offspring maintained ties with the United Kingdom for generations. One example was Emma Kalanikaumaka'amano Kaleleonālani Na'ea (1836–1885), a great-grandniece of Kamehameha I and a granddaughter of John Young. She directly challenged the increasing influence of white men of U.S. extraction. She was raised in the *hānai* (child adoption) system by her aunt Grace Kama'iku'i Young (1808–1866), who married an English medical doctor Thomas Charles Byde Rooke. Through her marriage with Kamehameha IV (Alexander Liholiho, reigned 1854–1863) in 1855, Emma became queen and encouraged her husband to embrace the style of the British monarchy but not American "democracy." While adopting a lifestyle of elegance, Emma and Kamehameha IV also took up modern philanthropic endeavors, appealing to their subjects and British residents for support. Furthermore, to strengthen an alliance with British settlers to resist the increasing power of American settlers, the royal couple invited the Anglican Church to Hawai'i and founded the Cathedral Church of St. Andrew in Honolulu.[58]

To save the kingdom, Hawaiian monarchs began reclaiming women's rank-based political rights and including Kamehameha's female descendants as candidates who were qualified to mount the throne. Contention between British and American traditions became evident over the possible emergence of a female monarch. As the advent of modern "civilization" had brought liquor, foreign diseases, and the novel custom of monogamy, the kingdom suffered not only a drastic decrease in the Native Hawaiian population but also a dwindling pool of possible heirs to the throne. In 1862, Emma's only child Albert, the prince and appointed heir to the throne, died at the age of four. In 1863, her husband, Kamehameha IV, followed the prince, passing away at age twenty-eight. Accordingly, his only surviving brother, Lot Kamehameha (1830–1872), ascended the throne, becoming Kamehameha V, but the bachelor king died in 1872. On his deathbed, Kamehameha V appointed Princess Bernice Pauahi (1831–1884) of the Kamehameha line as his successor. Nonetheless, Hawai'i's genealogy-based monarchical system was already strained under the influence of American gender ideology and cult of womanhood. Pauahi was Juliette Montague Cooke's favorite student at the Royal School and married Charles R. Bishop, a businessman from New England. She declined the appointment.[59]

Consequently, although the 1864 constitution stipulated that the legislature should elect a new king in the absence of a named heir, an unofficial plebiscite in 1873 elected William Charles Lunalilo (1835–1874) of the Kamehameha line, whose mother was Elizabeth Kīna'u (Ka'ahumanu II), to ascend the throne. The legislature validated the election result, but within a little over a year, King Lunalilo, also a bachelor, died without having appointed a successor.[60]

The succession decision was relegated then to the all-male, racially mixed members of the legislative assembly, and they chose David Kalākaua over Dowager Queen Emma in 1874. According to Hawaiian tradition, the monarchy was not a government office but "the symbol of the Hawaiian people, the bodily link to divine ancestors and greatness of the Conqueror and his times."[61] Emma, a Kamehameha descendant, was more qualified to ascend the throne than Kalākaua by Native Hawaiian tradition. Presumably, however, the white men of U.S. extraction were bothered that the Dowager Queen, a woman with strong ties to the British monarchy, was seriously considered a candidate for head of state. Initially, both Emma and Kalākaua used the slogan "Hawai'i for Hawaiians" and opposed concluding a U.S.-Hawai'i reciprocity treaty, which would grant duty free status to Hawaiian sugar businesses but also bring U.S. annexation a step closer. Kalākaua, however, withdrew his opposition in exchange for support from influential white men of American extraction. When the racially mixed, all-male legislature elected Kalākaua over Dowager Queen Emma, enthusiastic supporters of Emma attacked the Native Hawaiian representatives who went against their own tradition. With the landing of U.S. Marines, Kalākaua was sworn in as king. In 1875, the United States and the Kingdom of Hawai'i concluded a reciprocity treaty, accelerating the industrialization of the islands' sugar industry.[62]

King Kalākaua, however, had no intention of becoming a puppet of prosperous white settler men who supported his accession. He asserted his monarchal power and his kingdom's strength nationally and internationally by resorting to both traditional Hawaiian and modern Western ways. Aware of the necessity to have an heir apparent, he appointed his sister Lili'uokalani as the next heir to the throne. In 1881, he made a grand tour of the world, accompanied by missionary sons—his chamberlain Charles Hastings Judd (1835–1890), a culturally hybrid son of Laura F. Judd and Julie Judd Swanzy's father, and attorney general William Nevins Armstrong (1835–1905). Returning to the islands a year later, Kalākaua completed the construction of the modern Western-style 'Iolani Palace, where he held a grand ceremony for his coronation in 1883. He invited guests from around the world and revived public performances of the hula, which had been banned under the decades-long puritanical influence of American missionaries.[63]

Kalākaua also attempted to form an alliance with the "cognate race," the Hawaiian-led Polynesian federation of nations, to stand up against European colonizers, which outraged Germany, Great Britain, and France. He appealed to the international community that Western powers deal justly with countries in the Pacific.[64] During his 1881 world tour, Kalākaua also initiated an effort to establish an alliance with Japan and proposed marriage between his niece Princess Ka'iulani and Prince Yorihito of Japan. Although the proposal failed, their effort led to an 1885 agreement between the Japanese and Hawaiian governments for a contract to import Japanese laborers to Hawai'i.[65]

Kalākaua dissociated himself from the missionary circle that had become critical of not only his "lavish" spending and revival of Hawaiian cosmology but also his reliance on controversial white men—e.g., Claus Spreckels (1828–1908), a German-born financier linked with California's sugar-processing industry and a creditor willing to make personal loans to Kalākaua, and Walter Murray Gibson (1822–1888), who arrived in Hawai'i as a missionary for the Mormon Church. Kalākaua and his cabinet repealed the prohibition laws that kept liquor virtually inaccessible to Hawaiian commoners for many years and legalized the sale of opium by a licensing system. Such developments invited opposition not only from the missionary community but also from progressive Native Hawaiian nationalists—e.g., Joseph Nāwahī (Joseph Kaho'oluhi Nāwahīokalani'ōpu'u, 1842–1896), a graduate of a missionary-built boarding school on the island of Hawai'i—who believed the developments would endanger the survival and advancement of their nation.[66]

Cultural Imperialism and Transnational Networks: The Woman's Christian Temperance Union in Hawai'i

The Kalākaua cabinet's "immorality" and the "fearful increase of intemperance" symbolized not only Native Hawaiian resistance but also the growing influence of commercialism and non-Protestant moral values, which aroused a sense of mission among the missionary descendants. Those descendants turned to the Woman's Christian Temperance Union (WCTU), one of the most conspicuous women-conscious American social reform organizations of the time, to promote self-discipline among the multiracializing and multinationalizing population and increase labor productivity for their businesses. In 1884, the united efforts of the Honolulu YMCA and a male-led temperance group in the city, the Committee of Twenty-One, invited Mary C. Leavitt (1830–1912), a Bostonian and WCTU officer, to visit Hawai'i.[67] Leavitt was on a temperance lecture tour in California and extended her tour to the islands, where Kalākaua's legislature had allowed the sale of liquor to Native Hawaiians.[68]

Paradoxically, the WCTU, by hoisting the banner of temperance, a respectable secular cause, successfully moved out of the male-controlled denominational church structure and became an autonomous women's organization by and for women. Nonetheless, members believed in their cultural superiority and were willing to collaborate with temperate elite men who shared their evangelical sense of mission. Starting with its inception as a national organization in Cleveland, Ohio, in 1874, the WCTU pursued churchwomen's moral authority to make their own communities friendly to women of their own sort. Furthermore, under the motto of "home protection ballot," coined by its second president Frances E. Willard (1839–1898), the WCTU made suffrage a respectable women's cause for grassroots churchwomen nationwide.[69] Willard's encounter with opium dens in San Francisco's "Chinatown" in 1883 also led to the inception of the World Woman's Christian Temperance Union (World WCTU). Noticeably, Willard's aspiration for a transnational westward expansion coincided with intensifying U.S. imperialist interests in the Pacific and beyond. The World WCTU began expanding the WCTU's women-conscious, culturally imperialist movement across the Pacific to immigrant homelands.[70]

Arriving in Hawai'i in 1884, WCTU leader Leavitt showed women in Hawai'i how to promote temperance, assert moral authority, and influence politics. Lecturing throughout the islands, Leavitt called on local white churchwomen to form a Hawaiian branch (WCTU of the Hawaiian Islands, Hawai'i WCTU). Mrs. Mary Sophronia Rice Whitney (1835–1927), the first ABCFM-appointed missionary to Micronesia and wife of dentist John Morgan Whitney, assumed its first presidency.[71] Consequently, the Committee of Twenty-One disbanded "by mutual consent" and passed its archives to the Hawai'i WCTU as "its natural successor."[72]

Historian Patricia Grimshaw notes that "nearly all" Hawai'i WCTU members were "missionary descendants or married to missionary descendants," who were also active in the WBMPI-Honolulu.[73] Alarmed by surging waves of "heathen" workers and visitors and the increasing visibility of intemperance and "vice," they recognized the need to "emulate the example of Kamehameha III and the chiefs of his day," who were persuaded to use their influence for "temperance and righteousness." The Hawai'i WCTU used the WBMPI-Honolulu network to form branch groups by involving "good" Native Hawaiian and non–Anglo-Saxon settler men and women. Sharing the sense of mission in civilizing and uplifting the less civilized, the missionary circle in Hawai'i raised funds to assist Mary Leavitt in expanding WCTU's influence throughout the Pacific and the world.[74]

Women's Civilizing Mission and White Settler Colonialism

Leavitt's call for women's moral authority activated local churchwomen to support male family members as they challenged the "immorality" of King Kalākaua and his cabinet. Their sense of mission was grounded in a Protestant middle-class conviction of moral superiority. Their Orientalism and symbiotic relationship with white settler colonialism made them unconcerned about white settler men's thirst for wealth and power at the expense of Hawaiian land, foreign labor, and the marginalization of commoner Hawaiians. To retain tax-free sugar exports to the United States, planter oligarchs, including missionary descendants, left no stone unturned in renewing the reciprocity treaty and placing the kingdom's politics under their control. While Native Hawaiian nationalism was rising, the United States recognized the importance of Hawai'i for its expansion in the Pacific and demanded the exclusive lease of Pearl Harbor for the renewal of the treaty. This time, King Kalākaua, collaborating with his prime minister Walter Gibson, resisted. In response, during the absence of Queen Kapi'olani and her sister-in-law

Princess Liliʻuokalani, who had traveled to London to represent the kingdom at Queen Victoria's fifty-year jubilee, a small group of white men, led by missionary grandson Lorrin A. Thurston (1858–1931), forced Kalākaua to sign the "Bayonet Constitution" in July 1887. The constitution was so named because the king signed it under the threat of violence. It reduced the monarch to little more than a ceremonial figure.[75] The new constitution extended voting rights to wealthy male residents of "Hawaiian, American, or European birth or descent" who could read and write in "Hawaiian, English or some European language." The newly enfranchised did not need to swear allegiance to the monarch. Property and income requirements were tightened, and voters were required to swear to support the new constitution, which led to a dramatic reduction in the Native Hawaiian electorate. The Bayonet Constitution pushed kingdom politics to align with the racial reality of late nineteenth-century U.S. society, where politics was white men's business. Chinese and Japanese joined Native Hawaiians in opposing the new constitution but to no avail. In November 1887, the reciprocity treaty, with the Pearl Harbor amendment, was renewed for seven years.[76]

Hawaiʻi WCTU members were convinced of white women's moral authority and supported their family members in forcefully stripping power from the "uncontrollable" monarch and reducing the size of the "unrighteous" nonwhite electorate. When King Kalākaua signed the Bayonet Constitution in 1887, M. A. H. Green, a missionary daughter and secretary of the Hawaiʻi WCTU, recorded: "The women of this country owe a debt of deepest gratitude to those who so wisely planned and carried out the political reform. All honor to men who stood bayonet in hand ready to defend the cause and us. And now, may we not hope that the spirit of reform will enter into the social systems of this beautiful land of the Pacific, and make it the paradise it is by nature designed to be?"[77]

In 1888, a corollary of that "spirit of reform entered into Hawaiʻi's social system" and included an act "Relating to the Property and Rights of Married Women." It updated the kingdom's laws on women's coverture to align with legal changes in the United States. A married woman would be allowed to keep, gain, or sell her own property and retain her wages, but she could not sell or mortgage her real estate without her husband's consent.[78]

For Native Hawaiians, however, the Bayonet Constitution embodied escalating colonialism and "betrayal" by the missionary circle for whom Hawaiian royalty had been providing special favor. It threw Hawaiʻi into an era of political contention and instability. In 1889, Native Hawaiian Robert

Wilcox responded with an unsuccessful insurrection to replace the new constitution with the previous charter. The majority of Native Hawaiian people chose to recover their rights through the foreign system of party politics. Loyalist Native Hawaiian and settler men created party platforms to amend the Bayonet Constitution.[79] Concurrently, however, the McKinley Tariff Bill, enacted by the U.S. Congress in 1890, removed the tariff on raw sugar from all foreign countries but gave American sugar producers a bounty. Consequently, it wiped out the Hawai'i sugar industry's advantage, which was formerly assured in the reciprocity treaty. As negotiations for a new treaty floundered and the islands' sugar business fell into depression, radical white men of American extraction became increasingly convinced that overthrowing the monarchy and having the United States annex the islands was the only way to regain stability and prosperity for Hawai'i. In 1891, during the mounting crisis, King Kalākaua unexpectedly died in San Francisco, where he was receiving medical treatment.[80]

The eighth monarch and the first reigning queen of the Hawaiian Kingdom, Lili'uokalani, Kalākaua's sister, exemplified the Native Hawaiian tradition of women's leadership. She appointed her niece, Princess Ka'iulani (1875–1899), who was then receiving an education in England, as her heir.[81] Arguably, Lili'uokalani, who was educated at the Royal School, had emulated Anglo-Saxon liberal political ideals more than her white settler mentors.[82] Well-versed in Native Hawaiian and Western high culture, she married a white man of American extraction, but her cultural hybridity never diminished her sense of monarch, to be responsible for her nation and subjects. Presumably, Queen Lili'uokalani, who could rally Native Hawaiians to support her attempts at recovering monarchical and Native Hawaiian rights, irritated white settler annexationists more than her brother. On January 14, 1893, having received a number of petitions from her subjects and supported by the Hui Kalai'aina (Hawaiian Political Association), the queen, after a series of unsuccessful attempts in amending the Bayonet Constitution, made arrangements to promulgate a new constitution, which would restore the power of the monarch and the voting rights of the Native Hawaiian electorate. Although she backed off at the last minute as her cabinet refused to sign the new constitution, the incident provided an excuse for local white annexationists, led by Lorrin A. Thurston, to overthrow her government. Thurston and his group cast the queen as a "traitor" to the constitution for attempting a "revolution." Backed by expansionist U.S. minister John L. Stevens and the U.S. militia, the local white annexationists occupied 'Iolani

Palace. On January 17, 1893, they declared the formation of a provisional government, which they hoped would be under the protection of the United States.[83]

The queen temporarily surrendered to the United States but not to the provisional government. The incumbent president, Republican Benjamin Harrison, signed the annexation treaty with the provisional government, but he would soon be replaced by Democrat Grover Cleveland, who was to assume the presidency for a second, nonconsecutive, term. The queen counted on the U.S. president-elect, whom she had met along with his wife at the White House in 1887 when Cleveland was in office and Liliʻuokalani was on her way to London for Queen Victoria's jubilee.[84] Her surrender read, "I, Liliʻuokalani, by the grace of God yield my authority until such time as the government of the United States shall reinstate me as the constitutional sovereign of the Hawaiian islands." Princess Kaʻiulani, who was still in England for royal training, sailed to Washington, DC, to meet with President Cleveland and his wife. The president left the treaty unsigned and dispatched James H. Blount, U.S. Representative from Georgia, to Hawaiʻi for an investigation.[85]

According to historian Noenoe K. Silva, Native Hawaiians organized immediately after the coup to preserve their sovereignty. Men formed the Hui Hawaiʻi Aloha ʻAina (Hawaiian Patriotic League), with Joseph Nāwahī as its president. Women organized the Hui Hawaiʻi Aloha ʻAina o Na Wahine (Women's Hawaiian Patriotic League), and hybrid women of the privileged rank assumed leadership. Its first president, Emilie Kekauluohi Widemann Macfarlane (1859–1947), had a high-ranking chief mother from Kauaʻi and a German businessman/politician father, and Abigail Kuaihelani Maipinepine Bright Campbell (1858–1908), who succeeded Macfarlane, was a high-ranking Mauʻi chief married to a Scottish-Irish businessman. The two organizations carried out massive campaigns to explain the illegality of the coup and its provisional government. They rallied to win Blount's support for the restoration of the queen.[86]

Yet women from the missionary circle did not side with the queen and her supporters. They believed that their men were better suited than the Hawaiian monarch in upgrading Hawaiʻi's civilization.[87] According to historian Louise Michele Newman, whose work examines the racial origins of American feminism, white women activists were convinced of "their own race specific trait of moral superiority" and "thought of themselves as widely different from white men in sexual terms but fundamentally similar to white men in racial-cultural terms."[88] Queen Liliʻuokalani might have accepted Christianity but was never a monotheist. She was a member of the Strangers' Friend Society and the WBMPI-Honolulu at the time of the coup, and until then, she, in her own words, "was never appealed to in vain by the missionaries to give money or sympathy to all that was to be done in the name of Christianity."[89]

Unfortunately, the appeal for restoration waged by the queen and her loyal subjects was not enough to turn the tide. President Cleveland recognized the illegality of the provisional government of Hawaiʻi and made an official statement that Liliʻuokalani should be reinstated as the monarch of the Hawaiian Kingdom. However, the white revolutionists in Hawaiʻi had no intention of giving up their rule. Having failed in the United States' annexation of Hawaiʻi, they embarked on transforming their provisional government into the Republic of Hawaiʻi.

White Settler Anxiety and Woman Suffrage

In May 1894, President Dole and fellow white oligarchs of the provisional government declared a constitutional convention modeled after the founding fathers of the American republic. They appointed nineteen delegates to the convention and called for eighteen more to be chosen by popular vote. Male Hawaiians and Euro-American descendants could participate in the popular vote as long as they swore loyalty to the provisional government by promising to "oppose any attempt to reestablish monarchical government in any form in the Hawaiian Islands." The majority of Native Hawaiian men refused to make such an oath and were ineligible to cast a vote. Consequently, among the eighteen elected delegates for the convention, fifteen were born in Hawaiʻi, but only five were of Native Hawaiian descent.[90]

White settler colonialism in Hawaiʻi was opening up another outlet for white women activists' civilizing zeal: suffrage. Mary C. Leavitt, who had introduced the WCTU's social reform methods for morally "uplifting" the kingdom, returned to Hawaiʻi and promoted woman suffrage in the emerging "republic." In November 1893, the Hawaiʻi WCTU had held its annual meeting in the presence of Leavitt and formed the five-member Woman Suffrage Committee. Mary Sophronia Rice Whitney assumed its chair, and its members included influential missionary daughters, such as Mary Emma Dillingham Frear and Mary Tenney Castle.[91] Despite the efforts of Leavitt and her Hawai'i WCTU suffragist collaborators, local churchwomen in the runup to the Constitutional Convention were, in general, still cautious about asking for suffrage; rather, they were inclined to wait for an "opportunity." For example, Mary T. Knight Hyde, the WBMPI-Honolulu president, when addressing the June 1894 WBMPI-Honolulu annual meeting, insisted that women would have the political right when the time was ripe. Hyde argued that whenever "the occasion" arose, women proved their "ability" in "a wider sphere of influence than was [then] accorded to her" and their "fitness" in the new sphere "manifested itself."[92]

Ironically, although the male oligarchs had no intention of granting women suffrage, they appeared supportive of a small group of Hawai'i WCTU suffragists. They expected that the woman suffrage movement would make the overthrow a fait accompli and divert women's attention to the new cause, thus assisting the provisional government in establishing itself as a republic. Of course, Queen Lili'uokalani, to whom Native Hawaiians were still attached, opposed the movement.[93]

The Constitutional Convention, composed of male delegates from various racial backgrounds, was held from May 30 to July 3, 1894, in the face of outright opposition from Queen Lili'uokalani and her loyal subjects. While the settler men desired to bar the mass of Native Hawaiians and Asians from the electorate, they needed to bring corresponding bilingual elites to their side to justify forming a republic in Hawai'i. "Intelligence" and economic capability became the criteria for enfranchisement. The Hawai'i WCTU's Woman Suffrage Committee held a series of meetings in May 1894. Hawai'i WCTU suffragists, like their white mainland counterparts, envisioned that the people qualified to participate in creating the government were their own sort. They publicly asked for suffrage only for "women with a high educational and property qualification."[94] Importantly, culturally hybrid elite Native Hawaiian men and women could meet these qualifications.

White oligarchs were aware that woman suffrage bills and constitutional amendments were under deliberation in U.S. state legislatures. Some even predicted that it would soon become inevitable for the federal government to assure woman suffrage nationwide. On June 12, 1894, woman suffrage became an issue at the local Constitutional Convention when Article 74, on voter qualifications for Representatives, was discussed. Suffrage was ultimately limited to male taxpayers literate in either English or Hawaiian. While a motion to eliminate the word "male" immediately lost, Sanford B. Dole, who was "dubious" about woman suffrage, made another motion for an amendment to the article so that the legislature could extend the franchise to women in the future without amending the constitution. This motion, however, also met with opposition. For example, Mr. John William Kalua (1846–1928), a Native Hawaiian politician, insisted that his people had not "advanced far enough" to take part in politics and that the convention should not open "the door to extending the suffrage to women." Representative Henry Perrine Baldwin (1842–1911), a missionary son, knowing that local WCTU suffragists were preparing to present a petition, made another motion; the legislature "laid [the issue] on the table to be picked up and considered with any petition which may come in."[95]

On June 13, local WCTU suffragists submitted to the convention a petition with signatures from 173 women and 83 men for woman suffrage.[96] Yet they appeared half-hearted in their demand. The petition, reflecting deliberations at the convention, made two alternative requests: "Respectfully asking that by a provision in the Constitution women be entitled to the right of suffrage, with an educational and property qualification; or that the Legislature be authorized to grant such right hereafter."[97] The convention appointed a special committee and referred the petition to it. Invited by this special committee, local white woman suffragists attended its hearing and revealed their "settler anxiety."[98] When missionary son Samuel M. Damon asked them to explain which "women were to vote and under what qualifications," Mary Sophronia Rice Whitney, who led the Hawai'i WCTU's Woman Suffrage Committee, left out the "property and educational qualification" written into the petition. Although she referred to the positive social effects brought by women voters and juries in Wyoming, she defensively put off asking for the same voting privileges as men.[99] Whitney, joined by other Hawai'i WCTU members, argued that all they were asking for was "a clause in the Constitution" to allow future legislatures to enfranchise women. Consequently, the all-male special committee turned its attention to authorizing the legislature to grant woman suffrage at a later time.[100]

After the hearing on June 21, 1894, the Constitutional Convention again discussed woman suffrage based on two reports submitted by special committee members. There was no clear color line in the debate over woman suffrage. The majority report denied the first request for woman suffrage with an educational and property qualification. It endorsed the second request, adding a provision stating "the Legislature may enact laws extending the franchise to women" to Article 74 of the 1894 Constitution of the

Republic of Hawai'i.[101] The minority report, on the other hand, recommended tabling the petition, arguing that "woman's place [was] at home."[102]

Throughout the lengthy and complicated deliberations, the focal point of woman suffrage became whether the territorial legislature was authorized to enfranchise women in the future without amending the republican constitution. While each side included white settler and Native Hawaiian delegates, those who supported the majority report, for example, argued that nobody could stop the move for woman suffrage, that the amendment was not asking for woman suffrage at the present, and that it was desirable to add those women who were willing to assist in maintaining good government to the electorate. Writing for the majority, S. M. Damon argued that woman suffrage was "a move of right direction" with "the cause of civilization," which started at the time of Kamehameha II, freeing Hawaiian women from "the bondage" of *kapu*. Minority report supporters, in contrast, warned about the "unwomanly" affairs of politics, the existence of large numbers of "unintelligent" Hawaiian women with a property qualification, the possibility of splitting Native Hawaiian families in which women were as, if not more, politically active than men, and so on.[103]

Regardless, the all-male representatives unanimously opposed granting women suffrage at the time. Although Mr. John Kauhane, who recognized the fear of ladies' power among the delegates, suggested to "vote in such a way as will make the ladies your friends," the convention gradually inclined toward the minority report with arguments that the political situation in Hawai'i at the time was already complicated enough by the existence of antirepublic forces—namely royalists and Hawaiian nationalists, among whom women were politically active. Henry Perrine Baldwin, Mau'i resident and one of Hawai'i's most successful sugar planters, insisted, "we [had] no right to put a loose clause in here that [would] allow something that today our judgment [was] against." The minority report was adopted by a vote of 21 to 8; thus, the clause that would have enabled the legislature to extend suffrage to women never made it to Article 74 of the 1894 Constitution of the Republic of Hawai'i.[104]

When the Constitutional Convention was in session, Native Hawaiian men and women carried out political campaigns against establishing the constitution without the consent and participation of "the people." On July 2, 1894, two days before the promulgation of the new constitution, the opponents held a mass protest, which gathered five to seven thousand Native Hawaiians. Despite this massive demonstration of opposition, however, the constitution was promulgated on July 4 with the consent of only four thousand, most of whom were white settler men.[105] The 1894 constitution, published in both Hawaiian and English languages, enfranchised only taxpaying men (for the House of Representatives) and property-owning men (for the Senate). They had to have a command of English or Hawaiian to vote for the legislature. It barred all women, regardless of race or class, a substantial number of Native Hawaiian male citizens by the economic qualification, and virtually all Asian immigrant men by the language qualification. The constitution, however, granted alien men, regardless of race or proficiency in English or Hawaiian, whom the minister of interior judged desirable by their service to the government, all the privileges of citizenship, including suffrage. In the republic, multiracial/multiethnic Hawai'i, gender more than race became the decisive factor for full citizenship, and the constitution encouraged Asian settler men to be Americanized and faithful to the islands' white settler oligarchs.[106]

Not surprisingly, no lamentations came from Hawai'i WCTU suffragists. Mary Sophronia Rice Whitney expressed regret that they could not insert the clause allowing the legislature to grant women suffrage at a future time. But she seemed satisfied with their efforts, which she described as "an entering wedge." She expressed her optimistic expectation that "at some future time" women would "have the privilege of helping to make laws which [would] be for the uplifting of the Nation."[107]

This was the backdrop against which Queen Lili'uokalani signed the documents officially abdicating the throne on January 24, 1895. She realized the humiliating status of a woman citizen and the subordinate role assigned to her in the gender and racial system of the new republic. Weeks later, in February 1895, she was brought to trial on charges that weapons were found in the garden of her residence at the time of the counterrevolutionary attempt by Robert W. Wilcox. On trial days, according to Lili'uokalani's memoir, the palace's former throne room was filled with curious spectators, including diplomatic corps, "ministers of the gospel, and a liberal representation from all classes, including many 'ladies' of Honolulu society." The trial proceeded with Albert Francis Judd (1838–1900) testifying against Lili'uokalani.[108] He was another son of Laura F. Judd, who not only occupied high offices in the judiciary of the kingdom and later in the new republic but also served as the president of the Hawaiian Evangelical Association (HEA) that united various racial/ethnic Congregational churches in Hawai'i from 1883 to 1900.[109]

Although factors of race, ethnicity, gender, class, and nationality were intricately entangled in shaping Hawai'i's transformation from the kingdom to a republic, Lili'uokalani sensed a strong abhorrence against a female monarch among her accusers who placed her on trial. The former queen wrote:

> The only charge against me really was that of being a queen; and my case was judged by these, my adversaries, before I came into court. I remember with clearness, however, the attack upon me by the Judge Advocate, the words that issued from his mouth about "the prisoner," "the woman," etc., uttered with such affectation of contempt and disgust. The object of it was evidently to humiliate me, to make me break down in the presence of the staring crowd. But in this they were disappointed. My equanimity was never disturbed; and their own report relates that I throughout preserved "that haughty carriage" which marked me as an "unusual woman."[110]

Lili'uokalani was found guilty for misprision of treason, i.e., failure to report a treasonous crime, fined $5,000, and sentenced to hard labor for five years. Nonetheless, the sentence was never fully executed, and Sanford Dole's republican government pardoned and released her from house arrest half a year later in September 1895.[111]

Deposed and deprived of her kingdom and the privilege of her rank, however, the former queen did not intend to sit idly by watching her beloved nation and title of the Crown Lands become U.S. possessions without seeking recourse in law or fairness to herself or her former subjects, Native Hawaiians.[112] Although white oligarch attempts at having the United States annex Hawai'i had failed under the presidency of Democrat Grover Cleveland, Dole's government made another attempt when Republican William McKinley won the 1896 presidential election. Concurrently, Lili'uokalani left Honolulu in December 1896, with permission from Dole, allegedly for the purpose of visiting her relatives. In reality, she embarked on a campaign to preserve Hawai'i's independence, backed by supporters in Hawai'i and friends in the United States. In Boston and Washington, DC, she appealed to influential churchwomen and politicians to support the cause of the "real" people in Hawai'i.[113]

When Republican William McKinley was sworn in as the U.S. president in 1897, he concluded the annexation treaty with the Republic of Hawai'i and submitted the treaty to the U.S. Senate for ratification. Nonetheless,

Liliʻuokalani and her Native Hawaiian supporters kept their faith in the conscience of the American people. They endeavored to invoke the lofty ideal at the founding of the American republic, which declared that governments derive "their just power from the consent of the governed." As illuminated by historian Noenoe K. Silva, members of the Men's Hawaiian Patriotic League, the Women's Hawaiian Patriotic League, and the Hawaiian Political Association conducted a massive campaign to oppose annexation. Hybrid Native Hawaiian women activists—e.g., Abigail Kuaihelani Maipinepine Bright Campbell and Emma ʻAima Aiʻi Nāwahī (1854–1934), journalist from Hilo, the Big Island, and the wife of late Joseph Nāwahī—traveled the islands extensively to conduct mass meetings and collect signatures for their antiannexation petition drive.[114] Joining the antiannexation campaigns were non-American foreign settlers—e.g., Englishman Theophilus H. Davies, the guardian of Princess Kaʻiulani and the founder of Theo H. Davies & Co, one of the Big Five,[115] and German businessman and politician Hermann A. Widemann, whose hybrid Native Hawaiian daughters' activism will be discussed in the next chapter.[116]

Their efforts seemed to bear fruit, but only temporarily. On December 6, 1897, when the U.S. Senate began its session in Washington, DC, Liliʻuokalani presented petitions with over 38,000 signatures to the Senate and the president. Native Hawaiian efforts successfully prevented the annexation treaty from winning two-thirds of the Senate vote required for ratification. On the outbreak of the Spanish-American War in April 1898, however, Hawaiʻi became a strategically crucial site for U.S. imperial expansion and was annexed by an exceptional means—the Newlands Resolution, a joint resolution of the two Houses, despite the U.S. Senate's failure to ratify the annexation treaty.[117]

CHAPTER 2

The Politics of Woman Suffrage in the U.S. Territory of Hawai'i

After the overthrow of her government in 1894, Lili'uokalani, in her memoir, *Hawaii's Story by Hawaii's Queen* (1898), pleaded with the U.S. public for justice. She was appalled to see the annexation of Hawai'i becoming a matter of political parties in the U.S. Congress. In the book's last chapter, she pleaded with the U.S. people: "Oh, honest Americans, as Christians hear me for my down-trodden people! Their form of government is as dear to them as yours is precious to you. Quite as warmly as you love your country, so they love theirs."[1]

To the utter dismay of Queen Lili'uokalani and Hawaiian nationalists, however, her plea for independence failed to sway Americans, engaged as they were in a war against Spain in the Caribbean and the Pacific. They were much more concerned about matters immediate to their lives, status, and thriving empire than the will of the people in the remote islands of Hawai'i. Convinced of their civilizational superiority, many citizens of the "American Republic" turned their racialist gaze on Hawai'i and other new possessions brought by victory—Puerto Rico, the Philippines, and Guam. Rather than questioning the legitimacy of governing these islands against the will of the governed, many renewed their sense of mission to civilize and uplift their societies. Among them were suffragists.

Hawai'i—like Puerto Rico, the Philippines, and Guam—was composed of islands with a population mostly of people of color. Unlike other U.S.

"possessions," however, Hawai'i's multiracial population was dominated by an oligarchy of white settlers with close ties to U.S. political leaders. Accordingly, Hawai'i was incorporated as a U.S. territory with the potential to become a state. Nonetheless, Hawai'i, unlike other U.S. continental territories, was deprived of the privilege to write its own constitution, and the U.S. Congress assumed the prerogative. Accordingly, mainland suffragists felt inspired to pursue woman suffrage in Hawai'i as the first case of women enfranchised by federal action.[2]

In Hawai'i, under the pressure for globalization, white settler and Native Hawaiian women leaders sought ways to cope with rapid social transformation and shared philanthropic and maternalistic roles for the multiracial and multiethnic population of the islands. The kingdom's overthrow and subsequent annexation of the islands created a vast divide between them. Paradoxically, when mainland white suffragists embarked on their attempt to bring "the most civilized" aspect of the U.S. republic to Hawai'i, the high-ranking Native Hawaiian women enthusiastically responded to their call. They lost their traditional political and economic power under white settler colonialism and U.S. imperialism but were eager to recover their rights lawfully in the newly imposed U.S. system. In contrast, white settler women were unwilling to cast off the cult of true womanhood, which they saw as an indicator of their civilized status. Being a racial minority, they also harbored the settler anxiety about the fact that woman suffrage would double the already majority Native Hawaiian votes.[3]

Under the U.S. Orientalist gaze and its intensifying suspicion of Hawai'i's loyalty during World War I, Native Hawaiian and white settler women leaders were compelled to negotiate, reconcile, and collaborate for social integrity. To sustain Hawai'i's territorial status, they worked together to mobilize multiracial and multiethnic communities for the territory-wide war support efforts, strengthening ties with mainland suffrage leaders. Working under the white male oligarchy, Native Hawaiian women's enthusiasm for woman suffrage soon persuaded local white settler women to join their efforts to ensure women's rights. This chapter illuminates the rocky but steady process between 1898 and 1922 of women's collective influence and power-building among Native Hawaiian, local white, and mainland white women over the issue of women's political right to vote for and be elected to territorial public office.

Woman Suffrage: A New Cause for Women's Civilizing Mission

Mainland suffragists shared a conviction with Hawai'i's pioneer missionary wives of American civilizational superiority and, thus, remained oblivious to cultural inequalities experienced by high-ranking Native Hawaiian women. The Newlands Resolution (1898), which proclaimed the annexation of Hawai'i, established the all-male Hawaiian Commission to write the Hawaiian Organic Act, the constitution for the U.S. territory of Hawai'i. Lili'uokalani's well-organized antiannexation campaign, which had once prevented the U.S. Senate from ratifying the annexation treaty, must have impressed American women suffragists but not enough to stop the U.S. Congress from taking over Hawai'i by exceptional means. According to historian Allison Sneider, even some suffragists who stood firm for African Americans' human rights and who had initially opposed the Spanish-American War and U.S. imperialism focused their attention on the "strategic question" of how to set a precedent for the federal action of enfranchising women. It was the Jim Crow era when state laws were stripping away the voting rights of men of color and an expedient consensus was forming that voting was under state, not federal, jurisdiction.[4] In 1899, Susan B. Anthony, the president of the National American Woman Suffrage Association (NAWSA) and a veteran suffragist, along with her fellow NAWSA officers, presented a petition called the "Hawaiian Appeal" to Congress.[5] They demanded the omission of the word "male" in the proposed Hawaiian Organic Act and granting women suffrage "upon whatever conditions and qualifications the right of suffrage [was] granted to" men in Hawai'i.[6] Hawai'i's oligarchs were determined to uphold their white male supremacy by employing literacy and property qualifications, but mainland suffrage leaders did not touch upon the qualification issue.

In the imperial era, borrowing Sneider's words, voting had become "less a right of citizenship than of civilization" for woman suffragists in the United States. They came to define suffrage less by "universal inclusion than by a shared capacity to exercise the privileges of democracy based on a combination of racial traits and religious commitments."[7] During the antebellum era, the U.S. woman suffrage movement was initiated by a small group of white churchwomen in the U.S. Northeast whose evangelical impulses created women's auxiliaries to support male antislavery organizations.

They recognized similarities between themselves and enslaved people, and those involved in the Garrisonian wing of the abolitionist movement learned how to turn their evangelical thrust into social reform and ultimately a political movement.[8]

After the Civil War, however, the women's rights movement split over the Fifteenth Amendment, which assured freedmen's but not women's suffrage, creating two competing organizations: the New York–based National Woman Suffrage Association (NWSA), which had opposed the amendment, and the New England–based Republican-faithful American Woman Suffrage Association (AWSA), which had supported the amendment. In 1890, the two organizations merged into the NAWSA. During the course of rapid industrialization and the extension of federal outreach throughout the postslavery South, the West, and overseas, the women's rights movement accommodated to the prevailing evolutionary view of civilization articulated by social Darwinism. To win support of legislators, who were essentially white men, NAWSA members now advocated woman suffrage as the means for native-born white women to fulfill their mission in uplifting "less-civilized" Black, Native, and immigrant peoples. By the end of the nineteenth century, the U.S. woman suffrage movement under the NAWSA leadership had become more or less a white women's mass movement to execute womanly duties as guardians of home and civilization and to uplift uncivilized sections of their expanding settler nation.[9]

The NAWSA version of women's civilizing mission used woman suffrage as a parameter of an advanced civilization. As pointed out by Allison Sneider, this was evident in the "open letter," which NAWSA leaders wrote in January 1899 and sent to every member of Congress, deliberating on the proposed Hawaiian Organic Act. Prepared under the leadership of Carrie Chapman Catt, who would soon take over the NAWSA presidency from Susan B. Anthony, the letter remained mute about educational and property qualifications and demanded that the word "male" be omitted from the proposed territorial constitution: "The declared intention of the United States in annexing the Hawaiian Islands is to give them the benefits of the most advanced civilization, and it is a truism that the progress of civilization in every country is measured by the approach of women toward the ideal of equal rights with men. . . . Justice demands that we shall not offer to women emerging from barbarism the ball and chain of a sex disqualification while we hold out to men the crown of self-government."[10] Paradoxically, the same compulsive sense of "civilizing mission" had propelled white churchwomen to promote their cult of womanhood that served as the marker of their advanced civilization, stripping political and economic rights of Native Hawaiian women.

Regardless, the white oligarchs in Hawai'i, who had just deposed Lili'uokalani and established male monopoly on power in the islands' government, had no intention of meeting the demands of mainland suffragists nor of allowing woman suffrage to become the central issue of the territorial congressional debates. The Hawaiian Commission to write the Hawaiian Organic Act was composed of U.S. Senators Shelby M. Cullom (R-IL), John T. Morgan (D-AL), Congressman Robert R. Hitt (R-IL), Hawaiian Republic President Sanford B. Dole, and territorial Supreme Court Associate Justice Walter F. Frear. The bill proposed by the Commission in December 1898 used the word "male" "more frequently than in the Constitution of the United States or of any State." Replicating the 1894 Constitution of the Republic of Hawai'i, the proposed bill granted suffrage only to male citizens who met educational and property qualifications. Frear and Dole, possibly to appease women in Hawai'i or to avoid federal intervention, tried to make it possible for the territorial legislature to enfranchise women in the future, but their efforts fell short.[11] In fact, they were deeply concerned about politically active Native Hawaiian women of the chiefly rank and the multiracial demography of the islands, in which "whites" composed a minority.[12]

The Hawaiian Organic Act of 1900 made suffrage an exclusively male privilege. It also placed the elections and qualifications of electors of the territory under the jurisdiction of the U.S. Congress. To the oligarchs' dismay, however, suffrage was granted to male citizens of mature age regardless of economic means as long as they were literate in either English or Hawaiian. The act extended voting rights to formerly disfranchised male Hawaiian commoners with few economic means. According to author Lauren L. Basson, the elimination of property requirements for voting from the Hawaiian Organic Act was an "unexpected" result of party politics rather than the beliefs or preferences of individual policymakers in either camp. They essentially had agreed to maintain white male supremacy in the new "possession." While Republicans endeavored to keep the intelligence and property qualifications to exclude "undesirables" in the Hawaiian Organic Act, vengeful Democrats strongly opposed them. Throughout the Reconstruction era, Democrats had become resentful that Republicans had pressed them to provide full citizenship, including suffrage, to freedmen based on the universalistic principle of equality and justice. Democrats' spiteful action eliminated the property requirement for voting, granting suffrage to Hawaiian-speaking male commoners in the new territory.[13]

Nonetheless, the Hawaiian Organic Act required all legislative proceedings to be conducted in English, while allowing the use of Hawaiian only in times of necessity. The language requirement and the application of racist U.S. naturalization laws barred the expanding immigrant worker communities from gaining political power.[14] The U.S. naturalization law categorized foreign-born Asian immigrants as "aliens ineligible for citizenship" and thus already denied their voting right. The literacy requirement negatively affected substantial numbers of Portuguese immigrants and surging U.S. citizen children of Asian ancestry, who had insufficient command of English or Hawaiian. The Hawaiian Organic Act made it possible for their children to become full-fledged citizens but only after acquiring a command of English and American ways.

In 1901, the entire voting population quadrupled, and Hawaiian men constituted 73 percent of the territorial legislature, much more than during the final days of the monarchy and the republican era. Native Hawaiians composed a clear majority of voters until 1922. After that, they were the largest voter group by "race" until 1938, followed by the Portuguese.[15] Voters in the territory were authorized to elect one delegate to the U.S. House of Representatives, and Native Hawaiian Robert W. Wilcox of the Home Rule Party, who had led two unsuccessful insurrections against white oligarchic rule, was elected as the first territorial delegate to the U.S. Congress in 1900. As stipulated by the Hawaiian Organic Act, however, the delegate to the U.S. Congress had no voting rights.[16]

According to conventional Hawaiian history, the white settler men in the islands, who were affiliated with the Republican Party, managed to maintain their oligarchic rule in the territory. Under the Hawaiian Organic Act, the presidentially appointed territorial governor enjoyed much more power than any state governor ever had. Key organizations in Hawai'i, such as the Hawaiian Sugar Planters' Association (HSPA) and the Honolulu Chamber of Commerce, both of which were under the command of men with missionary connections, invested their wealth and connections in establishing offices in Washington and engaging in massive lobbying activities. Accordingly, the islands' white oligarchic men influenced the appointments of territorial governors by Republican presidents. By maneuvering around national and local politics and patronage in Hawai'i, local white oligarchs and the Republican Party wielded exorbitant power in island politics. Between 1910 and 1940, more than 80 percent of the candidates elected to the territorial legislature were Republicans.[17]

Accommodating to the political reality of the islands, Lili'uokalani and other royal family members were compelled to seek ways to gain justice within the new U.S. system. In an attempt to recover Hawaiian rights and sovereignty, nephews of King Kalākaua's consort Kapi'olani—David La'amea Kahalepouli Kinoiki Kawānanakoa (Prince David, 1868–1908) and his younger brother Jonah Kūhiō Kalaniana'ole (Prince Kūhiō, 1871–1922)—each affiliated themselves with one of the two U.S. political parties. While both had once worked with Wilcox in resisting white men's efforts to Americanize the islands, in the postannexation political realignment, Prince David affiliated himself with the Democratic Party, and Prince Kūhiō, the Republican Party. In the election of 1902, Kūhiō ran for the territorial delegate on a Republican ticket and defeated Wilcox. Kūhiō served nine terms in that seat until his unexpected death in 1922.[18]

Perpetuating the Spirit of Old Hawai'i: The Daughters of Hawai'i and the Daughters and Sons of Hawaiian Warriors

Women missionary descendants, who had embraced rank-based Hawaiian traditions and kingdom culture, sought reconciliation with privileged Native Hawaiian women to influence the territory's course. Since the arrival of U.S. missionaries in 1820, cultural hybridization had taken place in Hawai'i to form multiracial and multiethnic women's high societies. With a worldview that placed Anglo-Saxon middle-class civilization on top, high-ranking Native Hawaiian chiefs and commoner white missionary families from advanced civilization came to live in proximity to and intimacy with each other. These two groups of settler whites and Native Hawaiians exposed themselves to each other's languages and traditions. They stood well above Hawaiian commoners and Asian immigrants, most of whom lacked fluency in English or Hawaiian and modern Western ways. Besides, under the pressure of globalizing industrial capitalism, the Native Hawaiian families of chiefly rank sought to maintain their status by marrying their daughters to foreign merchants and businessmen. Landed Native Hawaiian families became racially mixed and culturally hybridized through intermarriages.[19]

In the period between the kingdom's overthrow and the U.S. annexation, hybrid Native Hawaiian and white settler women were in conflict. In the postannexation era, however, imposing the U.S. system of "democracy" compelled the two groups to work together to assert their collective authority over Hawaiian commoners and multiracializing and multiethnicizing settlers. They also felt that expanding foreign-speaking communities of immigrant families, who used their mother tongue at home and pidgin for interracial or interethnic communications, threatened their hybridized cultural hegemony. For instance, the Daughters of Hawai'i (DOH) was founded in December 1903 as an interracial organization of privileged women to "perpetuate the memory and spirit of Old Hawai'i and to preserve the terms and correct pronunciation of the Hawaiian language." Its seven missionary-daughter founders were each born during the pro-American reign of Kamehameha III and grew up on intimate terms with royal children and thus were fluent in Hawaiian language and culture.[20] They must have shared nostalgic feelings for the good old Hawai'i, a time before rapid commercialization and the large influx of immigrant laborers, when *ali'i* women accepted advice and assistance from American missionary women's circles and retained traditional power as *kuhina-nuis* and chiefs. In mending the rift, elite settler women endeavored to evoke this shared nostalgic memory of the good old days.

By restricting the DOH membership to those who were native-born and had family ties in Hawai'i as far back as 1860,[21] it aspired to become an organization of old-time white and Native Hawaiian women who were well versed in the hybrid high culture of the Hawaiian Kingdom. Although missionary daughter Emma Louise Smith Dillingham (1844–1920) served as its first regent, between 1903 and 1914, two hybrid Native Hawaiians succeeded her: Emilie Kekauluohi Widemann Macfarlane (in office, 1915–1916) and Irene Ha'alou Kahalelaukoa 'Ī'ī Brown-Holloway, *hānai* (adopted) daughter of Rev. and Mrs. C. M. Hyde (in office, 1917).[22] Among the early Native Hawaiian members of the DOH were descendants of the Kamehameha line; Princess Elizabeth Keka'aniau La'anui Pratt (1834–1928) and Princess Elizabeth Kahanu Kaleiwohi-Ka'auwai Kalaniana'ole (1878–1932), who married Prince Kūhiō.[23] The DOH members also included experts in Hawaiian traditions, who sought to preserve the history and culture of "Old Hawai'i." Among them were Emma Kaili Metcalf Beckley-Nākuina (1847–1929) and Elizabeth Lahilahi Rogers Webb (1862–1949).[24]

The hybrid Widemann sisters—the first Native Hawaiian DOH regent, Emilie Kekauluohi Widemann Macfarlane (1859–1947), and her sister, Wilhelmina Kekelaokalaninui Widemann Dowsett (1861–1929), who were both active in Hawaiian patriotic and antiannexation campaigns—played conspicuous roles in the reconciliation process between old-time elite white settler and Native Hawaiian women. Emilie had served as the first president of the Women's Hawaiian Patriotic League, and Wilhelmina would later lead the woman suffrage movement in Hawai'i. They were born to a high-ranking Hawaiian chief mother from Kauai, Mary Kaumana Pilahiuilani, and a German businessman and politician father, Hermann A. Widemann. Their father was a successful coffee and sugar planter on Kaua'i and occupied high-ranking offices in the kingdom government. He was once known as a "devoted royalist" and a "stalwart champion" of Lili'uokalani in resisting the overthrow, the formation of the republic, and the U.S. annexation of Hawai'i. Emilie's husband, Hawai'i-born British businessman Frederick Walter Macfarlane, was also known as a "staunch royalist."[25] Her sister Wilhelmina's husband, John McKibbin Dowsett, was also a Hawai'i-born British descendant businessman whose family had closely interacted with Hawaiian royalty.[26]

The cultural hybridity and political fluidity of the DOH membership was also exemplified in the family history of Julie Judd Swanzy (1860–1941)—granddaughter of Laura Fish Judd, trusted advisor of regent Ka'ahumanu and her successor Kīna'u. Julie Judd joined the DOH in 1906 and served as its fourth regent from 1918 to 1933. Her early life evolved close to the kingdom's high society but only at the periphery of the white women's missionary circle. Her missionary-doctor grandfather, Gerrit Parmele Judd, left his mission board in 1842 to become a leading counselor to Kamehameha III. Her parents also interacted closely with Hawaiian royalty. Her father, Colonel Charles Hastings Judd, served as chamberlain, privy councilor, and private secretary to King Kalākaua from 1878 to 1886 and accompanied the king on his world tour in 1881. Julie's mother Emily Catherine (Cutts) Judd (1840–1921) once served as a lady-in-waiting for Queen Lili'uokalani and participated in the kingdom's court. After attending Punahou School and then Mills College in Oakland, California, the first women's college west of the Rockies, Julie Judd spent a few years in Europe. When she returned to Hawai'i in 1887, she married Francis Mills Swanzy (1850–1917). Unlike other missionary descendants who married members of the American missionary circle in Hawai'i or their cohorts from or on the U.S. mainland, her husband was born and educated in Dublin under British colonial rule and worked for Theo H. Davies & Company, the only British enterprise among the Big Five. Francis Mills Swanzy played a role in introducing immigrant laborers from Asia and later became the managing director of Theo H. Davies.[27] Because of her cultural hybridity, Julie Judd Swanzy came to play a crucial role in mediating conciliation and reconciliation between the Native Hawaiian nobility and the missionary descendants to keep peace and unity among the multinational population in postannexation Hawaiʻi. As a long-time DOH regent, she fought for the preservation of Native Hawaiian historic sites and sought to raise multiracial island-born children into bona fide members of the U.S. territory. She led the free kindergarten movement as the longtime president of the Free Kindergarten and Children's Aid Association of the Hawaiian Islands (FKCAAHI) and served as the honorary president of the Pan-Pacific Women's Conferences (PPWCs), as will be discussed in the following chapters.[28]

Led by hybrid white settler and Native Hawaiian women of privileged rank, the DOH facilitated reconciling not only the once-divided two groups but also rival *aliʻi* families. The DOH produced a plaque for the birthplace of Kamehameha III, Keauhou, Kona on the Big Island, and held a ceremony on his birthday, March 17, 1914, at Kawaiahaʻo Church, a Congregational Church in Honolulu that had once served as the state church of the kingdom. It gathered over a thousand people, mostly Native Hawaiians.[29] According to the DOH record: "The most regal aspect of the ceremony was the presence of Hawaiʻi's highest *aliʻi*: Liliʻuokalani, the beloved former Queen, and High Chiefess Elizabeth Kekaʻaniau Pratt, a Daughter of Hawaiʻi member and a former classmate of the Queen at the Chiefs' Children's School. The two women, proud standard bearers of their race, sat on thrones draped with magnificent feather capes."[30]

The overthrow of Queen Liliʻuokalani ended the Kalākaua dynasty, which brought to the surface longtime rivalries among chiefs in Hawaiʻi. In a sense, by collaborating with white elite women in perpetuating and celebrating their memory of the old Hawaiʻi under monarchical rule, the highest-ranking Native Hawaiian women of rival bloodlines came together to assert their traditional authority together in relation to Hawaiian commoners and recently arrived settlers from all over the world. Consciously or unconsciously, however, they contributed to the reconciliation between Natives and settlers, ultimately normalizing the U.S. rule in multiracialized and multiethnicized Hawaiʻi.

Having been exposed to the mechanism of American "democracy" and realizing the political implications of such efforts, Prince Kūhiō initiated efforts to form a similar organization among ruling-rank Native Hawaiian women and men. In 1911, the Daughters and Sons of Hawaiian Warriors (DSHW, Māmakakaua), composed exclusively of descendants of female and male Hawaiian high chiefs, was inaugurated.[31] While hoisting its goal as the preservation of Hawaiian traditions and culture, like the DOH, the DSHW aimed to reconcile the descendants of the chiefs who had followed Kamehameha I and those who had opposed him and lost. It was an attempt to achieve collective Native Hawaiian political power. Influential Native Hawaiian DOH members, such as Emilie K. W. Macfarlane and Princess Kalanianaʻole (wife of Prince Kūhiō), likewise joined the DSHW. Emilie's sister Wilhelmina K. W. Dowsett was in the DSHW's position of *kuhina-nui* (premier/president) in 1912, and so was Emilie, later in 1917.[32] Among other notable Native Hawaiian women active in the DSHW was Emma Ahuena Davison Taylor (1867–1937), daughter of a chief mother with British heritage and an American father from Delaware, who served as the premier of the DSHW for many years.[33]

Carrie Chapman Catt and Native Hawaiian Women: Generating a Woman Suffrage Movement in Hawaiʻi

As the U.S. electoral system was introduced to Hawaiʻi, woman suffrage slowly drew attention from women in Hawaiʻi, where most of them were still either against or undecided about the issue as of May 1913.[34] By then, Native Hawaiian women had formed numerous suffrage groups throughout the islands—e.g., the Women's Equal Suffrage Association of Hawaiʻi (WESAH) headed by Wilhelmina K. W. Dowsett and the Women's Suffrage League headed by Mrs. Kali (most possibly Sera Kali). In June 1912, these groups appeared at a local Democratic meeting to press the cause. They formed the Women's Suffrage Association of Hawaiʻi (WSAH; aka, the National Women's Suffrage Association of Hawaiʻi). Possibly, the WSAH was to be an interisland umbrella organization. Dowsett assumed its honorary presidency, and Sera Kali shared the presidency with leaders of other organizations. The WSAH held the first woman suffrage *lūʻau* (Hawaiian feast) in Honolulu in August 1912.[35] Soon, the suffrage fervor reached women of other islands. In October 1912, the NAWSA–supported play, "How the

Vote Was Won," was performed at ABCFM missionary–initiated Church in Makawao, the island of Maui.[36]

To add to the mix, in late October 1912, Carrie Chapman Catt stopped briefly in Honolulu on her around-the-world tour. Catt twice served as NAWSA president from 1900 to 1904 and from 1915 to 1920 and was the president of the International Woman Suffrage Alliance (IWSA) from 1904 to 1923.[37] She recorded in her diary that she was greeted at the dock by two "half cast[e]" women and was welcomed at the Opera House by a "Hawaiian selection sung by a trio of Hawaiian women."[38] The news of her visit captivated Native Hawaiian women. One of the two women who had greeted Catt on her arrival at the dock was Wilhelmina K. W. Dowsett, the DSHW premier of the time. Dowsett also headed the WESAH and the WSAH and asked Catt to give a lecture at a meeting held under its auspices.[39] Dowsett and other suffrage leaders, who came to play a central role in generating a woman suffrage movement in Honolulu, were culturally hybridized and typically born to a Hawaiian mother and a father of non-U.S. extraction. They were eager to recover their rights lost in the new U.S. political system.[40]

At the moment when Hawai'i's representative government system was consolidating, white settler women and men became anxious at the prospect that granting woman suffrage would double the already majority vote of Native Hawaiians. It was quite threatening for them because Native Hawaiian women were much more enthusiastic and experienced in political leadership than white settler women.[41] Furthermore, situated at the "gender frontier" of Hawai'i, where the cult of womanhood and women's sphere functioned as indicators of their civilized status, white settler women were inclined to remain in the circumscribed sphere. According to the *Honolulu Star-Bulletin*, Catt's lecture meeting in Honolulu revealed that "though a large number of women prominent in the social circle of this city [were] interested in Woman's Suffrage, few [came] forward to take any important part in the work."[42]

Although Carrie Chapman Catt lacked full understanding of the territory's historical background, her visit successfully made woman suffrage a contemporary and crucial issue of the islands. On October 28, she lectured to a small but representative audience, mostly hybrid Native Hawaiian women but also missionary granddaughter Mary Emma Dillingham Frear (1870–1951). Mary E. D. Frear was a daughter of the DOH's first regent Emma L. S. Dillingham and the wife of Republican territorial governor

Walter F. Frear (in office, 1908–1913).[43] In mapping the world according to women's enfranchisement, Catt granted the leading position to Scandinavian countries and argued that American women were struggling because they had to rely on male voters, many of whom were naturalized foreigners. She insisted that it was strange that "a man from Italy who [had] remained in the United States long enough to become a citizen should have the right to vote on a ballot" but women, even "the daughters of the revolution whose ancestors came to America hundreds of years ago [should] not." In her view, women would vote in a "womanly" or nonpartisan way, independent of their husbands, and she argued that she knew of "a man who [was] a republican, his wife a democrat and his daughter a prohibitionist." For Catt, the coming of woman suffrage was "as certain as the rising of the sun," and she urged the women of Hawai'i to get their vote while Hawai'i was still a territory because it would be "far easier to do so now" than to do so when Hawai'i became a state and would have a larger population.[44]

Presumably, in the historical context of Hawai'i, Catt's argument appealed most to Native Hawaiian women, but not so much to local white men or women who were more likely to fall into the category of "naturalized foreigners," whom Catt criticized. Local Asians, who composed the majority of recent immigrants on the islands, were barred from naturalization and thus also from voting. Furthermore, the prospect of having politically active Native Hawaiian wives of Republicans voting for Democrats was a real concern of the local white oligarchy, and thus oligarchic Republican men became even more dubious about woman suffrage. Catt's lecture assured the legitimacy of Native Hawaiian women in demanding suffrage to participate in the territory's new political system.

Although Catt revealed her social Darwinist worldview of racial hierarchies—she noted in her diary that Polynesians were in a lower stratum[45]—she assisted hybrid elite Native Hawaiian suffragists in consolidating the newly formed WSAH and generating a movement. According to Catt, "the society formed" in Honolulu was "composed of native women mostly," and she instructed the WSAH in revising their constitution.[46] She promised to represent the new organization as a part of the NAWSA at its upcoming 1912 convention. The NAWSA, however, required affiliates to have a membership of at least fifty,[47] and it was not until the 1913 NAWSA convention that "for the first time Hawai'i took her place among the auxiliaries."[48]

Hawai'i's emerging woman suffrage movements willingly transcended the boundaries of race, class, and party, uniting "all women" with U.S. citizenship.

At the time of Catt's visit, Wilhelmina K. W. Dowsett asked Emma 'Aima Ai'i Nāwahī for her cooperation and advice in generating a woman suffrage movement. Emma 'Aima Ai'i Nāwahī's mother was a Hawaiian chief of minor rank and her father, a prominent Chinese sugar miller. In the 1890s, to preserve Hawai'i's sovereignty, Emma—along with Abigail Kuaihelani Maipinepine Campbell, president of the Women's Hawaiian Patriotic League—had led the antiannexation petition drive among the people of the islands. After the annexation, to promote the interest of Native Hawaiians under the new U.S. representative political system, she contributed to organizing the local Democratic Party in 1889.[49] Nonetheless, she understood the need of uniting women of various racial and social backgrounds, regardless of party affiliation, to gain political power. Calling for cooperation among "all women" in Hawai'i, she also warned: "All women throughout the Territory, who are American citizens, from the highest to the lowest, from the richest to the poorest, the whites, the Portuguese and the Hawaiians should stand shoulder to shoulder and advance together with accord and harmony."[50] Presumably, Nāwahī's call encouraged some white women whose husbands were active in the Republican Party to join the emerging woman suffrage movement in Hawai'i. For example, Mary Emma Dillingham Frear participated in a suffrage meeting held at the Dowsett's residence to speak for the cause and joined the woman suffrage movement under the Native Hawaiian women's leadership.[51]

Nāwahī's statement, however, also revealed the limitations of Native Hawaiian suffragists' strategy of the time. They recognized the importance of generating a bipartisan democratic women's movement uniting Native Hawaiian and white women citizens of all ranks, including the Portuguese, who constituted an important part of the plantation workforce and were labeled as a class "above" Asians but "less" than other whites. Although Emma Nāwahī herself was part Chinese and Asians composed over half of the population in Hawai'i, her understanding of "all women" at this point ironically did not refer to women of Asian ancestry.[52] In the bipolar plantation society, Nāwahī, a descendant of early Chinese settlers to the islands, was possibly distant in lifestyle and identity from recently arrived Asian settler women who spoke neither English nor Hawaiian and lived in ethnically segregated plantation camps. Furthermore, due to racially discriminatory U.S. laws, the new immigrants from Asia were barred from naturalization and citizenship, and the majority of their American-born daughters were still under the voting age. It required interracial and international exchanges during World War I for Native Hawaiian suffrage leaders to develop the concept of "all women" to include those without U.S. citizenship, most notably new immigrant women from Asia.

World War I and Women's Networking

During World War I, national and local pressure to prove Hawai'i's loyalty to the United States facilitated interracial and interethnic interactions and networking, consolidating Hawai'i's Republican oligarchy. While local branches of such organizations as the Red Cross and the U.S. Council of the National Defense (CND) were established and the territory-wide United War Work Campaign (UWWC) was launched, Native Hawaiian and white leaders were compelled to mobilize the ethnically divided population to carry out the patriotic wartime work. This gave leverage to bilingual high-society women linked to Republican oligarchs in Hawai'i but also facilitated a diverse collection of women to come together and collectively influence male territorial and national politicians.[53]

When war broke out in Europe in 1914, women in Hawai'i began their respective wartime contributions sporadically through the islands. For example, Native Hawaiian and immigrant women made hospital garments and collected donations to be sent to their respective homelands or allies. With U.S. participation in the war in 1917, the frenzy for Americanization and patriotism pressed Hawai'i's multinational population to demonstrate its loyalty to the United States. This top-down pressure for unity and efficiency brought multiple women's Red Crosses and other war relief organizations to take an auxiliary role to the male-led War Relief Committee of Hawai'i, which later became the American National Red Cross Hawaiian Chapter. Missionary grandson Alfred Lowrey Castle (1884–1972) became the secretary and executive officer of this male-led Honolulu-headquartered organization. His sister Alice Beatrice Castle (1888–1931) supervised the women's auxiliary work.[54] Hawai'i's participation in the UWWC—a nationwide fundraising drive and war-work campaign conducted by seven civic organizations, including the national YMCA and YWCA—came under the leadership of men and women who led local YMCA and YWCA movements.[55]

On the mainland, suffragists pressed President Woodrow Wilson to create the CND Women's Committee in 1917. Anna Howard Shaw, an ordained minister and physician who served as NAWSA president from 1901 to 1915, chaired the committee. The CND was composed of secretaries of the Treasury, War, Navy, Interior, Agriculture, Commerce, and Labor Departments. Its Women's Committee functioned as its advisory body coordinating women's wartime efforts.[56] Among the prominent committee women was Carrie Chapman Catt, who cofounded the Woman's Peace Party in 1915 but saw a need for patriotic war-support efforts for women to achieve full U.S. citizenship. By closely working with federal agencies and the U.S. Food Administration, the Women's Committee reached out to prosuffrage, neutral, and antisuffrage national women's groups and their local affiliates.[57] Although Hawai'i's territorial governor was unwilling to take up CND work, the CND's Women's Committee assigned Native Hawaiian suffrage leader Wilhelmina K. W. Dowsett to assume chairpersonship temporarily and form a division in Hawai'i.[58]

Prominent women from the missionary circle, such as Mary Dillingham Frear, who was active in the woman suffrage movement in Hawai'i and then served as the Honolulu YWCA president, also contributed to organizing the Hawaiian division of the CND Women's Committee. While Dowsett was chosen as its permanent chair and Frear as one of its vice chairs, several influential Native Hawaiian and white settler women assumed other offices of the committee. By establishing subcommittees in line with the CND's national Women's Committee, the Hawaiian division took charge of promoting territorial women's wartime work in home and foreign relief, liberty loans, food production and home economics, registration for service, child welfare, and so on. In fact, a small group of culturally hybridized women shared leadership in carrying out multiracial and multiethnic women's wartime work with the overlapping membership of local Red Cross, UWWC, and CND groups.[59]

Hybrid Native Hawaiian women, such as the German-heritage Widemann sisters, might have felt extra pressure to prove their loyalty to the United States, and they became a force in Hawai'i's patriotic war-relief and war-support endeavors. For example, on hearing that "the boys" of Hawai'i on duty were suffering from the cold weather, Emilie K. W. Macfarlane, assisted by Emma Ahuena Davison Taylor and other DSHW members, started a knitting unit, while Princess Kawānanakoa (wife of the late Prince David) secured wool during her visit to the mainland. With Lili'uokalani's alleged endorsement of American Red Cross work, knitting units mobilized Native Hawaiians, including not only women and girls but also men

KNITTERS AT MAKIKI FIRE STATION, HONOLULU

Figure 2.1 Knitters at Makiki Fire Station, ca. 1918.
Source: Courtesy of the Hawai'i State Archives.

and boys. Princess Kalaniana'ole (Prince Kūhiō's wife) came to head the 'Iolani Unit. When the Hawaiian Knitting Unit was organized in March 1918, Wilhelmina K. W. Dowsett became its president.[60] Promoted by these high-ranking Native Hawaiian women, the novel practice of knitting in tropical Hawai'i became a genderless patriotic effort (Figure 2.1).

Furthermore, under the collaborative leadership, bilingual elite women leaders of diverse ethnic and national backgrounds mobilized their respective ethnic communities to territory-wide women's war support, relief, and wartime fundraising endeavors. They did so to prove the loyalty of their respective ethnic communities and the territory to the United States. Non-English/non-Hawaiian–speaking Asian immigrant wives living in rural plantation camps were pressed to participate in wartime women's endeavors. Accordingly, intricate interracial, interethnic, and transnational networks of elite women exercising top-down influence over ethnic communities emerged.[61]

While Hawai'i carried out massive wartime campaigns among its multinational and multiracial populations, mainland woman suffragists turned their attention once again toward Hawai'i. In the late 1910s, suffragists came to Hawai'i to find the best way to assist the islands' suffrage leaders. For example, suffragist and peace advocate Alice Locke Park of Palo Alto, California, investigated the islands' situation in early 1915. Nonetheless, she failed to understand fully the peculiar condition of its white male oligarchy and formed an impression that the territory was ready to enfranchise women. Park reported similarities between Hawai'i's condition and Arizona's prior to its 1912 suffrage victory; she found "no excitement and no objection" on the issue.[62] In fact, by the end of 1915, local parties pledged to support votes for women, and the territorial legislature adopted a joint resolution requesting Prince Kūhiō, the territorial delegate to U.S. Congress, "to urge upon Congress the passage of an amendment to the Organic Act of this Territory, so that the right to vote be extended to women."[63] Kūhiō presented the resolution to Congress, but it received no attention at the national level. Two years later, the amendment to the Hawaiian Organic Act was still pending.

In 1917, mainland suffragists' optimistic reading of the islands' enthusiasm for suffrage inspired NAWSA leaders to believe that enfranchising women in Hawai'i could move from Congress to the territorial legislature. The central figure in this development was NAWSA activist Almira Hollander Pitman of Brookline, Massachusetts, who visited Honolulu in early 1917. Pitman was married to Benjamin F. Keolaokalani Pitman (1852–1918), a Native Hawaiian born to an American merchant father and a high-rank Hawaiian mother, Kino'ole-o-Liliha (1825–1855) of Hilo. Accordingly, she had a deep connection and interest in woman suffrage in the islands. After conversing with nearly all members of the territorial legislature at its opening, she became convinced of their support for woman suffrage.[64]

Pitman also reported the enthusiasm of elite-class white and Native Hawaiian suffragists. Describing the circle of local women who gathered to meet her, Pitman recalled a large reception given by "Madame Nakuina, who was known as the Court historian," possibly Native Hawaiian DOH member Emma Metcalf Beckley-Nākuina. Also among "all the women of the highest social circles in the Islands" who attended her reception "fête" were DSHW leaders Wilhelmina K. W. Dowsett, Emma Ahuena Davison Taylor, and missionary granddaughter Harriet Angeline Castle Coleman (1847–1924). Pitman held her first meeting at Dowsett's residence, followed by two more meetings: "one attended mostly by the middle class and the other by high caste Hawaiians and the 'missionary set.'" She was deeply impressed by the Native Hawaiian suffragists' fluency in English, world knowledge, and strong desire for the woman's vote. Pitman promised to meet their request to investigate the status of Hawai'i's territorial resolution on women's vote as soon as she returned home.[65]

From Washington, DC, to Honolulu: Peculiar Territorial Conditions and Suffrage Demand for "All Women" in Hawai'i

In Washington, convinced of the territorial legislature's willingness to grant women suffrage, Pitman advocated for territorial jurisdiction. Based on information Pitman provided, the chair of NAWSA's Congressional Committee, Maud Wood Park, raised the issue with the senator from Colorado, John F. Shafroth, chair of the Committee on Pacific Islands and Puerto Rico. On June 1, 1917, Shafroth introduced a bill presented by Kūhiō to the Senate, which asked to "grant the Legislature of the Territory of Hawai'i additional powers relative to elections and qualifications of electors" in order to enfranchise women. The Senate passed the bill without any discussion on September 15, but the House referred it to the Committee on Woman Suffrage, chaired by Judge John E. Raker. The committee held a hearing on April 29, 1918, in which Maud Wood Park, Anna Howard Shaw, and Almira H. Pitman were present.[66] Pitman believed that Hawai'i was ready to enfranchise women if it were left to its own devices, a view held similarly by Alice Park. Anna Howard Shaw, in her attempt to avoid arousing strong opposition, emphasized that the bill was not asking Congress to enfranchise the women of Hawai'i but to "permit the people of Hawaii to decide this question for themselves."[67] The committee recommended the passage of the bill, and Wilson signed it into law in June 1918. Territorial governor Charles J. McCarthy (in office, 1918–1921), an appointee of Democratic president Wilson, then recommended that the Hawai'i legislature use its power to confer woman suffrage.[68]

Mainland suffragist efforts to facilitate the process of enfranchising women in Hawai'i, however, ended up only transferring the prerogative from the U.S. federal government to the Hawaiian territorial government, which was under the firm grip of the local male Republican oligarchy. The territory indeed appeared ready to enfranchise women but, in reality, faced a strong undercurrent opposing their suffrage. Mainland efforts might have inadvertently assisted the islands' oligarchic men in postponing federal intervention on the issue. As 1919 unfolded, mainland suffragists diverted their attention away from Hawai'i, while local suffragists of various ethnic and racial backgrounds gathered together in the seemingly last stage of their movement so that they would be enfranchised in time for the approaching county and primary elections in May 1919. In February, territorial governor McCarthy, an advocate of statehood and woman suffrage, urged the legislature to enfranchise the women of Hawai'i without calling for a plebiscite vote on the subject.[69] Territorial senator Rev. Stephen L. Desha Sr. (R) introduced a woman suffrage bill to the territorial Senate (the Desha bill), but during deliberations of the territorial senate judiciary committee, Senators Manuel C. Pacheco (D) and Harry Alexander Baldwin (R) introduced an amendment to make the resulting law effective on July 1 after the upcoming county and primary election. Harry Alexander Baldwin (1871–1946), a son of Henry Perrine Baldwin, insisted that he was for woman suffrage but favored the postponement to provide enough time for registering women for the county election.[70] The delay tactic, however, also meant that women would not play a role in determining the candidates for their expected first vote.

Having learned the power of mobilization from their wartime experiences, Native Hawaiian women leaders transformed their concept of "all women" to include Asian women to regenerate a women's mass movement for suffrage. On the morning of the Senate vote on March 4, 1919, Wilhelmina K. W. Dowsett held a women's mass meeting at the capitol building to demonstrate the unity of women demanding suffrage.[71] At the meeting, which gathered representatives from the various ethnic communities, Dowsett declared the regeneration of the woman suffrage and advocated that "all" women cooperate.[72] Dowsett appealed to supporters for interracial and interethnic female solidarity. "Speaking as a Hawaiian Woman," she reminded "Sister Hawaiians, our foreign sisters are with us. . . . We are working all together, and we want the legislature to know this. And we must also remember our Oriental sisters, who are not here today but who will also unite this great cause."[73] The absence of Asian women at the site was because most foreign-born Asian women were barred by federal immigration law from citizenship, but Dowsett articulated a politics of unity. According to the *Maui News*, the Senate, having its chamber surrounded by "several hundred women," passed the bill that would make woman suffrage effective immediately.[74]

Although small in number, foreign-born Asian women had become U.S. citizens. Under the laws of the kingdom, the provisional government, and the republic, aliens, regardless of race or proficiency in English or Hawaiian, were to be granted all the privileges of subjects/citizens through their services to the respective government. The Organic Act declared that all citizens of the

Republic of Hawai'i as of August 12, 1898, were citizens of the United States and the Territory of Hawai'i.[75] Also, still small in number, children of Asian ancestry were granted U.S. citizenship. Once women were enfranchised in the territory, Asian women citizens of maturity would be able to vote after acquiring a command of English or Hawaiian. According to a newspaper article, in 1917, the estimated number of potential Asian women voters in the territory, for example, included 636 Chinese and 278 Japanese.[76]

To expedite the passage of the Territorial Senate suffrage bill in the Territorial House, Dowsett and her organization called another women's mass meeting in the throne room of the capitol on March 6, 1919. They adopted a resolution demanding that the House grant women the right and privilege of participating in the upcoming primary in May and the regular elections in June 1919. Among the speakers advocating the cause were Native Hawaiian clergymen, senator Rev. Stephen L. Desha Sr. and Akaiko Akana, and DOH and/or DSHW members, Emilie K. W. Macfarlane, Princess Kalaniana'ole, Elizabeth Lahilahi Webb, and Mary E. Dillingham Frear. Newly arrived mainland women professionals were also present to speak for woman suffrage, including Margaret Knepper, a teacher from California who had recently joined the faculty of McKinley High School, later known as "Tokyo High" due to its large student body of Hawai'i-born teenagers of Asian ancestry.[77]

Instead of promptly adopting the Territorial Senate Bill, however, the territorial house introduced another bill that referred woman suffrage to a plebiscite. According to the bill, the suffrage question would be submitted to the electorate at the time of the primary in May 1919, but the plebiscite would take place at the time of general election in June 1920.[78] In response, Dowsett, representing the island of O'ahu, and Louise MacMillan from the Big Island of Hawai'i conducted a mass agitation in the House chamber on March 23, 1919. According to the *Honolulu Star-Bulletin*, "nearly 500 women" of "various nationalities, of all ages" crowded onto the floor of the House, carrying "a huge banner bearing the words 'Votes for Women.'" Before the session opened, they filled the floor of the assembly hall and its outside *lanais* (terraces). Consequently, the House decided to hold a two-hour hearing on woman suffrage, inviting both supporters and opponents on the following day.[79] After the hearing, the suffragist leaders gathered a large crowd at A'ala Park in Honolulu.[80]

Nonetheless, the territorial legislature engaged in bitter "word wars" on suffrage, and the ultimate question to enfranchise women or not became secondary to who would be voting on the issue, how, and when. Consequently, this further delayed women's official participation in territorial politics.[81] By early April 1919, woman suffragists began losing their patience with the territorial legislature. In response, Dowsett began efforts to make suffrage a national matter; a plea for suffrage was drawn up and presented to the U.S. Congress through Prince Kūhiō, the territorial representative. To achieve woman suffrage in the new U.S. political system and to prepare themselves for the vote, suffragists in Hawai'i began to organize precinct clubs.[82] As deliberations in the two-chamber territorial legislature dragged on, however, local suffragists themselves divided over the question of how and when to decide on suffrage.[83] Hawai'i's high-spirited suffrage movement began to lose momentum, further delaying victory.[84]

Meanwhile, the Nineteenth Amendment to the U.S. Constitution, prohibiting the federal government and each state from disenfranchising women, passed both chambers by June 1919 and was ratified by three-fourths of the states in August 1920. This amendment, proclaimed by Secretary of State Bainbridge Colby on August 26, 1920, included U.S. territorial women. Thus, only through federal action, the Nineteenth Amendment to the U.S. Constitution, were women citizens in Hawai'i finally granted the right to vote.[85]

Although a few white women of missionary descent were present in the thick and thin of the woman suffrage movement, they, like their husbands, never fully eliminated their anxiety about being the islands' minority. According to historian Roger Bell, who examined the male statehood movement in Hawai'i, the early debate on statehood that emerged in the 1910s along with woman suffrage soon "submerged beneath a common concern: how to avoid or at least delay the triumph of the non-Caucasian majority in politics, economics, and society."[86] In fact, Hawai'i's white male oligarchy diffused increasing apprehension about Asian American girls with birthright citizenship, who were mostly still underage but would soon become eligible voters. They made surging numbers of *Nisei* (children of Japanese immigrants born in the United States) daughters a focal point in discussing the future electorate. According to an article in the *Hawaiian Gazette*, on September 18, 1917, granting woman suffrage would double the Hawaiian majority and then, with Japanese girls outnumbering Native Hawaiian girls under the age of twenty-one, hasten the advent of majority Japanese voters. The article attributed this ethnic disparity to a higher birth rate among Japanese immigrants than Native Hawaiians. The writer opposed woman suffrage and expressed a cultural and racial anxiety by cautioning readers that Japanese women would "overtake and outvote the other women considerably sooner" than Japanese men and that Japanese women and men combined would lead to "a Japanese majority over all."[87]

This information possibly discouraged local white women from advocating suffrage. Some might have collaborated with "antis" in the mainland and upheld their cult of womanhood to confine Native Hawaiian and immigrant daughters in women's private sphere. In fact, Massachusetts suffragist Almira H. Pitman recorded that "almost the first person" she saw in the islands during her visit in early 1917 was the field secretary of "the Massachusetts Association Opposed to the [Further] Extension of Suffrage to Women."[88] In February 1919, it was reported that among seventy-five women of the Outdoor Circle, a women's club in Honolulu under the leadership of white women of missionary heritage, only twenty supported the suffrage cause, with ten opposed and the rest undecided. Apparently, a substantial number of influential white settler women still remained hesitant about enfranchising women citizens in Hawai'i.[89]

Retrospectively recording observations of Hawai'i's politics in her diary, Alice Locke Park discussed the "peculiar situation" in Hawai'i, where Asians, comprising more than half of the population, were disfranchised, and politics were "nip and tuck" between "Hawaiians and whites." Park summarizes the situation:

> The Hawaiians see that it will be to their advantage to have votes for women and double their total vote—the solid vote. The whites all claim to be in favor of suffrage—sometimes—but are not eager to see it immediately in Hawaii. They are torn with conflicting emotions—for they can't oppose the movement when it is advancing all over the world. If the whites could restrict the vote to whites, both men and women, they would do so at once. But there is an awkwardness in the political situation, when the whites know that equal suffrage would double the solid Hawaiian vote, and give the whites a lesser number of new voters, and these of various opinions.[90]

Suffrage did not divide the women of Hawai'i wholly along color or party lines, but their suffrage movement "accepted or willing to acquiesce" the premise of Anglo-Saxon supremacist U.S. systems and "civilization."[91] For Native Hawaiian women leaders, suffrage was a crucial means for decolonization, to recover rights lost to white settler colonialism and U.S.

imperialism. Nonetheless, they were also concerned about the immediate need to bring Hawaiian commoners under their influence in the unfamiliar political system of U.S. "democracy." Furthermore, a surging number of Hawai'i-born daughters of Asian ancestry, who would soon reach voting age, needed education to be qualified voters in the territory. With the 1900 Hawaiian Organic Act, the command of either English or Hawaiian became a voter qualification, but English became the official language for legislative proceedings. Nonetheless, with the influx of immigrant labor, Hawai'i became a polyglot society, and pidgin was used for interracial and interethnic communication in rural plantation communities. Such circumstances narrowed the divide between Native Hawaiian and white settler progressive women leaders, who were equally conversant with each other's language and tradition. The same circumstances also compelled the Native Hawaiian women of the ruling rank and influential white settler women of missionary heritage to work with elite bilingual women of other ethnic communities not only to achieve woman suffrage but also to take charge of territorial "motherhood," as discussed in the following two chapters. Furthermore, although a viable woman suffrage movement initiated by hybrid Native Hawaiian suffragists fell short of achieving the goal by itself under white male oligarchic rule, the emerging interracial and interethnic women's political movement was gaining momentum, pressing male oligarchs to recognize the political power of women in Hawai'i.

The Politics of Women's Solidarity: Hawai'i's 1920 General and 1922 Special Elections

The bilingual woman suffrage movement in Hawai'i did not end with the U.S. secretary of state's proclamation ensuring suffrage for women citizens in the islands. Native Hawaiian women had ruled as chiefs, regents, and queens during the kingdom days, and they interpreted "woman suffrage" as women's rights to vote and to be elected for territorial public offices. They went ahead to run for election, which caused controversy. Although they transcended racial, ethnic, and party lines, they had experienced the reality of island politics that failed to enfranchise women. Privileged Native Hawaiian suffragist leaders were willing to collaborate with influential white women leaders to support and gain influence over local Republican oligarchic men to secure women's full suffrage.

The first postsuffrage election was to elect party nominees for delegate to the U.S. Congress and Territorial senators and representatives for the 1920 general election. Enthusiastic Native Hawaiian women placed their names as candidates for the territorial primary, which was scheduled for October 2, 1920. Helen Makakoa Sniffen of the island of Maui and Mary Ha'aheo Kinimaka Atcherley (1874–1933) of the island of O'ahu entered the race for the Territorial Senate on the Democratic ticket. Nonetheless, it did not mean that local Democrat men admitted women's claim for public office. They relegated the decision to whether women could hold office to the territorial court.[92]

Women's political enthusiasm also became evident when voter registration for the primary began on August 30. Native Hawaiian women rushed to the city clerk's office in Honolulu.[93] A dozen of them waited for the opening of the clerk's office, and the first woman to register was hybrid Native Hawaiian schoolteacher Louise Aoe Wong McGregor (figure 2.2).[94]

Figure 2.2 Hawaiian Women on Deck Early.
Source: *Honolulu Star-Bulletin*, August 30, 1920.

THE POLITICS OF WOMAN SUFFRAGE IN THE U.S. TERRITORY [67]

Although only a small number of Asian women, who were either born in Hawai'i or were naturalized before 1900, were eligible to vote, they too were enthusiastic to exercise their new right. The first woman of Japanese ancestry to register was Alice Sae Teshima Noda (1894–1964). As a dental hygienist and social activist in Honolulu, she contributed to ensuring the health, welfare, and education of Hawai'i's multiracial and multiethnic children.[95]

Unfortunately, however, multiracial women's enthusiasm for political participation once again encountered the islands' complex political undercurrents, which seemed best navigated by white male Republican oligarchs. Dowsett and Native Hawaiian suffragists in Honolulu, who canvassed downtown streets urging women to register, soon felt it necessary to facilitate the registration process. The islands' high ratio of cross-racial and cross-national marriages and different naturalization processes under its different governments must have added to the confusion in judging women's qualification for voter registration. U.S. laws at the time made a married woman's nationality and citizenship derivative of her husband's, with the exception of foreign-born wives of Asian descent, who, regardless of their husbands' nationality, remained ineligible for naturalization and citizenship. Furthermore, it must have been difficult for rural women voters to receive adequate registration information. Accordingly, Native Hawaiian suffragists requested the appointment of deputy clerks to facilitate the registration process, but Honolulu's Democratic mayor John H. Wilson rejected their requests. He insisted that City and County Clerk David Kalauokalani had "already made adequate provision" and that it was "up to the women to present themselves before the proper authorities."[96]

Concurrently, an editorial in the *Honolulu Star-Bulletin*, a newspaper under the influence of Republican settler men, accused the "women of Honolulu," specifically urban white citizen women, of "disheartening indifference to the primary duty of qualifying themselves as electors in the forthcoming elections by getting their names on the great register at the city clerk's office." Arguing that "flying squads of notaries canvas[ing] the city to register women voters" would "achieve nothing lasting nor worthwhile," the editorial encouraged "those women of Honolulu who had always taken an intelligent interest in civic affairs" to "take the lead in the vitally essential public service of arousing their sisters to the importance, the necessity, of using their ballots."[97]

On September 2, 1920, Wilhelmina K. W. Dowsett called a mass meeting at Mission Memorial Hall to encourage women to register for the

Figure 2.3 To Aid Women Politically.
Source: *Pacific Commercial Advertiser Second Section*, September 3, 1920.

upcoming primary and to demand more deputy clerks to expedite the registration of women voters (Figure 2.3). The mass meeting gathered "125 feminist voters" including Native Hawaiian and white settler suffrage leaders. It unanimously passed "a motion creating a committee of four to appeal for aid" in voter registration to the Honolulu mayor, the Chamber of Commerce, and the city clerk.[98] These suffrage leaders, however, refrained from supporting Native Hawaiian women candidates. In fact, along with privileged Native Hawaiian and white women leaders, who took the podium at the meeting, were a few white men who also gave speeches. Among the male speakers were Raymond C. Brown, Honolulu Chamber of Commerce secretary, and Lorrin A. Thurston, who had played a central role in the overthrow of the monarchy and the U.S. annexation of Hawaiʻi. While both men appeared to be supportive of the political participation of women in general, they lacked enthusiasm for Native Hawaiian women candidates, especially those affiliated with the Democratic Party. Brown promised that he would do all he could in assisting women's registration but did not challenge City and County Clerk Kalauokalani declining to appoint additional deputies.

Thurston welcomed Native Hawaiian women's enthusiasm for political participation but insisted that Secretary of State Bainbridge Colby's proclamation had not granted women citizens of Hawai'i the right to be elected. He argued that altering the Organic Act was necessary to "permit women to hold office" and suggested that women voters should pay attention to each candidate's stand "concerning such alteration."[99] In October, the territorial Attorney General Harry Irwin made a public statement that the Nineteenth Amendment affected "only the right of a woman to vote" and that the Organic Act needed to be amended to entitle women to hold public office, referring to Section 34 of the Act, which required male citizenship of the United States to be eligible for election as a territorial senator.[100]

Instead of supporting women candidates, high-society suffragists came to use women's votes to influence an oligarchic Republican man to achieve the women's full rights of suffrage. On the island of Maui, where Helen M. Sniffen was nominated to run as a senator on the Democratic ticket, missionary granddaughter Ethel Frances Smith Baldwin (1879–1967), upon the forming of the Maui Women's Suffrage Association in May 1919, had begun voter education. She endeavored to prevent party politics or sex wars by calling women to study community problems, solutions, and civil government. She assisted and influenced her husband by promoting women's causes. Her husband, missionary grandson Harry Alexander Baldwin (1872–1946), was an incumbent Republican territorial senator seeking reelection. The Baldwins, including his father Henry Perrine Baldwin, the "most successful sugar planter in the islands," had attained a status almost equal to the ruling families of the island of Maui.[101] Having been active in philanthropic and maternalist work, Ethel F. S. Baldwin had established collaborative relationships with Hawaiian nobility and gained substantial influence over the multiracial population of the island.[102] Being an influential member of the Maui Woman's Club, a women's civic organization, Ethel Baldwin formed a committee to hold meetings for women of various racial and ethnic backgrounds and to discuss political issues of women's concern.[103] Winning over numerous and politically enthusiastic Native Hawaiian women was essential for the victory in the upcoming election, and Ethel's efforts assisted her husband's reelection for territorial senator in the 1920 general election.

Native Hawaiian and white women suffragists' collaboration in the 1920 general election on the island of Maui pressed Hawai'i's white oligarchy to acknowledge the power of women voters in the following 1922 special election.[104] In January 1922, to fill an unexpected vacancy caused by the untimely death of Prince Kūhiō, a special election for territorial delegate to the U.S. Congress was announced for March 25, 1922. At that time, women's eligibility to hold public office remained unresolved. Pressed by women, territorial governor Wallace R. Farrington queried Washington. According to the answer he received, there was nothing preventing a woman from being a candidate for election as the territorial delegate to the U.S. Congress, but if elected, her eligibility would be judged by the U.S. House of Representatives.[105]

While Mary H. K. Atcherley of Oʻahu was determined to run for the 1922 special election, territorial senator Harry A. Baldwin, who won the seat in the 1920 general election, also entered the race. Culturally hybridized high-society women leaders continued to use their authority and influence over male Republican politicians to assure women's right to public office. Although Princess Kalanianaʻole, the widow of Republican Prince Kūhiō and a descendant of the Kamehameha line, was strongly urged to seek the seat of the territorial delegate long occupied by her late husband, she did not enter the race.[106] Meanwhile, Baldwin won the Republican nomination and received an endorsement from Princess Kawānanakoa, widow of Democrat Prince David.[107] Her mother, Maui chief Abigail Kuaihelani Maipinepine Campbell, had taken leadership in resisting white settler colonialism during the takeover of the Hawaiian nation.[108] With Princess Kawānanakoa's endorsement, Native Hawaiian and white settler women came together to support Republican nominee Harry A. Baldwin, instead of Mary H. K. Atcherley, a strong advocate not only for women's right to vote and seek office but also for workers' rights for a minimum wage and standard of living. Atcherley ultimately ran as an independent candidate.[109]

The power of women voters demonstrated in the 1920 general election urged Republicans in Hawaiʻi to seek mainland influence to win Native Hawaiian women's support for their candidate. In February 1922, Kathleen Dickenson, "a campaign worker and leader" from Virginia who worked for Republican U.S. President Warren G. Harding, arrived in Hawaiʻi.[110] In March, she spoke to women voters at Republican women's clubs, which had been formed on the major islands, and successfully pressed male Republican candidates to assure equal political rights for women.[111] Noticeably, these Republican clubs were composed mostly or entirely of Hawaiians from various racial, ethnic, and social backgrounds.[112]

On the island of Oʻahu, Honolulu suffrage leaders welcomed the effort to form women's block votes but also recognized the need for nonpartisan voter education. They began reorganizing women's political groups in Hawai'i. In the U.S. mainland, when suffrage came within sight, young radicals spun off from NAWSA to form the National Woman's Party (NWP), and the remaining members reorganized NAWSA into the nonpartisan National League of Women Voters (NLWV) in 1920. Under the presidency of New Englander Maud Wood Park, the NLWV set dual goals: "to develop the woman citizen into an intelligent and self-directing voter and to turn her vote toward constructive social ends."[113] Honolulu suffragists contemplated reorganizing the existing women's groups in line with the nonpartisan NAWSA by involving women voters throughout the islands. Stella Payne Noggle, a white settler woman who had attended the Honolulu women's mass meeting that Dowsett held on September 2, 1920, inquired about the possibility of affiliating the reorganized group with the NLWV.[114] The answer she received in March 1921 stated that the NLWV constitution should be amended as it assumed affiliation of a local League of Women Voters (LWV) only from each state and the District of Columbia.[115]

Meanwhile, forty representative women of diverse racial backgrounds throughout the islands gathered at the Library of Hawai'i in Honolulu on February 16, 1922, to discuss forming a postsuffrage women's organization in Hawai'i. The focus of the discussion became whether the new women's organization should be nonpartisan or not. Should it be composed of various women's clubs or individuals, and how much central control? Should it include men and nonvoter women? Present at the meeting was Republican Kathleen Dickenson, who insisted that "political parties are responsible organizations, and our place of influence [was] in them, forcing our ideas into the platforms and into the minds of the leaders." Others envisioned the new organization as Federation of Women's Clubs' affiliates, since women's clubs also served as important venues for Native Hawaiian women's political movements. Honolulu leaders envisaged the new organization to be a nonpartisan NLWV affiliate. Arguing that education would be the "keynote" of the new organization, Wilhelmina K. W. Dowsett insisted that the new organization should be "democratic in its ideals" and prioritize "education before all else." Furthermore, the meeting recognized the need to cultivate interest in civic affairs among women, including alien women. Gertrude D. Bunker—the wife of Dr. Frank F. Bunker, the educational specialist who led the federal Survey Commission to investigate Hawai'i's educational system in 1919, as will be discussed in chapter 4—concurred but argued that the new organization would accomplish much in "Americanizing the foreign population" by being democratic and admitting nonvoter women. Her suggestion was to keep the new organization "open to all women" but restrict officers to those who were voters. Julie Judd Swanzy "spoke in favor of a league of women voters as likely to be more effective than federation of clubs," and her daughter Rosamond Swanzy Morgan brought a motion to organize a league of women voters. After debating whether it should be "a league of women" or "a league of women voters," the meeting decided on the "league of women voters."[116]

This attempt at nonpartisan women's solidarity in Honolulu further pressed Republican men to work with women for women's causes. On March 16, 1922, on the island of Maui, the Women's Republican Auxiliary Club (WRAC) organized, gathering 250 to 300 women from Central and East Maui. Harry A. Baldwin endeavored to appeal to these women voters.[117] According to newspaper articles, incumbent territorial senator Baldwin was suspected of having a political stance against women and Hawaiians. The inauguration meeting of the WRAC in Maui "nailed" the campaign "lies" that territorial senator Baldwin "opposed woman suffrage and was unfriendly to (late) Prince Kūhiō."[118]

On the island of Oʻahu on March 20, 1922, a women's mass meeting was held at the Mission Memorial Hall in Honolulu to inaugurate the League of Women Voters of the Territory of Hawaiʻi (HLWV). Gathering "two hundred women, representing several races," Native Hawaiian women of the ruling rank and influential local white women, including DSHW premier Emma Ahuena Davison Taylor and DOH regent Julie Judd Swanzy, appeared on the platform. The meeting speakers included Gertrude D. Bunker, who pointed out "educational advantages," Kathleen Dickenson, who spoke on "Responsibility of Citizens," and Mrs. Charles M. Lea (Charlotte A. Brown Lea) of Pennsylvania LWV, who addressed the meeting on "the Relation of the League to Political Parties." In addition, two local Congregationalist ministers spoke. Rev. Akaiko Akana, a son of a Chinese father and Native Hawaiian mother, talked about "Cooperation and Unity," and Rev. A. W. Palmer, a son of a pioneer American missionary couple, discussed the "Importance of Voting." The women who filled the hall became charter members of the new organization, which allowed alien women to become associate members, and elected its officers to serve until its first annual meeting in May. At the end of the meeting, missionary granddaughter suffragist Mary E. Dillingham Frear, called on all members of the "Woman Suffrage Association," possibly the interisland WSAH organized in 1912, to remain after the meeting. Although the Honolulu-based WESAH president Wilhelmina K. W. Dowsett was absent, she requested its members to discuss dissolving their organization.[119] With the inception of the HLWV, the WESAH disbanded and merged into it. The Maui, Kaua'i, and Hawai'i groups assured their cooperation but remained independent of the Honolulu-based HLWV.[120]

On March 22, 1922, three days before the special election, the WRACs, under the leadership of Princess Kalaniana'ole (Kūhiō's widow), gathered a delegate from each of its precinct clubs for a rally in Honolulu to support Baldwin. Nonetheless, U.S. political party partisanship was not an issue for women in Hawai'i. Edith Stone, who visited the islands for Red Cross work, reported on the women's political enthusiasm during the meeting to the NLWV. According to her article in *The Woman Citizen*:

> About five hundred women composed the audience, filling the hall to capacity. They were Hawaiian and part-Hawaiian, varying from pure dark brown types to fair mixtures with English, American or Chinese.... Tiny brown babies were there in the arms of mothers who wore *lauhala* hats, around whose rims were yellow ribbons bearing the inscription, "Vote for Baldwin." There were young matrons and business women, some of them having so much white blood in their veins that they did not show their Polynesian ancestry. There were country women from distant sugar plantations who had come into Honolulu to take part in this political rally. There were in the gathering women of great wealth, whose ancestors had owned vast tracts of fertile land under the monarchy.... Seated on the platform were Governor Wallace R. Farrington and Mrs. Farrington and Senator L. M. Judd, together with a Chinese-Hawaiian Christian minister and six pure or part-Hawaiian women of education and ability. The meeting opened with a prayer in the Hawaiian language by the minister.[121]

Stone revealed a racially mixed and cultural hybridized women's political movement, which also suggested the influence of bilingual white settler women leaders and male Protestant clergy over Native Hawaiian women's daily lives. Lisa G. Materson, whose work examined Black Republican women in urban Chicago, described black clergymen as "primary political brokers between black neighborhoods and white city bosses."[122] A similar process unfolded in Hawai'i where Native Hawaiian clergymen and missionary heritage settler women shared or competed with each other to be political brokers between Native Hawaiians and white male oligarchs.

According to Edith Stone, "Like members of one family they seemed to cling together, coordinating their ancient traditions with present-day methods of government." The meeting was accompanied by artistic and musical entertainments and "adjourned with the singing of 'Hawaii Ponoi,' the national anthem," and thus, women participants appeared to enjoy the meeting as a Native Hawaiian event. "Enfranchised citizenship" was not about responsibilities, duties, or even privileges but "the normal, natural, joyful functions of community life." Stone also introduced "a feminine Hawaiian politician," Mary Haʻaheo Kinimaka Atcherley, the independent woman candidate for territorial delegate. Atcherley argued that Hawaiian women had the privilege "to reign as queens and the premier" and told their men how to conduct affairs. She also stated that women were generally considered the "brains of families" and that "the average Hawaiian man [would vote] as his wife tells him to."[123]

The concerted efforts of Native Hawaiian women led to Harry A. Baldwin's special election victory in a territorial landslide on March 25, 1922.[124] Stone felt a "pathetic touch" in the picture where "the remnant of a dying race . . . so loyally and staunchly [supported] the government to which the islands now [gave] allegiance." Her pessimism, however, quickly transformed into admiration for Native Hawaiian women transcending racial, gender, and party constraints of the U.S. political system. Commenting on Native Hawaiian women voters who supported "a white man, even though there were two Native Hawaiian candidates," she argued unironically that it was "indicative of their sincere and serious purpose to elect the best man without being swayed by any sentimental considerations." While insisting that Hawaiian women, who engaged themselves in "the masculine activities," were "no less feminine than the women of any race," she added, "Hawaiian women are so politically minded that they need not be urged, prodded, baited and educated to use the ballot. They cannot resist the ballot."[125]

Stone's article carried in the NLWV journal surely pressed mainland suffragists as well as Harry A. Baldwin to work for women voters in Hawaiʻi on Capitol Hill. During Baldwin's term as the territorial delegate, the U.S. Congress amended the Hawaiian Organic Act and made women in the islands officially eligible to hold public office. With President Warren G. Harding signing the bill on September 15, 1922, women citizens in Hawaiʻi were assured their right to hold elective office as a territorial representative, senator, or delegate to the U.S. House of Representatives.[126] Furthermore, after Harry A. Baldwin's wife, Ethel F. S. Baldwin, met Maud Wood Park in Washington, DC, and reported her impressions of NLWV social feminists' "tactful" and "wise" ways to HLWV members, the HLWV decided to become a Hawai'i affiliate of the NLWV in December 1922.[127] The HLWV, following the NLWV's nonpartisan principle, set out "to foster education in citizenship and to support improved legislation."[128] As of March 20, 1922, the list of HLWV officers included Harriet Cousens Andrews, president;[129] Princess Kalaniana'ole, first vice president; and Rosamond Swanzy Morgan, second vice president. Among its Finance and Membership Committees were Wilhelmina K. W. Dowsett, Mary E. Dillingham Frear, and Elizabeth Lahilahi R. Webb.[130]

When the amendment to the Hawaiian Organic Act that assured women's rights for elective office came into sight, Dowsett and Swanzy were asked to run for seats in the territorial legislature. They both declined but remained politically active.[131] Like Dowsett, Swanzy, who assumed the HLWV Legislative Committee's chairpersonship in 1922, was then most concerned about educating the multiracial and multiethnic islands' children to be bona fide citizens of the territory.[132] The HLWV became a venue for influential women in Hawai'i to discuss issues pertaining to women and children. Its white leaders endeavored to borrow mainland social feminists' methods and expertise to mobilize women voters to advance their maternalist and feminist causes on the islands. Nonetheless, their stance to emulate mainland white women's causes also brought their racist and racialist bias against people of color, leading to its disbandment in May 1936, as will be discussed in the epilogue.[133]

Backed by Native Hawaiian women's political enthusiasm, Rosalie Enos Lyons Keli'inoi (1875–1952), who was born to a Native Hawaiian mother and Portuguese merchant/rancher father in Maui, served as the first woman territorial legislature in 1925. She married and later divorced Democrat Benjamin Lyons, a prominent Maui politician and saloonkeeper. Then she married politically active Republican Samuel Keli'inoi in Kaua'i. Influenced by her new husband and supported by Kaua'i's eminent missionary heritage Rice family, Rosalie Enos Lyons Keli'inoi became active in elite interracial women's organizations, such as the DOH and the HLWV. Running for the 1924 election on Kaua'i's Republican ticket, she won the seat in the territorial house. During the term she served, she successfully passed four of sixteen bills that she proposed to advance women's causes. For example, although the bill she had introduced to recover women's right to serve on juries failed, she successfully amended the territorial laws to recover married women's property rights, including the right to sell her real estate without her husband's consent. She also secured laws designating funds for a program to promote the welfare and hygiene of infants and pregnant women and authorizing the territorial government to purchase and restore a Hawaiian royalty's summer vacation home, Hulihe'e Palace, to be managed by the DOH.[134]

CHAPTER 3

Territorial Motherhood's Double-Edged Sword

Women's Networks and Unequal Sisterhoods

In 1894, women from missionary families in Honolulu were deeply concerned about Hawai'i's future. After failing to have their provisional government annexed by the United States, male family members contemplated the formation of a new republic. Lili'uokalani and her loyal subjects resented and engaged in massive campaigns against such a move. Furthermore, the growing sugar industry had introduced substantial amounts of foreign labor. Hawai'i, especially Honolulu, one of the world's busiest globalization hubs, was rapidly multiracializing/multiethnicizing to be polyglot and divided. In February 1894, missionary daughter Harriet Angeline Castle Coleman (1847–1924) compared the situation to that of France a century earlier. She published "The Hope of the World Lies in the Children," a circular, in which she wrote: "the great cloud of anarchy that has been slowly gathering and spreading over the civilized nations of the earth would surely burst upon the heads of future generations, if not upon ours—as surely as in France, a century ago, . . . and our turn, or our children's, will come sooner or later unless we can do something to disperse it. But what can we do?"[1]

Coleman's answer was to bring together local women's voluntarism and contributions to kindergarten work,[2] a means found effective in acculturating immigrant children to be "bona fide" American citizens at U.S. urban centers. Her call prompted the WBMPI-Honolulu—the Congregationalist women's missionary board headquartered in Honolulu—to establish the Free Kindergarten Department in March 1894. It took over the kindergarten work that Rev. Frank W. Damon and his wife Mary R. Happer Damon had started in Honolulu in 1892 to serve the children of their Chinese congregation.[3] The WBMPI-Honolulu's new department built five separate kindergartens—for Chinese, Portuguese, Hawaiian, Japanese, and "poor" white children—and a school for kindergarten teacher training. Each kindergarten was conducted in the children's mother tongue according to the tradition of the American Board of Commissioners for Foreign Missions (ABCFM) of preserving converts' culture and language. In 1895, a year after the declaration of the Republic of Hawai'i, the Free Kindergarten and Children's Aid Association of the Islands of Hawai'i (FKCAAHI) incorporated itself as an independent, nonsectarian charity and took over the WBMPI-Honolulu's kindergarten work. The seed money for incorporation was a generous gift of $10,000 from Coleman's mother, Mary Tenney Castle. An additional $777.85 was donated by native and settler—including white, Native Hawaiian, and Asian—women, showing the racial and national diversity of Honolulu women who supported the FKCAAHI's incorporation. Relying on members of the Congregational Central Union Church in Honolulu for its officers, pioneer missionary Mary T. Knight Hyde became the first president and Coleman, its financial secretary.[4]

During kingdom days, Hawaiian queens and chiefesses performed the role of benevolent motherhood and asserted their royal authority, while assuring their subjects' welfare in all aspects. They took care of the education, health, and welfare of their people in their lifetime and left their landholding to Native Hawaiians in the form of permanent charitable trusts upon their death.[5] After the kingdom's overthrow, Queen Lili'uokalani's private landholding was confiscated and transferred to the territorial government. White settler women leaders joined Native Hawaiian leaders to share the responsibility and authority of territorial motherhood to extend education, health, and welfare to every child on the islands. Amid the political upheaval at the turn of the twentieth century, women's territorial motherhood was double-edged. Building common ground for the ethnically divided children for social integrity also facilitated Anglophone cultural hegemony and, thus, multiracial/multiethnic settler colonialism and U.S. imperialism in Hawai'i. Through FKCAAHI's kindergarten efforts and Honolulu YWCA International Institute's immigration work, missionary heritage leaders from Honolulu pursued this double-edged territorial motherhood, especially among U.S. citizen children of Asian ancestry whose parents were aliens racially ineligible for citizenship.

Under the pressure of globalization in the late modern era, interracial and interethnic interactions took place to forge women's networking and collaboration. Thriving patriarchal industrial capitalism in Hawai'i had caused massive human movements and ensuing demographic and social changes, creating new opportunities and responsibilities for women's civilizing mission. Located in Honolulu, on the frontline of cross-cultural interactions, Native Hawaiian, white settler, and Asian settler women leaders became culturally hybridized. Furthermore, with missionary-pioneered trans-Pacific women's networks linking local ethnic communities and their homelands, they together were able to mobilize women's voluntarism and carry out territorial motherhood.

This chapter examines men and women of diverse backgrounds who supported or participated in Honolulu's Free Kindergarten Association and Young Women's Christian Association (YWCA) International Institute movements from local, national, and transnational perspectives. It asks how they affected the lives of native and settler women and children. A light is shed on the women's networks and activism linking Honolulu, Chicago, Kobe, and Yokohama, which all served as missionary outposts and globalization hubs at the turn of the twentieth century. It also interrogates how the territorial motherhood that the trans-Pacific women's collaboration carried out in Hawai'i was related to thriving transnational industrial-capitalist ventures and to the rising colonialist and imperialist aspirations of the United States and Japan—the homelands of two of Hawai'i's settler groups.

Kindergarten Education: Multifaceted Public Motherhood

The kindergarten initiative, which defined itself as a liberal educational movement at the turn of the century, had its roots in religious and political dissension and embraced transnational and multifaceted dimensions as it diffused across the globe in the nineteenth century. It borrowed ideas and practices developed in Germany, where Friedrich Froebel (1782–1852) rejected the religious conviction that children were inherently sinful and insisted that they were essentially good in nature and that a child's will should not be broken but rather molded by education. He promoted rationality rather than religious obedience and appealed to women intellectuals who deplored the destruction of the French Revolution. Providing children of all classes with kindergarten education, but not daycare facilities just to keep working-class children, was envisioned as a solution to class conflicts and social divisions. Women activists who engaged in this free kindergarten movement also sought women's socialization and emancipation. In the aftermath of the unsuccessful 1848 German revolution, religious and political dissenters dispersed to other countries, bringing with them liberalized child education ideas. In the United States, progressive educator Elizabeth Peabody built the first Froebelian kindergarten for Anglophone children in Boston. After the Civil War, native-born, middle-class mothers embraced the kindergarten movement to secure a liberal preschool education for their own children. By targeting the impressionable minds of young children, kindergarten education also proved an effective means to evangelize and "civilize" non-Protestant natives and settlers. Supported by the wealth and voluntarism of upper-middle-class white women in the growing federal republic, the kindergarten movement expanded to the frontline of white settler colonialism and U.S. westward expansion.[6]

Promoting child education and welfare was a part of American missionary "woman's work for woman and children" and a way to build women's autonomous sphere in male-dominant missionary efforts at home and abroad. Starting in the late 1870s, women's boards of American missionary enterprises began running charitable daycare and tuition-based kindergartens.[7] Congregationalist churchwomen were especially active in promoting Froebelian kindergarten education and teachers' professionalization through globalizing missionary networks. National and transnational Woman's Christian Temperance Union (WCTU) and YWCA movements expanded in their wake and further promoted the kindergarten movements nationally and internationally.[8] By collaborating with liberal male clergies and educators, women-led kindergarten movements sought and promoted scientifically proven pedagogy for child development and socialization, which appealed to middle-class mothers who desired a head start for their children.

At the turn of the twentieth century, U.S. commercial and industrial centers also experienced a large influx of immigrant labor. Concurrently, the daughters and granddaughters of churchwomen, who had pioneered charity and evangelical efforts at home and abroad, were receiving college and postcollege education. These "New Woman" progressives incorporated German-origin kindergarten education into the England-origin settlement movement and American public school systems. In urban Chicago at the turn of the century, after Jane Addams opened Hull House to provide services to wage-earning immigrant families in 1889, Alice Harvey Whiting Putnam (1841–1919), who managed the Chicago Froebel Association Training School, moved her training class to Hull House. Froebelian ideas, which encouraged secularism, empiricism, and kindergarten work, further evolved by involving University of Chicago psychologists and educationalists, such as G. Stanley Hall and John Dewey. While engaging in settlement work in urban immigrant neighborhoods, New Woman progressives became students and experts of emerging new academic subjects, such as early education, child psychology, home economics, nursing, hygiene, public health, and social work. Consequently, they became the backbone of progressive maternalists, who established and expanded women's autonomy in fields pertaining to women and children. Embracing and transforming Dewey's pedagogy and philosophy, they also pushed liberalism and "democracy" in their kindergarten and settlement movements.[9]

The free kindergarten movement promoted by progressive Chicagoans, however, was multifaceted. It was based on elite women's genuine concern for the welfare of immigrant mothers and children and their sense of mission in providing them with care and education. Nonetheless, it disseminated their own gender norms, bolstering the white- and male-dominant U.S. social order. For example, psychologist G. Stanley Hall, who contributed to establishing child study as a women's subject, believed in separate social functions for men and women. He insisted that mothers should stay at home with their infants and thus promoted the middle-class norm of the gender-based separate sphere.[10] Meanwhile, John Dewey envisioned education and schooling as instrumental to social change and reforms.[11] Accordingly, progressive Chicagoans directed free kindergarten education toward children in the lower strata of the social hierarchy and made it an experimental ground for new approaches for uplifting and civilizing immigrants. While they insisted on the value of kindergartens in Americanizing immigrant children, families, and communities, they also argued that early education was a "birthright" of children. As early as 1892, these multifaceted, charitable kindergarten efforts persuaded the Chicago Board of Education to integrate ten privately sponsored kindergartens into its public school system.[12]

In the runup to the twentieth century, mothers' clubs and parent-teacher associations sprang up in the expanding U.S. system, promoting colonialist and imperialist public motherhood and an English-medium child education based on "love and science." Founded in 1897, the National Congress of Mothers, which evolved into the National Congress of Mothers and

Parent-Teacher Association (PTA), disseminated modern scientific methods of child-rearing, popularized parent education, and expanded public health, education, and welfare services throughout the nation. Many of these mainland maternalists—working with the U.S. Bureau of Education, the National Education Association, and the National Kindergarten Association—successfully integrated kindergartens into their local public schools in the 1910s and 1920s.[13]

Progressive maternalist efforts made their way to Honolulu via Hawaiʻi's missionary families and their descendants who were rooted in ancestor-pioneered trans-Pacific networks. These descendants closely interacted with their mainland counterparts while studying at mainland colleges and universities. For example, Henry N. Castle (1862–1895), the younger brother of Harriet Castle Coleman who initiated the FKCAAHI, was an Oberlin and Harvard roommate of George Herbert Mead, who became a leading pragmatist philosopher and University of Chicago professor. Mead later married Henry's sister Helen Castle (1860–1929), also an Oberlin graduate. Through Henry's friendship with Mead, Harriet Castle Coleman was introduced to John Dewey and his ideas for progressive kindergarten education.[14] After organizing the FKCAAHI, Harriet participated in a month-long seminar at the Chicago Froebel Association Training School in 1896. There, she recruited Frances Lawrence (1876–1935), a graduate of the Chicago Kindergarten College, who served as the superintendent of FKCAAHI kindergartens and the director of its training school from 1896 to 1935.[15]

Kindergarten advocates emphasized education, "democracy," and shared "moral ethics" in building a common ground for the islands' multiracial and multiethnic children.[16] Their effort, however, was double-edged and never deviated from their movement's goal to acculturate and Americanize their families and communities. This is evident, for example, in a speech by Harriet Park Thomas, who spoke at the FKCAAHI annual meeting in Honolulu in 1913. Thomas, a colleague of Jane Addams and wife of University of Chicago sociologist William I. Thomas, believed in the contemporary psychological studies that assured the effectiveness of the "universal application" of "a carefully worked out educational system." In her speech, Harriet Park Thomas showed her sympathy for immigrant mothers who lacked social links to the "great strange world." She envisioned children of immigrants serving as "interpreters to their parents of our (American) civilization, of the friendliness and helpfulness of a great strange community." At the same time, however, she thought that children were the "property of the community" to be utilized as objects of study and the means for social reform. In Thomas's vision, the free kindergarten movement was another means for white settler women leaders to enact their colonialist and imperialist projects and to reform their clients' society. In Hawai'i, children of Asian settler and Native Hawaiian families were mediators for cultural negotiations between biological mothers from the "old world" and those who advocated modern American values and practices.[17]

Paternalism Versus Maternalism in Bipolar Plantation Society

In the U.S. territory of Hawai'i, missionary descendant men were equally enthusiastic in civilizing and uplifting the population. They constituted the core of territorial oligarchs who had planter philanthropy and Protestant church evangelism at their disposal.[18] Both charity kindergarten and settlement work began as church projects in Honolulu during Hawai'i's turbulent 1890s, with rural plantation daycare and schooling resting largely on planters' paternalism. Historically, planters assisted their workers in building ethnic schools to provide daycare and education for workers' children to be taught in their mother tongue. This practice was agreeable to parents who had initially intended to make fast money and then return to their homelands. The planters' ulterior motive, however, soon surfaced to segregate plantation camps by ethnicity to spur interethnic rivalry for higher productivity and to prevent workers from engaging in transethnic labor agitation.[19]

Meanwhile, missionary descendant women incorporated the FKCAAHI as a women's enterprise through their separate sphere strategy. Nonetheless, especially in its early days, FKCAAHI's leaders had to work closely with male family members and bilingual Protestant clergies to reach out to settler labor families. When the FKCAAHI began managing the five ethnic kindergartens in Honolulu, each was segregated by ethnicity and language. To rally voluntarism and contributions, it had an advisory committee composed of five "gentlemen"—bicultural clergymen or lay elite leaders, each representing a specific ethnic community.[20] In 1897, when the Ewa Plantation Company in Honolulu opened its kindergarten, Frank C. Atherton (1877–1945), a son of missionary daughter Juliette Montague Cooke Atherton (1843–1921) and director of the company, allowed the FKCAAHI to provide liberal preschool education, with the company paying all its expenses.[21] FKCAAHI leaders envisioned their kindergarten's role as the "opening wedge in the district where it [was] placed" to promote their brand of liberal kindergarten education.[22] Collaborating with these men, it slowly extended its influence over the ethnic communities' preschool children and their parents.

White settler paternalists and maternalists collaborated in carrying the colonialist and imperialist burden of establishing common ground among the islands' multiethnicized and multinationalized children. Consequently, the FKCAAHI's effort facilitated the transfer of sovereign authority from Native Hawaiian royalty to white settler oligarchs. Their efforts had gained impetus from the U.S. annexation of Hawai'i and the 1898 landmark U.S. Supreme Court decision *United States v. Wong Kim Ark*, ruling that U.S.-born children of alien parents could not be stripped of their birthright citizenship.[23] Within the sugar plantation communities, Native Hawaiian and Portuguese overseers managed the plantation workforce, of which 70 percent were Japanese in 1902. Within the next two decades, Filipinos would outnumber Japanese.[24] As pidgin became the de facto language for interracial and interethnic communications and networking, the FKCAAHI began using "individual" progress instead of ethnicity for their kindergarten classification criterion. The FKCAAHI declared that its kindergartens were a "very early 'melting pot'" and "seedbed of democracy." The Hawaiian Organic Act required English or Hawaiian literacy to be a qualified voter and mandated English as the medium for legislative proceedings in the territory. The FKCAAHI pressed English as the language of instruction in its kindergarten classes with the prospect that surging numbers of alien settler children with birthright U.S. citizenship would soon be the majority of Hawai'i's electorate (Figure 3.1).[25]

Hawai'i's liberal progressive maternalists were willing to bear the burden and authority in pursuing the double-edged territorial motherhood. They facilitated prevailing Anglophone cultural hegemony and transethnic settler colonialism in Hawai'i, while assisting the islands' children in acculturating themselves to the forging mainstream of territorial Hawai'i. Honolulu-based FKCAAHI leaders enthusiastically adopted progressive liberal theories and practices that had been developed in urban Chicago to democratize their kindergarten efforts. "A constant succession of financial crises" also pressed FKCAAHI's free kindergarten efforts to become secular and culturally and racially inclusive. The FKCAAHI's funding, especially in its early days, largely

"Future Voters of Hawaii."

Figure 3.1 FKCAAHI Future Voters of Hawai'i, Calendar (1918–1919), 57.
Source: Courtesy of KCAA Preschools of Hawai'i.

came from the family trusts of prominent missionary families and was supplemented with donations from Native Hawaiian and settler community leaders of the upper middle class. It also received funding from local umbrella charity organizations such as the Associate Charities of Hawai'i and, later, the United Welfare Fund; both organizations were formed and managed under the leadership of missionary descendant men.[26] At the same time, FKCAAHI actively sought contributions from native and settler parents. As stipulated in its constitution and bylaws, although the association's work was "in accordance with Christian principles and methods," FKCAAHI membership was open to any woman who pledged and paid the annual dues.[27] These contributions, dues, and funding were further supplemented by client children and parents who paid tuition, contributed skills, and raised funds. The FKCAAHI adopted Native Hawaiian court rituals and transformed them into fundraising events, in which native and settler children and parents of diverse backgrounds celebrated and showcased their cultural traditions.[28]

FKCAAHI work remained under the purview of women's voluntary efforts for a period much longer than similar efforts in progressive mainland cities and counties. They gained some degree of autonomy and successfully networked among "prominent" women from Honolulu's ethnic communities to carry out public mother work. Arguably, however, they were unable to overcome the heavy weight of the "cult of womanhood," which proved the racial, class, and cultural superiority of women by their commitment to "altruistic" voluntarism. By upholding the conventional white middle-class assumption of woman's innate selflessness, FKCAAHI leaders enticed racially and ethnically diverse mothers and daughters to emulate their voluntarism and self-proclaimed altruism. Accordingly, kindergarten staff and assistants, although on the FKCAAHI payroll, were in reality "volunteers" and received only a pittance of a salary. Its leaders believed that charitable endeavors "instilled in the hearts of those able to help, a greater desire to be of service to those less fortunate." Accordingly, the movement, while inclusive in terms of race and ethnicity, failed to question the racialist and sexist assumptions of the time. Instead, they proudly acknowledged that "the Department of Education could not maintain the kindergartens so cheaply and likewise maintain present standards . . . nor could it furnish the personal interest for the children afforded through the unselfish work of the women now handling the schools." In the minds of Hawai'i's white maternalist leaders and perhaps those of their nonwhite women collaborators, "selfless" women's voluntarism was nobler than paid work.[29]

FKCAAHI leaders began serious efforts to integrate kindergarten education into Hawai'i's public school system only in the 1910s. The outbreak of World War I compelled Hawai'i's society to become more American and Anglophone. Furthermore, as women's voting came into sight, they recognized the urgency of Americanizing islands' mothers and children from diverse backgrounds. To use the lingering federal pressure in the post–World War I era as a backwind, Julie Judd Swanzy, who served as the FKCAAHI president from 1915 to 1934, collaborated with the Department of Public Instruction's (DPI) superintendent Vaughan MacCaughey (1887–1954; in office, 1919–1923). They endeavored to reform Hawai'i's polyglot school system, while pressing the integration of kindergarten education into the territorial public school system.[30] Nonetheless, their collaborative attempts struggled against complex local, national, and transnational male political maneuvering, which unwittingly caused Hawai'i's so-called foreign language school controversy, as will be discussed in chapter 4. Undeterred, FKCAAHI leaders tirelessly continued their efforts in making the territorial government responsible for providing preschool English education to every child in the islands. They successfully had a bill introduced in the territorial legislature in 1923 and 1927 that would appropriate funds for transforming a limited number of kindergartens into public schools, but their efforts bore no fruit. In 1923, Territorial Governor Wallace R. Farrington supported FKCAAHI's efforts by arguing for public kindergarten education, but the territorial legislature defeated a bill that would have appropriated funds for seven kindergartens. The opponents of the bill accused MacCaughey of "trying to run away with the government in his enthusiasm for 'fads and frills'" and pressured the legislature to set the requirement for compulsory school to begin at age six. In 1927, the FKCAAHI led another campaign emphasizing the benefits of kindergartens, and Native Hawaiian Representative David K. Ewaliko (D) introduced a bill to provide funding for ten kindergartens. Facing strong opposition again, the bill failed in 1929, ostensibly on fiscal concerns from the Chamber of Commerce and the Hawaiian Sugar Planters Association.[31]

Opposition to kindergartens involved multiple factors. Although recognizing the need for their children to master English, non-Anglophone parents prioritized that their children acquire command of their mother tongue. Also, Native and settler parents, who were concerned about their own language and cultures on the verge of obliteration, opposed English-medium preschool education. Nonetheless, of all the forces of opposition, paternalism seemed to be the most formidable foe of FKCAAHI's maternalist drive to integrate kindergarten education into the territorial public school system. Liberal male oligarchs shared the same sense of mission as their female counterparts in uplifting and civilizing multiracialized and multinationalized Hawai'i under U.S. colonial rule. However, they were unwilling to let women, who were more experienced in providing preschool education, begin claiming their autonomous space in the territorial bureaucracy. Furthermore, these paternalistic progressive Republicans ran Hawaii's sugar industry, the economic backbone of the territory. As such, they shared planters' fear that the FKCAAHI work would inspire the children of field hands to leave the plantations for better career opportunities or would facilitate transethnic labor movements. Many planters, unwilling to use public funds for early education, especially liberal and democratic versions thereof, were resentful of those who supported the efforts. It is not surprising that Hawai'i's planter class, including its liberal progressives wing, shared the same mindset as their mainland industrialist counterparts. They engaged in progressive reforms but only when those reforms met their interests.[32]

Philanthropy played a crucial role in social control. Liberal progressive men in Hawai'i were much more persistent than their female family members in providing early education only as private benevolence rather than a public responsibility.

Mainland Maternalism's Rippling Effects on Hawai'i

In the continental United States, Jane Addams and her New Woman cohort began building women's dominion out of their ancestors' voluntary "woman's work for woman and children" in the male empire of policy-making. Hull House alumnae and residents employed the separate sphere strategy and engaged in interclass and interethnic women's interactions to ease immigrant families' transitioning to modern industrial lives in U.S. urban centers. To assure the health and welfare of wage-earning women and children, they established federal agencies headed by and staffed with women.[33] Intertwined with the development was the YWCA movement, which thrived by hiring New Woman professionals. Their efforts were still influenced by American middle-class norms and thus double-edged, but they nonetheless worked for industrial democracy.

During World War I, mainland women progressives endeavored to provide services to immigrant and migrant wage-earning women nationwide. Their efforts affected local maternalist efforts in Hawai'i, especially through the YWCA's expanding network and its thriving International Institutes. The YWCA movement on the U.S. mainland, like the one in the United Kingdom, originated in two competing but complementary Christian women's movements: (1) a student-based movement with an evangelical emphasis and (2) a city-based movement to protect "women adrift." An example of the city association work was the New York Travelers' Aid Society, which formed in 1903 to reach out to the native-born women arriving at train stations from rural areas and foreign-born women disembarking at ports. The two movements merged to form the National Board of the YWCA (National Board/National YWCA) in 1906.[34] The newly formed National YWCA established its Industrial Department in 1908 to develop the city-based movement. Headed by Florence Simms (1873–1923), the YWCA's industrial work catered to increasing numbers of working women in booming Midwest industrial towns and pushed the National YWCA to meet the needs of wage-earning women and children. In 1911, the YWCA National Convention adopted a resolution supporting legislations that set a minimum wage, maximum hours of labor, and women's right to a living wage.[35]

To facilitate work among immigrant women, the first International Institute opened in New York in 1910 under the auspices of the National YWCA. By modeling itself after settlement houses and recruiting Hull House residents and alumnae, the International Institute functioned as a service and adjustment agency for non-Anglophone immigrant families. Under the directorship of Edith Terry Bremer (1885–1964), a Hull House graduate, fifty International Institutes opened nationwide. Bremer loosened and dropped strict Protestant Church membership requirements. Instead, staff were expected to be committed to professional social work standards in promoting immigrant welfare. Under her leadership, the International Institute movement became a force fighting against anti-immigrant sentiments and agitations in the United States.[36]

The YWCA's immigrant work and expanding national networks began affecting local and transnational women's social activism in U.S. globalization hubs. Founded in 1900, prior to the incorporation of the National YWCA, the Honolulu YWCA had aimed to cultivate Protestant religiosity and a self-denying sense of mission among young women of their own sort. Composed of women members of the Central Union Church, the Honolulu YWCA in its early days functioned as a subordinate to the Honolulu YMCA. After establishing ties with the National YWCA's growing network and movements, the Honolulu YWCA began conducting work independently of the Honolulu YMCA. In 1916, it joined associations in California, Arizona, and Nevada to constitute the Pacific Coast Field of the National YWCA movement.[37] To meet the needs of an increasing number of picture brides of immigrant men in Hawai'i and on the U.S. Pacific coast, the National YWCA dispatched its secretaries to San Francisco and Honolulu. Helen Topping went to San Francisco, where, *Issei* (a first-generation immigrant of Japanese ancestry) churchwomen had formed the San Francisco Japanese-in-America Young Women's Christian Association (SF Japanese YWCA) in 1912 to "protect" a small number of middle-class female students from Japan under their supervision.[38] The National YWCA also sent Helen Salisbury to the Honolulu YWCA in 1916 to reach out to the growing numbers of Japanese and Korean picture brides disembarking at the port in Honolulu. To assist Salisbury, the Honolulu YWCA hired Japanese Tsuru Masuda Kishimoto (1857–?), who became the first woman of Asian ancestry to be on its paid staff. In consultation with the Japanese Consulate in Honolulu, Salisbury and Kishimoto launched Traveler's Aid to monitor and protect the picture brides coming to or passing through the city.[39]

During World War I, the American public became concerned about the loyalty of foreigners and the unity of the nation. The National YWCA's "foreign community work" played a double-edged role in acculturating immigrant women and mobilizing them for wartime patriotic work to assure their loyalty to the United States. The National YWCA increased its presence and influence by carrying out the 1918 United War Work Campaign (UWWC), a national drive for fundraising and wartime work to uphold civic patriotism and servicemen's morale. Among the seven civic organizations authorized by the Departments of War and the Navy to conduct UWWC efforts, the YWCA was the only women's group headed by women. In parallel with suffrage leaders, who took up conspicuous roles in the presidentially appointed Council of National Defense Women's Committee (CND Women's Committee) to promote women's war-relief and war-support endeavors, the National YWCA was entrusted with a large portion of public funds and led young women in UWWC's wartime efforts. It created visitor centers called "Blue Triangle Houses"—venues for women working in war industries to meet, relax, and participate in "wholesome" recreation. The National YWCA also organized the Patriotic League/Girl's Reserve and Hostess Houses. The Patriotic League/Girl's Reserve promoted patriotism and the ideal American womanhood/girlhood among young women between the ages of twelve and twenty. Hostess Houses provided appropriate accommodations, care, and wholesome entertainment to servicemen and their families at military camps. Many women who took up military-industry work came from immigrant communities. Servicemen and their families who used Hostess Houses as well as women who provided services also came mainly from immigrant communities. Accordingly, YWCA's wartime work facilitated transracial and transethnic women's networking, while fanning American patriotism among immigrant women and families.[40]

In Hawai'i, a small circle of women closely linked to prominent missionary families, in collaboration with influential Native Hawaiian women, took leadership in the local wartime efforts of the UWWC, the CND, the American Red Cross, and the Honolulu YWCA.[41] They developed networks with women representatives of ethnic churches, clubs, and civic organizations to mobilize women members of each ethnic community to participate in women's wartime efforts. As the island of Oʻahu accommodated air, naval, and military bases, young women were mobilized to entertain enlisted men who were to be sent to the front. Paradoxically, *Nisei* daughters, who constituted a majority of "girls" recruited for the work, were encouraged to play Asian women's stereotypical role as a companion, entertainer, and facilitator of male socialization but only in an American and wholesome way. Under the supervision of respectable women leaders who had embraced white racialism and gender stereotypes, nonwhite "girls" pursued their patriotic duty by providing recreation for U.S. servicemen.[42]

Arguably, these wartime contributions from local "girls" also helped their community and the territory win local and national approbation for their generous war support. In return, the National YWCA Board opened the forty-first International Institute in Honolulu in May 1919 to provide services to immigrant women and their daughters. Honolulu in the 1920s saw increasing picture bride arrivals from immigrant homelands and a rise in pidgin-speaking daughters escaping rural plantation camps throughout the islands. Honolulu YWCA's territorial motherhood aimed to make them useful full-fledged citizens and to integrate them into the territory's mainstream society. It promoted modern American girlhood/womanhood while encouraging them to retain their cultural "pride." Nonetheless, the Honolulu YWCA movement bred class consciousness among immigrant women and their daughters by managing two institutions for women with different degrees of Americanization. The Honolulu YWCA had invested in a modern new building designed by pioneer woman architect Julia Morgan, which promoted its bourgeois image. This modern downtown edifice offered business courses mainly for Anglophone city girls. The foreign-born and the daughters from rural communities were offered classes on the English language, housekeeping, and child-rearing at the International Institute.[43]

During World War I, the National YWCA worked with other women's groups in support of the Sheppard-Towner Maternity and Infancy Act, the first federal social security legislation, enacted in November 1921. The National YWCA also contributed to the successful transformation of the U.S. Labor Department's Woman in Industry Service—the temporary wartime federal division, tasked with conducting a study on women's working conditions—into a permanent agency, the U.S. Women's Bureau, in 1920. The Women's Bureau, just like the U.S. Children's Bureau founded in 1912, was headed by and staffed with women and constituted "female dominions" in the male empire of social reform policymaking in the federal buraucracy.[44] Under the directorship of Mary Anderson, who served as a World YWCA advisory secretary during the war, it aimed to establish standards and policies to promote the welfare of wage-earning women and improve their working conditions.[45] Concurrently, prominent national social-feminist and maternalist groups—e.g., the National League of Women Voters (NLWV), the WCTU, the PTA, and the Women's Trade Union League (WTUL)—formed an umbrella organization, the Women's Joint Congressional Committee (WJCC), in 1920 to lobby Congress.[46] The National YWCA joined the WJCC in 1921 and established the legislative service division as "a clearinghouse" in educating YWCA members on federal and state laws.[47] The WJCC, through collaboration with women policymakers of the Children's Bureau and the Women's Bureau, lobbied and campaigned to secure funding by the Sheppard-Towner Act for the state's efforts in developing infant healthcare programs. Mainland social feminists' power, however, climaxed in the early 1920s and slowly declined in the late 1920s until Frances Perkins assumed the U.S. Secretary of Labor in 1933.[48]

The expanding YWCA work during and after World War I and its connection to the WJCC's campaigns affected Hawai'i's maternalist efforts. Children attending FKCAAHI kindergartens were "weighed, measured, and compared with mainland norms." This led to the shocking discovery that most of the island's children fell short of the mainland standards. Local maternalists rolled up their sleeves to promptly rectify the "deficiency" via proper nutrition and dental hygiene. For example, nutritionist Mrs. James (Nellie R.) Russell, the YWCA cafeteria director and a leader in Hawai'i's wartime food production and conservation efforts, was "loaned" to the FKCAAHI to conduct nutrition classes for mothers and children.[49]

In Honolulu, a multiracializing and multiethnicizing commercial and industrial center, women's pursuit of territorial motherhood rested on cultural mediation provided by elite, bilingual women from diverse ethnic backgrounds. As privileged white and Native Hawaiian daughters upheld high-society lifestyles to engage in volunteer work, paid occupations in the expanding public mother work were filled by women experts from the mainland and local bilingual settlers and Native Hawaiian commoners. They all came to share maternal responsibility and authority in carrying out territorial motherhood and established and expanded the women's sphere while attaining some degree of their own autonomy in the white-male dominant empires of professionalism and bureaucracy.

Japanese, Korean, Filipina, and Chinese immigrant women, who were hired by the Honolulu YWCA to serve as International Institute nationality secretaries, filled the bottom strata in the organization and took charge of day-to-day operations among their fellow immigrant women. They worked under local volunteers, who served on the Honolulu YWCA's executive board or the International Institute's management committee, and professionally trained national workers dispatched from the National YWCA. Unlike white national workers who had a high turnover rate due to insufficient funding from the National Board, foreign nationality secretaries, for example, Japanese Tsuru Kishimoto and Korean Ha(i) Soo Whang (aka, Hwang Hae-su, 1892–1984), remained in their positions for more than two decades.[50] They were invaluable in filling linguistic and cultural gaps between Honolulu Anglophone society and foreign language–speaking immigrant communities. Entrusted by white local leaders, Kishimoto and Whang, like other nationality secretaries, gained substantial discretion and authority in their respective immigrant community.[51]

After World War I, educated-in-Hawai'i immigrant women and daughters also became visible in maternalist efforts in Hawai'i and the Pacific. Among them was Alice Sae Teshima Noda (1894–1964), a dental hygienist for the territorial DPI. She was also "the first Japanese woman to register" for the first post-woman-suffrage territorial election in 1920.[52] When deplorable dental hygiene conditions among the islands' children came to light, the philanthropy of Helen Strong Carter (1866–1945) established the Honolulu Dental Infirmary in 1920 and opened the Infirmary-associated Honolulu Dental Hygiene School in 1921. Helen S. Carter was a daughter of an Eastman Kodak cofounder and president and the wife of a missionary grandson, George R. Carter (1866–1933), who served as territorial governor between 1903 and 1907. Alice S. T. Noda became one of the first graduates of the Dental Hygiene School and subsequently worked as a dental hygienist. She then headed the Dental Hygiene School and assumed the presidency of the Dental Hygienists' Club, which was organized in 1922.[53] Local women's efforts pressured the territorial government to create full-time, women-dominant civil service positions in order to provide dental hygiene education in public schools.[54]

Furthermore, when these efforts obtained federal funding through the Sheppard-Towner Act administered by the Children's Bureau in 1925, Hawai'i's Territorial Board of Health established the Bureau of Maternal and Infant Hygiene in 1926 to reduce infant mortality rates on Hawai'i's four major islands: Oʻahu, Maui, Kauaʻi, and Hawaiʻi.[55] Dr. Vivia B. Appleton, a mainlander who had recently returned from her work in China for the U.S. Council on Health Education and the National YWCA, became the first director of the bureau.[56] In 1927, Hawaiʻi's Board of Health also created the Department of Public Health Nursing, and Mabel Leilani Smyth (1892–1936), a daughter of an Irish-English father and a Native Hawaiian mother, became one of the first Native Hawaiian women to be certified in public health nursing and the first director of the Public Health Nursing Department.[57]

With collaboration from territorial agencies, as well as from the Honolulu YWCA's International Institute, parent volunteers, nutritionists, dental hygienists, and dentists, FKCAAHI health work became the "most fruitful" of its activities.[58] It organized home visits and mothers' meetings to reach out to "ignorant" mothers and promoted vaccinations and immunizations, "general habits of cleanliness," and physical and dental checkups for children (Figure 3.2). The FKCAAHI also provided free snacks and lunches to its kindergartners. "Cooked rice with sugar and milk" might not have complied with the tastes and customs of immigrants but was nutritious and filled the stomachs of children.[59]

Figure 3.2 A mothers' meeting at the Muriel Kindergarten. A Palama Settlement nurse is bathing a baby. Mrs. Kishimoto is interpreting for her. The meeting was to show how to deal with rampant impetigo sores. FKCAAHI Mother's Meeting, Calendar (1929–1930), 38.
Source: Courtesy of KCAA Preschools of Hawaiʻi.

Nonetheless, interethnic and transnational collaboration in assuring the health, education, and welfare of the islands' multiethnic children was hierarchical and failed to rectify racial, cultural, and national inequalities under the Anglophone-dominant globalization pressure of the early twentieth century. For example, historian Bruce Bottorff discovered the conceptual gap between local members of the Honolulu YWCA's executive board and national leaders who pushed "cultural pluralism" or "cultural democracy." He pointed out that local Honolulu YWCA executive board members lagged behind national workers dispatched from the National YWCA in promoting cultural and industrial democracy.[60] As immigrant women workers with various religious backgrounds became the clients of YWCA's city work, the National YWCA loosened its Protestant Church membership requirement and shifted its board membership from privileged women—who themselves hired domestic servants at home and whose male relatives employed factory girls—to middle-class activists and professionals who were more knowledgeable about and sympathetic to working-class women.[61] Having been active in social gospel endeavors, the National YWCA was a member of the Federal Council of Churches of Christ in America (the FCC)—an ecumenical partnership organized in 1908 among thirty denominations and two lay organizations, the YWCA and the YMCA. In an attempt to substitute YWCA industrial work for trade unionism, the National YWCA adopted, in 1920, the FCC's sixteen-point platform of labor reforms, known as the "Social Creed of the Churches," declaring its support for such issues as the abolition of child labor and workers' rights to organize and to demand shorter hours.[62]

In contrast, the Honolulu YWCA's executive board was still essentially composed of relatives of paternalistic planter oligarchs. These local Honolulu YWCA board members envisioned domestic labor as a benevolent "opportunity" for young women of diverse ethnic backgrounds to learn modern American women's civility and to attain social upward mobility. Accordingly, they were negligent in addressing the heartbreaking reality of immigrant daughters who, even with high school diplomas and business training at the downtown Honolulu YWCA, were able to find jobs only as household labor.[63]

Historian Judith D. Gething Hughes highlights the limitations and contradictions of women's civilizing efforts in the life of Elsie Hart Wilcox (1879–1954), a missionary granddaughter from the island of Kaua'i who served as the first executive of the Honolulu YWCA's International Institute. Wilcox was also a founder of the Kaua'i YWCA in 1921 and became the second elected female territorial legislator in 1933.[64] According to Hughes, Wilcox's concern for the poor and enthusiasm in making changes were genuine, but her proposed changes were "slow in coming and incremental." White women leaders in Hawai'i worked hard to civilize and uplift immigrant mothers and children, but they were often "the direct beneficiary of the status quo" and social injustices and thus reluctant to bring about drastic changes to the territory's white male oligarchy.[65]

Nonetheless, some Asian immigrant women and their daughters found a silver lining in working as a "schoolgirl"—a part-time housemaid who did housework in exchange for lodging—for benevolent mistresses. Although some faced malicious whims and even sexual exploitation, these schoolgirls attended high schools, while assisting their mistresses in managing the households, and learned middle-class American ways.[66] For daughters of rural plantation camps, it was a way to leave camp communities and be integrated into the mainstream territorial society. By mastering the English language, American civility, and even professional and academic expertise, some became entrusted members of interracial and interethnic elite women's communities, sharing civic responsibility and authority. They contributed to uplifting and civilizing their own community in Hawai'i and their ancestors' respective motherlands, and thus, entangled themselves with the Western-advanced and white-dominant globalization process.

To fully understand the transnational aspects of racially inclusive maternalist work in Hawai'i, consideration should be given to the immigrant communities and their transnational networks that intersected with Hawai'i's white settler women's pursuit of territorial motherhood. The following section examines the development of trans-Pacific women's networks in the case of the Japanese, who composed the largest ethnic group in turn-of-the-century Hawai'i, to analyze the complex workings of globalizing industrial capitalism, women's separate sphere strategy, and women's pursuit of the civilizing mission.

Globalization and Unequal Sisterhoods: A Case Study in U.S.-Japan Trans-Pacific Capitalist Ventures and People's Movements

From a trans-Pacific Japanese perspective, the turn-of-the-twentieth-century phenomenon that historian Robyn Muncy termed "female dominion building" can be traced back to American churchwomen's separate sphere strategy.[67]

The resulting women's networks and forging of sisterhood were complicit with globalizing Western-origin capitalist industrialism and Anglo-Saxon liberalism. The transnational sisterhood was unequal because of social and cultural disparity that favored more freedom, material wealth, and comfort in the modern industrializing West. It coincided with the prevailing subliminal terrain for unequal national, race, gender, and cultural relationships. Coming from a Western nation with more advanced stage of industrialization, American missionaries and their descendant progressives assumed the roles of benevolent mentors, benefactors, and/or employers of Asian and Asian American women and sometimes even of men. These white women mentors were enthusiastic about transferring "civilized" and scientific ways to improve the status and welfare of their protégés, who, when successfully uplifted, would share the burden of mediating the globalizing tide of industrial capitalism and its ensuing social changes. Recognizing the efficacy of their mentors' ways and strategy in coping with rapid social changes, missionary protégés joined transracial and transnational women's networks and movements. Those Japanese women, who forged sisterly relationships with American mentors, were women-conscious but also patriotic and nationalistic. They were most eager to assist Japan's efforts to fend off Western imperialism and stand on par with Western powers.

The phenomenon can be illuminated by the trans-Pacific lives of pioneer culturally hybrid women of Japanese ancestry—Ito(ko) Ozawa Imanishi (1872–1925), Fuji Koga (1857–1938), Yeiko Mizobe So (1865–1932), and Tsuru Masuda Kishimoto. Imanishi was a *Nisei* daughter, while Koga, So, and Kishimoto were immigrated from Japan, where they came under the influence of ABCFM missionaries in Kobe, Japan. These bilingual elite women, along with their mentor/employer American women activists, participated in transnational liberal kindergarten, WCTU, and/or YWCA movements, linking port cities in Hawai'i, the U.S. mainland, Japan, and beyond at the turn of the twentieth century.

Nisei daughter Ito Ozawa Imanishi was born to Japanese contract workers, referred to as *gannenmono* (the first-year people) because they arrived in Hawai'i in 1868, the first year of the Meiji era (1868–1912). They were sent to Hawai'i without the Meiji government's permission. Recruited from diverse walks of life, many vocally complained about the harsh working conditions. The Meiji government reacted by repatriating those who wished to return to Japan and discouraged further emigration of Japanese laborers until 1885.[68] Many of the *gannenmono* were bachelors and became field hands at Hawai'i's sugar plantations, but Ito's parents, Kintaro and Tomi Ozawa, and their newborn son became live-in house servants for Briton Richard F. Bickerton (1844–1895), who became a judge in the Hawaiian Kingdom. Born in Hawai'i in 1872, Ito became one of few children of Japanese ancestry in the islands during the 1870s and 1880s. She was raised under the influence of the Bickertons and culturally hybridized, mastering English, Hawaiian, and Japanese. Consequently, she came to play a crucial role as a generational and cultural mediator in the Hawaiian Kingdom and Japan and later, for Japan and the world. At age twelve, she began working as an interpreter for Robert Walker Irwin, an Irish-American businessman.[69] Stationed in Japan, he married a Japanese woman, Iki Takechi, and was appointed as the Hawaiian Kingdom's consul general on the eve of King Kalākaua's visit to Japan in 1881. While assisting Irwin, Ito stayed with his family, including Sophia Arabella "Bella" Irwin (1883–1957), who later became a kindergarten specialist in Japan,[70] and Marian Irwin (later Dr. Marian Irwin Osterhout, 1888–1973), a physiologist and faculty member of Rockefeller University who later contributed to founding the Women's Peace Association in Japan (Nihon Fujin Heiwa Kyōkai), Japanese affiliate of the Women's International League for Peace and Freedom (WILPF).[71]

Working for the Bickertons and the Irwins encouraged Ito Ozawa to be culturally hybridized and linked her to the transnational women's communities emerging on the frontline of cultural exchanges. When the Congregationalist Woman's Board in Honolulu (WBMPI-Honolulu) took over the charity kindergarten project and opened the Honolulu Kindergarten Training School in 1894, Ito Ozawa attended the school and became one of its first ten graduates. The FKCAAHI's 1896 annual report listed Ito as a principal of its kindergarten for Japanese. Ito, however, soon resigned, after marrying Kenji Imanishi, a Japanese bank representative in Honolulu.[72]

While in Hawai'i, Ito Ozawa assisted her husband, who assumed the presidency of the Japanese Benevolent Society (JBS; Nihonjin Jizenkai), in its male-led community efforts.[73] Soon, she left Honolulu to accompany her husband to world commercial centers—Tokyo, Hong Kong, and New York—and ultimately settled in Tokyo in 1918. Having emulated American upper-middle-class volunteerism and enthusiasm for women's civilizing mission and dominion-building efforts, she remained socially active at these globalization hubs. She was a founding member of the Tokyo YWCA, an officer of the Japanese affiliate of the WILPF, and a supporter of women's schools, including Tsuda College and St. Luke Hospital's Nurse Training

School in Tokyo, which rested on American-Japanese sisterhood and funding from capitalist-philanthropists.[74]

The expanding trans-Pacific networking of American and Japanese women for the "woman's work for woman and children" went hand in hand with thriving trans-Pacific economic ventures and accompanying male networks. Teenager Ito Ozawa's employer, Robert Walker Irwin, played a key role in reaching an agreement between Hawai'i and the Meiji government to resume procuring labor from rural Japan for Hawai'i's booming sugar industry. Meiji Japan was drawn into the modern capitalist system while retaining its traditional feudalistic human and social relationships. Some 29,000 *kanyaku imin* (government-contracted laborers) relocated from Japan to Hawai'i between 1885, when the agreement went into effect, and 1894, when the inauguration of the Republic of Hawai'i nullified it. By 1894, Hawai'i's plantation workforce had become predominantly Japanese, and an additional 40,000 Japanese contract laborers, mostly men, were brought under the auspices of private emigration firms until 1900, when Hawai'i's new status as a U.S. territory abolished the quasi-slavery contract labor system.[75]

Although plantation labor in Hawai'i appeared to be an attractive economic opportunity for Japanese workers, Irwin along with his collaborators, Japanese politicians and businessmen, were the ones who made a fortune from procuring Japanese labor for the plantation industry.[76] Accordingly, they assumed a paternalistic role to protect laborers from planters' cruel treatment.[77] To avoid the fate experienced by the *gannenmono*, who suffered poor health, communication problems, and harsh working conditions, they pressed the Hawaiian Kingdom government's immigration bureau to hire bilingual Japanese inspectors and physicians and to mediate between planters and workers.[78] Among these mediators was Dr. Iga Mori, a U.S.-educated physician who later assumed a leading role in representing Hawai'i's Japanese community and in establishing and sustaining amicable interracial and international relations between Japan, Hawai'i, and the United States, as will be discussed in chapter 4.[79]

In Hawai'i, culturally hybridized descendants of pioneer missionary families also assumed the role of cultural mediators by involving bilingual nonwhite elites from Hawai'i's ethnic communities and their homelands. When the Republic of Hawai'i came into being in 1894, the Hawaiian Evangelical Association (HEA) began reaching out to Hawai'i's growing foreign communities. As a part of this effort, the HEA had established the Japanese Department in 1885 and called on Rev. Orramel H. Gulick

(1830–1923) and his wife Ann Eliza Clark Gulick (1833–1938) who both worked as missionaries in Japan. While assisting her husband, Ann E. C. Gulick engaged herself in the FKCAAHI's Japanese kindergarten work.[80] After Ito Ozawa Imanishi left the Japanese kindergarten, FKCAAHI leaders resorted to the transnational missionary network to find her replacement. Her replacement, Fuji Koga, had studied and worked at the Woman's Board of Missions of the Interior (WBMI-Chicago)–funded female mission school in Kobe, Japan's port city, accommodating an ABCFM mission station. Through the missionary network, American kindergarten experts disseminated their knowledge and movements.[81] Among the experts were Frances Lawrence, who moved from Chicago to Honolulu to serve as FKCAAHI's superintendent and training school director; Fuji Koga; and Annie Lyon Howe, who went to Japan to promote the WBMI-Chicago–funded Froebelian kindergarten movement.[82]

Emerging in and around the missionary-pioneered women's network were efforts to build exclusively women's fields in academia, professions, and voluntarism, providing a theater for transnational women's career development and social movements. Fuji Koga had lost her father at an early age and came under ABCFM missionary families' influence. She worked as a nursemaid for the Gulicks and gained firsthand experiences of American ways in child-rearing. Winning trust and favor from her employers, Koga was granted the opportunity to study at WBMI-Chicago's female mission school in Kobe, upon its establishment in 1875, and became one of its first boarding students. In the summer of 1877, she accompanied another missionary family on furlough to San Francisco, while working as a nursemaid. Through her close interaction with American missionaries, Koga became a Christian, an entrusted protégé, and an invaluable assistant to their evangelical, civilizing, and female dominion building efforts. She served as a matron for boarding students of her alma mater between 1879 and 1886. Then, she was sent for further training to Boston from 1887 to 1890 to become a kindergarten teacher. After her return to Japan, she assisted A. L. Howe in Kobe and Methodist N. B. Gaines in Hiroshima, each of whom built a kindergarten and a kindergarten teachers' training school.[83] Then in 1897, she sailed to Honolulu to become the new director of FKCAAHI's Japanese kindergarten. In 1902, Koga attended the University of Chicago to further her studies in liberal kindergarten education theories. Returning to Japan in 1906, she became the first head of the kindergarten attached to the Japan Women's University (JWU) in Tokyo.[84]

As for Yeiko Mizobe So, she was widowed at a young age and came under the influence of the Gulicks who, without their own children, treated her like their own daughter. Upon the Gulicks' return to Hawai'i from their missionary work in Japan in 1894 to take charge of the HEA's work among Japanese, they called on Yeiko to work as a "Japanese helper" for Ann E. C. Gulick.[85] Tsuru Masuda Kishimoto, who worked as the Honolulu International Institute's nationality secretary, also received education at the WBMI-Chicago's female mission school in Kobe. After graduating from Kobe College, she taught at her alma mater and other Congregationalist female schools in Osaka, Japan, and Honolulu, Hawai'i. After her husband, whom she met and married in Hawai'i, died, she joined the Honolulu YWCA's staff to assist in its new travelers' aid work and became a nationality secretary with the opening of the Honolulu YWCA International Institute.[86]

Japanese women, who were "fortunate" to be successfully integrated into the expanding Anglo-American–origin women's networks, became enthusiastic advocates of modern womanhood that would fit the missionary propagated ideals of companionate marriage and "Christian Home," the autonomous sphere of women granted with moral authority. Their efforts, however, were multifaceted. In a sense, they presented a feminist challenge to Japanese feudal and patriarchal "household." Japan's rapid modernization and industrialization relied heavily on remittance from Japanese immigrants who toiled overseas. Among them were daughters from rural peasant families, whose patriarchs sold them into various forms of servitude on the frontline of globalization. Japanese women, who had emulated Anglo-Saxon liberalism and moral values, joined American churchwomen activists in "rescuing," sheltering, and liberating indentured prostitutes. Their efforts also assisted Japan's nationalistic attempts at repairing its "degraded" image, which anti-Asian exclusionists often exploited to fan the American public's anti-Japanese sentiments. Having emulated Protestant moral values and middle-class civility, Japanese female mission school graduates participated in trans-Pacific efforts and exercised moral authority to "protect" and "uplift" those Japanese women. In doing so, they also strengthened prevailing American middle-class cultural hegemony and thus bolstered class, race, and national inequalities.[87]

In Honolulu, Yeiko So engaged in these multifaceted women-conscious efforts through transnational WCTU movements. The Japanese WCTU movement, introduced by Mary C. Leavitt in 1886, invested its efforts in social reform attempts to prohibit overseas emigration of Japanese prostitutes, correct Japan's sexual double standards, and abolish Japan's licensed prostitution. With funds and guidance from the World WCTU network, the Japan WCTU also built and managed women's homes in Tokyo for "rescued" women.[88] In Honolulu, Yeiko So mobilized *Issei* churchwomen for this line of work and managed a women's home to shelter Japanese prostitutes. Later, it extended services to abused picture brides and neglected children. They participated in forming the interisland WCTU of the Territory of Hawai'i in 1926.[89]

Integrating themselves in the expanding missionary-pioneered women's networks, these bilingual Japanese women came to share authority and responsibility in acculturating Japanese migrants and settlers to their multiracializing and multinationalizing host societies and globalization hubs. In Honolulu, they joined the wife of Japan's consul general to institute the Japanese Women's Society (JWS; Nihonjin Fujinkai). To prove the Japanese community's loyalty to the territory of Hawai'i during World War I, highly elite JWS members represented and led local "Japanese women" in territorial war-relief and war-support endeavors under white women's leadership.[90] They also sat on committees for FKCAAHI's Japanese kindergarten work and for the Honolulu International Institute. Internalizing their American mentors' worldview, these Japanese bilingual elites became convinced of the efficacy of a white, Protestant, middle-class brand of womanhood and voluntary activism as the criterion for "civilization." Accordingly, they were intent on forging and promoting modern Japanese womanhood that met the white middle-class standard. By doing so, they hoped to disprove the exclusionists' claim that the Japanese race was "unassimilable" to America. Indeed, bilingual Japanese elite women, who shared the burden and authority in conducting territorial motherhood, were more committed to advancing the status of their communities and nation than to meeting the individual needs of women whose bodies and labor were exploited for development. By emulating white racism and Anglophone racialism, they had no intention of turning the tide of its globalized status quo.

CHAPTER 4

Elusive Collaboration for Anglophone Hegemony

Maternalists, Liberals, and Internationalists

In August 1921, the first Pan-Pacific Educational Conference convened in Honolulu. The Conference was called by the U.S. Department of Education and held under the auspices of the Pan-Pacific Union (PPU), a Honolulu-based male organization that explored international friendship and transnational business opportunities in the Pacific.[1] At the opening ceremony of the Conference, PPU's director Alexander Hume Ford (1868–1945) insisted on the importance of education and the Pacific region to bring world unity:

> Only education can now salvage the world. . . . Nearly two-thirds of the inhabitants of this planet live adjacent to Pacific waters. In the Pacific, the oldest and the newest civilizations meet. Here must be worked out the great world problems of inter-racial cooperation. Unless the children now born and being born are guided aright by you educators in Pacific lands, both the old and the new civilizations are in danger of disappearing in chaos. . . . Perhaps you may lead in the way of creating a real Patriotism of the Pacific. If you can do this, a World Patriotism will be the next step. . . . Our name means peaceful. Will you lead us into the ways of peace and knowledge of that which is good in each of us?[2]

Along with Ford, the Conference proceedings carried opening messages from two influential missionary granddaughters born and raised in

Hawaiʻi—the longtime Free Kindergarten and Children's Aid Association of Hawaiʻi (FKCAAHI) president and Daughters of Hawaiʻi (DOH) regent Julie Judd Swanzy, who chaired the Conference's entertainment subcommittee, and Mary Emma Dillingham Frear, who officially represented the National Young Women's Christian Association (YWCA) for the Conference and also served on the entertainment subcommittee and the permanent organization committee.[3]

This chapter examines the motives of influential women leaders in Honolulu and their male collaborators in promoting English-medium preschool education in Hawaiʻi under its local oligarchy and U.S. colonialism. The male colleagues were white settler liberals recruited from the U.S. mainland and internationally minded nonwhite settler elites who were active in male-led transnational PPU networks initiated by Hawaiʻi's capitalist-internationalists. It examines elusive relationships among the three groups active on the networks—Honolulu women, white settler liberals, and nonwhite settler internationalists—and argues that Honolulu women's bitter experience in this cross-gender and interracial collaboration inspired them to convene the women-only Pan-Pacific Women's Conferences (PPWC) in 1928 under the theme of "Mother and Child Welfare."[4]

This development in Hawaiʻi intersected with the thriving Young Men's Christian Association (YMCA) and YWCA movements and the revival of an evangelical civilizing mission among their college student members on the U.S. mainland and worldwide. Organized in 1886, the Student Volunteer Movement for Foreign Missions (SVM) sent young students, mostly YMCA/YWCA members, abroad. Their efforts led to the inception of the World Student Christian Federation (WSCF) in 1895. In parallel were attempts for worldwide interfaith dialogue, which were exemplified by and diffused through the 1893 World Parliament of Religions held in Chicago. Major Protestant churches and lay organizations transcended denominational differences in their social gospel endeavors to form the Federal Council of Churches of Christ in America (FCC) in 1908. Religious and intellectual leaders on the frontline of transcultural interactions engaged in numerous movements in a quest for mutual understanding and world unity. With the eruption of the Great War in Europe, these movements became a force in generating a rising tide of internationalism, leading to the formation of a set of intergovernmental institutions in Geneva.

The PPU's advocacy of "Pacific patriotism" as a step toward "world patriotism" linked progressive but monotheistic efforts to find a universal principle for world unity. By then, the globalizing industrial capitalism and ensuing movements of peoples had created urgent social ills and intensifying conflicts. Incorporated in 1917, the PPU initially sought tourists, investors, and migrants from white settler nations in the Pacific to diversify Hawai'i's industry and Anglo-Saxonize its population. Hawai'i's booming sugar business, however, became increasingly dependent on Asian labor, while trans-Pacific business partnerships thrived. Concurrently, postrevolution political turmoil in China and the Great War in Europe prompted interethnic discord and U.S.-Japanese imperialist rivalries, creating volatile racial, ethnic, and national relationships in Hawai'i and the Pacific. Surging numbers of born-in-Hawai'i children of Asian settlers, most conspicuously Japanese, in the 1910s and 1920s drew mainland exclusionists' suspicion. Planters' strategy of "segregation by ethnicity" caused the prevailing use of pidgin as a common language in rural plantation communities. Subsequent interethnic attempts at labor strikes alarmed Hawai'i's planter oligarchs. Now they embarked on using the PPU network to gather bilingual elites from local ethnic communities and their homelands to promote not only free trade and business ventures but also Anglophone cultural hegemony and the peaceful integration of Hawai'i into the globalization process.[5]

Although no permanent organization resulted from the PPU's 1921 Pan-Pacific Educational Conference, participants recognized the importance of education for international/interethnic understanding and cultural hegemony in forging or resisting settler colonialism and imperialism. In the face of recurring anti-Asian exclusionism in the United States, Hawai'i's planter oligarchs began another effort to convene a Pan-Pacific YMCA meeting to promote "Christian citizenship" among young people in Hawai'i and the Pacific. Their efforts soon went beyond their original scope to discuss social, political, and economic issues, leading to the inception, in 1925, of another Honolulu-based, male-led international organization, the Institute of Pacific Relations (IPR). The IPR was separate from the YMCA and the PPU but involved the same line of elite internationalist men: board members of Protestant/pro-Christian organizations, capitalist-philanthropists, bureaucrats, diplomats, educators, and professionals.[6] Accordingly, Honolulu also became the venue for the convening of IPR's first two conferences. The PPU and IPR meetings gathered leaders linked through trans-Pacific male networks radiating from Honolulu.[7] Their conferences were open to women, but the PPU became the so-called father organization of the women-exclusive PPWC and its permanent organization, the Pan-Pacific Women's Association (PPWA).[8]

The immediate concern for the Honolulu women who bore the burden and authority of territorial motherhood was pidgin-speaking children overcrowding public schools. Especially during and after World War I, Honolulu saw an influx of migrant families attracted to its booming wartime businesses or evicted from rural plantation communities due to their participation in the island-wide 1920 O'ahu Strike.[9] Public schools in the city became crowded with *Nisei* (second-generation Japanese American) children, who spent many hours at ethnic schools learning in their parents' mother tongue and tradition. In the frenzy of 100 percent Americanism, the federal call for English to be the first language of U.S. citizen children pressed the territorial Department of Public Instruction (DPI) to reform its polyglot school system.[10] FKCAAHI leaders intensified their advocacy of liberal kindergarten education and its incorporation into the English-medium public school system. They avidly supported PPU director Alexander Hume Ford in his calling for Pacific patriotism and DPI superintendent Vaughan MacCaughey (1887–1954; in office, 1919–1923) in his territorial school reform.

Also collaborating with Honolulu women leaders were internationally minded elite Japanese men who had a stake in amicable relationships among the United States, Hawai'i, and Japan. These Japanese internationalist men, who became active in the PPU's transnational networks, were not necessarily Christians. Nonetheless, they typically had Anglo-Saxon missionaries or their cohort teaching them English and Western knowledge in their youth. Many of them were involved in a thriving YMCA movement in Japan at the turn of the twentieth century. Due to racial, class, and gender inequalities in Hawai'i, old-timer missionary descendant women, liberal male recruits from the mainland, and Japanese male internationalists occupied similar positions in the islands' social hierarchy. White Honolulu women leaders, who struggled with the planter oligarchy and the feudalistic values of local Asian settlers, hoped that collaborating with these liberal progressive men would increase their influence in territorial policymaking. It would also facilitate mobilizing Asian women's voluntarism in entertaining guests and participants of PPU-sponsored events and conferences. Their collaborative efforts should enable women to wedge into the emerging Hawai'i-centered internationalism.

Nonetheless, this cross-gender collaboration in expanding English-only early education to every child on the islands was elite, urban, and elusive. It remained aloof from the daily lives of plantation worker families and thus oblivious to inner-communal/national rivalries and multilayered inequalities in Hawai'i and the Pacific. As a result of the bitter experiences of their attempts at navigating the local male oligarchy, feudalistic human relationships among local settler workers, and Pan-Pacific patriarchy, Honolulu women leaders were inspired to convene the women-only gathering and carve out an interracial and interethnic women's sphere in the thriving male-dominant Pan-Pacific movements.

The PPU, Alexander Hume Ford, and Trans-Pacific Networks

Alexander Hume Ford, who in the 1920s collaborated with Honolulu women leaders as the PPU's director, was born in 1868 to a prominent family from the U.S. South and settled in Hawai'i in 1907. By then, he had experienced postbellum devastation in Charleston, South Carolina, embraced social gospel zeal in New York and Chicago, and explored career possibilities in playwriting and journalism while traveling in Pacific countries.[11] Arriving in Hawai'i for a new job—promoting the islands to white tourists, residents, and investors—he created the Outrigger Canoe Club in 1908 to preserve and promote Hawai'i's disappearing surfboard riding and canoeing as tourist attractions and world sports. In addition, he founded, in 1911, the Hands-Around-the-Pacific movement with the formation of Pan-Pacific clubs in Honolulu and Sydney. Entrusted by missionary grandson Lorrin A. Thurston, publisher of the *Pacific Commercial Advertiser*, Ford took charge of the Hawai'i-promoting monthly journal, *The Mid-Pacific Magazine*.[12]

Ford successfully involved elite Asian settlers, many of whom had come under the sway of American missionaries, to reach not only tourist bureaus but also business, political, and civic leaders who became active in thriving trans-Pacific YMCA networks.[13] The Hands-Around-the-Pacific movement expanded to the Asian settlers' homelands. In 1917, the year of the Bolshevik Revolution and U.S. entry into World War I, Hands-Around-the-Pacific turned into the Pan-Pacific Union (PPU) to be a world peace center. Headed by Walter Francis Frear, ex-governor of the Territory of Hawai'i, the PPU enlisted Hawai'i's influential male leaders, many of whom were also active board members and trustees of the Honolulu YMCA.[14] While Ford assumed the modest position of corresponding secretary, he became an advocate of the Pacific as a center of world peace. He fantasized about the Pacific as a place for "democratization" without war:

> Revolutions are accomplished in the Pacific, racial rivalries brought about without armed conflict. Here, every man's life is liable to have its great dramatic moments in peaceful thrills. Sun Yat Sen, son of a Chinese peasant in Honolulu, became the first president of China after a practically peaceful revolution; the Shoguns quietly restored the Emperor to power in Japan; a few Americans peacefully dethroned the Hawaiian queen. The Pacific itself is being made democratic, and we of the Pacific look for the dramatic moment in our lives in thrills of peace rather than in the terrors of war.[15]

Ironically, however, "democratization" in the Pacific was neither peaceful nor democratic for everybody, as in the case of Hawai'i. The advent of technologically advanced Western powers that embraced "democratic" ideas shook premodern or early modern social foundations. Debates over the modernization process ensued, and rifts occurred between those who profited from and those who were marginalized by modern globalization processes. Furthermore, unlike Hawai'i, the social divide led to a civil war in China and military coups in Japan that waged wars against China and the United States. In this historical context, the expanding networks of the YMCA/YWCA, the PPU, and the IPR promoted intellectual exchanges and explored religious, economic, and political liberalism in the Pacific. Culturally hybridized Asian elite internationalists were expected to participate in this social gospel endeavor to mend existing rifts and to take on leadership for the peaceful integration of their communities and nations into the globalizing industrial capitalism and human movements.

After World War I, the Euro-centric Paris Peace Conference and the resulting Treaty of Versailles paid little attention to the Pacific, where victor nations' colonialism and imperialism preyed on the colonized, the defeated, and the "less civilized." Woodrow Wilson's principle of "self-determination" inspired anti-imperialist attempts in Korea, China, India, and the Philippines and among African Americans in the United States. Still, white racism and Japanese racialism quelled them. The major powers at the Paris Peace Conference—France, Britain, Italy, the United States, and Japan—ignored pleas for independence voiced by the uninvited delegation of overseas Korean nationalists residing in Japan, China, and Hawai'i. At the same time, the Conference refused to lend an ear to China's appeal to recover its sovereignty. Instead, it essentially abided Japan's imperialist demands on China and U.S. claims that the Philippines remained its "protectorate."[16] Nonetheless, Japan was irritated as its call for a racial equality clause in the covenant failed. These decisions inflamed nationalism, anti-colonialism, and anti-imperialism in Asia and the Pacific. They also pitted people of color against white racism and Japan against the United States over the Chinese market.[17] Hawai'i's planter oligarchs became concerned about relations among their majority Asian workers, who might lapse into interethnic hostility or pan-Asian solidarity.[18]

In this sociohistorical context, the PPU's Alexander Hume Ford, with support from Hawai'i's missionary descendants, promoted a "Patriotism of the Pacific" as the first step for world patriotism. While facilitating their trans-Pacific economic and political interests, he hoped that the world's Anglo-Saxon leadership would appeal to colonialist/imperialist internationalists who desired to acculturate the multiracial and multiethnic populations in their settlements, colonies, countries, or empires to the emerging post–World War I world order. The PPU's first objective was bringing together delegates from all over the Pacific to discuss and advance common interests.[19] As historian Paul Hooper pointed out, Ford envisioned that by collaborating with the Pan-American Union (PAU), official agency of the International Union of American Republics, the PPU would generate an international movement on par with European-centered internationalism.[20]

The PPU's secular attempt at intergovernmental cooperation in the Pacific intersected with the growing social gospel zeal of liberal American Protestants, a driving force of American progressivism. In the face of rising popular nationalism, anticolonialism, anti-imperialism, and radicalizing labor movements worldwide, it promoted a Christian spirit. It hoped to soothe the oppressed and exploited and alleviate social ills caused by global-scale industrialization. Among Hawai'i's missionary descendants were the Gulicks, who carried on the torch of missionary work. The most visible in the early twentieth century was Sidney Lewis Gulick (1860–1945)—a nephew of Orramel H. Gulick, who initiated the Hawaiian Evangelical Association (HEA) work among the Japanese. Born in the Marshall Islands to missionary parents, Sidney L. Gulick worked as a missionary and theology professor in Japan for almost twenty years between 1887 and 1913.[21] After returning to the United States, he took a position in the FCC headquartered in New York. The FCC was organized in Philadelphia in 1908 by major Protestant churches and lay organizations that transcended denominational differences in their social gospel endeavors. Its leadership criticized laissez-faire capitalism, appealed for the elimination of racial discrimination, sought to alleviate the hardships of labor, and tried to calm volatile labor and race relations.[22] The FCC had supported the U.S. entry into World War I and Wilson's ideal of collective security but advocated its own vision of the post–World War I world order by extending its influence on "all matters affecting the moral and social condition of the people." To accomplish this, it formed committees and commissions to study international issues, promote international justice and goodwill, and improve race relations in the United States and the world. By engaging in these efforts, Sidney Gulick, along with Hawai'i's prominent missionary families and their protégé Asian elite internationalists, became active in trans-Pacific efforts to fight Asian exclusionist forces and form secular organizations for the purpose. Consequently, he forged loose connections with liberal American men and women of prominence. Among them was Lillian D. Wald—the Henry Street Settlement founder, community nursing pioneer, and gender and racial equality advocate—who joined the National Committee for Constructive Immigration Legislation (NCCIL), for which Gulick served as its executive secretary. At Gulick's initiative, Jane Addams and Carrie Chapman Catt listed their names as honorary members of the National Committee on American-Japanese Relations.[23]

Ford was hardly free from social Darwinist views but developed sympathy and friendship with local Asian elites and their homeland dignitaries. He perceived plantation workers as "colored labor" who received "more generous treatment and higher wages" in Hawai'i than anywhere else in the world but whose public school–educated children were tempted to leave the plantation.[24] Still, he became sympathetic toward Hawai'i-born Asian youth who, along with their immigrant parents, were labeled "inassimilable" to America even after mastering the English language and American democratic principles. To mitigate their "unfortunate and often cruel treatment," he started monthly 12-12-12 meetings, which "gathered twelve leading Anglo-Saxons, twelve foremost Japanese, and as many prominent Chinese, each pledged to speak his mind honestly and freely." In the face of Hawai'i's need to prevent interethnic hostility among peoples from the Pacific nations, the meetings developed into Good Relations Clubs, adding Korean and Filipino representatives.[25]

After the Paris Peace Conference adjourned, Ford did not miss the chance to catch the rising tides of internationalism to advance the PPU's effort for interracial and interethnic understanding. Arriving in the islands after the U.S. annexation, Ford was exempted from the political entanglement that might have constrained Hawai'i's settler oligarchs from promoting the rosy picture of "democratic" Hawai'i. Being "innovative" and "always miles ahead of his contemporaries," Ford became "Hawaii's best booster."[26] In November 1919, Ford, as the PPU's secretary-director, traveled to Pittsburgh to attend the third World Christian Citizenship Conference, promoting Hawai'i as "the Radiating Center of Pan-Pacific Civilization."[27] Also present at the Conference was Sidney L. Gulick, who delivered his report as a chair of the World Commission on Immigration.[28] Gulick, as a NCCIL board member, was then engaged in a battle against exclusionists at the House Committee on Immigration at Capitol Hill.[29]

Ford extended his trip to Washington, DC, in early 1920 to advocate for "a Pacific League of Nations." He accompanied Charles J. McCarthy, the Wilson-appointed territorial governor and the PPU president, and Prince Kūhiō, territorial delegate to the U.S. Congress. There, he successfully convinced Massachusetts senator and chair of the Committee on Foreign Relations Henry Cabot Lodge that the Pacific, not the war-ridden Atlantic, was "the place to begin the work of a real League of Nations." The PPU won a federal appropriation, which was supplemented with territorial appropriations, and began holding a series of gatherings for representatives from nations in the Pacific. Later, his suggestion for a "Congressional junket to the Orient" materialized into a three-month journey to Hawai'i, the Philippines, China, Korea, and Japan in 1920.[30] Ford himself joined the junket to promote the PPU and facilitated U.S. congressmen in establishing friendships with political dignitaries and YMCA leaders from the countries they visited.[31] During its heyday, the PPU listed the names of dignitaries as its honorary presidents and vice presidents. Among them were President Woodrow Wilson, Secretary of Interior Franklin K. Lane, Jonah Kūhiō Kalaniana'ole (Prince Kūhiō), and the prime ministers or presidents of Australia, Canada, China, Japan, and New Zealand.[32]

The consolidation of the PPU's trans-Pacific networks was effective in recruiting participants to PPU-sponsored meetings and conferences. Also, revenues from subscriptions to *The Mid-Pacific Magazine*, which carried PPU-related articles and pages, went to funding Pan-Pacific conferences, as did donations from governments, private organizations, and capitalist-philanthropists. The first Pan-Pacific Educational Conference, held in August 1921, was the second in a series of such PPU-sponsored international conferences, following the 1920 first Pan-Pacific Science Congress.[33]

Pan-Pacific Patriotism Versus 100 Percent Americanism

Honolulu maternalist leaders embarked on carving out a women's sphere in the thriving male-led Pan-Pacific movement. The most conspicuous leader in this effort was culturally hybridized Julie Judd Swanzy, the longtime FKCAAHI president and DOH regent and an active participant in the League of Women Voters of the Territory of Hawai'i (HLWV).[34] Her love for swimming and involvement in the interracial DOH to "perpetuate the memory and spirit of Old Hawai'i" led Swanzy to befriend Alexander Ford, who had formed the Outrigger Canoe Club. As the club's membership was limited to men, Swanzy organized the Outrigger Club's Women's Auxiliary in 1909 and secured a part of the club's ground for a grass hut for women to use.[35] FKCAAHI kindergarten teachers and students of the teacher-training school, who came from various racial and ethnic backgrounds, enjoyed picnics and wholesome recreation on the club's beach. Ford, in later years, remembered that it was "Swanzy's purse and the Women's Auxiliary members" that saved the club's property when it went bankrupt.[36] Presumably, after the inception of the PPU in 1917, activities at the Outrigger Canoe Club were linked to Pan-Pacific banquets. With multiracial and multiethnic women's voluntarism, the women's auxiliary contributed to entertaining dignitaries from Pacific nations and to Pan-Pacific luncheon and dinner meetings for local, ethnically diverse male elites.[37]

By supporting Ford's PPU work, Swanzy and her Women's Auxiliary members slowly gained leverage over the emerging male-led Pan-Pacific movement. According to FKCAAHI organizational records, Swanzy was "in a position to arouse the interest and cooperation of persons from all walks of life in whatever project she had in hand." In fact, the FKCAAHI was "only one of the many agencies through which she worked toward the betterment of the peoples and institutions of her beloved Hawaii." Because of her "indefatigable energy" and "indomitable spirit," she became a "formidable opponent when crusading against what she believed wrong, and a powerful ally for any cause she espoused."[38]

With the eruption of the Great War in Europe, Swanzy worked with Ford to create a Pan-Pacific patriotism and "to imprint the spirit of harmony" among the islands' children, whose parents were mostly settlers and some of whom were from the nations at war. Possibly through her DOH connection, Swanzy and her maternalist cohort persuaded former Queen Lili'uokalani to lend a hand in a pageant at 'Iolani Palace in 1915, promoting friendship among Hawai'i's diverse children. For the occasion, Lili'uokalani returned to the palace and reoccupied her throne for about an hour to receive the flags and homage from children representing each country (Figure 4.1). Paradoxically, however, the pageant, organized by the PPU's predecessor Hands-Around-the-Pacific Club, claimed to commemorate Vasco Núñez de Balboa, Spanish explorer and conquistador who crossed the Isthmus of Panama in 1513 and "discovered" the Pacific.[39]

In the war-time frenzy of Americanization, efforts promoting Pan-Pacific solidarity and "racial harmony" among the islands' children assumed an additional role, disproving U.S. military intelligence claims against Japanese immigrant communities and mainland Americans' suspicions that multiracial and multiethnic Hawai'i was disloyal to the United States. The U.S. Bureau of Education in the Department of the Interior aggressively promoted English-language education and formulated national standards and

The late Ex-Queen Liliuokalani at her last appearance in public, again on the throne.

Figure 4.1 Former Queen Lili'uokalani back to her throne for a PPU-sponsored pageant, promoting unity among a multiracialized and multinationalized Hawaiian community after the eruption of the Great War in Europe.
Source: "Queen on the Throne," *Mid-Pacific Magazine* 15, no. 2 (February 1918): 127.

methods to nurture patriotism. As early as the spring of 1914, the Bureau of Education involved state and private organizations to inquire into local educational needs and conditions. When the war began, multiple federal agencies linked with the Council of the National Defense intensified the Americanization movement as part of wartime patriotic endeavors.[40] When U.S. Secretary of the Interior Franklin K. Lane (1864–1921) officially visited Hawai'i in May 1918, the PPU organized another pageant gathering children and representatives of "all Pacific nations," each carrying their national flag. As Queen Lili'uokalani had passed away the year before, the flags were submitted to Franklin K. Lane (Figure 4.2). Lane agreed to deliver them to President Woodrow Wilson on his return to Washington and pass on a request that Wilson become the PPU honorary president.[41]

PPU efforts favorably impressed Secretary Lane and assured him that the islands' multiethnic population was loyal to American principles. At the after-the-ceremony banquet attended by male representatives of the islands' ethnic communities, Lane promoted Wilson's claim that the war was to end all wars and that it would make the world safe for democracy. Lane also revealed his elation at the scene where culturally hybridized

Figure 4.2 After the U.S. participation in World War I, the pageant took a new role in proving Hawai'i's loyalty to the United States. In May 1918, U.S. Secretary of Interior Franklin K. Lane, promoter of the "One Country, One Language, One Flag" movement, visited Hawai'i. Children dedicated the flag to the secretary to be delivered to President Wilson. *Source*: "Pageant with Lane," *Mid-Pacific Magazine* 16, no. 3 (September 1918): 216.

men—including Australasian, Chinese, Japanese, Korean, Portuguese, Filipino, and Hawaiian—spoke English "not only with fluency" but "in the spirit of the highest American Christian civilization." He insisted that God had given man "a power of Will" and "adaptation" so that he could "change himself" and "blend intellectually and spiritually" with those "around him."[42] After his return to the mainland, Lane stated in his first public address, "Nowhere have I found in all my travels more intelligently patriotic and devoted people than our citizens in Hawaii."[43] Lane never questioned the superiority of "American Christian civilization" nor the benefit for natives and settlers to conform to its spirit and standard. Unlike many of his contemporaries, however, he affirmed the will and ability of nonwhite Asians and Polynesians to assimilate into U.S. society.

Secretary Lane's favorable comments on Hawaiʻi and his successful effort to have President Wilson assume the PPU's honorary presidency inspired the PPU and its women supporters to collaborate with Lane and his Department of the Interior. The department, however, stressed "one nation, one flag, and one language" for wartime Americanization efforts. Ford's call for Pan-Pacific patriotism might have embraced a radical edge in asserting Pan-Pacific transnationalism under the guardianship of Hawaiian royalty. It attempted to accommodate itself to the national and ethnic pride of the peoples of the Pacific. Now, the Pan-Pacific patriotism was subjugated to the U.S. president and assured U.S. hegemony in the Pacific. On July 4, 1918, the PPU held another ceremony, "A Pan-Pacific Declaration of Independence," at the home of Walter Francis Frear, Hawaiʻi's ex-governor and the PPU president. The Declaration of Independence, which called for the independence of "United Colonies" almost 150 years earlier, was read in twelve languages, including English, Hawaiian, Chinese, Japanese, Korean, and Portuguese, while "men and maids of Pacific lands in national costume came forward" and "the girl and boy scouts lowered their respective flags" and put them in a large box to be delivered to President Wilson.[44]

"One Nation, One Flag, and One Language": Securing Anglophone Cultural Hegemony in Hawaiʻi

In the frenzy of 100 percent patriotism, Hawaiʻi's missionary descendants and Japanese liberal internationalists linked by the PPU network found a common goal in the Americanization of *Nisei* children, whose parents composed over 70 percent of the plantation workforce in the early 1900s.[45] Although the system of promoting English over Hawaiian had been installed in the republic days, the growing pidgin-speaking population alarmed Hawai'i's white oligarchy. In 1896, school attendance had become mandatory and English was used as the medium of public instruction. Although the 1900 Organic Act required literacy either in English or Hawaiian to be qualified for suffrage, all territorial legislative proceedings would be conducted only in English, and Hawaiian became supplementary to be used only when necessary.[46] Hawai'i's public education system was introduced in the kingdom days but only slowly reached the settler children of rural plantation communities. Growing up in rural multiethnic environments, these children were first exposed to their parents' mother tongue and then pidgin used in interracial and interethnic communication. Accordingly, pidgin was establishing itself almost as their first common language, Pidgin.[47] Pidgin-speaking children also concerned ethnic community leaders, who mediated between white planter oligarchs and plantation workers. Japanese mediators appealed to planter paternalism to assist workers in building Japanese-medium ethnic daycares and schools to keep children off the streets. These schools were usually funded with fees paid by parents, subsidies from planters, and aid from the Japanese consulate or affiliated religious organizations. While public education became available to children, working parents sent them to foreign language-medium ethnic schools before and after public school hours. These arrangements were essential to non-Anglophone parents who needed their children to acquire a command of their mother tongue and cultural tradition. The foreign-language schools also met the interest of planters who desired to keep workers ethnically segregated to avoid interethnic labor movements.[48]

After the U.S. annexation, Hawai'i's public school system for the four major islands was centralized under the DPI's supervision, but foreign language schools remained outside of DPI's direct purview.[49] In the 1920s, the federal pressure to reform the polyglot territorial school system was amplified by local white families. Hawai'i's old-timer elite and a small quota of highly Americanized ethnic families with social connections sent their children to prestigious private English-medium schools on the islands. Nonetheless, Anglophone settler families without the privilege or resources had to rely on public schools. They complained that the schools were crowded with Pidgin-speaking pupils who might "contaminate" their children's language. Their pressure moved the DPI to designate the Central Grammar School as an experimental school that would require an oral English entrance examination. Soon, the white settler families would demand more schools like Central Grammar, and once children of non-Anglophone families began to pass the examination, their demand would escalate to openly segregate public schools by ethnicity, regardless of English proficiency.[50]

In this sociohistorical context, Hawai'i embarked on reforming the polyglot educational system, while exploring ways to secure qualified English-medium education for children from diverse racial and ethnic backgrounds. This was another means to consolidate American cultural hegemony in the territory and embrace paternalistic and maternalistic intentions. Because members of the missionary circle were involved in procuring foreign laborers for Hawai'i's sugar industry or led the kingdom's overthrow, some might have felt responsible for raising children of those settler laborers and displaced Native Hawaiians to be full-fledged U.S. citizens of the territory.[51] Their progressive and colonialist/imperialist efforts became imperious, reflecting the pressure from the national frenzy for 100 percent Americanism and the call for "one nation, one language." In 1919, the territorial legislature had multiple bills introduced to tighten DPI control over schools, including foreign-language schools, but passed none of them. Instead, it authorized the territorial governor to request the federal Department of the Interior's Bureau of Education to conduct a survey in Hawai'i.[52]

Honolulu women leaders found an opportunity in the federal pressure to step up their territorial motherhood and integrate Pidgin-speaking children into the fast Americanizing Hawai'i. For them, the battleground became preschool education. They sought collaboration with Vaughan MacCaughey, who was appointed as the DPI's new superintendent in 1919. MacCaughey, a Cornell graduate from South Dakota, arrived in Hawai'i in 1910. He served as a professor of botany at the College of Hawai'i (renamed University of Hawai'i in 1919), a vice president of the Territorial Normal School, and the director of the Hawai'i chapter of the National Education Association.[53] MacCaughey and his wife closely interacted with members of the islands' prominent missionary families, including Julie Judd Swanzy and her fellow FKCAAHI supporters.[54] MacCaughey also worked with the PPU and sympathized with Ford's Pan-Pacific ideas. In June 1919, he contributed to the PPU's *Mid-Pacific Magazine*, arguing for "a great and unescapable responsibility" of multiracial Hawai'i to educate "a rising generation of American-born young people, in the best Americanism, the finest inter-racial good will, [and] the highest pan-Pacific friendliness." He insisted on the importance of "children of many races, in a common peaceful and equable environment," to "live and play and study and grow up together, as chums—as friends—as native-born to Hawaii," as it was difficult "to change the adult mind." MacCaughey acclaimed the Pan-Pacific idea "as a dynamic educational force of incalculable power for good" not "a hollow phrase" of "a glittering generality."[55]

In October 1919, the U.S. Department of the Interior Bureau of Education Survey Commission arrived in Hawai'i to inspect and make recommendations on the educational situation in the territory.[56] By then, Japanese language schools, staffed by 449 teachers, enrolled about 20,000 pupils, and another 2,000 Korean and Chinese children attended their respective language schools in Hawai'i. The commission, headed by urban education specialist Dr. Frank F. Bunker, came with a liberal ideal of "Americanization" promoted by Franklin K. Lane, Secretary of the Interior, and Philander P. Claxton, Commissioner of Education. They envisioned Americanization as "a process of education, of winning the mind and heart through instruction and enlightenment," and thus with "no use of force." While "some common method of communication to convey the thought of the Nation" was necessary for children with birthright citizenship, Americanization was "what these persons do for themselves when the opportunity [was] offered and they [were] shown the way," and thus, the function of the agencies interested in Americanization was "to offer the opportunity, make the appeal, and inspire the desire."[57]

The federal Survey Commission espoused the double-edged progressive educational ideals of middle-class white settler families in America, and it requested three prominent civic organizations in Hawai'i—the Aloha Chapter of the Daughters of the American Revolution (Aloha-DAR), the Chamber of Commerce, and the Ad Club that was under the presidency of MacCaughey at the time—make legislative recommendations for foreign-language schools. Among the three, the Aloha-DAR issued the most forceful statement, insisting that foreign-language schools were "not only unnecessary, but a menace to the unity and safety of our Nation and the peace and prosperity of our people." They opposed "all foreign-language schools of whatever nationality." The Chamber of Commerce prioritized vocational education and recommended that "no instruction in any language other than English should be allowed in any public or private school in the Territory in any grade lower than the seventh grade." However, it, along with the Ad Club, argued for regulation rather than cancelling foreign-language schools.[58]

Little is known about the Aloha-DAR, but it could be an organization at the disposal of Hawai'i's planter oligarchs of missionary heritage. Possibly affiliated with the Daughters of the American Revolution (DAR), which organized in Washington, DC, in 1890 among patriotic women descended from active participants in the War for Independence, the Aloha-DAR formed in 1897 during the days of the Republic of Hawai'i. In the United States, DAR membership was primarily composed of middle-class, Anglo-Saxon Protestant women of diverse feminist consciousness, including women's rights activists. In Hawai'i, Albert Francis Judd I (1838–1900), missionary son and Julie Judd Swanzy's uncle who was then the republic's chief justice and the HEA president, founded the Hawai'i Chapter of the Sons of the American Revolution in 1895.[59] The Aloha-DAR formed with thirteen charter members at Judd's residence, and his wife, Agnes Hall Boyd Judd (1844–1934), a daughter of a Presbyterian minister from New York, assumed its first regency.[60] On the U.S. mainland, DAR membership attracted antisuffragists after the Nineteenth Amendment and increasingly became a white supremacist, antipacifist, and antisocialist/anticommunist organization.[61] Presumably, distant from such development on the metropole, the DAR's persistent advocacy of the conventional gender system, motherhood, individualism, property ownership, capitalism, Christianity, and republicanism sustained the membership of Honolulu maternalists of differing feminist consciousness.

The Survey Commission's final report was published in 1920. Its analysis and recommendations were essentially supportive of the DPI and the FKCAAHI leaders who endeavored to integrate liberal English-medium kindergartens into the public school system. It highly valued their tireless efforts in Americanizing the plantation's multiracial and multiethnic children. After recognizing that only 2 or 3 percent of the islands' children spoke English when they entered school at six or seven years of age, the Survey Commission's report stated that "many of those who come with some knowledge of English would better not have any at all," as "the jargon of the plantations and the 'pidgin English' of the streets" should be eliminated "in the end." The report emphasized that "no more important single step in Americanizing the children of the foreign born can be taken than in the establishment of a kindergarten or kindergartens in every settlement in the Territory." Furthermore, the report recommended that training teachers for kindergarten should be a part of the university's education department.[62] It echoed the opinions of territorial school authorities, who listed necessary reforms that required funding. Among these were increasing teacher salaries, raising teachers' training and qualification standards, reducing the size of elementary school classes, and providing permanent and modern school buildings.[63]

At the same time, the Survey Commission's report accommodated Hawai'i's various, even conflicting, civic causes. On the one hand, it normalized and bolstered Anglophone cultural hegemony and the plantation's bipolar social structure in its recommended Americanization process. Concerning foreign-language schools, it proposed that they were "certainly un-American if not anti-American" and that "all foreign language schools" for children with birthright citizenship should be abolished at the next session of the territorial legislature. Recognizing the need of "some common method of communication" to convey "the thought of the Nation," the commission insisted that English should be the medium of instruction for future citizens of the United States. It suggested that foreign-language education should be provided at public schools under the DPI's supervision only for pupils who were making satisfactory progress, and its expenses would be covered by a monthly fee paid by parents. Responding to white migrant families' desire for separate schools for Anglophone children, the report also suggested that students attending the same high school should be grouped according to their English proficiency. At the same time, the report accorded planter oligarchs' need to secure labor and raise future workers for Hawai'i's sugar and pineapple businesses. So, it included a suggestion for lengthening "the school day to seven or eight hours" so that "agricultural, industrial, manual, and play activities" could be provided for children whose parents worked in the fields and who might otherwise be running about the streets without such opportunities.[64]

Still, the Survey Commission's final report reflected progressive liberal educators' aversion to hierarchical human relationships based on Confucian morality and their attempt to liberate children of Asian ancestry from it. The report paid close attention to early childhood education and strongly objected to the rigid method employed by Japanese-language schools and the hierarchical teacher-children relationships that mirrored Japan's feudalistic household system, which required household members' absolute loyalty to the patriarch. Rote learning conflicted with "the spontaneous expression" public school teachers sought "in the child's own language." The report sympathized with public school teachers who found that foreign-language schools diverted children's attention, particularly those of Pidgin-speaking young children.[65] It argued that no people would "be transformed into Americans by a course in school" as it was "a matter of touch, of feeling, like the growth of friendship." The report called for turning the "schoolhouse" into a "community center" where there would be "no fear, no favor, no ulterior motives, and above all no soul insulting patronage of poor by rich, of black by white, of younger by elder, or foreign born by native born" and "all feel entitled to use."[66]

Anticipating planter opposition to the territorial educational reforms, the Survey Commission report also made hopeful comments. Employers were urged to reject the idea that success depended on "cheap, ignorant, illiterate, alien laborers who stick to their jobs only though fear of want and through inability to do anything else." It argued that when education fully functioned in the lives of employers, employees, overseers, and field hands, "all will be working as free men." Whatever the occupation, they would have "an enlarged individuality, a wider range of thought and action, a higher and more permanent peace." When "the true purpose of education" was achieved, the public schools of Hawai'i would no longer "be justly charged with educating the youth of the islands away from those occupations which require toil with the hands and making them relatively inefficient, 'white-collared folk.'"[67]

At any rate, the liberal educators from the U.S. mainland proved their genuine motive to provide U.S. citizen children with quality liberal education for the better future of their expanding republic. Local Free Kindergarten Association leaders were encouraged by the federal Survey Commission's high regard for their efforts and intensified their call for public kindergarten education in English. For long time, the FKCAAHI cherished the belief that kindergarten education with "the use of English and the training of hand and eye, as well as improved health" would enable first graders to make a "flying start" in public schools.[68] Siding with these FKCAAHI leaders were urban elite families of diverse ethnic backgrounds, whose mothers could afford to stay home and teach children their cultural tradition and language. They also saw a problem in overcrowded public schools populated by children without a proper command of English or their mother tongue.

PPU Networks and Elite Internationalists:
Race, Ethnicity, Gender, and Class

In pressing the maternalist cause, Honolulu women leaders developed a connection with Japanese male internationalists. These men were the prime participants in the expanding Japanese-American PPU/IPR networks and recognized the need to Americanize *Nisei* children in their fight against recurring anti-Asian agitation.[69] In Hawai'i, because nearly all Japanese laborers came from farming villages where a Buddhist temple was at the center of a community, the majority of them sent their children to schools or daycares affiliated with Buddhist missions.[70] In the early 1900s, anticipating American prejudice against Buddhism, bilingual *Issei* leaders who clustered around the Japanese consulate introduced Japanese Ministry of Education (JMoE)–certified textbooks and teachers from Japan in an effort for secularization. Ironically, the JMoE had mythologized the emperor as the lineal descendant of the Sun Goddess Amaterasu and imposed emperor-worshiping rituals on its public school system to nurture absolute loyalty among its subjects. In the 1910s, as the nationality and allegiance of U.S. citizen *Nisei* children came under suspicion, *Issei* leaders declared that the purpose of Japanese schools was solely to provide language education and began revising JMoE-certified textbooks to be suitable for the education of future American citizens.[71]

Honolulu's elite Japanese families joined this effort by showcasing support for the territorial educational reform prioritizing English-medium education. Sponsored by *Issei* businessmen in Honolulu and following the Survey Commission's report, the Japan Women's Society (JWS; Nihonjin Fujinkai), the most elite Japanese women's association in Hawai'i, took charge of opening the Nuuanu kindergarten for Japanese children in 1920. JWS's president, Chiyoko Yada, the wife of the Japanese consul general in Hawai'i, relegated its management to the FKCAAHI so that the children would learn standard English under the guidance of Frances Lawrence.[72] Although their fundamental motives differed, inculcating children with the English language and American ways served as an intersectional point for FKCAAHI leaders and urban elite Japanese families. FKCAAHI leaders aimed to turn the islands' children into "bona fide" members of the U.S. territory and disprove mainland suspicions of multiracial Hawai'i's disloyalty to the United States. For Japanese urban elites, however, it was a way to attain upward social mobility for their children, family, community, and the Japanese "race" and to refute the exclusionist claim of the Japanese as a race unassimilable to America.

Nonetheless, this transnational gender-and-race-mix network came to demarcate transnational class boundaries. Unlike the urban Japanese middle class, Japanese wives of plantation workers engaged in field labor although paid less due to their sex and ethnicity. They joined their husbands in labor strife, unlike other ethnic groups.[73] In the 1910s, during Hawai'i's rising labor movement, Buddhist churches and Japanese-language schools became venues for labor organizing. During World War I, although prosperous planters provided bonuses, they were not enough to keep up with rampant wartime inflation. Japanese workers petitioned for higher wages, shorter working hours, child daycare, maternity leave, and so on but to no avail. Japanese union leaders, for the first time, decided to link their movement with other ethnic groups. When three thousand Filipino workers, whose demands were also rejected, put their tools down in January 1920, their leader Pablo Manlapit called other ethnic groups to join, and three hundred Portuguese, Chinese, Puerto Rican, Spanish, Mexican, and Korean workers participated in the strike. In response, five thousand Japanese workers conducted a large-scale Japanese strike on O'ahu in February 1920. While Manlapit yielded to planters' pressure to call off the strike, Japanese strikers were persistent. The planter oligarchs insisted that the strike was anti-American, even suspecting Japanese government involvement. Japan's consuls general, Chonosuke Yada and his predecessor Eiichi Furuya, chastised the Japanese strikers, claiming that the strike was destructive to the Japanese community. To avoid the exclusionist forces from condemning the strike, bilingual *Issei* leaders, who were considered Christian or pro-Christian, joined the consuls general in mediating between the strikers and the Hawaiian Sugar Planters' Association (HSPA). They worked with Rev. Albert W. Palmer of the Honolulu Central Union Church. Mediation between employers and strikers, however, bore no fruit. The planters, despite the protest of Acting Governor Curtis P. Iaukea (D), evicted the strikers and their family members who were already suffering from the Spanish flu pandemic. After six months of struggle, the 1920 O'ahu Strike finally ended on July 1, causing a huge loss to the HSPA and no immediate gains for the strikers. Only three months later, the HSPA increased wages by half and improved working and living conditions in plantation communities while seeking their primary source of labor from the Philippines under U.S. colonial rule.[74]

While Japanese workers' distrust of the consuls general and *Issei* internationalists deepened during the island-wide strike, Honolulu's major newspapers, the *Star-Bulletin* and the *Advertiser*, attacked Buddhist temples, Japanese-language schools, and the Japanese-language press for their role in organizing labor resistance.[75] The territorial legislature, called to special session, refused to abolish the foreign-language schools outright; instead, it passed a compromise bill in November 1920, Act 30 (S.B. 32), which took effect in July 1921.[76] The legislature claimed that Act 30 would regulate rather than abolish foreign-language schools—schools teaching in any language other than English or Hawaiian except for Sabbath schools—so that the "Americanism of the pupils may be promoted." It required foreign-language school teachers and administrators to apply and obtain a DPI permit and place their school textbooks and curriculum under the DPI's jurisdiction. Only those with a command of English, belief in the ideal of democracy, and knowledge of American history and institutions—to a level satisfactory to the DPI—could receive the DPI's "basic license" for teaching at foreign-language schools. Nonetheless, Act 30 also stipulated that the schools should be open only after public school hours and only during term times. Pupils could attend classes a maximum of one hour a day for a total of six hours a week. Any person who violated the provisions would be guilty of a misdemeanor punishable by a fine.[77]

To bring the foreign-language schools under the DPI's supervision, superintendent MacCaughey resorted to the PPU's interracial and international network. Japanese internationalists—Consul General Chonosuke Yada and his bilingual wife Chiyoko, along with Honolulu *Issei* elites in the PPU network—were pressed to mediate between the DPI and Japanese immigrant communities.[78] Dr. Iga Mori, who had become an invaluable agent of the PPU's Pan-Pacific movement, formed and headed the Teachers' Training Committee (Kyōiku kōshū iinkai) to assist Japanese teachers adjusting to the changes. The committee, in consultation with the DPI, offered courses. The first exam allowed Japanese teachers lacking a command of English to use interpreters so that they could obtain a DPI's license for a year. After the first exams, the Yadas held a reception for three hundred Japanese teachers who had taken the exam. At the reception, Dr. Mori congratulated teachers, stating that "the Americans met you more than half-way and you went the rest of the way, but now you must keep up with the spirit."[79] To organize the joint American-Japanese committee on the revision of textbooks and Japanese-language school curriculums, MacCaughey requested Chonosuke Yada recommend Japanese members and Walter Francis Frear—the former territorial governor who was then the chair of the Honolulu YMCA Citizenship Education Committee—recommend American members.[80]

Arguably, as a part of this interracial, transnationalist endeavor, the Pan-Pacific Educational Conference convened under the auspices of the PPU in Honolulu in August 1921.[81] The conference attempted to facilitate interethnic and international mediation among education specialists in reforming Hawai'i's educational system. Vaughan MacCaughey took charge of organizing the conference, in cooperation with Dr. Frank F. Bunker who had directed the federal Survey Commission and remained in Hawai'i until 1923 to serve as the PPU's executive secretary.[82] By gathering internationally minded progressive educators, the DPI and its collaborators looked for a way to build cultural common ground among the polyglot population.

The U.S. Federal Bureau of Investigation (FBI) suspected the Pan-Pacific Educational Conference was a front for pro-Japanese sentiments, noting that the conference had more delegates from Japan than any other nation.[83] Instead, the conference attempt rested on growing recognition among internationalists and imperialists in the Pacific of the need for a common ground—a religious, spiritual, or ethical base—for amity and prosperity. After experiencing the nativism and prejudices of both their own and host communities in the Pacific, white and Asian internationalists active in missionary-pioneered transnational networks began exploring thriving ecumenical, unitarian/universalist, and pantheist movements. In Japan, they came under the sponsorship of Viscount Eiichi Shibusawa (1840–1931), "the father of Japanese capitalism," who dedicated his wealth and time in retirement to promote private diplomacy for the improvement of U.S.-Japan relations and Japan's reputation in the world. Accordingly, businessmen, diplomats, bureaucrats, educators, and religious leaders, who clustered around Shibusawa, composed the Japanese delegation to the Pan-Pacific Educational Conference. These Japanese internationalists were expansionists who were willing to adopt Anglo-Saxon liberalism to Japanese aspirations for colonialist and imperialist expansion. Nonetheless, from the Japanese public perspective, they were "pro-American/Western" and/or "Christian/pro-Christian."[84]

The Pan-Pacific Educational Conference became a venue for these Japanese internationalists to learn about various imperialist and colonialist attempts at establishing linguistic and cultural hegemony. As the post–World War I world order prevailed under the leadership of Anglo-American liberalism, the Japanese colonial government in Korea switched its longtime suppressive colonial policy based on military force to one that was equally forceful but was more conciliatory for cultural integration. Against this backdrop, Korean delegate H. Heung-Wo Cynn, a University of Southern California graduate and the general secretary of the Seoul YMCA, insisted on the need for more schools but also for the use of the Korean language in schools. Responding to Cynn was Masaharu Anesaki (1873–1949), Shibusawa's son-in-law and a Tokyo University religious studies professor, who insisted on the benefit of Japan's colonialism while paying lip service to Korean agony under Japan's colonial rule and Korean fear of losing their identity and cultural pride. He argued that the "people in Korea"—i.e., "the Korean people themselves, and the Japanese residents and settlers in Korea"—would "soon be able, under the present plan of education, to understand each other" while admitting that school language issues were "delicate and difficult," as in other countries.[85] As for the Americanization of U.S. *Nisei* citizens, Japanese consul general Chonosuke Yada asserted that his government had no intention of keeping them Japanese but viewed them as "a medium" for improving U.S.-Japan understanding.[86]

Arguably, these Japanese leaders' statements upset the Japanese immigrant community but facilitated territorial efforts to Americanize the islands' children. While some scholars have pointed to MacCaughey's Anglo-centric views and prejudice against non-Christian religions, others considered him as "extremely liberal."[87] MacCaughey was conciliatory in establishing Anglophone hegemony in Hawai'i and doing his best to appease every group involved in or affected by the DPI's educational reform effort. At the Pan-Pacific Educational Conference, MacCaughey insisted, "there [was] no other part of the United States of America where public education [was] more democratically administered and distributed than in Hawai'i." He praised "a high order of intelligence, remarkable courage and heroic spirit" of "old Hawaiians," who achieved trans-Pacific voyages and developed "a type of civilization, a type of education . . . we [could not] afford to forget or lose." MacCaughey also attributed the rapid progress of popular education after the coming of the missionaries to "the innate intellectual, spiritual and civic capacities of the Hawaiian race." Discussing the foreign-language schools, which had "many features of merit" but were "much misunderstood," he argued that the problem was caused by "stress, misunderstanding, and difficulties" typical of any transitional period when "foreign laborers," who had once intended to work in Hawai'i only for a few years and then return to their homelands, had now decided to remain in Hawai'i. MacCaughey went on to praise the "cordial spirit" of cooperation among Japanese teachers who were preparing themselves for "new conditions" under the leadership of "prominent men." At the same time, while explaining the highly centralized territorial public school system, he emphasized kindergarten education's ability to reach children during their "plastic" and "impressionable" age and hoped to "have a public kindergarten in every public school" within the next few years.[88]

As for female education, MacCaughey was reluctant to challenge socially assigned conventional gender roles, reflecting the patriarchal milieu of the Pan-Pacific internationalists' network and Hawai'i's upper-middle-class maternalist community. In his presentation, he argued that "recognition of the women's subjects in education" made "significant strides" and insisted that "girls should be trained in home-making, and in dress-making, and in cooking and sewing, and in civic affairs, and everything else that she is going to participate in."[89] Developed under the patriarchal control of American Protestant missionary enterprises and capitalist/imperialist ventures in the Pacific, transracial and transnational women's communities in Honolulu and other port cities utilized, rather than challenged, the assigned women's sphere and roles to build women's collective influence and autonomy on womanly issues to achieve women's causes.

Under the leadership of Julie Judd Swanzy and Mary Emma Dillingham Frear, local women leaders of different ethnic backgrounds worked together to provide food and entertainment for the Pan-Pacific Educational Conference. In return, they gained influence over its agendas and carved out space for their causes in the male-led Pan-Pacific movement. They successfully pressed the PPU to discuss preschool education and invite women education specialists to speak on the issue at the conference. Delegates from the U.S. mainland included Julia W. Abbott, chief of the Kindergarten Division of the Federal Bureau of Education; Barbara Greenwood of the University of California, Los Angeles, who represented the International Kindergarten Union; and representatives of the Association of University Women, the National Congress of Mothers and Parent-Teacher Associations, and the National League of Teachers' Associations. FKCAAHI's Frances Lawrence, an official delegate, presented a paper on kindergartens in Hawai'i.[90]

Through the Pan-Pacific Educational Conference, Hawai'i's women leaders were excited to reform Hawai'i's polyglot school system and establish personal ties with U.S. women education specialists and organizations. Explaining Hawai'i's kindergarten situation, Frances Lawrence emphasized that providing physical care to preschool children, disseminating knowledge for hygiene and healthcare to their mothers, and mixing preschool children of different races to create "pleasant and harmonious" interracial relations were as important as exposing preschool children to proper English.[91] Her argument about the need for and benefit of early education was further substantiated and universalized by mainland kindergarten experts. For example, Julia W. Abbott insisted that "no individual [could] become a worthy member of society unless he [had] been given the opportunity for self-realization," and she stressed the importance of early education "by the way of the child's own self-activity." While explaining the historical development of mainland kindergarten education, Abbott was sympathetic to FKCAAHI leaders who had developed schools that represented "the best in modern thought" but were still struggling to have them integrated into the territorial public school system. According to Abbott, before the introduction of kindergartens, states had fixed the starting age for school, and thus thirty-two states had to pass special legislation so that general school funds could be used for preschool-age children. By the time of the Pan-Pacific Educational Conference, all but four of these states had passed such laws, and the establishment of kindergartens within public schools spread in cities and in many small towns with populations of less than 2,500.[92] Furthermore, Barbara Greenwood of the International Kindergarten Union (IKU) introduced its new slogan, "a kindergarten for every child in the world," and its efforts to serve as "a medium for the general exchange of ideas" on early education. While stressing that kindergartens assumed "a grave responsibility" to help establish the habits of "ideal citizenship," she argued that the IKU's "quiet" efforts "scattered all over the world" would promote the peace that nations yearned for.[93] Such arguments from mainland experts must have encouraged DPI and FKCAAHI leaders to renew their efforts to reform Hawai'i's territorial schools so they could catch up with mainland developments and promote world citizenship.

Hawai'i had an urgent need to expand public school education for the surging numbers of children. Observing the island's children, Frances Lawrence believed that the lack of English proficiency caused student "repeaters" who clogged the lower grades, causing a shortage of rooms and thus blocking six-year-olds from receiving a proper education. Emphasizing that children's ability to acquire a new language peaked before their sixth year, she insisted that opening English-medium kindergartens throughout the territory "as soon as expedient" was not only imperative but also "cost-effective." She publicly voiced the FKCAAHI's support for public kindergartens, which also required trained teachers. Lawrence declared that the FKCAAHI was "ready in every way it [could be] in the establishment of sufficient kindergartens and in securing and maintaining as high a standard of efficiency as possible."[94]

Urban Internationalists Versus Rural Plantation Worker Parents: Kindergarten Education and Foreign-Language School Controversy

By assisting Ford in the Pan-Pacific movement and MacCaughey in the territorial educational reform, Honolulu women leaders successfully made promoting liberal preschool public education a territorial, national, and transnational issue. Their progressive efforts were linked closely to male networks serving the interests of industrial capitalists pursuing transnational ventures. Furthermore, their advocacy of a white middle-class standard of family life and quality liberal English-medium early education was desired by urban elite Japanese families but not necessarily by plantation worker parents. Honolulu's maternalist leaders unwittingly played a part in exacerbating multiple rivalries in local Japanese communities; for example, Christian clergies sided with Hawai'i's missionary descendants versus Buddhist missions and affiliated schools preserving Japanese traditions, and urban internationalists versus rural plantation workers. The rivalry also extended to the two ethnic newspapers *Nippu Jiji* and *Hawaii Hochi*. Arguably, the resulting so-called foreign-language school controversy provided Honolulu women leaders and their collaborators with additional impetus to convene an exclusively women's Pan-Pacific conference.

The controversy started in July 1922 when the DPI hastily drew up a set of new regulations based on the recommendations submitted under the DPI-appointed joint American-Japanese committee's name. The regulations included the elimination of foreign-language school classes for preschoolers and first graders and ultimately for second graders. Although Act 30 (S.B. 32) of 1920 had already limited foreign-language school instruction hours, the schools continued to care for and discipline preschoolers during their parents' work hours. According to Japanese records, white members of the DPI-appointed joint committee drafted the recommendations and asked its Japanese members for approval before submitting it to the DPI.[95] The Japanese-language school principals on the committee, who made up a minority of the Japanese members of the joint committee, insisted that they had never approved the recommendations that were submitted under the joint committee's name. Accordingly, the DPI's obtrusive action prompted contention among the council general–recommended Japanese members of the joint committee.[96]

Concurrently in July 1922, DPI's MacCaughey called for the "urgent desirability" of public kindergartens throughout the territory.[97] Had the DPI, its maternalist supporters, and Japanese internationalists expanded public school kindergarten education promptly, the Japanese community might not have been as agitated. The DPI attempted to prohibit private foreign language–medium education for preschoolers and first graders without securing alternative English-medium education on public funding. Hawai'i's public schools were supported by general property taxes, of which a substantial amount came from the Big Five and other sugar-related industries.[98] The 1920 O'ahu Strike had caused a huge loss to the island's sugar industry, and in 1921, the United Welfare Fund drastically cut funding for the FKCAAHI work.[99] Furthermore, the planter class had now hardened its attitudes toward not only unruly Japanese immigrant workers but also maternalist leaders who had increased their presence in the public sphere to pursue their causes independently of men. Planter oligarchs were unwilling to increase appropriations for providing modern liberal public education in English to young children, which they felt would "ruin plantation labor."[100]

Preschool education became the controversy's focal point. To the surprise of Honolulu's maternalist leaders, the DPI's attempts not only failed again in making private liberal kindergarten effort a public responsibility but also faced strong opposition from children's parents and the *Issei* community. While their efforts were based on a white middle-class gender system and family practices, they intended to liberate Japanese wives and *Nisei* children from the feudalistic patriarchal household tradition. For example, the virtue of "filial piety" obliged local immigrant families to make large remittance to homeland siblings who took care of their aging parents, often forcing wives to work for wages. In fact, *Nisei* writers made the suffering caused by the feudal family obligation a topic of their work.[101] Furthermore, when the DPI needed a larger budget to expand the public schools for surging numbers of *Nisei* children, Japanese immigrants' remittances to their homeland were drawing public attention.[102] Nonetheless, the DPI's hasty move to abolish foreign-language kindergartens without providing an alternative triggered an explosion of plantation-worker families' pent-up resentment against urban Japanese internationalists, who had spoken on behalf of the white planter oligarchs during the 1920 O'ahu Strike and, this time, for the DPI.

In the face of vehement opposition, the PPU's Alexander Hume Ford offered to assist Japanese internationalists in their mediation efforts. After meeting Keiichi Yamasaki, Japanese consul general in Honolulu (in office, 1922–1924), Ford argued that a solution could be found "through the friendly informal conferences conducted in the spirit of the Pan-Pacific Union." While MacCaughey declared that the DPI would not change its new regulations but would make efforts to provide public kindergarten education, Yamasaki requested that the territorial authority promptly establish public kindergartens so that young Japanese children could receive the same care as they received in language schools. He also asked Japanese parents to abide by the new regulations and cooperate with American efforts, while suggesting that alternative services could be provided by plantation-operated daycares and kindergartens.[103]

Despite this attempt at conciliation, rural plantation worker families felt estranged as their acculturation efforts were denied. The local Japanese press spoke for the community. *Hawaii Hochi*, the newspaper that rivaled Yasutaro Soga's *Nippu Jiji*, vocalized their indignation. Fred Kinzaburo Makino, the publisher of *Hawaii Hochi*, was a racially mixed and culturally hybridized *Issei* community leader born in Japan to a British trader father and a Japanese mother. Makino must have agreed with an editorial arguing that Japanese immigrants should "destroy the habit of worshiping the consul-general" and the belief that he would "act as a final arbiter of every problem." The editorial inspired Japanese immigrants in Hawai'i to stand up as they were "cast away" by the Japanese government, which prioritized diplomatic and international issues rather than the welfare of their people.[104]

MacCaughey blamed Yasutaro Soga, the publisher of *Nippu Jiji*, for its inability to "sell their idea to their own community." Soga was one of the Japanese members of the DPI-appointed joint American-Japanese committee, who approved the recommendation drafted by its white members, and a member of the first Pan-Pacific Educational Conference's International Publicity Committee.[105] The DPI expected him to promote its cause and win support for the recommendations submitted under the joint committee's name. Soga's editorial supporting the DPI's policy, however, fueled indignation of Japanese immigrants who vented about "weak-kneed," urban elite *Issei* leaders who had been serving as mediators between mainstream Anglophone society and Japanese-speaking immigrant communities.[106]

Against this backdrop, the DPI adopted the new regulations without any changes in August 1922, by which foreign-language kindergartens were to be abolished without an alternative on September 1, 1922 (the enforcement date later extended to January 1, 1923). In an attempt at appeasement, the

DPI also adopted "the policy of providing suitable supervision and activities for kindergarten-primary children after public school hours" and authorizing the DPI's superintendent to "proceed in devising ways and means to this end, cooperating with all interested agencies."[107] To keep children off the streets, the City and County of Honolulu provided public funding for a recreation commission to manage municipal playgrounds. Julie Judd Swanzy became its first chair and Frances Lawrence its secretary. Prominent missionary family members, including Swanzy, made their property available for children's playgrounds.[108] Meanwhile, the Hawaiian Education Association insisted that kindergarten education was the "best kind of educational investment of the territory."[109] FKCAAHI's Lawrence argued that "the only hope of providing education for all the pre-school age children" was "the establishment of public school kindergartens."[110] Nonetheless, the DPI's effort—despite support from the FKCAAHI, the PPU, and Japanese elite internationalists—fell short of meeting the needs of rural plantation worker parents. For example, in January 1923, Mrs. M. Yamada of Pepeekeo Japanese Language School on the Big Island had to dismiss nearly sixty young children to abide by the new regulations. She wrote directly to MacCaughey, expressing an urgent need for an alternative to care for the dismissed children.[111]

Concurrently, Makino's newspaper became a venue for local Japanese educators and parents to discuss establishing an education system independent of American or Japanese control so that *Nisei* children could become hybrid, "bona fide" U.S. citizens with *Yamato damashii* (Japanese spirit). Makino began collecting donations to file litigation against the DPI regulations. In December 1922, Palama Japanese Language School on Oʻahu, which had no religious affiliation, sued Governor Wallace Farrington in the Hawaiʻi Territorial Circuit Court. In 1923, schools affiliated with the largest Buddhist congregation in Hawaiʻi joined the lawsuit, and ultimately eighty-eight schools, nearly two-thirds of all Japanese-language schools, joined the lawsuit. The U.S. Supreme Court settled the "foreign-language school controversy" with the *Farrington v. Tokushige* decision in 1927, declaring Hawaiʻi's foreign-language laws unconstitutional.[112] Along with *Meyer v. Nebraska* (1923), which concerned anti-German sentiment, and Oregon's *Pierce v. Society of Sisters* (1923), dealing with anti-Catholic sentiment, the *Farrington v. Tokushige* case secured a victory over coerced Americanization.[113] Hawaiʻi's foreign-language school controversy showcased *Issei* parents' determination to raise their children to be bona fide U.S. citizens and their desire to pass down their cultural values and traditions. It also revealed the existence of multiple voices and motivations in local Japanese communities that Honolulu maternalist leaders encountered in their liberal but still imperialist attempts to integrate polyglot Hawai'i's multiethnic children into Anglophone society.

The PPU, the HLWV, and the Nationality of Sons of Japanese Ancestry

In March 1922, prior to the start of the foreign-language school controversy, Honolulu suffragists had inaugurated the League of Women Voters of the Territory of Hawai'i (HLWV). The HLWV's inception reflected their aspiration to introduce mainland feminists' expertise for voter education to achieve their causes. FKCAAHI leaders were also engaged in this effort. Besides pressing for bills to integrate kindergartens into the territorial public school system, the HLWV would work for various women's causes, such as women's jury right, child welfare, school building expansion, health education, and the widest education opportunities for surging numbers of school-age children. To prevent juvenile delinquency, it also sought to extend compulsory education from age fifteen to seventeen.[114]

In the face of growing controversy over the DPI's polyglot school reform attempts, Honolulu white women leaders also developed a link to Japanese internationalist men through the PPU's network. They came to assist trans-Pacific Japanese internationalists' effort to secure *Nisei* children's U.S. nationality. International tensions between the United States and Japan were building in the 1910s and 1920s, and *Nisei* children's dual nationality became a crucial issue. On September 12, 1922, Vaughan MacCaughey brought the matter to the HLWV's first board meeting.[115] *Nisei* children's dual nationality derived from the two nations' conflicting systems for determining nationality: Japan's practice of *jus sanguinis* (right of blood) granted nationality to children born to Japanese fathers regardless of their birthplace, and the U.S. practice of *jus soli* (right of soil) granted nationality to children born in the United States regardless of their parents' nationality.[116] Japanese internationalists on the U.S. Pacific Coast had been worried that *Nisei* children's dual citizenship could become another pretext for exclusionists' anti-Japanese agitation. After establishment of the alien land laws—first in California in 1913 prohibiting the ownership and long-term leasing of agricultural land by aliens racially ineligible for U.S. citizenship—the Japanese farming industry on the Pacific Coast increasingly became dependent on the U.S. citizen status of their children.[117] In 1916, *Issei* leaders, in collaboration with Japanese consuls, successfully petitioned the Japanese imperial government to revise its nationality law so that guardians of children born to Japanese fathers in countries with *jus soli* could renounce their children's Japanese nationality with approval from Japan's Home Affairs Minister. After the age of fifteen, these dual citizens could self-renounce their Japanese citizenship. Japan's revised Nationality Law of 1916, however, excluded men between the ages of seventeen and thirty-seven from the dispensation in order to prevent draft-dodging.[118]

In the U.S. mainland, however, exclusionist efforts to prohibit Asian settlers from owning and leasing agricultural land intensified. California, where alien Asians were already prohibited from owning land or leasing it for more than three years, established the new alien land law in 1920 to forbid alien Asians from leasing and sharecropping entirely.[119] In the same year, exclusionist forces also began demanding a new federal immigration law to exclude Japanese immigration along with a constitutional amendment to bar children of aliens racially ineligible for naturalization from holding citizenship.[120] Concurrently, *Issei* leaders filed multiple lawsuits to nullify alien land laws and to grant citizenship to sufficiently Americanized but foreign-born Japanese. Nonetheless, the courts denied their claims, one after another. The *Issei* quest for U.S. citizenship ended with the Supreme Court decisions, *Ozawa v. United States* (1922) and *Baghat Sing Thind v. United States* (1923), which denied naturalization of aliens of color from the "Asiatic" zone.[121]

In this context, trans-Pacific Japanese internationalists mobilized their networks to petition the Japanese government to further revise the 1916 Japanese Nationality Law to allow male subjects between seventeen and thirty-seven to renounce their Japanese nationality. As Japan's imperialist aspirations in the Pacific became conspicuous during and after World War I, the dual nationality of *Nisei* sons became a crucial diplomatic issue.[122] Anxious about the "possibilities of the domination of the Territorial electorate by representatives of a single racial group, such as the Japanese," the federal Survey Commission report also addressed the "great importance" of nationality in its analysis.[123] While seeking a solution to the foreign-language school problem, the Japanese consul general in Hawai'i, Chonosuke Yada, thought that the fundamental issue was American suspicion of Japanese government control over *Nisei* children with dual nationality.[124]

The growing distrust of American citizens with dual nationality affected the lives of Asian individuals in Hawai'i, for example, public school teachers and war veterans. In accordance with the Survey Commission report, which explored the dual nationality issue, Hawai'i's territorial DPI prohibited, in April 1920, American citizens with dual nationality from being admitted to the Normal School or becoming public school teachers.[125] Furthermore, although Judge Horace Vaughn of the U.S. District Court in Hawai'i had granted U.S. citizenship in November 1919 to about four hundred *Issei* veterans, his judgment was never carried out. The debates continued about whether alien veterans of Asian ancestry had the same rights as alien soldiers of the "white race" or "African descent" to become naturalized citizens. In 1920, the Americanization Committee of Honolulu Post No. 1 of the American Legion, a World War I veterans' organization, formed the Society of American Citizens of Japanese Ancestry (SACJA) and required its members to "publicly declare [their] undivided and wholehearted allegiance to the United States of America and her government and to publicly renounce any allegiance to Japan." The SACJA also joined trans-Pacific internationalists in petitioning the Japanese government to revise its 1916 Nationality Law.[126] In 1922, however, the new territorial governorship of Republican Wallace Farrington nullified the U.S. citizenship of *Issei* veterans. The Supreme Court decision *Toyota v. United States* (1925) confirmed the status of *Issei* veterans as aliens racially ineligible for U.S. citizenship. *Nisei* youth in Hawai'i became a force in SACJA's petitioning for the further revision to the 1916 Nationality Law,[127] and Alexander H. Ford made the dual nationality issue a topic at the PPU's 12-12-12 meetings.[128]

Appearing at the HLWV's first board meeting, Vaughan MacCaughey raised the possibility that U.S. citizen *Nisei* could be "legally claimed" as subjects of the emperor of Japan because of their dual nationality status. MacCaughey estimated that more than half of the 48,000 children attending public schools in the territory could be "claimed by a foreign empire."[129] In response to his report, HLWV board members inquired about the issue to experts, some of whom had attended the Pan-Pacific Educational Conference held in Honolulu in August 1921.[130] Among the experts whom the HLWV consulted was Rev./Dr. Tasuku Harada—an American Board of Commissioners for Foreign Missions (ABCFM) missionary ordained minister and U.S.-educated professor teaching Japanese literature and history at the University of Hawai'i. He reported about ongoing trans-Pacific efforts in petitioning the Japanese government to revise its 1916 Nationality Law.[131]

In their efforts, HLWV leaders also met with Baron Yasushi Togo, a member of the House of Peers of the Japanese Imperial Diet and the Pan-Pacific Association of Japan, when he visited Honolulu to attend the first Pan-Pacific Commercial Conference in 1922. Asked for his opinion, Togo responded that a resolution from the HLWV would be helpful in drawing the attention of Japan's House of Peers' American-Japanese Relations Committee to the issue. In December 1922, HLWV leaders, after consulting with territorial governor Wallace R. Farrington and local male civic leaders and businessmen, handed Togo a resolution requesting that necessary and "proper" actions be taken to solve the dual nationality problem.[132]

In support of the trans-Pacific efforts of Japanese internationalists, the HLWV successfully added pressure on the Japanese Imperial Diet to revise the 1916 Nationality Law. Revisions would take effect in December 1924 to eliminate the provision that prohibited draft-age *Nisei* sons from renouncing their Japanese nationality. Furthermore, a child born to a Japanese father in the United States would lose Japanese nationality unless the parents registered such a child at a Japanese consulate within fourteen days of birth. Also, those who had dual nationality could renounce their Japanese nationality without approval from the Home Affairs Minister through a simple procedure.[133] At the October 1924 HLWV executive committee meeting, a message from Colbert Kurokawa, a YMCA Nuuanu Branch *Nisei* staff member and one of his generation's most enthusiastic Americanization advocates, explained the revised Japanese Nationality Law and expressed his gratitude to the HLWV.[134] Despite the 1924 Revised Nationality Law, however, the number of renunciation applications remained low in the late 1910s and 1920s, possibly due to rural plantation families' distrust of Japanese and *Nisei* internationalists and YMCA leaders.

Noticeably, the mixed-gender trans-Pacific collaboration forged between Honolulu women leaders and Japanese male internationalists through the PPU-YMCA network only secured draft-age *Nisei* sons the same right to renounce their Japanese nationality that other-age-group *Nisei* had obtained. They paid no attention to the ordeals of *Nisei* daughters who lost their birthright U.S. citizenship by marrying *Issei* men. At that time, the postsuffrage mainland feminist campaign had successfully established the Cable Act in September 1922. It secured individual nationality for white, married women citizens. Prior to the 1922 Cable Act, the nationality of a white woman in the United States was a mere reflection of her spouse's status.[135] With the establishment of the Nineteenth Amendment in 1920,

Congress opened a debate over married white women's naturalization and expatriation rights. In support of women expatriates who had lost their citizenship through marriage to foreign men, both the National League of Women Voters (NLWV) and the National Woman's Party (NWP) campaigned, although separately, for married women's independent nationality rights. In the process, the possibility of U.S. women citizens holding "dual nationality" and alien wives having "statelessness" was debated because wives' nationality depended solely on their husbands' nationality in most nations at the time. The Cable Act of 1922 required white alien wives to emulate American ways and to take the same naturalization process as white alien men.[136] The Cable Act of 1922, which made the nationality of a married woman independent of her husband's, remained tainted with racism. The act only applied to women citizens who married alien men racially eligible for naturalization. Accordingly, it did not address the problems of U.S. citizen women who lost their U.S. citizenship by marrying foreign-born Asian men or alien Asian women who remained racially ineligible for naturalization whether they were married to American citizen men or not.[137]

The HLWV had only been organized in February 1922. Although HLWV leaders were also active in the FKCAAHI and Honolulu YWCA movements serving alien Asian women and their U.S. citizen daughters, they failed to recognize their gender- and race-specific ordeals at this point. Their collaborators, Japanese and *Nisei* internationalist men were only concerned about the nationality of *Nisei* sons and naturalized *Issei* veterans and had no intention of granting wives or future wives the right to act independently of their husbands. Consciously or unconsciously, the HLWV did not extend its attention to the nationality issue of U.S. citizen Asian daughters who married Asian men racially ineligible for naturalization. Nor were they concerned about Asian immigrant women racially ineligible for U.S. citizenship.

Inspired to Convene a Women's Pan-Pacific Conference

While collaborating with the PPU's and DPI's white male recruits from the mainland and the Japanese internationalist men in the PPU's network, Honolulu women leaders also endeavored to strengthen their national and international women's networks. They first attempted to call a Pan-Pacific YWCA meeting in the city but to no avail. Prior to the first Pan-Pacific Educational Conference in June 1921, Honolulu YWCA board member

Mary Emma Dillingham Frear and Honolulu YWCA general secretary Grace Channon visited the National YWCA's Pacific Coast Field Committee in San Francisco to discuss convening a single-gender YWCA Pan-Pacific Conference in Hawai'i. Consequently, Mrs. Walter G. Barnwell, chair of the committee, and Grace Love, an executive of the committee's Immigration and Foreign Community Department, each sent letters to the National Board in New York recommending a conference that was more like "a friendly gathering of the people who [were] distinctly affecting women in the Pacific." According to Love, Hawai'i was "one of the most strategic points from which" the YWCA could do "constructive work." While referring to Hawai'i as a "human laboratory where the yellow non-Christian civilization [had] met the white Christian civilization," she argued that in Hawai'i, women of various nationalities were "rapidly awaking to a new life," bringing "new responsibilities and new opportunities" to the YWCA, which was to be a great "World's Christian Organization." By introducing a "great" Pan-Pacific Educational Conference scheduled for August 1921, Love fulfilled the committee's resolution and recommended that a pan-Pacific conference be held to consider "the present status of women in the Pan-Pacific world, with a study of their existing problems, economic, educational and social."[138] Although the National YWCA's response to the Honolulu YWCA's request is unknown, it is certain that the YWCA's gender-specific pan-Pacific conference never materialized in Hawai'i. Possibly, progressive members of the territorial oligarchy decided to hold a pan-Pacific YMCA conference, thereby submerging the Honolulu YWCA's call for a pan-Pacific conference. Local YMCA member efforts led to the inception of the Institute of Pacific Relations in 1925.

Honolulu YWCA leaders explored ways to increase their influence in the PPU. So, Mary Emma Dillingham Frear attended the PPU's first Pan-Pacific Educational Conference in 1921 as an official delegate representing the National YWCA, as mentioned at the beginning of this chapter. She also served on the conference's permanent organization committee, which unsuccessfully recommended that the PPU establish a permanent educational organization to arrange future educational conferences, facilitate exchanges among teachers of diverse backgrounds, and promote successful teaching methods.[139] Frear was also on the conference's Entertainment subcommittee chaired by Julie Judd Swanzy. To facilitate women's interracial, interethnic, and international exchanges, these women leaders, with support from women's voluntarism from Honolulu ethnic communities, repeatedly entertained the predominantly male participants to pan-Pacific gatherings and conferences.

In 1922, the Pan-Pacific Aloha and Entertainment Committee, in which "the influence and work of the women predominate[d]," was organized to welcome and entertain delegates to pan-Pacific conferences.[140]

Nonetheless, it required more negotiations and maneuvering for Honolulu women leaders to convene a pan-Pacific women's conference. They were committed to the separate sphere strategy and desired to act independently of men for women's autonomy but without confronting them. Some were conservative, but all were prudent in unshackling themselves from the socially assigned wife's role as her husband's "helpmate." For example, Gertrude D. Bunker, the wife of Dr. Frank F. Bunker, advocated the conventional missionary idea of "women helping men." She insisted that women "were not fighting with men" but "anxious to help them" to enact "constructive" legislations, especially for "international cooperation for the prevention of war, [and] schools and laws having to do with women and children."[141] After her husband worked for the PPU to convene the 1921 Pan-Pacific Educational Conference, Gertrude took up the HLWV presidency and stayed in the position until they left Honolulu in 1923.[142]

Aspirations for a women's pan-Pacific conference revived in August 1924, when Honolulu women successfully influenced Mark Cohen, a New Zealand participant in the PPU-sponsored First Pan-Pacific Food Conservation Conference, to propose a women's conference to "consider problems of mother and child welfare." He made his proposal at a luncheon for conference participants sponsored by the Outrigger Club's Women's Auxiliary. In response to Cohen's call, the PPU promised its funding and named Julie Judd Swanzy as the temporary president of the proposed women's conference.[143] In December 1924, a "group of determined women"—including prominent missionary descendants, professionals recruited from the mainland, and Honolulu YWCA workers from local ethnic communities—met for a luncheon, where the PPU's Women's Auxiliary was formed to launch the planning of the conference.[144] The PPU's Women's Auxiliary eventually developed into the organizing committee called Conference Committee for the Pan-Pacific Women's Conference (PPWC).[145] Swanzy became the honorary chair and Honolulu YWCA president Harriet Cousens Andrews (1875–1963), the chair for the committee.[146]

Ironically, the strongest impetus for convening a gender-specific conference came from the dampening effect that mixed-gender collaboration had on building interracial women's solidarity. Asian men were willing to collaborate with influential white women, but Ford observed that "so many of the Oriental women would not attend meetings where there were men." In fact, although women internationalists from Asian communities had participated in early Conference Committee meetings, men replaced women in representing their ethnic communities.[147] These male internationalist leaders, however, faithfully constituted a part of the male pan-Pacific network and spoke for male interests more than they did for women of their community. For example, present at the Conference Committee meeting held in January 1925 were two Asian men, Japanese Tasuku Harada and Chinese Shao Chang Lee. Both were Yale graduates and University of Hawai'i faculty active in the PPU and the IPR. While Lee questioned "a real need" for a women's conference, Harada expressed his hope that the women's conference would only deal with limited topics such as "health, child welfare, eugenics, and birth control" because the scheduled male-led conference would discuss "racial, economic, and ethical" issues.[148]

Under the directorship of Alexander Hume Ford, the PPU became the "father organization" of the PPWCs and their permanent organization, the PPWA, which would form in 1930. In an attempt to facilitate women representing their respective communities in the upcoming PPWC, Ford, who had once promised that the PPU would not interfere but only raise money for the PPWC,[149] began monthly women-only luncheon meetings, called the Pan-Pacific Women's Club, in September 1926. At the same time, he insisted that the PPWC "must be in the thinking of all the women in the community; it must be in the thinking of all nationalities if we are going to get the most out of it."[150] Assisting the efforts of the PPU and its Women's Auxiliary was Ann Yardley Satterthwaite (1892–1964), a Swarthmore graduate from the Pennsylvania Quaker community who was hired in 1919 to become Ford's right hand.[151] Committed to the women's separate sphere strategy, the Hawai'i's Conference Committee soon secured Jane Addams's agreement to be the PPWC's international chair.[152]

The theme for the 1928 PPWC was set on "motherhood and child welfare,"[153] and its round-table discussion topics included health, education, women in industry and profession, women in government, and social work.[154] As for "health," the PPWC specifically addressed the health "of mother and child" but excluded the topics of medicine or health in general, as the PPU was in the process of organizing the Pan-Pacific Medical Conference scheduled for Honolulu in 1929.[155] Organizers also reserved such current and controversial topics as immigration, race, and international politics for male-led IPR conferences in 1925 and 1927.[156]

CHAPTER 5

Forming the Delegation to the 1928 Pan-Pacific Women's Conference

United States, Hawai'i, Japan, and China

The primary goal of convening the exclusively women's conference for Honolulu leaders was to forge transnational women's solidarity and autonomy to facilitate their territorial mother work. However, they recognized the need to find local, national, and international niches for their gender-specific pan-Pacific women's attempts to call for international participation. Hawai'i's male leaders had already formed two international organizations—the Pan-Pacific Union (PPU) and the Institute of Pacific Relations (IPR)—whose international conferences were open to women. Furthermore, with the outbreak of World War I in Europe, growing calls for social justice and world peace caused a rising tide of internationalism. It further created "multivalent and even contradictory currents," regrouping and reorganizing women's movements worldwide. The bourgeois women leaders who were active in trans-Atlantic women's networks were inspired to "truly" internationalize their movements and expanded networks to women in Asia, Africa, and the Middle East.[1] Concurrently, these Euro-American leaders endeavored to participate in world policymaking at the newly organizing intergovernmental bodies, e.g., the League of Nations and the International Labour Organization (ILO).[2] Although the U.S. government joined neither the League of Nations nor the ILO in the 1920s, postsuffrage U.S. women leaders, supported by their nation's economic power, assumed conspicuous roles in these international women's endeavors.

The rise of women's internationalism led to the formation of "super-international" women's coalitions in Geneva, e.g., the Joint Standing Committee of the Women's International Organizations (JSCWIO or Joint Standing Committee) and the Liaison Committee of Women's International Organizations (LCWIO or Liaison Committee). The Joint Standing Committee was formed in 1925 to facilitate women's appointments to the League of Nations Secretariat staff, to its commission and committee members, and to national delegates of intergovernmental organizations and their international conferences. The Liaison Committee would be formed in 1931 to coordinate increasing numbers of international women's organizations that engaged in intergovernmental debates.[3]

In the struggle to build common ground among multiracialized and multiethnicized Hawai'i's population, Honolulu women hoped to catch the mounting tide of internationalism and broaden their perspectives. Fortunately, they found enthusiasm and cooperation from white and nonwhite women active in and around the networks pioneered by Anglo-Saxon missionaries. Nonetheless, convening the Pan-Pacific Women's Conference (PPWC) in Honolulu required the volunteerism of local women and coordination among women leaders of participating countries. Furthermore, winning support and funding from local male oligarchs and community leaders, who had already started to use the pan-Pacific movement to promote trans-Pacific dialogues for men and women, would be essential.

By focusing on women who became active at multiracial and multiethnic urban centers in Hawai'i and the U.S. mainland, Japan (Tokyo), and China (Shanghai International Settlement), this chapter interrogates the effect of the late modern phase of globalization on the lives of women in the Asian Northeast and the ensuing transnational and international women's movements. In doing so, this chapter illuminates the multifaceted and multilayered aspects of women's activism and movements that emerged on and around missionary-pioneered trans-Pacific networks in facilitating, adjusting, and resisting multiple colonialist and imperialist attempts in the Pacific. It also describes how women's interactions at the PPWCs contributed to intersecting social reform, suffrage, motherhood, labor reform, and peace advocacy, and how they broadened the scope of women internationalists who engaged in global women's collective power building for the benefit of women and children.

Feminism, Backlash, and Growing Interest in the Pacific: The 1928 U.S. and Hawaiian Delegations

The victory of the Allied powers in World War I and the emerging postwar new world order under British-American hegemony began pressing Pacific nations to emulate Anglo-Saxon liberalism. Meanwhile, progressive social feminists from the United States were experiencing backlash from right-wing and antifeminist social forces. In the United States, the eruption of the Bolshevik Revolution in Russia caused a Red Scare, disaffecting maternalist causes and achievements. The Keating-Owen Act of 1916, the first federal statute that addressed child labor, went into effect in 1917, but the U.S. Supreme Court struck it down only nine months later in 1918.[4] Subsequent social feminist endeavors to safeguard their causes led to the passage of the Child Labor Tax Law in 1919, which levied a tax on employers using child labor. However, once again, in 1922, the U.S. Supreme Court declared it unconstitutional. Undaunted, the Women's Joint Congressional Committee (WJCC)—an umbrella organization of U.S. national social feminist groups—successfully pressured Congress to pass a constitutional amendment to allow the federal government to regulate child labor in 1924, but the amendment failed to win three-fourths of the states for ratification.[5]

In the postsuffrage United States, women's increasing presence in national and international arenas also invited a strong backlash from male medical professionals, state-rights advocates, and industrialists. Maternalists' hard-won Sheppard-Towner Maternity and Infancy Protection Act of 1921—which provided matching funds to states, including the territory of Hawai'i but not until 1925, to enhance the health and welfare of mothers and children—also fell victim to the backlash. Antifeminist forces claimed that Carrie Chapman Catt, Jane Addams, Children's Bureau directors Julia Lathrop and Grace Abbott, and WJCC member organizations—including the National League of Women Voters (NLWV), National Congress of Mothers and Parent-Teacher Association (PTA), Women's International League for Peace and Freedom (WILPF), Woman's Christian Temperance Union (WCTU), Young Women's Christian Association (YWCA), National Women's Trade Union League (NWTUL), and National Consumers' League (NCL)—were all under the influence of communism and socialism. Despite this criticism and in the face of a backlash from the right, social feminist and social gospel groups fought for continued federal Sheppard-Towner funding beyond June 1927. They only succeeded in winning an extension to June 1929.[6]

Undaunted, U.S. women progressives, who were steadily entering federal bureaucracies, sought international collaboration to assure human rights, gender equality, and the welfare of wage-earning women and children. These publicly funded policymakers, along with American activists supported by the widows and daughters of wealthy industrialists and the voluntarism of middle- and working-class women, attended Geneva-based intergovernmental conferences in official and unofficial capacities. They urged American women into advisory commissions and committees to pressure the ILO and the League of Nations to work for the well-being of women and children.[7]

Among these American women policymakers on the international scene were Anglo-Saxon YWCA industrial reformers who strengthened the World YWCA's industrial work. Founded in 1894, the World YWCA's original purpose was to evangelize and promote Protestant morality and middle-class womanhood among young women worldwide. In the face of industrial globalization, however, the World YWCA's main focus shifted to the protection of wage-earning women and children. In 1920, the World YWCA gathered delegates from its member nations and held an executive commission meeting at Champéry, Switzerland, where it adopted a policy to fight for universal ILO-established labor standards for working women in their respective country and to encourage them to raise voices in self-advocacy. In 1921, the World YWCA formed the International Industrial Committee and appointed American Mary A. Dingman (1875–1961), U.S. Women's Bureau director Mary Anderson's old friend, as its industrial secretary.[8]

Ironically, however, increasing women's visibility and activism in the national and international male public sphere eroded the efficacy and legitimacy of women's conventional separate sphere strategy in forging cross-cultural interactions and solidarity. The tendency for younger women activists to enter into the male sphere of political, economic, and civic affairs for the advancement of their causes was aided by trends in mass-consumer culture that reformulated traditional religious, moral, and gender norms in the advanced industrial nations, where women were less willing to be selfless and domestic. Scientific and professional expertise replaced moral authority in legitimizing women's entry into the public sphere, and liberal Christians engaged in ecumenical, unitarian/universalist, and pantheist movements. These changes undermined the separate spheres tradition in missionary and related cross-cultural work. The women's boards of American Protestant missionary enterprises, both for domestic and foreign fields, had once enjoyed a high degree of autonomy defined by grassroots donations and voluntarism, but their work and identity merged into the general boards.[9] Compounding the problem, American missionary, social gospel, women's education, and progressive humanitarian efforts were all increasingly dependent on funding from capitalist-philanthropists, and thus, they not only escaped from women's control but also met diversifying women's voices.[10]

Hawai'i's female internationalism was not exempt from such world trends. The male-led PPU and IPR conferences were open to women's participation and were attended by women leaders in the Pacific. In fact, IPR convened two conferences, in 1925 and 1927, and brought prominent women leaders to Honolulu prior to the first PPWC. In 1925, the PPWC Conference Committee invited the IPR's first conference participants to its meeting and sounded out the desirability of a women-only conference. There were opinions for and against gender specificity. For example, Mrs. Parker S. Maddux, former president of the San Francisco Central League of Women Voters (LWV), expressed "a fear that a separate women's conference would do more harm than good." Yau Tsit Law, general secretary of the Canton, China, YWCA,[11] also voiced her great interest in "equal opportunity for men and women." In contrast, Janet Mitchell, assistant secretary of the Council of the Victorian League of Nations Union and organizing secretary of the Melbourne YWCA Educational Department, emphasized "the importance of separate men's and women's conferences to train for leadership among the women." She also insisted that each country's delegation should include "at least one woman in close touch with industry, preferably one who worked her way up through the factory as a factory hand to a position in one of the trades councils."[12]

Further complicating the situation was intensifying rivalry and competition among American former suffragists who had split into two groups—younger generation "individual-right feminists" who led the National Woman's Party (NWP) and older generation "social feminists" who led the NLWV and the WJCC. The NWP leaders introduced the Equal Rights Amendment (ERA)—a U.S. constitutional amendment bill guaranteeing equal legal rights to all citizens regardless of sex—in 1923 but rejected motherhood-based rhetoric to promote the ERA nationally and later the Equal Rights Treaty (ERT) internationally.[13] The two groups competed for influence over Latin American women, resulting in personal and organizational contentions. Although the NLWV initiated pan-American women's networking and organized the Pan-American Association for the Advancement of Women in 1922, the NWP took over the effort and formed the Inter-American Commission of Women (Comisión Interamericana de Mujeres), which became an official agency of women delegates for the intergovernmental Pan-American Union (PAU, which later became the Organization of American States, OAS) at its sixth conference, held in Havana in 1928.[14]

Possibly, such developments inspired social feminists to turn their attention to the Pacific, where the PPU had aspired to be the Pacific version of the PAU and together become the "true League of Nations."[15] While women leaders were still divided over the gender specificity of the Honolulu-initiated pan-Pacific women's meeting, the World WCTU made its workers travel through the islands to revive the local WCTU movements. They formed the WCTU of the Territory of Hawai'i and affiliated it to the U.S. National WCTU in July 1926.[16] Around the same time, the U.S. branch of the WILPF successfully involved a missionary daughter, Caroline Dickinson Castle Westervelt (Mrs. W. D. Westervelt, 1859–1941), in sounding out the possibility of convening its meeting in Hawai'i.[17] In 1927, the male-led IPR's second conference, held again in Honolulu, brought additional prominent women to Honolulu to participate in it. Among them was Carrie Chapman Catt, the honorary president of the NLWV and the International Woman Suffrage Alliance (IWSA); Grace Abbott; NLWV president Belle Sherwin (1869–1955); NWP member Elizabeth Green (Elizabeth Green Kalb Hardy, 1896–1973); Mary Emma Woolley (1863–1947), former president of Mount Holyoke College and head of the American Association of University Women (AAUW); and World YWCA officers, including Mary Dingman; American Maud Russell (1893–1989), student secretary for China YWCA; and Korean Helen Kim (aka, Kim Hwal-lan, 1899–1970), a founder of the Korea YWCA and dean of the Methodist-affiliated Ewha College in Seoul.[18] Nonetheless, this did not mean that they all welcomed the thriving Hawai'i-centered pan-Pacific movement.

These women responded differently to the attempts of Honolulu leaders to create a women's autonomous sphere in the emerging pan-Pacific movement. Grace Abbott supported the upcoming women's conference and brought the U.S. Children's Bureau's special request to the PPWC Conference Committee to discuss "National Standards of Child Labor as an International Problem" at the upcoming conference.[19] Nonetheless, Carrie Chapman Catt was especially skeptical. She detected contradiction in the pan-Pacific movement, which was originally meant to facilitate transnational industrial ventures but now worked for world peace. She was also against adding yet another women's peace group. Catt, along with Jane Addams who would serve as the first PPWC's international chair, had founded the Woman's Peace Party in 1915. With U.S. participation in World War I, however, pragmatic and expedient Catt, unlike pacifist Addams, led women's nationwide war support efforts and pressed President Wilson to work for their suffrage cause in return. For Catt, the vote was essential but not "the sole aim of the movement." After winning hard-fought suffrage for U.S. women citizens, Catt anticipated that "peace" would unite fragmented women's groups to gain collective power. Reflecting on her personal experience that former suffragists and activists working for peace and protective legislations all fell victim to misogyny and red-baiting capitalists, Catt made special efforts to rally "respectable" women's organizations, including those from missionary groups, for this purpose. Resigning from the IWSA presidency in 1923, she held a meeting a year later of nine U.S. women's organizations to cooperate, reduce duplication of peace work, and convene the first Conference on the Cause and Cure of War. Held in Washington, DC, in 1925, this first conference resulted in the inception of the Catt-chaired National Committee on the Cause and Cure of War (NCCCW), which ultimately was composed of eleven women's organizations.[20] The NCCCW advocated for the U.S.-led Kellogg-Briand Peace Pact, which would outlaw war and be signed by sixty-two countries.[21]

Representing the NCCCW, Carrie Chapman Catt appeared at the 1927 IPR conference and expressed her apprehension about the pan-Pacific movement initiated by Hawai'i's "sugar barons" and funded by the generosity of lucrative trans-Pacific capitalist ventures. Catt saw that the elusive relationship between thriving international peace movements and growing imperialist aspirations could once again cause military conflict. In speaking at the second IPR conference, Catt fearlessly argued that "powerful groups in the United States [were] economic imperialist without apology" and questioned the ultimate goal of capitalist-philanthropists: "Were these men all dangerous foes of better things, they might be restrained in the interest of society; but very many are not only gentlemen of a high cultured order but they give freely of their surplus to Churches, missions, many good causes, and especially to political party funds. Doubtless, some of them have made this Institute of Pacific Relations possible. These are the reasons why ideals wax dim and foreign policies grow timid at times." Catt requested that the

IPR "face the really fundamental problem of the world." She argued that "unrest and innumerable problems" caused by intense international suspicion would only find relief in "changed standards and systems of international relations."[22]

Catt further emphasized voter education and public opinion as the true means of "defense" for enfranchised peoples to protect "weaker peoples" from the exploitation of powerful groups and the dangers of war caused by their economic imperialism. Catt argued:

> What defense [have] smaller or weaker peoples against exploitation by this power? . . . The chief defense . . . is public opinion in the United States. Monied interests do not own or control the United States. Ours is a self-governing country where men and women citizens vote. . . . Other nations, wishing to do business with the United States, must deal with Mr. Coolidge, the Congress, and the Republican Party now in power, . . . but Presidents and Parties come and go—the people alone keep on forever. . . . The people are often ignorant and are usually indifferent, but they are capable of understanding and they can be aroused. The people, in endless procession, marching generation after generation through school houses to their places in the world, . . . the people are the United States. A general said, "The people are not always right, but give them time and they will wobble right." Governments must not be permitted to wobble, but because the people may, there always lies among them new hope.[23]

Presumably, this message delivered by Catt should have encouraged many of Hawai'i's women leaders in forming a permanent organization out of the first PPWC, but they soon faced Catt's opposition.

In finalizing the first PPWC conference agenda, the PPWC's Conference Committee, outside the purview of the IPR conference site, sought opinions and support from American women leaders. The League of Women Voters of the Territory of Hawai'i (HLWV), under the presidency of Julie Judd Swanzy's daughter, Rosamond Swanzy Morgan, invited Catt and Mary Emma Woolley to give talks to its members.[24] While HLWV leaders and Catt agreed on the importance of education, Catt, as a seasoned organizer, expressed her candid opinion that cooperation with an already existing society would be a better solution than forming a new organization.[25] Possibly Catt's strong objection affected NLWV members who were reluctant to participate in the first PPWC scheduled for 1928. Their concern for Latin America and domestic voter education for the 1928 U.S. presidential election may also have been factors.

Furthermore, another 1927 IPR conference participant, NWP member Elizabeth Green, expressed her low opinion on the women's conference, which a "women's auxiliary or separate groups" convened. She felt that "participation in general [IPR] organization was of far greater moment."[26] After the second IPR conference, Green remained in Honolulu to join the IPR staff to take charge of the IPR's house journal and develop it into the renowned international journal, *Pacific Affairs*.[27] Green, however, would ultimately recognize the value of holding the gender-specific PPWCs and forming its permanent organization, as discussed in the next chapter.

In the face of the mainland suffragists' reluctance, PPU's secretary Ann Yardley Satterthwaite traveled to the U.S. mainland and held a meeting in New York, which was attended by Jane Addams and Hull House graduate labor reformers.[28] By then, U.S. mainland labor reformers had been exposed to the different milieu for wage-earning women in various parts of the world and renewed their recognition of the need for the separate sphere strategy. On October 28, 1919, the NWTUL sponsored the International Congress of Working Women (ICWW) in Washington, DC, with funds from its wealthy president Margaret Dreier Robins (1868–1945). The conference took place because the Commission on International Labor Legislation, over which Samuel Gompers presided, marginalized women in drafting the ILO constitution. The ICWW had convened just a day before the opening of the ILO's first international conference—the International Labour Conference (ILC)—which gathered women representatives from the United States and European nations as well as from Canada, India, and Japan in Washington, DC. Although the ICWW resulted in a permanent organization that was independent of men's organizations, the U.S. failure to join the League of Nations forced the ICWW to relocate its headquarters to London.[29] It assumed a new name, the International Federation of Working Women (IFWW), and was absorbed by the European-based, male-led labor organization, the International Federation of Trade Unions (IFTU), in 1924.[30] U.S. Women's Bureau director Mary Anderson (1872–1964; in office, 1920–1944), who was present at both the ICWW and the ILC in Washington, DC, in 1919, recorded that she felt that women of some European countries, particularly Great Britain, were "much more integrated in the labor movement than American women were" and, thus, they "did not realize how much on the fringe [women unionists] in America still were."[31]

At the same time, Anderson became cognizant of the horrendous situation in Japan, where women's voices were suppressed and male bureaucrats and experts were afraid to address the conditions of Japan's wage-earning women and children. At the ILC, she witnessed the Japanese delegation's attempt to stop Takako (Takanashi) Tanaka (1888–1966) from revealing the harsh reality of Japanese women textile workers. Tanaka was born to a grandniece of capitalist-philanthropist Eiichi Shibusawa and one of his wives and had studied English at Stanford University and received a master's degree in sociology from the University of Chicago.[32] Before attending the ILC, Tanaka participated at the ICWW, accompanying Setsu Ogata, a young woman with experience as a textile factory worker. Tanaka was a nonvoting "advisor" at the ILC who served solely as a translator for the Japanese delegation. The delegation members were appointed by the Japanese government and included no representatives elected by workers, despite the ILO's "tri-patriotism" requirement that each national delegation to the ILC be composed of representatives of the government, employers, and workers. Fluent in English, Tanaka was the only female member of the government-appointed sixty-member Japanese delegation. She was expected to read an English translation of the prepared statement for Japanese delegation head Eikichi Kamada. His statement was to justify Japan's unique condition regarding its delay in introducing night work laws.[33] Instead of reading the translation, Tanaka began delivering her own message in English, revealing the harsh conditions of female textile workers and the need for the immediate abolition of night work in Japan. The Japanese delegation became aware of Tanaka's conduct and stopped her. They insisted that she was ignorant of the Japanese situation due to her long absence from the country and dismissed her from the delegation.[34] Margaret Dreier Robins and Mary Anderson, however, successfully intervened to reinstate Tanaka. In Anderson's observation, "the Japanese women were not free, they always had to be careful that they did not say anything that might be derogatory to the Japanese government."[35] Arguably, through such experiences, Anderson and her fellow women policymakers became convinced of the need to investigate labor conditions in Asia and the rest of the world and to set a universal standard and regulations. Accordingly, Mary Anderson was "quite taken" with the idea of a pan-Pacific women's conference when she received an invitation from the PPU's secretary Ann Yardley Satterthwaite.[36]

Not surprisingly, the U.S. mainland delegation to the conference was composed mostly of social feminist bureaucrats, professionals, and activists, who desired to make health and welfare of wage-earning women and children a well-recognized pan-Pacific issue. Despite Satterthwaite's repeated requests, the NLWV failed to send its own representative to the 1928 PPWC. It asked a U.S. delegation member, Katherine Philips Edson, who represented the California State Division of Industrial Welfare, also to represent the NLWV. The U.S. delegation was headed by Dr. Valeria H. Parker, chair of the National Council of Women. Other delegation members included Mary Anderson; Caroline Manning, industrial supervisor of the U.S. Department of Labor Women's Bureau; Dr. Louise Stanley, U.S. Department of Agriculture Home Economics Division chief; and Dr. Ellen Smith Stadtmuller, California State Board of Health, Child Hygiene Bureau pediatrician.[37] They were joined by representatives of allied women's organizations in the United States such as Grace Coyle, Education and Research Division of the National YWCA; Elizabeth Christman, secretary-treasurer of the NWTUL; and labor activists under their patronage such as Jo Coffin, printer and member of the International Typographical Union in New York.[38]

While securing a niche in American women's international efforts, Honolulu women leaders applied a new scheme, adopted by trans-Atlantic women's organizations at the end of World War I, to recruit delegates representing "countries" that did not conform to the conventional notion of an independent sovereign state.[39] Hawai'i obtained the "country" status to form its delegation to the PPWC.[40] They decided that Hawai'i's delegation would be composed of women, half of whom had European or American origins and half of whom were from other races on the islands.[41] The arrangement reflected the disproportionate presence of minority Euro-American–origin women in local leadership and in the rising tide of women's internationalism. At the same time, placing Native Hawaiian women in the category of "other races" on the islands assured transnational settler colonialism over the land of Native Hawaiians.

Nonetheless, the Hawaiian delegation revealed the culturally hybridized women leaders who shared the authority and burden of territorial motherhood so that they could tackle the pressing problems of the islands' population. As mentioned at the beginning of this book, the dedication ceremony to the restoration-in-progress Hulihe'e Palace, a former residence of the highest-rank Native Hawaiian rulers, showcased the importance of Native Hawaiian's support to realize the first PPWC. The ceremony was held by the Daughters of Hawai'i (DOH), the chief contributor to the restoration, in collaboration with the Daughters and Sons of Hawaiian Warriors (DSHW), about two month before the opening of the first PPWC. Julie Judd Swanzy, DOH regent and honorary chair of the upcoming PPWC, stood next to a *kāhili*, a Hawaiian signifier of *ali'i* chiefs.[42]

The Hawaiian delegation was headed by Harriet Cousens Andrews, president of the Honolulu YWCA. Among the white settler members were missionary descendants Rosamond Swanzy Morgan, the HLWV president at the time, and Beatrice Castle. Also on the delegates list were local progressives who had migrated from the mainland: Frances Lawrence of the Free Kindergarten and Children's Aid Association of the Hawaiian Islands (FKCAAHI); Catherine McAlpine Crane Farrington, the wife of former territorial governor Wallace R. Farrington; Dr. Vivia Belle Appleton, who, after a four-year stint in China for the New York–based Council on Health Education and the U.S. National YWCA, directed the Hawai'i Board of Health's Maternal and Infant Hygiene Bureau; and Grace Channon, National YWCA secretary working at the Honolulu YWCA.[43]

The delegation held a place for hybrid Native Hawaiians, e.g., Elizabeth Lahilahi Rogers Webb, a former lady-in-waiting in Queen Lili'uokalani's court and a member of the DOH and the HLWV. Also among the delegates were bilingual women leaders representing Hawai'i's ethnic communities, e.g., Filipina Petra Ligot, wife of Cayetano Ligot who was the Filipino Resident Commissioner for Hawai'i; Tai Heong Kong Li, the first Chinese woman to practice Western medicine in Hawai'i;[44] Saki Harada, the wife of Rev./Dr. Tasuku Harada; and Japanese Tsuru Kishimoto and Korean Ha(i) Soo Whang, who were both YWCA nationality secretaries of the Honolulu YWCA's International Institute. There were also U.S. citizen Asian daughters, e.g., Dr. Ellen F. L. Leong, the first Hawai'i-born Chinese woman doctor trained on the mainland,[45] and Alice Sae Teshima Noda, a dental hygiene specialist and pioneering cosmetologist active in Hawai'i and Japan.[46]

For the Empire More Than the People: The 1928 Japanese Delegation

The PPU's secretary Ann Yardley Satterthwaite, assisted by mainland social feminists, reached out to women in the Pacific countries to send delegates to the first PPWC. Its director Alexander H. Ford also traveled to Asia to promote the PPWC along with other scheduled PPU conferences.[47] In Japan, by then, Western-educated internationalists, by adopting Western systems and expertise, contributed to establishing an oligarchy in the form of a constitutional monarchy. Modeled after the Prussian system, Japan promulgated the Imperial Constitution in 1890. Creating a modern myth of the nation around the emperor and the everlasting imperial reign instigated a nationalistic and imperialistic fervor to achieve rapid industrialization and militarization. By 1911, Japan nullified the unequal treaties, by which the foreign powers established extraterritoriality and deprived Japan's tariff autonomy, while imposing similar unequal treaties on its neighbors—Korea as early as 1876 and China in 1895. Through fighting two wars, the Sino-Japanese War (1894–1895) and the Russo-Japanese War (1904–1905), Japan colonized Taiwan in 1905 and Korea in 1910. The rise of imperial Japan, however, demanded a heavy sacrifice from its subjects and the colonized. The victory of the Allied nations in World War I and the emerging new world order under Anglo-American leadership pressed Japan to emulate Anglo-Saxon liberalism for its modern empire building. Universal manhood suffrage was established in 1925, quadrupling the voter population. At the same time, Japan's colonial governments transformed policies from "rule by force" to "rule by civilization" for assimilation of the colonized. Elite internationalist men sought to bring Japan in line with the world trend toward liberalism, international cooperation, and peace.[48]

Nonetheless, Japan's oligarchy never loosened its control over the subjects. Its so-called security laws—e.g., the Police Security Law (Chian Keisatsu Hō) of 1900 to control political and labor movements and the Peace Preservation Law (Chian Iji Hō) of 1925 to suppress socialist and communist movements—were in operation. Enforced by the *Tokkō* (the secret Special Higher Police), which was formed in 1911 after the disclosure of a "plot" to assassinate the emperor (the High Treason Incident of 1911), the laws made it difficult for grassroots social and labor reform activists to engage in movements suspected of any connection to communist, socialist, or truly egalitarian movements.[49] While Japan's Ministry of Education (JMoE) promoted the modern Japanese womanhood ideal of "good wife and wise mother" to replace the feudalistic women's role of bearing a male heir and serving the husband's household, it also revived the feudalistic human relationships requiring absolute loyalty of each household member to the patriarch and every subject to the national patriarch, the emperor. Female mission schools, which had thrived in the 1870s and 1880s by promoting women's education and social activism, now struggled from the backlash—the state-fostered patriarchal nationalism combined with escalating anti-Western/Christian nativism at the turn of the twentieth century.[50]

Female mission schools had once served as cradles for Japan's modern women's education and social reform activism. Now they became reluctant to perform that role, hoping to avoid public resentment and JMoE intervention. Instead, Japanese internationalist men recognized the need to produce Japanese "New Women" to showcase Japan's modern civilized status. They initiated efforts to build institutions that could provide college-level female education. One of the most conspicuous internationalist men in these efforts was Inazō Nitobe (1862–1933), agriculturalist, educator, bureaucrat, and diplomat. Baptized in Japan, he received his education in the United States and Germany. Nitobe had once worked for Japan's colonial government in Taiwan to promote sugar production and would later serve as the League of Nations undersecretary (1920–1926).[51] He owed much of his international presence to his wife Mary Patterson Elkinton Nitobe (1857–1938), who hailed from an orthodox Quaker family.[52] Mary came from Philadelphia's Quaker community, where philanthropist Mary H. Morris, a founder of the Foreign Missionary Association of Friends of Philadelphia, generously supported Japanese students studying in the area. Inazō Nitobe was one of its beneficiaries, along with Umeko Tsuda (1864–1929), one of the first five Japanese girls sent to the United States for a ten-year stint of female education and an additional three-year graduate education at Bryn Mawr. Returning to Japan, Tsuda received funding and support from the Philadelphia Quaker community and its international network to open a school for English learning in Tokyo, which later became Tsuda College in 1900. Mary H. Morris tightened the Tokyo-Philadelphia relationship by establishing the "Japanese Scholarship" so that one Japanese student at a time could come to the Philadelphia area for American education. The Nitobes remained Tsuda College's crucial supporters and influencers.[53] Furthermore, when the Tokyo Woman's Christian College (TWCC) was established in 1918 through the interdenominational efforts of the women's missionary boards of six American Protestant churches, Inazō Nitobe served as its first president.[54]

The Nitobes also helped in the inception of other women's colleges in Tokyo. They helped Jinzo Naruse (1858–1919) establish the Japan Women's University (JWU) in 1901. Naruse was an educator ordained in the Congregationalist tradition. He founded Kiitsu Kyōkai (Association Concordia), a short-lived syncretist or pantheist organization.[55] Japanese capitalist-philanthropists, such as Viscount Eiichi Shibusawa and businesswoman Asako Hirooka, contributed to sending Japanese women for Western education and hiring those Western-trained Japanese women for the JWU faculty. Among them were Hideko Inoue (1875–1963), a JWU alumna and home economics professor who had studied at Columbia Teachers College and the Chicago Normal School on funds secured by JWU Japanese supporters,[56] and Fuji Koga, who had once served on the faculty of the FKCAAHI Japanese kindergarten in Honolulu and was hired by the JWU to manage the JWU-attached kindergarten.[57]

This small group of Japanese New Women, along with older generations of female mission school alumna whose social activism had already established their public personas, took crucial roles in generating voluntary women's Christian and secular organizations and movements. For example, when Canadian YWCA worker Caroline Macdonald (1874–1931) arrived in Japan to organize the Japan YWCA movement, Mary P. E. Nitobe and Umeko Tsuda joined founding members of the Tokyo YWCA and the Japan YWCA at Macdonald's residence in 1905.[58] In 1912, Tsuda College faculty member Michi(ko) Kawai (1877–1953), who had studied at Bryn Mawr on the "Japanese Scholarship," became the first Japanese to assume the World YWCA position of general secretary in Japan's YWCA movement.[59]

When elite Japanese women failed to accept an invitation from Aletta Jacobs to attend the 1915 Women's Congress at The Hague, where WILPF was incorporated, the Nitobes mediated the WILPF's attempt. They gathered elite Japanese women at their residence to study international affairs. After the Nitobes moved to Geneva, Itsuko Mekata, whose husband Tanetaro Mekata had represented Japan at the League of Nations, hosted a study meeting at her residence. The Nitobes' efforts led to the inception of the Women's Peace Association in Japan (JWPA, Japan's WILPF, Nihon Fujin Heiwa Kyōkai) in 1921.[60] The JWPA's first presidency was assumed by Hideko Inoue. After Jane Addams's landmark visit to Japan, the JWPA became the Japanese affiliate of the WILPF in 1924. The JWPA presidency was succeeded by Japan YWCA's Michi Kawai in 1930 and Japan WCTU's Tsune(ko) Gauntlett in 1933.[61]

These women internationalists in Tokyo supported Inazō Nitobe when he served as the League of Nations undersecretary (in office, 1920–1926) in charge of the International Committee on Intellectual Cooperation, which later became UNESCO under the United Nations' mandate. They joined male internationalists in assisting Nitobe in representing Japan. They became active in Japan's semi-governmental League of Nations Association (Kokusai Renmei Kyōkai), which formed student associations and held lecture meetings to promote the spirit of the league and the study of international affairs in Japan.[62] Furthermore, to generate an international education movement, Japan's affiliates of the World WCTU, YWCA, and WILPF, along with male-led internationally minded groups, organized the Japan International Education Association (Nihon Kokusai Kyōiku Kyōkai) in 1922.[63]

Nonetheless, working closely with internationalist men who prioritized advancing Japan's status in the international arena, these elite women internationalists, many of whom were faculty members of prestigious women's schools and colleges, subordinated young women's yearnings to social norms and national needs. When JWU graduate Raicho Hiratsuka (1886–1971) published the magazine *Seito* (*Bluestockings*) to liberate women's literary talents in 1911, they were harshly critical of her, especially of her flamboyant behavior challenging Japan's traditional household system and the JMoE promotion of the womanhood ideal, "good wife and wise mother." The JWU alumnae association expelled her from membership. Japan YWCA secretary Michi Kawai, and even Umeko Tsuda, an advocate of women's independence, condemned Hiratsuka and her cohort's "false" view of women's self-realization and liberation and lamented their disreputable influence on young women.[64]

In early twentieth-century Japan, a growing nationalistic fever whipped up by the government, along with Japan's patriarchal and feudalistic human relations, made addressing human rights or the lamentable conditions of wage-earning women almost a taboo. Japan's modern nation-state builders were mostly from the ruling samurai class and now advancing themselves to be the ruling elites. They enthusiastically promoted Japan's rapid modernization, industrialization, and militarization, which depended heavily on the blood and sweat of rural, tenant farmer families, especially their daughters, who were often indentured to work as prostitutes or mill hands in emerging globalization hubs in Japan and abroad. Although these indentured girls were locked up in brothels or prison-like dormitories at the risk of physical or sexual abuse, the men of the ruling elites, who grew up in the premodern patriarchal caste system, were oblivious about human rights. Instead, they encouraged the public to treat those girls as commendable filial daughters and patriotic subjects.[65]

Japan's misogynistic and antiunionist attitudes slowly changed only with influential male internationalists recognizing the world's progressive trend for human rights and egalitarianism. To catch up with the trend, Japanese Ministry of Agriculture and Commerce (JMoAC) bureaucrats drafted a factory law, which passed the Japanese Diet in 1911. Although the law gave factories a forbearance period of fifteen years, it faced strong opposition from business leaders, including internationalist-capitalist-philanthropist Eiichi Shibusawa.[66] Making any improvement in labor conditions or women's status required endorsement by these influential internationalist men. Although they desired to keep the state-centered probusiness economic milieu for Japan's rapid industrialization and militarization, the thriving international efforts for industrial democracy pressed them to support something of a labor movement in Japan.

The Yūaikai (Friendly Society), a workers' mutual aid and self-help society, assumed the role as Japan's labor organization. The Yūaikai was founded by Bunji Suzuki (1885–1946) at the Tokyo Unitarian Church in 1912, during the labor movement's bleakest era triggered by the 1911 High Treason Incident. It engaged in modest labor reform and unionism under the purview of Japanese and American internationalists who embraced the ideas of the social gospel and labor liberalism through missionary-pioneered networks.[67] According to historian Yuji Ichioka, Bunji Suzuki was an "intellectual social reformer rather than a worker" or labor leader. Suzuki was a Tokyo Imperial University graduate and worked as a personal secretary to Pennsylvania-born Clay MacCauley (1843–1925), the Tokyo Unitarian Church minister and the president of the American Peace Society of Japan. As a part of trans-Pacific internationalists' fight against anti-Asian exclusionist forces, Suzuki, funded by Eiichi Shibusawa and aided by Sidney L. Gulick, attended the California State Federation of Labor and the American Federation of Labor (AFL) conventions in 1915 and 1916. Although his presence did not affect the AFL's Asian-exclusionist stance,[68] his exposure to the American labor movement inspired him to allow women to participate in Yūaikai activities. The Yūaikai formed a women's department in 1916. Suzuki, however, still regarded women's factory work as transient and promoted "self-cultivation" to be a future "good wife and wise mother" among women workers.[69]

In 1916, the factory law that had passed the Japanese Diet in 1911 finally went into effect after numerous concessions to businesses. The 1916 Factory Law did little to help working women and children because of many exceptions, especially in industries, such as textiles, where the labor force was predominantly women. For example, the 1916 law set the maximum working hours at twelve per day, but the silk industry was exempted from the rule and operated on a system that kept workers on fourteen-hour shifts. Furthermore, the minimum age for workers was twelve, except for the light industry, where the minimum age was ten years. As for night work, the law prohibited women under the age of sixteen from working between 10 P.M. and 4 A.M. but exempted factories operating on a shift system.[70]

In 1919, as Japan became an ILO founding member, Japanese labor and women revived their movements under international pressure. Yūaikai changed its name to Dai-Nihon Rōdō Sōdōmei-Yūaikai (Greater Japan Federation of Labor Friendly Society, or Sōdōmei-Yūaikai for short). Sōdōmei-Yūaikai claimed to be a full-fledged labor organization and rejected socialism, anarchism, and communism.[71] It adopted a platform that included the principles in the ILO constitution's preamble, and its women's division hired Fusae Ichikawa (1893–1981) as its secretary. Fusae Ichikawa—a female mission school dropout and a primary school teacher who would become a well-noted Japanese suffragist—yearned for modern Western knowledge, which led her to the Tokyo Unitarian Church, the birthplace of the Yūaikai, and thus to its networks of internationalist men and women. Although the Sōdōmei-Yūaikai took time to correct Japan's violation of ILO's "tripartite" rule (i.e., national delegations of government, employer, and workers representatives), the internationally concerted efforts of women labor reformers fast revealed the two-faced attitude of the Japanese government.[72] By then, the Geneva-based Joint Standing Committee (JSCWIO) had successfully made the ILO constitution require its advisors, who accompanied national delegation to the ILC, to include at least one woman. When Takako (Takanashi) Tanaka, Eiichi Shibusawa's grandniece, was appointed as an advisor to the all-male Japanese delegation to the first ILC, Ichikawa convened a women's labor meeting in her home prefecture to invite Tanaka and encouraged her to accompany a woman worker to the ILC. The direct interactions with women laborers at the meeting must have inspired Tanaka, as noted earlier, to expose the harsh reality of Japanese mill operatives at the ILC.[73]

Charlotte H. Adams, a U.S. National YWCA religious education worker who toured Japan and China, confirmed the horrific conditions in Japan's textile mills in 1919. She reported that Japan was "rising with great rapidity into an industrial nation on 'the backs of its toiling women and children'" and that their conditions were "not paralleled in the world" without any "legislative safe-guards" for their help or protection.[74] These exposés led Ernestine L. Friedmann to visit Japan and China in early 1920 to investigate the situation further. Her report for the Federation of Women's Boards of Foreign Missions disclosed the grim facts that Japanese village girls worked on contracts signed by their patriarchs but not themselves, that government regulations did not prohibit women from working fourteen hours a day or at night, and that many children ten years old or younger regularly worked in silk filatures.[75]

Nonetheless, the unsuccessful large-scale strike by two thousand workers (four hundred men and sixteen hundred women) to unionize at a cotton-spinning factory in 1920 invited harsh criticism against women's unionism as unwomanly conduct, and it devastated the Sōdōmei-Yūaikai women's division. Consequently, some unionists joined the women's sections of socialist, anarchist, and/or communist groups, but they experienced dissolution and reorganization under increasing government suppression. Some went underground.[76] In the persistently patriarchal, nativist, and antiunion social milieu of early twentieth-century Japan, even the Japanese YWCA movement, with its extensive international connections, was reluctant to shift its middle-class student focus to take up labor reform. Convinced of the need to investigate labor conditions, internationally active social feminists visited Japan, China, and the rest of Asia and the Pacific. U.S. YWCA workers, who visited Japan in the late 1910s and 1920s, reported their astonishment at seeing that both Anglo-Saxon missionaries and their protégé Japanese YWCA members were clueless about the laboring women's devastation. Neither national nor city associations in Japan had even investigated the harsh working conditions of wage-earning women and children. In fact, because of "the absolute lack of any standards for social and business relationships between men and women," middle-class, student-focused Japanese YWCA leaders busily drafted a behavioral guide for white-collar "business girls" to protect themselves from sexual harassment in their workplaces. They also became concerned about the well-being of members who visited textile mills to conduct prayer meetings and self-cultivation classes for "factory girls."[77]

The exposé at the ILC ruined Tanaka's respectability and Ichikawa's position at the Sōdōmei-Yūaikai. Undaunted, the two joined Raicho Hiratsuka in founding the New Women's Society (NWS, Shin Fujin Kyōkai) in 1920 to revive the socialist-origin campaign to amend Article Five of the 1900 Police Security Law, which prohibited women from participating in and holding political gatherings.[78] Fusae Ichikawa, however, also became critical of Hiratsuka's bourgeois flamboyant lifestyle and left the NWS to cross the Pacific for the firsthand experience of American society.[79] While women educators and YWCA officers were critical of Hiratsuka and unwilling to support the NWS, Japan WCTU officers revived their past fruitless efforts to amend Article Five.[80] Introduced by Mary C. Leavitt in 1886, the Japanese WCTU movement pioneered volunteer Japanese women's social activism and established its national organization, Japan WCTU, in 1894. During the Russo-Japanese War, it established a reputation as a respectable women's organization through its support of Japan's colonialist/imperialist aspirations.[81] In the face of the post–World War I rise of women's internationalism for world peace, however, its officers made efforts to have a Japanese women's presence. Japan WCTU's long-time president, eighty-seven-year-old Kajiko Yajima (1833–1925), accompanied by its officer Tsune(ko) Yamada Gauntlett (1873–1953), a Japanese woman married to a Briton, attended the 1920 World WCTU Conference in London. Gauntlett extended her trip to Geneva for the IWSA conference. There, she met IWSA president Carrie Chapman Catt, who advised her that woman suffrage was the means to attain world peace. The following year, the Japan WCTU established its peace department, and Yajima crossed the Pacific to attend the Washington Naval Conference to deliver a petition for world peace signed by over ten thousand Japanese women to U.S. President Warren G. Harding.[82] Concurrently in Japan, Gauntlett persuaded fellow Japan WCTU officer Ochimi Kubushiro (1882–1972) to support woman suffrage. They formed a Japan WCTU subgroup for woman suffrage.[83] These Japanese WCTU suffragists supported the NWS, which successfully amended Article Five of the 1900 Police Security Law, securing women's rights to hold and participate in political gatherings, in April 1922.[84]

Instead of these Japanese activists, Canadian Caroline Macdonald, who had withdrawn from the Japan YWCA in 1915, began work committed to factory workers and prisoners in Tokyo. She held Wednesday meetings at her residence, which gathered diverse groups of men and women. By mid-1919, Macdonald established collaborative relationships with influential internationalist men in Tokyo and Sōdōmei-Yūaikai leaders. She launched settlement work at the Shinrinkan (Friendly Neighborhood Hall) to provide a wide range of services, including "labor classes." In the antilabor milieu of the time, Macdonald's work at Shinrinkan was not to raise class consciousness or solidarity for labor unionism but to reform workers' ways and to protect strikers and unionists from police abuse.[85] Concurrently, the

Japan WCTU's foreign auxiliary, which was composed of Western missionary women and church members, embarked on urban settlement work in Tokyo, providing dispensary, day nursery, and kindergarten services.[86] While socialists, anarchists, communists, and tenant farmers engaged in more radical labor movements in the early 1920s, the ILO Conventions adopted at the first ILC in 1919 rattled the Japanese government, pushing it to narrow the disparity between Japan's reality and the world standard. In addition, the visit by World YWCA's industrial secretary Mary Dingman, on her Pacific tour in 1922, awakened Japanese YWCA staff to the importance of industrial work among women factory workers.[87]

Joining these Western women seeking influence over Japanese internationalist men and women was Mary Ritter Beard (1876–1958), a historian, suffragist, progressive social and labor reformer, and the wife of the historian Charles Beard (1874–1948).[88] The Beards visited Japan in 1922 and 1923, at the request of Shimpei Goto (1857–1929), an influential and multifaceted member of the internationalists' circle.[89] Their first visit (September 1922 to March 1923) took place when Goto was Tokyo mayor and willing to emulate American progressive urban planning methods. Their second visit (October to December 1923) was to assist Goto, the Home Affairs minister in charge of metropolitan reconstruction, after the Great Kanto Earthquake of September 1, 1923. The earthquake caused massive devastation in Tokyo and its vicinity, especially among the poor. Rampant nativism, racialism, and antilabor prejudice spread false rumors, causing the massacre of Korean workers and the murder of labor activists, Chinese students, and socialists, including anarchist-feminist Noe Ito.[90]

Through their visits, the Beards encouraged the internationalists to step up their engagement in labor reform and social gospel endeavors. Immediately after the earthquake, Christian and non-Christian religious associations as well as voluntary, semi-governmental, alumnae, professional, and worker women's groups in Tokyo came together in relief work. They coordinated with government efforts and led the inception of the Tokyo Federation of Women's Organizations (TFWO, Tokyo Rengō Fujinkai) in October 1923. In November 1922, Japan's Ministry of Home Affairs (JMoHA) won jurisdiction over the Social Bureau that took charge of public hygiene, child protection, social welfare, and labor issues, including labor investigations and inspections, labor laws, and international labor relations.[91] After Goto assumed the post of Home Affairs Minister, Caroline Macdonald's Shinrinkan settlement work received generous subsidies to obtain a new building and was integrated into the public welfare system in 1924.[92] Nonetheless, although the 1916 Factory Labor Law was revised to narrow the gap with the international standard, it was not until 1929 that the ban on engaging women and minors under the age of sixteen in night work between the hours of 10 P.M. to 5 A.M. was put into effect, again with an exception for the cotton industry, which was allowed to keep them working one hour later until 11 P.M.[93]

Mary Beard approached a broad spectrum of women activists, including Baroness Shizue Kato (1897–2001), a birth control advocate; Kikue Yamakawa (1890–1980), a Tsuda College alumna who became a noted socialist theorist; Yayoi Yoshioka (1871–1959), an indigenously trained medical doctor who founded the Tokyo Women's Medical College in 1900; and Utako Shimoda (1854–1936), the president of the semi-governmental Patriotic Women's Association (Aikoku Fujinkai). While promoting American progressive maternalist methods, Mary Beard inspired Japanese women to pay more attention to hygiene, health, education, comfort, and welfare, especially among wage-earning mothers and children. The first official meeting of the TFWO (Tokyo Rengō Fujinkai), held in January 1924, elected Japan YWCA's Michi Kawai president and created four departments: employment and labor, social work, education, and political affairs.[94]

While aiding and praising Japanese women's collaboration, Mary Beard also insisted that suffrage was overdue. Facilitated by women's networking through the TFWO's post-earthquake relief efforts, the Japan WCTU suffrage subgroup merged Christian and non-Christian suffragists to organize the League for the Realization of Women's Suffrage (the Woman Suffrage League or the WSL; originally Fujin Sanseiken Kakutoku Kisei Dōmeikai and later renamed Fusen Kakutoku Dōmei) in December 1924. Japan WCTU's Ochimi Kubushiro became WSL's first president.[95] Concurrently, the first general election after the establishment of the 1925 universal manhood suffrage law gave a few seats in the diet to members of "proletarian"—socialist, labor, and tenant farmer, but not communist—parties that had publicly endorsed woman suffrage. Accordingly, woman suffrage became a national issue.[96]

International pressure on labor reform in Japan also led to the opening of the ILO Tokyo Office in 1924. It recruited Fusae Ichikawa from the United States as its only female staff member. After crossing the Pacific in 1921, Ichikawa worked as a "school girl," part-time housemaid, for families in Seattle, Chicago, and New York, using her free time to attend civic activities, meet American women leaders, visit the headquarters of various organizations—e.g., Hull House, the Industrial Workers of the World (IWW), the NWP, the LWV, the PTA, the YWCA, and the WCTU—and contribute articles to newspapers and journals in Japan.[97] In one article, she pointed out the gap between Japanese "slave-like" housemaids and American housemaids, whom she felt were well-paid with ample time for themselves.[98]

Returning to Japan in 1924, Ichikawa worked for the ILO Tokyo Office for three years, pressing the Japanese government and business to improve women's labor conditions. She also reconnected with women's groups and leaders in Tokyo to form a Women's Labor Commission in March 1927. Taka Kato (1887–1979), a Tsuda College alumna who was trained at the U.S. National YWCA's Training School and then served as the general secretary of the Tokyo YWCA, assumed the chairpersonship of the committee, with Ichikawa serving as its secretary.[99] Working alongside Ichikawa were Japan WCTU's Ochimi Kubushiro; Canadian Caroline Macdonald; Yoshiko Shoda (1877–1942), a Cornell University graduate and JWU faculty who was well-versed in American labor issues and fluent in English; and labor reformer Tsuneko Akamatsu (1897–1965), a Buddhist women's school dropout who worked with Toyohiko Kagawa, Christian labor reformer and pacifist, in his settlement work in Kobe and with Macdonald in Tokyo, before serving as the secretary of the revived women's department of the Sōdōmei (the successor of the Sōdōmei-Yūaikai, which was reorganized and renamed after purging its left- and right-wing members in 1921).[100] Members of the Women's Labor Commission visited coal mines and textile factories for firsthand observations of labor conditions. As a result, the committee adopted resolutions that included not only a ban on women's labor in coal mines, prohibition of night work, and limiting work hours to eleven hours, but also the improvement or prohibition of the indentured labor system practiced in Japan at that time. Their efforts, however, did not immediately establish official regulations; nonetheless, they encouraged women's labor movements. In December 1927, Ichikawa resigned from her high-salary position at the ILO Tokyo Office to lead the woman suffrage movement and assumed the Woman Suffrage League's presidency in 1930.[101]

In 1927, the World YWCA urged the Japan YWCA to form a labor investigation commission. Headed by Yoshiko Shoda, it carried out surveys at the request of the World YWCA to produce reports for the ILO.[102] Concurrently, elite YMCA and YWCA college student members cultivated an interest in labor issues and engaged in settlement work. They also affiliated themselves with the globalizing gender-mixed Student Christian Movement, which had established the World Student Christian Federation (WSCF) in 1895.[103] Students reached out to wage-earning workers and formed groups to study labor issues, including Marxist theories. However, the JMoE prohibited such activism, as communism was banned, and a few members, including female college students, were arrested in 1928.[104] While a small group of "proletarian" women, who insisted that women were subjugated by capitalism, sustained their movement, they became the only force publicly committed to woman suffrage, labor reform, and unionism in the late 1920s. These proletarian women activists experienced not only government attacks but also sexist male labor leaders who treated them as "housekeepers" and sexual partners.[105] Arguably, Japan YWCA leaders and the faculty of women colleges became even more pressed to keep their students away from assisting women's labor reform efforts in Japan.

Against this backdrop, in June 1927, Prince Iyesato Tokugawa, president of the Japan Pan-Pacific Association (Japan PPA) and chair of the House of Peers, received the PPWC's official invitation, in the name of Hawai'i's territorial governor Wallace R. Farrington.[106] A small group of internationalist women leaders in Tokyo were then entrusted to invite civic, professional, and college alumnae groups to represent Japan at the PPWC. The original Japanese delegation formed in early 1928 was headed by Hideko Inoue, the incumbent president of the JWPA (Japan WILPF).[107] It was composed mainly of women leaders in the Tokyo metropolitan area who had joined the TFWO's post-earthquake rescue efforts, including Fusae Ichikawa; Taki Fujita, a Tsuda College alumna and English literature professor who had studied at Bryn Mawr and taken leadership positions in the Japanese YWCA movement; Tsune(ko) Yamada Gauntlett, then serving as an officer of the Japan WCTU and the JWPA; and Yayoi Yoshioka, medical doctor and founder of the Tokyo Women's Medical College.[108] Through the male network extending to the Pan-Pacific Club in Kobe, Kikue Ide—an alumna of a Canadian Methodist mission school in Tokyo who had studied at Wellesley and received a master's degree from Columbia and then taught at Mary Lambuth Girls' School in Kobe—joined the delegation.[109]

Presumably, the lack of a Japanese representative for wage-earning women fell short of satisfying the international women's community, which paid close attention to the convening of the first PPWC. But the most vocal opposition to the urban, elite, and bourgeois nature of the original list of delegates came from Kyo Kiuchi (1884–1964), a secretary of the National

Federation of Primary School Teachers' Association (NFPSTA; Zenkoku shōgakkō rengō jokyōinkai). Kiuchi protested that their organization had not received an invitation even though NFPSTA had actively participated in the TFWO's earthquake relief work. Founded in 1924, NFPSTA had quite possibly the largest working women's membership in Japan at the time. Nonetheless, it was not a teachers' union but rather subordinate to the Imperial Education Society (IES; Teikoku kyōiku kai). NFPSTA's primary school teachers played a crucial role in promoting public education, public health, and social hygiene nationwide. Furthermore, its members also filled the ranks of Shojokai (Maiden Association), a semi-governmental young women's organization that engaged in promoting modern womanhood and motherhood under the supervision of the JMoE and the JMoHA.[110]

This development suggests the attempt by Japanese internationalist men, who participated in the pan-Pacific movement and became active in the PPU and the IPR, to obtain influence over the PPWCs. The NFPSTA's father organization, the IES, was headed by Masataro Sawayanagi, a former JMoE bureaucrat responsible for Japan's forceful colonialist education policy in Korea and creating the Japanese womanhood of "good wife and wise mother." Nonetheless, accommodating the emerging new world order and the Japanese colonial government's new policy for assimilation, Sawayanagi became an advocate of liberal education and promoter of the Japan-led international education movement. Rather than challenging Anglophones' cultural dominance in the globalizing Pacific, they found common interests with white settler colonialists in seeking nonviolent means to integrate the multiethnicizing population of their empire. Sawayanagi took a leading role in the IPR's Japanese Council.[111] Eiichi Shibusawa and his internationalist cohort procured funding to send six Primary School Teacher Federation (NFPSTA) members to the first PPWC. Possibly, internationalist men and women in Hawai'i and Japan desired to have transnational exchanges among school teachers to facilitate the Americanization of *Nisei* children. The NFPSTA continued to send its member school teachers to all PPWCs held before World War II.[112]

The process of forming the Japanese delegation drew wide publicity in Japan, and the lack of a Japanese representative for wage-earning women became an issue. In an attempt to rectify Japan's original bourgeois-oriented list of delegates, a Japanese newspaper company conducted a popular vote to elect a woman who would be suitable for the industrial section of the first PPWC. The woman who was elected was not a unionist but a bilingual

JWU faculty member, Yoshiko Shoda, who headed the Japan YWCA's labor investigation commission and was willing to speak for women laborers. Shoda thus joined the delegation and traveled to Honolulu to be present at the first PPWC. There were also Japanese participants without delegate status. Among them were a freewheeling journalist Kaneko Kitamura (1903–1931) and Chiyoko Yada, the wife of the former Japanese consul general to Hawai'i who had assisted the PPU and Hawai'i's Department of Public Instruction (DPI) in their territorial educational reform effort.[113]

Sending the Japanese delegation to the 1928 PPWC prompted varied reactions from Japanese women activists. Among the supporters were Akiko Yosano (1878–1942), a well-known feminist writer who assisted Ichikawa in raising funds; and Waka Yamada (1879–1957), a former resident of the Presbyterian rescue home in San Francisco and an advocate of protective laws for women and children in Japan, who advised delegates to seek mutual understanding. The objectors included Kikue Yamakawa, the socialist theorist for the National Women's Federation (NWF, Zenkoku Fujin Dōmei), a "proletarian" women's group, who disparaged the PPWC as a "bourgeois" women's gathering.[114] The loudest opposition came from the NWF, which struggled with government suppression and sexism from the male-led labor movement. It declared "absolute opposition to the convening of the PPWC" under the high-sounding phrase "for mutual understanding and friendship." The NWF argued that those who remained firm in opposing the 1927 expedition of Japan's troops to China's Shangdong Peninsula were proletarian women, not bourgeois women who had enthusiastically supported the so-called Peace Conferences. The NWF insisted that "friendship and peace," the words that "spokespersons for the imperialist bourgeoisie consistently used," were "deceptive."[115] Japan sent the third largest foreign delegation, after Australia and New Zealand, to the first PPWC.[116]

National Versus Transnational Identities: The 1928 "Chinese" Delegation

Unlike the emerging Japanese empire, the Chinese empire, embracing five major ethnic groups in its vast continental landmass, was slow to recognize the need to adopt Western systems and expertise. Forming a Chinese delegation to the first PPWC rested on the transnational women's community forged under foreign settler colonialism. In early 1927, Alexander

Ford continued his Pacific tour to Shanghai, one of China's semi-colonial treaty port cities, where PPU's Chinese branch, the Pan-Pacific Association of China (China PPA), had already been in existence. Ford was welcomed at a lunch hosted by the Joint Committee of the Shanghai Women's Organizations (JCSWO, Shanghai Joint Committee), under the courtesy of the American Women's Club.[117] The JCSWO was an umbrella organization of twelve women's groups of various nationalities, with a total membership of thirty-one hundred.[118]

Prosperous women's international communities owed their existence to the foreign exploitation of Chinese land and resources. After two Opium Wars (1839–1842 and 1856–1860), Qing China was forced to conclude unequal treaties with the British government and other imperialist nations. Foreign traders, diplomats, missionaries, capitalist-industrialists, and laborers began to pour in. The imperialist powers established extraterritoriality in the foreign settlements, i.e., lands carved out for private lease to qualified settlers. Although the settlements initially excluded local Chinese, Qing China's unstable political situation caused the entry of Chinese refugees and migrants in and around the settlements.[119] In 1854, the consuls of British, U.S., and French settlements agreed to write a land regulation and elect a municipal council to protect their interests from the Chinese populace. While the French dropped out of the agreement, the British and U.S. settlements, along with other imperialist powers, merged into the Shanghai International Settlement, where privileged foreign rate (tax) payers could elect councilors to the international colonial body, the Shanghai Municipal Council (SMC). The International Mixed Court, an international court presided over by Western judges involving Chinese administrators deciding on Chinese laws, was also established to handle legal cases involving Chinese residents. The SMC took charge of providing basic public works and infrastructure to foreign businessmen and supervising the quasi-military police force to protect their interests. The SMC's administrative responsibility expanded with the growth of the settlement over time but also accommodated itself to changing local, national, and international situations.[120]

Shanghai, like other treaty port cities in the Pacific, served as a steppingstone for ongoing "woman's work for woman and children" that was undertaken by Anglo-Saxon Protestant missionary women. These cities also served as a window on foreign-origin religious, political, and economic ideologies—and to modern consumer lifestyles and comforts. Without centralized government control, Shanghai became a "hotbed" for Christian, feminist, revolutionary, nationalist, labor, and communist movements. While the Qing Court did not start educating girls until 1907, female mission schools sprouted in these port cities, promoting women's Christian education starting in the mid-nineteenth century. Mission school teachers, graduates, and students joined expanding transnational women's organizations—e.g., the World WCTU, the World YWCA—and promoted anti-opium, anti–foot-binding, and anti-concubinage women's causes.[121] After its defeat in the Sino-Japanese War (1894–1895), Qing reformists encouraged upper-class women to go to nearby Japan. There, they were expected to emulate Japan's modern womanhood of "good wife and wise mother" to assist China's modernization and civilization. Instead, they became captivated by Western liberal political theories and feminist ideas, already introduced to Japan. In the early twentieth century, Chinese women found increasing opportunities to study in Western nations. Returning to China, these foreign-educated women engaged in various women's social movements. Many of them joined revolutionary movements and demanded gender equality and women's rights.[122] In 1912, when Carrie Chapman Catt toured China right after the 1911 Republican Revolution, she was deeply impressed with Chinese women activists pursuing woman suffrage in their republic-building efforts.[123]

Nonetheless, although the Republican Revolution ended Qing rule, the ensuing power struggles among warlords in the north and rising nationalism and labor radicalism divided China and plunged it into civil war. This enticed further foreign imperialist/colonialist interventions. The women's movements for equal rights and freedom embraced anticolonialist causes of national unity and sovereignty, while progressive intellectuals engaged in the anti-Confucian New Cultural Movement in the late 1910s. After World War I, when the Paris Peace Conference refused to nullify Japan's imperialist demands on China's northeast, women students in Beijing, Shanghai, and Tianjin became a force in boycotting Japanese goods and carrying out massive demonstrations and strikes, which developed into the May Fourth movement. The movement led to the U.S. "Open Door Policy" and the 1921 Washington Naval Conference that forced Japan to relinquish many of its newly obtained rights in China.[124] This development, along with the racist 1924 U.S. immigration law, exacerbated Japanese anti-Western sentiments and aspiration to stand on par with Western imperialists.

While these events were transpiring, "troubled China" became the outlet for American students charged with social gospel zeal on college campuses.

The new generation of American missionaries, many of whom were YMCA/ YWCA workers and active in the Student Volunteer Movement for Foreign Missions (SVM), arrived in China to evangelize the people while assisting in modernization. These New Woman missionaries with academic knowledge and professional skills took a lead in building China's women colleges and medical schools, while promoting the Student Christian Movement on campuses. Chinese alumnae found opportunities for further study and training in the United States. Their collaborative efforts played a crucial role in producing Chinese New Women who would contribute to China's struggle for national unity and sovereignty. They worked not only for the welfare of Chinese women and children but also for nationalistic and anti-imperialist causes. The transnational efforts that were forged under foreign imperialism also assisted Chinese women to insert themselves as policymakers in local and national governments of New China.[125]

Noticeably, unlike Japan, which introduced the German medical system under rigid state control,[126] China's treaty port cities became major outlets for Western women doctors' talent and maternalist zeal, as they were barred from their own nations' sexist medical societies. Building modern social infrastructure for hygiene and public health was crucial for local Chinese people and settler colonialists to prevent pandemics among the rapidly internationalizing populations at international settlements.[127] Western women doctors and their Chinese women specialist protégés played an indispensable role in this effort. Assisting these transnational women's endeavors were "benevolent" American capitalist-philanthropists, such as the Rockefellers, whose family foundation invested its wealth worldwide, and Levi Lewis Barbour, the University of Michigan regent who funded the Barbour Scholarship for the education of women in the "Orient." They were generous, especially in building modern medical and public health systems and training experts in the field, all essential in preventing epidemics and protecting the lives and interests of both native peoples and settlers in international globalization hubs worldwide.[128]

In the early twentieth century, the Shanghai International Settlement was embedded in a system of laissez-faire capitalism-industrialism and imperialism. The unequal treaty imposed by Japan after the First Sino-Japanese War gave Japan and other imperialist powers, through most-favored-nation treatment, the right to open factories in the settlements. Wealthy foreign investors took advantage of this new privilege, and the Shanghai International Settlement rapidly industrialized and modernized, accompanying both prosperity and misery caused by thriving industrial capitalism and its exploitation of Asian labor.[129] During World War I, when European powers were busy fighting each other, the militarily neutral Shanghai International Settlement saw sprouting Japanese and Chinese factories, which shared feudalistic patriarchal family ideologies and exploited rural peasant daughters in quasi-slavery conditions. The settlement had not yet instituted laws to regulate labor conditions.[130]

With growing interest in labor conditions in Asia, the London-based World YMCA recruited British labor reformer Agatha Harrison (1885–1954) to investigate Shanghai in 1921. Harrison had worked as a teacher and a welfare worker at a tin-box company and was the first "University Welfare tutor" at the London School of Economics.[131] Arriving in Shanghai in 1921, she encountered the destitute conditions suffered by women and children working in textile mills. She urged the women's community in the Shanghai International Settlement to pressure the SMC to introduce labor provisions. For this purpose, the Joint Committee of the Shanghai Women's Clubs (JCSWC, the precursor of the Shanghai Joint Committee, JCSWO) formed to coordinate five women's organizations—the American Women's Club, the British Women's Association, the Japanese Women's Societies, the Shanghai Women's Club, and the Shanghai Chinese YWCA.[132] Thus, when the World YWCA industrial secretary, American Mary Dingman, visited Shanghai in 1923 on her Pacific tour, Shanghai's transnational women's network had already embarked on labor reform.[133]

The JCSWC was headed by bilingual and culturally hybrid Chinese Anna Fo-Jin Kong Mei (1891–1958), who had embraced the social gospel fervor on U.S. college campuses. She was born in Hong Kong, lost her preacher father at a young age, and crossed the Pacific with her remaining family to live with an uncle, a rector of St. Peter's Episcopal Church in Honolulu.[134] After graduating with honors from McKinley High School in Honolulu, she became the first Chinese woman to graduate from Barnard College for Women in New York. In 1915, she returned to China to teach at mission schools and then married Hua-chuan Mei (Dr. H. C. Mei), a San Francisco–born U.S. citizen lawyer of Chinese ancestry who had studied law at Columbia and New York University. Both Anna (Fo-Jin) Kong and H. C. Mei embraced social gospel zeal on American college campuses to become active in the YWCA/YMCA and SVM. Although H. C. Mei was admitted to the bar of New York State Courts, he had difficulty practicing law there because of his race. He sought opportunities in Shanghai, where he passed bars to be qualified to serve for the British Court, U.S. Court, and the International Mixed Court. In Shanghai, H. C. Mei assumed leadership in the Chinese YMCA movement, and Anna, in the YWCA movement.[135] Anna Kong Mei became the chairman of the National Committee of the China YWCA and the honorary vice president of the World YWCA Far East. In addition, she was active in the American Association of University Women and American Women's Federated Mission Boards until she left Shanghai in 1937.[136]

The JCSWC, with support from the World YWCA, pressured the SMC to introduce labor regulations to abolish children's night work, to provide part-time schools in factory districts, and to supervise health and safety in factories. JCSWC leaders also made labor reform one of their patriotic causes of the National Christian Council in China—a permanent organization that resulted from China's first National Christian Conference in 1922, an ecumenical attempt to unite Chinese Protestant Churches and foreign missionary societies. To facilitate child labor reform efforts, the organization brought Dame Adelaide Anderson (1863–1936), another British labor reformer—active in British colonies, dominions, and settlements—to the Shanghai International Settlement in 1923. The SMC was thus pressured to establish the Shanghai Child Labor Commission to investigate labor conditions and appointed British and Chinese women activists—including Agatha Harrison, Dame Adelaide Anderson, and Mei-ling Soong, a young Wellesley alumna who would later marry Chiang Kai-shek—along with foreign male industrialists to its membership.[137]

Their collaboration, however, made little progress for multiple reasons. First, the complexities in the SMC's governing mechanism and its elusive relationship with the Chinese government made any legislation extremely difficult. The authority of the SMC derived from its bylaws and the Land Regulations that were established in 1854. Attempts at change or additions to the Land Regulations required consent from "a special meeting of the rate payers, of the Consular Body in Shanghai, of the Diplomatic Body in Beijing, and of the Chinese Government." Second, during a time of rising nationalism and anti-imperialist feelings among the Chinese, the Chinese government resisted SMC regulatory expansion to industrial labor and factory workers. Third, many families needed their children's wages, regardless of how meager they were. Fourth, a ban on child labor aroused fear among both foreign and Chinese factory owners operating in the settlement that they would lose their international competitiveness. Finally, the misogynistic resentments that men harbored worked against women, especially women's entry into the male public sphere that regulated labor.[138]

The Shanghai Child Labor Commission successfully urged a British firm to eliminate child labor for boys under ten and for girls under twelve. It also pressured the SMC to summon a special meeting of rate payers to discuss child labor regulations in 1925. Nonetheless, a scheduled special meeting failed to achieve a quorum because the May Thirtieth Incident stirred China. The incident started when a Chinese striker at a Japanese factory was killed on May 25, and then SMC-supervised Indian mercenary police killed eleven protestors on May 30, 1925. The development ignited massive nationalist and anti-imperialist movements and strikes throughout China, some of which were organized by the Chinese Communist Party (CCP).[139]

After failing to enact child labor regulations, the JCSWC disbanded in 1925 but reassembled in 1926 into a permanent entity, the Joint Committee of the Shanghai Women's Organizations (JCSWO or Shanghai Joint Committee), which hosted a luncheon for Alexander H. Ford, as mentioned at the beginning of this section. Anna Kong Mei remained as the president of the JCSWO. American Addie Viola Smith (1893–1975) became the new organization's corresponding secretary, and Australian Eleanor M. Hinder (1893–1963) served as its recording secretary.[140]

Smith and Hinder were rooted in transnational social feminist networks committed to labor reform and linked to the labor reform efforts of the ILO. Smith started her career in the U.S. government with a probationary appointment at the Children's Bureau, headed by Julia Lathrop, and attended the first ILC held in Washington, DC, in 1919. Smith, however, cultivated her path in the U.S. Department of Commerce and pioneered women's participation in the U.S. Foreign Service. Working as a trade commissioner in China, she was also active in the China PPA, the male-led PPU's Chinese branch.[141] Eleanor M. Hinder was her lifelong partner and a committed labor reformer. Hinder worked as a biology teacher and then a welfare supervisor at Farmer's, a large department store in central Sydney. Hinder was affiliated with various Australian branches of international women's organizations, for example, the World YWCA and the International Federation of University Women (IFUW). The World YWCA Industrial Secretary Mary A. Dingman's visit to Australia on her Pacific tour led Hinder to work for child labor reform in China. In 1924, Hinder traveled to Oslo to represent Australia at the IFUW congress and then to Shanghai to study and report on the conditions of women and children factory workers for the World YWCA. After returning to Sydney, she made her way back to Shanghai in 1926. Sponsored by the Rockefeller Fund and appointed by the World YWCA, Hinder became the Shanghai YWCA's industrial secretary.[142]

The international women's community of the JCSWO, like the privileged foreign rate payers' community of the SMC, transcended national and racial boundaries but was multilayered and multifaceted in its members' causes and intentions. Both Anglo-Saxon and Chinese leaders, however, were compelled to mediate Native Chinese nationalism and anti-imperialism, foreign settler colonialism, and transnational feminism for world peace. At the time of the May Thirtieth Incident, World YWCA leaders believed that forging solidarity among elite Chinese, Japanese, and Korean women internationalists was essential for the peaceful integration of the "Far East" into the globalizing industrial capitalism and the emerging new world order under the Euro-American leadership. Accordingly, when the Japan YWCA convened its first annual meeting in October 1925, Anna Kong Mei represented the China YWCA, and Helen Kim represented the Korea YWCA as guest speakers.[143]

The May Thirtieth Incident politicized students, workers, and peasants to demand social justice, equal rights, and freedom. It also revived the Republic of China's ruling party, the Chinese Nationalist Party (CNP), and led to the formation of a CNP-CCP United Front, which engaged in military campaigns to vanquish northern warlords and promote national unity. The United Front Northern Expedition, however, was enthusiastically embraced by workers and tenant farmers who also took up violent anti-Christian and antiforeign uprisings. In January 1927, under the pressure of escalating nationalism and anti-imperialism, the foreign powers in Shanghai abolished the International Mixed Court, and three Chinese men were added to the SMC's board of directors. American YWCA and YMCA members and missionaries also voiced their opposition to extraterritorial rights and pressed the U.S. government to end its extraterritoriality.[144]

In the face of national turmoil, the National Committee of the China YWCA sent a cable in January 1927 to various international women's organizations' member countries asking for support for China's complete independence and for cooperation to prevent their respective government from intervening in China's domestic affairs. In response, U.S., British, and French YWCAs approached their governments to support China, and the YWCAs of Canada, New Zealand, Norway, Japan, India, Burma, and Ceylon expressed their support for the China YWCA's appeal.[145] Nonetheless, the escalating popular uprisings culminated in the Nanjing Incident of 1927, where several foreigners and Chinese Christians were killed in the treaty port of Nanjing in March 1927. The imperialist powers—Britain, the United States, France, and Japan—sent troops to the city, ostensibly to "protect" their citizens. Fearing communism, Chinese and foreign businessmen, along with YMCA and YWCA workers, supported Chiang Kai-shek, the CNP army general. Chiang brutally eradicated communists, CNP leftists, and the anti-Chiang faction, which led to the execution of New Woman activists including French- and Soviet-trained Xiang Jingyu (1885–1928). The CNP-CCP United Front broke down. After bringing the CNP under his control, Chiang's troops resumed the Northern Expedition for national unity.[146]

Although Chinese New Women displayed diverse forms of feminist consciousness in the face of the bloodshed, those who had embraced American middle-class social gospel aspirations turned inward and sustained their faith by promoting a "Christian Home." This was a less-controversial and safer way to advance women's rights and welfare. China's feudalistic past was symbolized in the patriarchal households, where concubinage persisted as an avenue to secure male heirs, and in destitute households, daughters were indentured to servitude at brothels, private homes, or factories.[147] Anna Kong Mei, in articulating a social feminist vision, argued that realizing a "Christian Home" would make "slavery in any form utterly impossible." She wished that the "stiff formalities" of patriarchal household relationships would become "more mutually respecting," "frank and companionable," and "patient and considerate." She argued that Christian women should make the home an example of "a training school in Christian virtues." Such an approach would be more effective than women's political "agitation" in assuring the "health, comfort, and welfare" of servants and factory and mill workers.[148] At the same time, YWCA leaders also saw that expanding the school system was an urgent issue not only to achieve equality but also to prohibit child labor. Their campaign to ban child labor faced working parents' concerns that their children would be released from factory labor and be left adrift on the streets.[149] The China YWCA's Western secretaries transferred leadership to Chinese women, who shifted their focus from middle-class women students to female factory workers and peasant women.[150]

This was the historical context for Alexander Ford's visit to Shanghai in 1927 promoting the first PPWC, where A. Viola Smith was active in the China PPA.[151] In response to the invitation to the PPWC, the JCSWO formed the pan-Pacific subcommittee to prepare for the PPWC in 1928, and A. Viola Smith chaired the China Preparation subcommittee.[152] JCSWO president Anna Kong Mei, along with Mrs. Chindon Yui Tang of the Shanghai Women's Club[153] and National YWCA General Secretary Shu-ching Ting, expressed hope that Chinese women would "gain" and "give" something at the PPWC.[154] Along with Smith, Hinder, assuming the role of 1928 PPWC program secretary and a Conference (Executive) Committee member, engaged in the preparation work to convene the first PPWC in Honolulu.[155] Nonetheless, Hinder and Smith had difficulty in finding Chinese participants to form a delegation.[156]

The five-member "Chinese" delegation to the PPWC, funded by the China PPA and its network, embraced the paradox of Chinese women's nationalism and transnational feminist imperialism in the Shanghai International Settlement and the emerging pan-Pacific women's community. The delegation included two "delegates"—Dr. Me-Iung Ting (1891–1969, Ding, Maoying), the director of the Beiyang Women's Hospital in the treaty port city of Tianjin in the north, and Bae-tsung Kyong, the industrial secretary of the Shanghai Chinese YWCA and the chair of the JCSWO subcommittee on child labor—and three "resident delegates"—Eleanor M. Hinder, A. Viola Smith, and Mrs. Ella P. Ely, who was affiliated with St. John's University, Shanghai.[157]

The racially mixed Chinese delegation exemplified the mutually beneficial but unequal nature of transnational sisterhood that had been forged by women's separate sphere strategies. The semi-colonial globalization hubs allowed transnational ventures to thrive, but an ensuing influx of foreign settlers and migrant workers resulted in crowded living and poor working conditions, epidemics, and devastation, especially among laboring women and children. Anglo-Saxon New Woman medical professionals and labor reform experts who found freedom and fulfilment in the foreign fields found outlet for their modern scientific knowledge and expertise. With assistance from these women professionals and experts from the West and funding from transnationalizing capitalist philanthropy, Chinese New Women adopted modern, Western skills and scientific expertise to advance China's anti-imperialist struggle for full sovereignty. Facing the dilemma of Chinese nationalism and feminist globalism, Chinese and Anglo-Saxon New Women, both working for the betterment of Chinese women and children, developed relationships that were symbiotic but elusive. This became evident during the first PPWC.

CHAPTER 6

Pan-Pacific Women's Voices and Global Feminism

In August 1928, the first Pan-Pacific Women's Conference (PPWC) convened in Honolulu under the auspices of the Pan-Pacific Union (PPU). With Jane Addams serving as the international chair, the PPWC gathered delegates representing eleven "countries" in the Pacific. At the opening ceremony, PPU's director Alexander H. Ford, in his greetings, implored the participants not to be afraid but "to give birth to a new Pan-Pacific organization." He encouraged them to form a permanent organization out of this gathering and to join PPU efforts in creating "a patriotism of the Pacific."[1]

As enthusiastic as Ford in forming a permanent organization out of the first PPWC was Eleanor M. Hinder, Australian labor reformer and a "resident delegate" representing China. Committed to improving the deplorable working conditions of wage-earning women and children in the Shanghai International Settlement and its vicinity, she recognized the need for trans-Pacific women's collaboration to set international labor standards.[2] As the corresponding secretariat of the Joint Committee of the Shanghai Women's Organizations (JCSWO or Shanghai Joint Committee), Hinder communicated with the Joint Standing Committee of the Women's International Organizations (JSCWIO), a Geneva-based "super-international coalition" that aimed at women's global networking and collective action to influence male-dominant intergovernmental organizations. She also engaged in preparation work for the first PPWC as the conference's program secretary and an executive committee member. Accordingly, she was well aware of Geneva-based feminist internationalists' strong interest in the Pacific as well as objection to forming another international organization to avoid duplication of work. Hinder conceived a blueprint of the permanent organization to justify the new organization in the Pacific. She published a booklet in May 1928, prior to the opening of the first PPWC, and insisted that with the crucial exception of the Young Women's Christian Association (YWCA), all the notable women's international organizations—the International Council of Women (ICW), International Woman Suffrage Alliance (IWSA), and Women's International League for Peace and Freedom (WILPF)—were headquartered in Europe and had little contact with Asian women. Thus, a permanent follow-up organization should be Pacific focused. It would be regionally limited but able to receive international recognition as "a clearinghouse" for not only materials produced in European-centered agencies but also "constructive Pacific thinking" made available to European women. Hinder argued for a pan-Pacific women's community that would not compete with but complement Geneva-based women's global collective power-building efforts. She insisted that they should form a permanent organization as an outcome of the first PPWC; if not, a continuation committee to prepare for future conferences should be elected.[3]

Nonetheless, Honolulu local Julie Judd Swanzy, the PPWC's honorary chairperson, and her fellow women organizers were apprehensive.[4] Hinder's message revealed her Eurocentric sense of mission to guide peoples in the Pacific toward feminist internationalism. Based on her brief experiences in the Shanghai International Settlement, Hinder agreed with Institute of Pacific Relations (IPR) member Herbert Croly, who described cultures in the Pacific as "both more primitive and more worn out, both more ancient and more modern than those of any European countries." Hinder advocated for "the aid of human efforts" to guide the most diverse groups of people in the Pacific, who were still oblivious about the vast changes and social transformations caused by rapid globalization.[5] Honolulu women leaders, who also experienced diverse women's causes and strategies in preparing for the first PPWC, were concerned about how linking trans-Pacific women's movements to Eurocentric women's internationalism would affect multiracial Hawai'i and non-Western cultures in the Pacific. At the same time, Honolulu women leaders, working under Hawai'i's male oligarchy and trans-Pacific patriarchy, were still committed to the separate sphere strategy to ensure women's autonomous sphere and to scoop up voices of women with diverse backgrounds. At the opening of the PPWC, the conference organizers followed Hinder's suggestion to appoint a "continuation committee" but instructed its members "to 'keep its ear to the ground,' but to avoid any appearance of forced growth, or the stimulating of further work if such were not felt to be warranted."[6]

PPWC organizers, along with its participants of varying feminist consciousness and divergent interests, who gathered in Honolulu, slowly recognized the value of the gender-specific pan-Pacific women's conference. It was a rare opportunity to inspire and negotiate for collaboration in improving the status of children, women, and "humanity in general." The Pan-Pacific Women's Association (PPWA) formed at the second PPWC in 1930 to coordinate participating countries for future PPWCs. It embraced the international aspirations of Anglo-Saxon women leaders, while lending an ear to nonwhite women elites of colonizing and colonized countries in the Pacific. As such, in a departure from the Euro/American centricity of trans-Atlantic feminist internationalism, the PPWA facilitated the emergence of feminist globalism by recognizing national, class, racial, and ethnic diversities and seeking common intersectional points for women's solidarity. By examining the two PPWCs held in Honolulu in 1928 and 1930, this chapter illuminates how the experiences there persuaded local, national, and international participants to form a permanent organization. It also provides an overview of the following two PPWCs held in the turbulent 1930s.

Sharing Multiple Causes and Multilayered Women's Voices in the First PPWC in 1928

Convening the PPWC relied on the male initiative of paternalistic and patriarchal aspirations for Hawai'i-centered internationalism and the separate sphere strategy of women leaders in carving out women's autonomous sphere in the opening-up international arena. By adhering to the sex-based separation of spheres, the first PPWC carried out official presentations and discussions in its five sections—education, industry, health, government, and social services—in a diplomatic manner. Nonetheless, women participants created room to raise controversial issues and exchange candid opinions. Some faced unequal racial, ethnic, class, national, and cultural relationships; others grappled with who would represent a nation or country and how.

Nonetheless, they made careful efforts to understand the complexity, diversity, and commonality of women's experiences in Hawai'i and other Pacific countries. For example, Mary Anderson was warmly welcomed at Honolulu's port, receiving "eighty leis," but quickly sensed the probusiness and oligarchic milieu of Hawai'i. She had recruited Caroline Manning, a field agent of the Women's Bureau, and Elizabeth Christman and Jo Coffin from the National Women's Trade Union League (NWTUL) to survey women's working conditions during their stay in Honolulu. Soon she learned that "there had been considerable opposition in some quarters to [her] coming because [she] was supposed to be a labor leader and the [local] employers were afraid [she] would stir up troubles."[7]

Anderson remained diplomatic when speaking of the situation on the mainland, while stressing the importance of learning about women's working conditions in the Pacific countries.[8] As the chair of the PPWC's Industrial Section, Anderson ensured that PPWC participants freely addressed the problems they viewed as urgent. As a result, Japanese delegate Yoshi(ko) Shoda reported on the impoverished conditions women faced in Japan's textile and coal mining industries. While mentioning the "remarkable progress" attained after the 1919 International Labour Conference (ILC) and "rapidly changing" recent conditions, Shoda revealed the dangerous, unhealthy, backbreaking, and low-paid work of women employed in these industries. Arguably, the most shocking news was that "a great number of workers [gave] their lives as the victims." According to her report, the ratio of women textile mill workers who died of tuberculosis had risen from 3.6 percent in 1922 to 9.7 percent, and half of those developed the disease within a year of working. The percentage of those who developed tuberculosis-related respiratory diseases was 76.4. As for Japan's mining industry, which primarily operated in a two-shift system, women constituted 24 percent of the workforce of 296,015, and the great majority worked in coal mines. They worked "only about 15 or 20 days or little more a month," mainly due to "illness and personal or domestic affairs." Furthermore, 175,000 Japanese mine accidents were reported in 1924.[9] Before their departure, Anderson's team also discovered that women's working conditions in Hawai'i were "bad in many ways" and that the "most deplorable" conditions existed not in canneries or the sugar cane or pineapple fields, but rather among Japanese women workers in the garment and service industries.[10]

Chinese delegate Bae-tsung Kyong reported on "girls of 7 or 8 years of age working day and night" under exploitive conditions in textile mills in

China. She argued for an international standard for wages and living because low industrial and living standards in one country drove down standards in other countries. She insisted, furthermore, that the fundamental cause of the discriminatory immigration policies of white settler nations was that the lower standards of wages and living in China and other nonwhite nations made immigrants willing to accept wages that were much lower than host nations' standards. Accordingly, "the industrial problems of China [were] not only China's problem but rather problems of the world."[11]

These reports and discussions at the Anderson-chaired Industrial Section opened the eyes of many social feminist participants about the urgent need for adequate standards for working conditions in booming Pacific industrial centers.[12] According to Eleanor M. Hinder, "a prominent and wealthy woman of Honolulu," commented that Anderson and her cohort "have made us the friend of the employed woman for life—or rather they have made the employed women our friend."[13] Local organizers in Honolulu, who were primarily concerned about the acculturation of multiracial island children, became convinced of the need for continuous study and international coordination to improve volatile class, race, and national relations in the Pacific and the welfare of women and children worldwide.[14]

Fusae Ichikawa did not miss the astonishment of the women participants who listened to Japanese delegates' presentations on child labor, factory hygiene, mother-children suicides, and licensed prostitution in Japan. She hoped that the "disclosure" tactics that were often used by "proletarian movements" would positively affect women's labor conditions in Japan.[15] While women factory workers fought a hard battle and proletarian parties vocalized worker's voices, discussions at the PPWC's Industrial Section added pressure on the Japanese government, which was greatly concerned about its international reputation.[16] In 1929, the 1923 revision of the 1916 Factory Law, which prohibited night work for women and forbade minors under the age of sixteen from working between 10 P.M. and 5 A.M., finally went into effect. Still, the cotton industry received a special exemption to keep them working until 11 P.M.[17]

Ichikawa was somewhat disappointed by the Government Section Roundtable. Colonialist Australian, New Zealand, and Japanese delegates extended their discussion to cover woman suffrage in their respective settlements and colonies. Nonetheless, the roundtable discussion emphasized Japanese women's priority in reforming the feudalistic household system. The system, like the one in China, was based on the neo-Confucian principle of "obedience and filial piety," facilitating the absolute patriarchal control of the household and the nation.[18] To increase Western women's understanding on this point, National Woman's Party (NWP) member Elizabeth Green's *Pacific Affairs* published Japanese delegate Kikue Ide's article, in which she explained why Japanese suffragists focused on reforming the private sphere of the "household." Somewhat like Chinese Anna Kong Mei, who had insisted on replacing the household system with a more mutually respectful and companionable family system, Ide argued in her article that for Japanese suffragists to "reform" or "destroy" the patriarchal household system was as important, if not more so, as demanding women's right in the public sphere.[19] In fact, the woman suffrage bill that Ichikawa's Women's Suffrage League (WSL) managed to have submitted to the Japanese Imperial Diet would pass the House of Representatives in 1931, but only with numerous revisions, including the condition of "with her husband's consent." The revision was in no way acceptable to the suffragists.[20]

Arguably, the exchange of ideas continued through personal interactions outside of the conference sites and through correspondence after the meeting. For example, Ichikawa recorded that she enjoyed off-conference time with NWP member Elizabeth Green.[21] Although the conference proceedings listed "married women's status" as one of the Government Section's roundtable discussion topics, it carried no report on the discussion.[22] Nonetheless, returning to Japan, Ichikawa, along with another 1928 PPWC Japanese delegate Taki Fujita, visited the Japan Ministry of Foreign Affairs (JMoFA) Treaty Division Head to petition for (1) independent and equal nationality rights for men and women, an issue that would be dealt with at the upcoming Hague Conference for the Codification of International Law (1930 Hague Codification Conference), and (2) support for Japanese participation in women's organization conferences such as the ICW. Ichikawa also contributed an article analyzing international debates on women's independent nationality. Obviously, Ichikawa obtained information on the issue through personal efforts.[23]

Furthermore, although Japan barred Korea from representing itself, the conference proceedings' education and industry sections carried reports authored by Helen Kim. Kim, a graduate of the Methodist Ewha Girls' School in Seoul, studied at Wesleyan and received an MA in philosophy from Boston University and a PhD in education from Columbia University. She eventually headed Ewha Women's University.[24] The proceedings' education section also included a report by Japanese school teacher delegate Fusa

Ishikawa (not Fusae Ichikawa), introducing an attempt by Japan's Imperial Education Society (IES) president Masataro Sawayanagi at liberal education that emphasized individuality among children of the urban upper-middle class. Active PPU-IPR member Sawayanagi was also responsible for imposing a Japan Ministry of Education (JMoE)–administered unified public school system in the Japanese empire in the 1900s and 1910s. While Helen Kim's report made "a rough appraisal" of Japan's colonial policy of expanding public schools to Korea, she expressed Korean fear of "distinct racial obliteration." Kim stated: "The policy of assimilation of the Korean people on the part of the Japanese authorities dominates the educational program to such an extent that a distinct racial obliteration is feared by the formers. The death of a race that has had a large share in the upbuilding of civilization would be a loss to the world as well as to the race in question. The civilization of the world is a totality of the contributions made by each race for the benefit of all."[25] Her statement crystalized the deep concern of not only Koreans, whose civilization verged on extinction under Japan's colonial rule, but also of Native Hawaiian and various ethnic settler parents who opposed Hawai'i's English-only education policy.

Various women's experiences also revealed complicated dynamics of intercultural exchanges between women with diverse backgrounds. Another Japanese school teacher delegate, Kyō Kiuchi, spoke for non-English speakers who felt estranged among bilingual elite PPWC participants. She recognized the importance of learning English, the sympathy conveyed by Anglo-Saxon organizers, especially Eleanor M. Hinder, and the invaluable assistance provided by local Japanese residents. Still, Kiuchi, on return to Japan, insisted that the PPWC's cause of peace and harmony would only be obtained by assuring equality and including women of different races and all classes, even those who did not have enough time or money to learn English. She suggested that future PPWCs should use the language of the conference site for communication and provide interpreters, use a new international language (such as Esperanto), or invent and install simultaneous translation devices. Although none of her suggestions were immediately feasible, when the PPWA later formed and instituted bylaws, they stipulated that interpretation and translation be arranged for those not proficient in English. The bylaws also noted that when the language of the host country was not English, the business and program should be bilingual.[26]

Possibly, the most controversial issue at the first PPWC was who would represent a nation or a country and how, which involved the paradox of nationalism, colonialism, imperialism, and feminist internationalism. This complexity surfaced again when China's Anglo-Saxon "resident delegates"— Eleanor M. Hinder and A. Viola Smith—extended the invitation from the China Pan-Pacific Association (PPA) to host the following PPWC at Shanghai in 1930 without first consulting their fellow Chinese delegates. A. Viola Smith served as the chair of the PPWC's Continuation Committee. Both Smith and Hinder led organizing the Chinese delegation for the conference as officers of the Shanghai-based JCSWO and the China PPA, the male-led PPU's affiliate in China that funded the Chinese delegation. They had worked closely with Alexander Ford. Ford thought that Shanghai, more specifically its International Settlement, was the ideal setting for the second PPWC, much more than any city in the United States, where organizers had to comply with restrictive U.S. immigration laws. With his encouragement, they drafted a PPWC resolution calling for the acceptance of the China PPA's invitation and submitted it to the PPU-PPWA joint meeting, where Ford promised that the PPU would offer clerical and all other support.[27]

Hearing the decision, the head of the Chinese delegation, Dr. Me-Iung Ting, vehemently objected to what amounted to symbolic, white settler feminists' imperialistic attitudes and the PPWC's collaboration with the PPU's capitalist-imperialist network.[28] Ting's frustration also exemplified the dilemma of the transnationally bred Chinese New Women. She had studied at a female mission school in Shanghai[29] and at Mount Holyoke College in Massachusetts and received a medical degree at the University of Michigan on a Barbour Scholarship. Returning to China, Dr. Ting became the director of Beiyang Women's Hospital, one of the first public Chinese women's hospital to be equipped with a state-sponsored health department and nursing school in the city of Tianjin. Ting's professional expertise owed itself to the complex networks of capitalist-imperialist philanthropy, feminist evangelism, and separate sphere strategies.[30] Nonetheless, Chinese women joined China's national struggle for full sovereignty and were compelled to use their modern medical and hygiene expertise to deter imperialist/colonialist powers that argued they were "uplifting" China's "backward" public health system via invasion.[31] The incident at the first PPWC pressed PPWC women organizers to recognize that China's settler "resident delegates" were seeking reform in transnational laissez-faire capitalism-imperialism. They also saw that China's native delegates were fighting for their national sovereignty to make decisions by themselves.

Although the two groups were working together for women and children, they held differing views when it came to the meaning of "China."

With little prospect of delaying the schedule to hold the second PPWC in Shanghai, Ford, as the PPU director, offered the PPU's services "in calling and financing" the second PPWC and asked the first PPWC's executive committee and local committee to act in advisory capacity. Hinder agreed to serve as the honorary secretary of the PPU-appointed executive committee for the 1930 meeting, which also functioned as a temporary continuation committee.[32] The committee would continue "consultation with national and international groups" to "determine what, if any permanent Pacific Women's organizations should be set up by the second PPWC." Hinder suggested organizing "a Joint Standing Pacific Committee, functioning somewhat along the lines of the Joint Standing International Committee [possibly referring to the Geneva-based JSCWIO]."[33]

Hinder remained in Honolulu to lead the continuation work toward forming a permanent women's organization. She struggled, however, with the unchallengeable power structure forged by local oligarchic families and their extensive pan-Pacific networks.[34] Against her will, she had to leave the city by the end of 1928. The reason for her sudden deportation remains a mystery, but Ford's answer to Hinder's inquiry was that she "put the cart before the horse."[35] Perhaps her settler colonialist claim to represent "China" invited criticism from local and pan-Pacific communities. Or her willingness to assert leadership by collaborating with Ford and male-dominant PPU networks did not sit well with the PPWC's commitment to a separate sphere strategy. Or her advocacy of the international labor standard could have posed a threat to trans-Pacific capitalists who preferred paternalism to improve labor conditions. Regardless of why, Hinder returned to Australia to continue her work for the 1930 PPWC and then traveled to Shanghai to commit herself to labor reform in the International Settlement.[36]

Hinder's insights into feminist globalism contributed to the inception of at least two organizations affiliated with the Geneva-based JSCWIO in the Pacific before the second PPWC, one in Australia and the other in Japan.[37] For example, Japan's JSCWIO affiliate, the Japan Women's Committee for International Relations (JWCIR; Kokusai Renraku Fujin Iinkai), was formed in 1929 in response to a call that arrived through the World YWCA network.[38] The JWCIR, an umbrella organization that was independent of any specific international or Japanese women's organization, sought to connect organizations and individuals in Japan with those in other countries.[39]

Headquartered at the Japan YWCA, the JWCIR was unable to free itself from Japan's patriarchal social milieu and influential elite internationalists' paternalism, nor could it transcend its bilingual elites' racialism and "bourgeois" nature. Nonetheless, Japan YWCA leaders, especially the wives and daughters of YMCA officers, were occupied with accompanying YMCA men attending the IPR conferences. Accordingly, the JWCIR took charge of gathering women activists of a little broader backgrounds to form Japanese delegations for future PPWCs. The JWCIR also responded to inquiries and invitations from foreign women's organizations that had no Japanese affiliates. Under the close eye of the JMoFA and its consuls general abroad, the JWCIR, while collaborating with male internationalists, sought its autonomy and authority in deciding who in the burgeoning women's international arena would represent Japan and how.[40] Ironically, when the JWCIR openly recruited the Japanese delegation for the second PPWC, one of the requirements to be an official delegate was to have a command of English. Those who did not were only allowed to be "associate delegates."[41] With influential male internationalists' support, Japan's National Federation of Primary School Teachers' Association (NFPSTA) continuously sent its members to the PPWCs but only in an associate capacity. Furthermore, the JWCIR disqualified women who sought to represent "Japanese women" at international conferences without JWCIR endorsement.[42] Although the JWCIR was increasingly expected to serve as the government's international spokesperson, it kept Japanese women visible in the pan-Pacific women's community and sisterhood. Fusae Ichikawa committed herself to serve as the JWCIR's secretary and corresponded as much as possible with various women's groups, including the ICW, the egalitarian British Sixth Point Group, and the All-Asian Women's Conference.[43] She also made efforts to inform the Japanese public about international feminist issues by contributing articles to socialist, feminist, and apolitical women's magazines.[44]

Pan-Pacific Feminists' Identity and Feminist Internationalism: The Second PPWC and PPWA's Inception in 1930

The second PPWC, held again in Honolulu in 1930, gathered 157 delegates from eleven countries in the Pacific along with British Dame Rachel Crowdy, who represented the League of Nations. Convened during the

Great Depression and the year of U.S. presidential election, the second PPWC had less of a U.S. mainland labor reformer presence than the first. Instead, the attendance of women linked to YWCA networks became more evident, lending credence to the validity of the YWCA's separate sphere strategy and its extensive transnational network in building the pan-Pacific women's community.[45] The diffusing effects of the Great Depression made local support and voluntarism as well as women's skillful maneuvering even more important for holding the second PPWC in Honolulu and forming a permanent organization out of it. In preparing for the conference, Ford's right-hand secretary Ann Satterthwaite worked closely with women leaders from participating countries to coordinate with Geneva-based feminist globalism. To investigate the status of women and children, they conducted pan-Pacific surveys on the issues of education, cinema, standards of living, diet, dental hygiene, industrial hygiene, wages, social services, and government.[46]

At the opening of the second PPWC in August 1930, Julie Judd Swanzy asked participants whether the PPWC would continue and where, when, and how? Concurrently, Wallace R. Farrington, former territorial governor and the current PPU president, and Lawrence M. Judd, Swanzy's cousin and the incumbent territorial governor, gave welcoming speeches and encouraged the formation of a permanent pan-Pacific women's organization. Still, the two men reminded women of their proper roles, i.e., supplementing and assisting the male-led pan-Pacific movement. Governor Judd expressed his pleasure at seeing that "the women of the world [were] taking their rightful place in the activities of world affairs, state affairs, and territorial affairs." Meanwhile, Farrington praised women's focus on "those subjects that [dealt] most directly with the health and economic welfare of the homes and home makers in the Pacific."[47]

The conservative turn in the official outlook of the PPWC was also evident as Margaretta Willis Reeve (Mrs. A. H. Reeve), who headed the National Congress of Mothers and Parent-Teacher Association (PTA) and the International Federation of Home and Schools, succeeded Jane Addams as the international chair of the second PPWC. Dr. Mary E. Woolley had initially been slated to assume the role.[48] Woolley, a daughter of a Congregational minister, turned out to be a noted educator and mediator. She transformed Mount Holyoke from a female mission school promoting Protestant womanhood and civility into a women's college providing academic education equal to male colleges. In the process, her resistance to introducing a home economics department to Mount Holyoke had invited strong criticism from conservative colleges' board members. As a member of the Foreign Missions Conference of North America Educational Commission to China, she visited colleges in China and Japan in 1921 and served as the American Association of University Women (AAUW) president (1927–1933).[49] Woolley, a colleague of Carrie Chapman Catt, had frowned upon NWP members' militancy during the suffrage campaign and joined social feminists supporting protective legislation. When she attended the 1927 IPR conference in Honolulu, however, she insisted that the contention between NWP egalitarian feminists and social feminists, who sided with the National League of Women Voters (NLWV), was "tearing down the fabric" of American women's organizations and remained a big problem. She called for adjusting their two different views over the Equal Rights Amendment (ERA) and protective legislation.[50]

While the reason for the last-minute change requires more research,[51] selecting Reeve as the international chair for the second PPWC revealed the urgency that Honolulu women leaders felt for the peaceful integration of Hawai'i's multiethnic population into the U.S. territory. In January 1927, the U.S. Supreme Court ruled in *Farrington v. Tokushige* that Hawai'i's Americanization efforts, including the ban on foreign-language preschool education, were unconstitutional.[52] In April 1927, right before the IPR's conference, Honolulu hosted the First Pan-Pacific Conference on Education, Rehabilitation, Reclamation, and Recreation (PPCERRR). The conference was called by U.S. President Calvin Coolidge. Possibly, the PPCERRR's purpose was to discuss how to rehabilitate natural and human resources displaced or strained in the modern phase of globalizing. Present at the PPCERRR was Margaretta Willis Reeve, who presented a paper in its Education Section and advocated "nursery school" instruction by trained teachers and health education for mothers and children. She expected education to "favorably affect the formation of habits, attitudes, knowledge, and skills, with regard to community as well as personal health."[53]

In multiracial and multinational Hawai'i, dependent on the agricultural industry, the social feminist versus individual-right feminist or conservative versus progressive binary became elusive. While in Honolulu as the first PPWC's international chair, Jane Addams recommended the PTA as "the most satisfactory means yet devised of bridging the gap between foreign-born and bred parents and their Americanized children."[54] Reeve was known as "less a feminist than a committed advocate of early childhood education" and critical of prevailing mass and consumer cultures.

Under her leadership, the PTA campaigned against purportedly immoral children's books and movies, and the second PPWC added "home economics" and "cinema" to the five themes of the first PPWC—education, government, health, industry, and social service. In her presidential address at the second PPWC, Reeve emphasized the need for parents to participate in social services and argued that education began "not at school age but at birth," and that the "most enduring teaching [was] done before the child enter[ed] school."[55] The PTA's precursor organization, the National Congress of Mothers, was the driving force in the 1910s for the establishment of mothers' pensions and the expansion of public school kindergarten education throughout the U.S. mainland.[56] Yet Reeve and her predecessor PTA president, Hanna Kent Schoff (1853–1940), took a stand against national labor regulations. Historically, social gospelers viewed rural agricultural labor as salutary for rehabilitating children of urban factory labor who had been exploited under laissez-faire industrial-capitalism. The PTA officials opposed prohibiting labor under eighteen years of age, as it would deprive children's "freedom" to "earn their living by honest work."[57] Reeve's stance must have pleased those who opposed the labor legislations—ERA advocates and Hawai'i's internationalist oligarchs who needed young agricultural labor and who procured funding for the second PPWC.

The U.S. delegation to the second PPWC was headed by NLWV representative Alice Parsons (Mrs. Edgerton) and composed mainly of bureaucrats who had carved out policymaking positions in U.S. federal and state agencies. Among them were Dr. Louise Stanley, director of the Home Economics Bureau of the Department of Agriculture; Bess Goodykoontz, Assistant Commissioner of Education, the Department of Interior; and Agnes Peterson, Assistant Director of the Women's Bureau, the Department of Labor.[58] Although Mary Anderson, who contributed to the second PPWC's preparation work by directing the Industrial Section's standards of living and wage project, could not travel to Honolulu, her deputy Peterson attended on Anderson's behalf.[59] A good part of the Home Economics Section under the chairpersonship of Dr. Louise Stanley dealt with living and dietary standards, which supplemented the Industrial Section's intensive study on living and wage standards.[60]

Chinese and Japanese delegations to the second PPWC were both headed by U.S.-educated medical doctors. An increasing risk of pandemics caused by rapid industrialization and urbanization highlighted the importance of social hygiene and public health for both nations. The five-member

"Chinese" delegation was headed by Dr. Zen Way Koh (Zung-wei Koh), a Barbour scholar who was then the acting chief of the Division of Maternity and Child Welfare of the National Ministry of Health. She attended the second PPWC on her way to the University of Michigan for further study as a Barbour fellow. The remaining delegates included two alumnae of U.S. missionary–founded Jinling (Ginling) College in Nanjing: Siao-sung Djang, another Barbour scholar and educator at Jinling, and Gwan Fan, who was then affiliated with the Bible Seminary of New York City. In addition, there was one "resident delegate," Geraldine Townsend Fitch (Mrs. George Ashmore Fitch), whose husband was a foreign secretary of the Nanjing YMCA; and one local resident, Mrs. Fred K. Lam, possibly Ah Chin Loo Lam, who was the wife of a local medical doctor active in the IPR.[61]

The Japanese delegates included two Barbour scholar medical professionals: Dr. Kameyo Sadakata, a physician at St. Luke's International Hospital's Pediatrics Department, and her colleague Midori Saito (later Midori Saito Hirano), who headed the St. Luke's Nursing School Public Nursing Department.[62] St. Luke's International Hospital, an American medical system enclave in Tokyo, was built with funding from Japanese and American capitalist-philanthropists and with endorsements from influential Japanese internationalists. The hospital gained a reputation for providing professional nurse training under the management of American missionary doctor Rudolf Bolling Teusler (1876–1934).[63] Headed by Dr. Sadakata, the Japan delegation included Yukiko Kimura, a Japanese National YWCA secretary who had worked at Australian and New Zealand YWCAs,[64] and Shizuko Kawasaki, a Hawai'i-born *Nisei* daughter who founded the Buddhist Musashino Girls' Seminary in Tokyo.[65] Also joining them were four associate delegates, who were school teachers and one more delegate, Honolulu resident Dr. Toshiko Yamaguchi, who worked for a Japanese hospital in the city.[66]

Japan was intensifying its colonial and imperialist schemes, and the second PPWC again dropped any Korean name from its list of delegates by country. Nonetheless, the Educational Section report included a short article by Nodie Kimhaikim (Sohn), the Superintendent of the Honolulu Korean Institute who was known for her efforts in the Korean independence movement. Her message revealed the Japanese colonial government's control over "the policy, administration, and curricula" extended to private Korean schools. Passing the Japanese language test was required for students to enter secondary schools. Nonetheless, thanks to an easily learned Korean alphabet, once regarded as "women's letters," 90 percent of Korean people, including those who failed the test, were literate and able to sustain their cultural pride.[67]

One international feminist issue discussed at the conference this time was women's independent nationality. American social and individual-right feminists disagreed over the ERA and protective federal legislations. Both groups had worked to revise the 1922 U.S. Cable Act, but the act still fell short of eradicating the disparity in male and female citizens' nationalities. In March 1930, the Cable Act was again amended to repeal the provision that caused U.S. women citizens to lose citizenship if they married non-nationals abroad. Nonetheless, this U.S. action led to the statelessness and dual nationality of women because many countries held married women's nationality derivative of their husbands' nationality. While independent women's nationality drew national and international attention, NWP and NLWV leaders, who vied with each other personally and organizationally, endeavored, although separately, to make the cause of assuring independent and equal nationality for men and women an international cause.[68]

The second PPWC in Honolulu created a rare occasion for the married women's nationality issue to be examined from multiple perspectives. The papers prepared on this topic were published in the August 1930 issue of Ford's *Mid-Pacific Magazine*. An article by Australian Anna Brennan discussed a British Dominion woman becoming stateless by marrying a U.S. citizen in the United States.[69] Another article by Hawai'i-born Chinese Ruth L. T. Yap explained the legal status of alien and U.S.-citizen Chinese women in Hawai'i. Yap, an assistant professor of mathematics at the University of Hawai'i and a member of the Hawaiian delegation, prepared her paper with Dr. T. Chen, a visiting professor from Tsing-Hua University, Beijing. Yap's paper provided a brief historical overview of Chinese women's experiences and mainly dealt with Chinese women in China but also revealed that the 1930 Revised Cable Act did not address the problems of a U.S. citizen woman of Chinese ancestry who would still lose her birthright citizenship by marrying an alien Chinese man who was ineligible for U.S. citizenship. Yap also discussed the class-based injustices caused by the 1924 Immigration Act that denied reentry of these Chinese American women who had lost their American citizenship through marriage but allowed, by treaty provision, the entry of alien Chinese wives, along with her minor children, who accompanied their merchant class husbands. She argued for an additional amendment to the Revised Cable Act of 1930.[70]

Again, despite the officially conservative outlook of the second PPWC, feminist ideas circulated on and off the conference site through publications and in-person exchanges. The 1930 PPWC's official "resolutions and recommendations" included the statement that "nationality shall be determined without discrimination on the ground of sex" but remained mute about the injustices caused by race or class.[71] Nonetheless, personal interactions and discussions on and off the conference site must have contributed to further amending the Revised U.S. Cable Act of 1930, which did not address the ordeal of U.S. citizen women who lost their citizenship by marrying alien men racially ineligible for nationality. In March 1931, with support from various national women's organizations—including the NLWV, the NWTUL, the National YWCA, the National Woman's Christian Temperance Union (WCTU), the AAUW, and the NWP—the U.S. Cable Act of 1930 was once again amended, this time to guarantee the independent nationality right of all women who were "citizens at birth." Now U.S.-born women of any race could retain and regain their citizenship even after their marriage to alien men racially ineligible for citizenship.[72] Still, it was not until 1932, when another amendment was made to the Cable Act, that the older generation of Native Hawaiian women, who had become U.S. "citizens by the acts of Congress," gained the same nationality right.[73]

Gertrude Scott Straub (Mrs. George Straub), a League of Women Voters of the Territory of Hawai'i (HLWV) member and president of the local branch of the WILPF, held a meeting at her residence.[74] Gertrude Scott Straub was a born-in-Japan daughter of Marion McCarrell Scott (1843–1922), an educator who had worked as an advisor to Japanese government in establishing the modern school system in Tokyo and taught and headed McKinley High School in Honolulu.[75] Although speculative, she also played a role in sharing the experiences of U.S. citizen women of Asian ancestry with PPWC attendees. The 1931 issue of *Pacific Affairs*, the IPR's house journal edited by NWP member Elizabeth Green in Honolulu, carried an article titled "Women and Nationality: Toward Equality in Citizenship Laws," written by NWP headquarter legislative secretary Emma Wold, a member of the U.S. delegation to the 1930 Hague Codification Conference. It argued that the most "obnoxious" item in the U.S. Cable Act was the provision distinguishing between women who marry aliens eligible for U.S. citizenship and those who marry aliens racially ineligible for citizenship. According to Wold, "the provision that seemed originally intended to penalize a marriage of American women of the Caucasian race with Asiatics became in reality a heavy penalty upon American-Chinese and American-Japanese girls for marrying aliens of their own race."[76]

The 1930 PPWC also provided an opportunity to discuss issues affecting the lives of indigenous women. Gertrude Scott Straub served as the 1930 PPWC's international project leader and the Government Section chair.[77] In the Straub-chaired Government Section, Australian Constance M. Ternent Cooke (1882–1967) reported her firsthand observation of the destitute conditions of aboriginal women in central Australia. The conference's official proceedings included its resolution calling for "just and generous legislative measures" to promote "the welfare of indigenous peoples" and its "strict enforcement."[78] Furthermore, local HLWV leaders secured NLWV's support in pressuring the U.S. Congress to amend Hawai'i's Organic Act to recover women's right for jury service.[79] That, along with women's property rights, had been a cause for native and settler women in Hawai'i. Hybrid Native Hawaiian Rosalie Enos Lyons Keli'inoi, Hawai'i's first elected woman territorial legislator, championed both causes in 1925 but recovered only property rights.[80] According to an after-conference report by NLWV's Alice Parsons, "the American group took the opportunity to urge by letters and resolutions to Senator Bingham and the Committee on Insular and Territorial Affairs that the women of Hawai'i have the right of jury service."[81]

With the presence of Rachel Crowdy—the only woman who headed a League of Nations Secretariat Section, the Social Welfare Section—the 1930 PPWC's Social Service Section also addressed trafficking in women and children, opium trafficking, intellectual cooperation, and refugees. Supporting Crowdy, the U.S. delegation urged President Hoover and the secretary of state to accept U.S. participation in the League of Nations Commission on opium trafficking.[82]

In all, the PPWCs served as invaluable occasions for women with diverse backgrounds and feminist consciousness to learn from each other and to be aware of old and new inequalities and disparities experienced by women in the rapid social changes brought about by globalization. This was especially true for women who interacted with each other as colonizers/settlers and colonized/natives who were to discover multiple positionalities and realize the importance of seeking common ground in their respective circumstances.[83]

Such pan-Pacific women's efforts impressed the participants with the desirability of forming a permanent organization. According to Georgina

Sweet, president of the Australian YWCA and head of the 1930 PPWC Australian delegation, many participants still doubted the "need, value and desirability" of continuing the women-only conferences at the beginning of the second conference. It was because the male-led IPR worked for similar purposes and gathered prominent Anglo-Saxon feminist leaders to discuss international and feminist issues. The IPR, however, was more focused on "matters likely [to] cause frictions between countries," and many women did not or could not find a place in their respective male-controlled national IPR organizations. After seven days of working together, even those who initially had doubts, including League of Nations representative Crowdy, accepted the desirability of forming a permanent organization.[84]

Formed in Honolulu, the PPWA embraced an idealistic evangelical vision for transracial and transethnic pan-Pacific women's exchanges, networking, and negotiations that transcended communal and national borders. The PPWA's constitution stipulated that "countries, dominions, colonies, territories, or dependents" were entitled for membership as a "country." Emphasizing personal experience and face-to-face meetings, the PPWA strove "to strengthen the bonds of peace among Pacific people by promoting better understanding and friendship among the women of all Pacific countries." It promoted "cooperation among the women of the Pacific region for the study and betterment of existing social conditions."[85]

Inaugurating the PPWA at the end of the conference, the assembly elected Julie Judd Swanzy as its first honorary president. Also, with each national delegate casting a vote, Australian Georgina Sweet was elected president; American A. H. Reeve, first vice president; and Chinese Dr. Me-Iung Ting, second vice president. Although the Japanese consulate and local community were unhappy with the election results—objecting and demanding that "appropriate attention" should be paid to Japan—the PPWA stood firm and refused the male nationalistic intervention in the appointment of its officers. To appease Japanese disappointment and indignation, two Japanese delegates publicly vindicated the election result in the local community.[86] They explained that of the four nominees—not only a Japanese but also an American and a Canadian—all lost the second presidency to Dr. Me-Iung Ting. According to them, the reasons why Japanese Tsune Gauntlett was not elected were because (1) China won Korea's vote; (2) Japan could not receive Hawaiian support largely because Tsuru Kishimoto, an eminent local Japanese who worked as a Honolulu YWCA's nationality secretary, was absent from the Hawaiian delegation on the election day due to a car accident; and

(3) possibly the name of the Japanese candidate, Tsune Gauntlett, did not sound very Japanese. At any rate, the inception of the PPWA made preparing future PPWCs "an essential means of attaining its objectives," and the second PPWC passed a resolution to convene a third conference again in Honolulu, with Ford's promise of PPU's assistance and funding.[87]

The Turbulent 1930s and Efforts for Mutual Understanding

In the 1930s, the impact of the Great Depression left the masses destitute. Collaboration among white and nonwhite liberal internationalists disintegrated when the exploited populace in the Pacific vented their pent-up frustration and resentment in growing movements of labor radicalism, anti-imperialism and anticolonialism, ethnic identity, nationalism, or ultranationalism. In Hawai'i, while money and enthusiasm from local planter oligarchies waned for Ford's pan-Pacific movement, Ford took a long journey to Asia for support and funding. His effort brought his PPU under substantial influence from Japan and a further flight of support from local, national, and international dignitaries.[88]

The PPWA's inception in 1930 highlighted the efficacy of women's separate sphere strategy in recruiting bilingual elite women from countries with patriarchal state and family systems for the collective efforts to cultivate common ground and causes for women in the Pacific. The Democratic Franklin Delano Roosevelt administration appointed workers-right advocate Frances Perkins as the Secretary of Labor, which opened up a new era for U.S. mainland labor reformers. Nonetheless, the Great Depression caused an unprecedented crisis in the modern phase of globalization in the Pacific, revealing the fundamentally unequal structure of thriving women's internationalism. The forging of friendship and solidarity among high-spirited, elite women internationalists was still white and Euro-American centric, indebted to Anglo-Saxon liberalism, and complicit with globalizing industrial capitalism and ensuing multinational colonialist/imperialist aspirations. During the turbulent era before World War II, women internationalists in the Pacific took trial and error to ameliorate social disparities. The PPWA convened the two additional PPWCs—the third in Honolulu in 1934 and the fourth in Vancouver in 1937—while sustaining its friendly and diplomatic atmosphere.

For Chinese and Japanese women internationalists, the decade of the 1930s was especially difficult. In 1932, Chinese women internationalists were appalled by Japan's military aggression and the establishment of "Manchuria," a puppet state of Manchus in China's northeast. Chinese women's organizations with international connections—namely the YWCA of China, the WCTU of China, the Chinese Women's Suffrage Association, and the National Council of Women of China—sent a telegram to women's organizations in Japan and the world, protesting Japan's violation of China's sovereignty and the Kellogg-Briand Pact.[89] Nonetheless, having embraced imperialist and colonialist aspirations, Japanese internationalist women were susceptible to Japan's imperialistic assertion that its military actions in Manchuria were only to "protect" its vested interests and did not violate the Kellogg-Briand Pact.[90] Unfortunately, they served as spokespersons for the Japanese government by promoting its image at international gatherings as a modern, civilized, peace-loving empire.

In 1930, for example, the Japan WCTU's two vice presidents, Tsune Gauntlett and Utako Hayashi, attended the London Naval Conference and the annual meeting of Carrie Chapman Catt's National Committee on the Cause and Cure of War (NCCCW) in Washington, DC, to demonstrate Japanese women's efforts for world peace. They brought huge bundles of signatures petitioning for world peace to the conferences, and Gauntlett crisscrossed the U.S. northeast, promoting peace and the League of Nations. The internationalist Japanese envoys signed the London Naval Treaty, but the treaty limited Japan to a smaller tonnage of cruisers and destroyers than either Britain or the United States. The ratification of the treaty added fuel to the indignation of Japanese nationalists, ultra-nationalists, and hawkish navy officers. Ironically, the interwar effort of elite internationalists to align Japan's system to the world trend for liberalism only temporarily sustained Japan's reputation as a "civilized" modern nation but fell short of eliminating poverty among the subjects. It also failed in erasing white racism toward their nonwhite nation or Japanese racialism toward their "less advanced" neighbors. Unfortunately, it promoted repeated military terrorism against the civilian government and the subsequent escalation of Japan's militarism and ultra-nationalism. Japanese women internationalists consequently became defensive not only to protect their nation but also themselves.[91]

Japanese women leaders appealed for international sympathy for their difficulty as they incurred strong criticism from the public who felt that the world order was Anglo-American dominant and discriminatory to the Japanese race. When a foreign missionary organization in Boston asked Japan WCTU's Ochimi Kubushiro and Japan YWCA's Michi Kawai to write about the situation of Japanese women, they stressed the "difficult position" of Christian activists who were under the scrutiny of non-Christian people in Japan and Christians in the West. On the one hand, Japanese nationalists regarded Christians, who promoted international harmony, as dangerous and disloyal and labeled them as "Communists." On the other hand, "the peace workers and pacifists of other countries" branded Japanese Christian workers as cowards, "kowtowing humbly before militarism."[92] Arguably, this dilemma was shared by all PPWC participants and feminist internationalists, who endeavored to mediate between patriotism, nationalism, transnationalism, and internationalism to benefit women in their country, the Pacific, and the world.[93]

In the face of Japan's intensifying aggression, however, Chinese internationalists were enraged by Japan and disappointed with the League of Nations and the international feminist community that had failed to take decisive measures against Japan. Furthermore, the ongoing contention between Chinese Nationalists and Communists and ideological differences among the leaders deepened their national crisis. According to historian Karen Garner, the ideological rift among China YWCA workers also became apparent when World YWCA leaders clung to their stance of promoting Christian sisterhood among women in the "Far East." On one side of Chinese YWCA workers were women leaders such as Chinese Deng Yuzhi (aka, Cora Deng, 1900–1996) and American Maud Russell, who became critical of the antilabor Chinese Nationalist Party (CNP) and the globalizing capitalist system. At the China YWCA's annual convention in August 1933, Deng Yuzhi stressed the need for a "fundamental reorganization of the economic system" in China. She had previously led China YWCA's student work promoting Christian womanhood for students and urban elite women, but China's changing circumstances made her more politically and socially conscious. After studying at the London School of Economics on a YWCA scholarship, Deng headed the Industrial Department to develop programs for worker education that embraced anti-Japanese patriotism, labor reform, and unionism.[94] YWCA night schools became a venue for the Chinese Communist Party (CCP) to raise political awareness of factory workers and peasant women to participate in the Communist revolution.[95] In her 1934 publication, Deng declared the need for "the followers of Christ" to help people to "be free from the exploitation of the profit-making system."[96]

On the other hand, Mei-ling Soong, who had sat on the Shanghai Municipal Government Child Labor Commission in 1925, married General Chiang Kai-shek on December 1, 1927. In 1934, she traveled to the United States to directly appeal to American Christians for their sympathy and support for the CNP under her husband's leadership. At that time, the CCP pushed ahead of the CNP in liberating women from conventional Chinese womanhood and marriage practices and recruited women to the party and the Red Army. In contrast, the CNP was more inclined to combat social "ills" caused by modernization and industrialization, e.g., spreading labor unrest, Communist influence, modern consumer culture, and "declining" morality. In 1934, Chiang Kai-shek embarked on the New Life Movement, tightening control over people's daily lives for the guise of national unity against Japanese aggression. The movement promoted a modern Chinese version of the "cult of womanhood" that combined white, middle-class, Protestant womanhood and neo-Confucian female virtues, and Mei-ling Soong led the CNP's New Life Movement's Women's Department.[97] Following the advice of her American missionary friend Geraldine Fitch, a Chinese "resident delegate" to the second PPWC, Soong appeared in the U.S. media and before the public to ask for support for New China. Confessing her Christian faith and recognition of the God-given role of supporting her husband for the transformation of China, Soong inspired American zeal for the civilizing mission and its focus on China's role in creating a future market and becoming a young democracy.[98]

While these Chinese and Japanese women in missionary-cultivated transnational networks competed with each other in appealing for international support and understanding, women's movements in Hawai'i came under the spell of feminists' racism. In the 1930s, the HLWV began taking up issues discussed by their national cohort, including the ERA and stylization.[99] Soon, however, men and women in Hawai'i realized intersectional injustices through the development of the so-called Massie Affair. The infamous affair started in September 1931 with Thalia Massie's false rape claim against five local men—two Hawaiian, two Japanese, and one of Chinese-Hawaiian ancestry. Massie was the wife of a Navy lieutenant stationed at Pearl Harbor. In the trial in December in Honolulu, the local multiracial male jurors failed to reach a verdict, causing racist uproars among the white public in Hawai'i and on the mainland. Meanwhile, the local police caught four whites—Thalia's mother, Grace Hubbard Fortescue from a prominent mainland family, Thalia's husband, and two Navy men—in a car carrying the corpse of Joseph Kahahawai—one of the five acquitted in the rape case in January 1932. The four whites were then brought to trial on charges of murdering Kahahawai, and the all-male but racially mixed jurors—three Chinese, one German, five Americans, one Native Hawaiian, one Portuguese, and one Dane—reached a verdict in April 1932. Despite intense pressure not to convict, all defendants were found "Guilty of manslaughter. Leniency recommended." Still, the crime of whites murdering a person of color seemed unimaginable, especially if the accused included a socialite. The criminal charge and conviction in the multiracial U.S. territory were unacceptable to the racist and classist mainland white public at the time. Thus, order and law enforcement in the territory came under the scrutiny of the U.S. Navy and Congress, and Hawai'i was on the verge of being placed under martial law.[100]

This incident took place when volatility in the Asian northeast reaffirmed Hawai'i's strategic importance to U.S. security and when white supremacists were irritated by African American antilynching campaigns disclosing the "threadbare lie" of Black men raping white women. The mainland white press fanned the image of multiracial Hawai'i as occupied by "degenerative natives" and men of color who preyed on the purity of white womanhood.[101] To avoid martial law, territorial governor Lawrence M. Judd yielded to pressure from President Herbert Hoover, the Navy, and the mainland public's racist frenzy. Judd commuted the prison term from ten years to one hour, and the four convicts took the first available boat to San Francisco, where they received a hero's welcome. Furthermore, the mainland press and Washington congressmen accused Governor Judd of having branded the defendants as convicts, which led to the Territory hiring the Pinkerton Detective Agency to prove that Thalia Massie's allegation of rape by the islands' five men in October 1932 was false.[102]

At the time, the longtime HLWV cause of recovering women's right to jury service was gaining momentum. At the 1930 PPWC, the American group promised to pressure the U.S. Congress on behalf of the women of Hawai'i.[103] In January 1932, the HLWV was elated to hear that Victor Stewart Kaleoaloha Houston (R), Territorial Delegate to the U.S. Congress, reintroduced a bill to amend Hawai'i's Organic Act to allow women to serve on juries. In February, HLWV leaders welcomed the news from NLWV president Belle Sherwin, and the bill quickly rallied mainland women's support. At the time, however, they did not question Thalia Massie's allegation. Rather, they saw the allegation and acquittal of the five men as "an excellent basis for pressing the juror bill."[104] Furthermore, when Hawaiʻi's territorial status was in jeopardy due to the Massie Affair, the HLWV, whose members became primarily white by then, prioritized protecting Hawaiʻi's territorial status over confronting mainland racism. The HLWV took a stand against any implication of abridging Hawaiʻi's territorial status. They adopted a resolution in November 1932 to petition the national office to change a section of the NLWV bylaws from "Hawaiʻi and other Territorial Dependences" to "Hawaiʻi and other territories."[105] In December 1932, the HLWV adopted another resolution to protest any action on the part of the federal government or the adoption of any bills in Congress that would change Hawaiʻi's territorial form of government.[106]

With the startling development of the Massie Affair, Princess Abigail Kawānanakoa (wife of late Prince Kūhiō), who had once expressed sympathy for Thalia Massie, publicly opposed the commutation given to the Kahahawai murderers and the U.S. legal system's double standard: "one for the favored few and the other, for the mass."[107] According to historian David E. Stannard, the Massie Affair cracked the monolith of oligarchic Republican rule, allowing voices against the powerful business oligarchy to be heard. The Massie Affair further convinced people from diverse backgrounds that their common interests were more important than their differences.[108] In addition, surging numbers of born-in-Hawaiʻi Asian youth, who had reached voting age, joined the Democratic Party and contributed to shaking Republican dominance in island politics. With a record number of local nonwhites voting in 1933, an unprecedented number of Democrats and an equally remarkable number of Asians swept into office.[109] Because of the changing political dynamics, when HLWV's vice president Gertrude M. Damon publicly supported Republican Victor S. K. Houston in the 1932 election, it caused controversy. Gertrude Scott Straub claimed the HLWV officer's partisanship violated the NLWV's nonpartisan principle. The HLWV slowly lost its membership, ceased its activity, and disbanded in May 1936.[110]

Hawaiʻi's women leaders deepened their recognition that the endeavors to build pan-Pacific feminist consciousness still rested on the subliminal terrain which looked up to the modern advanced Anglo-Saxon "civilization" of metropoles. At the same time, PPWC organizers realized that each settler community in Hawaiʻi looked to their respective homeland's metropole for ethnic pride and identity. They were inspired to focus their renewed efforts on peoples from diverse backgrounds in Hawai'i and the Pacific in an attempt at mutual understanding and pan-Pacific women's solidarity. The 1934 PPWC official conference proceedings for the first time listed the Korean delegation on the participant list, despite the Japanese government's opposition.[111] At the same time, possibly pressed by Japan and its local settler community in Hawai'i, PPWC organizers assigned (Constance) Tsune(ko) Yamada Gauntlett to take leadership in mending the strained international relationships in the Asian northeast and easing interethnic tensions in Hawai'i. According to Gauntlett, the day before the election, she was invited by Julie Judd Swanzy, who was at her residence due to illness, and asked about her intention of assuming the presidency if she was elected. Although Gauntlett was reluctant since it would be a large burden to bear, Swanzy insisted that it was time to have an "Oriental" president. After consultation with Yasutaro Soga, the PPU-active publisher of *Nippu Jiji*, a Japanese newspaper in Honolulu, Gauntlett was persuaded to assume the role.[112] At the third PPWC in 1934, held under the international chairpersonship of Australian Georgina Sweet, nine out of ten participating countries voted for Gauntlett as the international president for the fourth PPWC. Despite strong opposition from the Chinese delegation, Gauntlett saw that clarifying what she perceived as a foreign "misunderstanding" of Japanese acts was her patriotic duty, especially after Japan's withdrawal from the League of Nations in opposition to its resolution denouncing Japan's military invasion of China in 1932.[113] As the PPWA bylaws stipulated a quorum in order to convene a PPWC, securing the attendance of the Chinese delegation to the fourth PPWC in 1937 became her first task. Gauntlett, along with PPWA's honorary secretary Ann Satterthwaite, went to great lengths to achieve it.

Nonetheless, the trans-Pacific women's community's condescending attitude in promoting transnational sisterhood placed Chinese internationalists in even more difficult positions. Chinese YWCA General Secretary Shu-ching Ting, after attending the National Convention of the Japan YWCA in 1935 as a representative of the World YWCA, died suddenly in 1936.[114] According to historian Elizabeth A. Littell-Lamb, Ting "came away" from the Japan YWCA's convention "with renewed hope, because the Japanese women she met had been eager to know the truth about the situation on the Chinese mainland, which their own press failed to report." She felt that "a spirit of friendship had permeated their discussion of the difficult subject of Japanese aggression."[115] Nonetheless, she had to face the unchanging reality in China. Historian Karen Garner attributed Ting's death to her trip to the Japan YWCA convention, which "took a toll on her physical and emotional health."[116]

Gauntlett, who was kept oblivious about Japan's military conduct and atrocities by government press control, pursued her faith in transnational Christian sisterhood. In early 1937, she traveled to China to visit the urban industrial centers of Shanghai, Nanjing, and Beijing to persuade Chinese leaders to send a delegation to the fourth PPWC. Although she was unable to fully unshackle herself from the Japanese version of the racialist idea of "civilization," her tour and exchanges with Chinese women exposed her to the essence of China's great civilization from which Japanese culture had developed. She realized the need for the Japanese to correct their "ingratitude" to the civilization, now staggering through modern nation-building efforts.[117] Consequently, Anna Kong Mei, who had her residence destroyed by Japan's air raids on Shanghai in 1932, was obliged to lead the Chinese delegation to the fourth PPWC, as she had high positions in various international and transnational women's organizations, including the Shanghai Joint Committee, the World and Chinese YWCA, and the PPWC's China Preparation Committee.[118] In advance, she sought the Conference Committee's assurance that the PPWC would not be used by Japan as a means to have "Manchukuo" recognized as an independent country.[119]

The fourth PPWC convened in Vancouver, Canada, in July 1937 under the theme, "Practical Ways and Means of Promoting Peace." It gathered delegates from eight countries. Held outside of Hawai'i for the first time, the primary leadership changed hands from those in Hawai'i and the U.S. mainland to those in the British Dominions. Tsune Gauntlett was determined to do her best to fulfill her role but was shocked to see the front-page news of Japan's massive aggression in China's northeast on the morning of the second conference day. The CNP and the CCP had been negotiating with each other about cooperating against Japanese attacks since late 1936. Now Japan's action facilitated the process, triggering an all-out war between Japan and a united China.[120] According to the Australian delegate Doris McRae, "The Chinese women were weeping, and they were comforted by the Japanese women. 'It [was] not the people who [were] fighting each other, but our governments,' they said to each other."[121]

Nonetheless, the fourth PPWC's concern with Japan's military aggression in China was upended by another surprising event staged by a group of African Americans.[122] Although published records written by Gauntlett have no mention of it, the official minutes of the conference had the following one-paragraph record of the event in the section that reported on roundtable discussions on the Technique of Developing Public Opinion, chaired by American Josephine Schain (1890–1920), the NCCCW chair (in office, 1936–1941): "At the final forum, a representative of the Negro race made an appeal to international women to 'join hands and hearts together and find the cause of the broken peace.' She urged the right of dark people everywhere to be considered a free people 'to have equal opportunity for education and equal chance to develop in every direction.'"[123]

The representative was Pearl B. Sherrod (Mrs. Pearl Takasaki), who made an unannounced appearance at the conference site to bring up the issue of racial violence in the United States. Historian Fiona Paisley found the conference diary of New Zealander Elsie Andrews, the PPWA's program chair in the 1930s. Sherrod led a well-dressed African American women's group from Detroit, which arrived in a chauffeur-driven car. Andrews wrote about the stir caused by their appearance and the shiver she felt when she saw press clippings on lynching brought by Sherrod's group.[124] The *Vancouver News Herald* covered the incident and Pearl Sherrod's speech. According to its article, she stated that "the dark nation" should be able to make "the same claim to be called men as the Europeans themselves" and that it was unreasonable for one to dominate the other. She also asked in her address:

> Have you stopped to consider that injustice has caused nations to grow restless. Injustice has been the cause of many innocent men to lose their lives without even a fair trial. Discrimination and injustice are causing a confusion all over the universe. Now I am appealing to you international women to let us join hand and heart together and find the cause of the broken peace which is injustice and discrimination and let us kill the germ of it. Then, and only then, will we cure the pain of war and have peace all over the world when justice is given all mankind.[125]

Sherrod's presence and address not only shifted participants' attention away from Japan's military aggression in China but also created room for Chinese and Japanese delegates to imagine themselves as fellow Asians of the "dark race."

Sherrod's antilynching speech challenged the PPWC's diplomatic scheme to transcend racial, ethnic, cultural, and national differences to build women's common ground and solidarity. It awakened the participants to Black people's experiences, but the 1937 PPWC failed to take a stand against lynching Black people. Still, Sherrod's action gave another lesson to realize multiple and multilayered inequality and injustices among multiracializing and multiethnicizing populations under globalization pressure. Canadian Violet McNaughton, who reported about the Technique of Developing Public Opinion roundtable discussion, mentioned the "not-identical" status of modern development and public opinion building and the need to study "the degree to which world opinion influences national thought, questions of racial feeling and historical background." She also called for "serious thought" in "deciding whether a common platform can be found in all the countries upon which to build up a 'Pan-Pacific public opinion.'"[126] In fact, many recognized the necessity to continue cross-cultural interactions, share experiences, and further diversify participants. Speaking about the past four PPWCs in general, former international chair Georgina Sweet described delegates to the PPWCs as "women of high intellect, trained minds, and wide experience in world affairs." She wrote that "some of these conferences [had] shown how, in spite of difficulties and tensions in political, international, and inter-racial relationships, a determined will to understand one another's difficulties and a friendly attitude [had] enabled the spirit of appreciation and goodwill to bring about a real friendliness of thought and feeling."[127] The Vancouver conference subsequently decided to convene a fifth PPWC in New Zealand in 1940.[128] Sadly, the fifth PPWC only convened in 1949, after World War II.

Epilogue

In the modern phase of globalization, pioneer missionary women from the northeast United States successfully used women's separate sphere strategy for transracial exchanges and networking to build women's solidarity. This strategy was effective in transcending the boundaries of class, race, and nation in expanding "woman's work for woman and children" toward and across the Pacific. Nonetheless, the trans-Pacific women's community that resulted in the early twentieth century was not demarcated by a gender line to replace the Du Bois-advocated global color line. As Amy Kaplan observed, it represented "a network of power relations that change[d] over space and time and [was] riddled with instability, ambiguity, and disorder, rather than as a monolithic system of domination."[1]

Women's solidarity building was complicit with multiracial and multinational capitalist-industrialist ventures that rested on global movements of peoples, goods, and ideas. Committed to women's separate sphere strategy, they successfully built "women's dominions" in male-dominant empires that exploited native resources and settler labor. Missionaries' faith in the almighty Anglo-Saxon ways contributed to white settler colonialism and U.S. imperialism but waned through interactions with native and settler peoples whom they encountered. Under accelerating globalization pressure that prompted multiple forms of settler colonialism, nationalism, imperialism, and countercolonialism/imperialism in the Pacific, missionaries' descendants, collaborators, and protégés came together to build common ground among the fast multiracializing and multinationalizing population at various globalization hubs in the region. During the interwar years, they aspired to collaborate with Atlantic-based women leaders to have pan-Pacific women's voices reflected in the opening of the international arena for women.

Women leaders, who sought agendas to advance the status of women from diverse backgrounds in Hawai'i and the Pacific, recognized the difficulty and the need for venues for their friendly exchanges. Accordingly, the pan-Pacific women's community avoided controversy, which proved to be slow and insufficient in correcting myriad forms of inequality and injustices. Their commitment to the separate sphere strategy also propagated the "cult of womanhood" and the white middle-class ideals of companionate marriage and "home" as a woman's autonomous space, which assured Anglo-Saxon cultural authority and women's dependence in the modern phase of globalization. Nonetheless, the Pan-Pacific Women's Association (PPWA), which resulted from ongoing "woman's work for woman and children" was resilient to the turbulent 1930s and 1950s. It sustained its potential to participate in global feminism of the contemporary era. Among the three international organizations formed in Honolulu in the early twentieth century—the Pan-Pacific Union (PPU), the Institute of Pacific Relations (IPR), and the PPWA—only the PPWA evaded the fatal blows from the Pacific War and the Cold War. Alexander Hume Ford and the PPU were slow to question the legitimacy of Japan's militarism in the 1930s and disappeared by the end of the Pacific War. The IPR moved its international secretariat from Honolulu to New York in 1934 and avoided Japan's influence but fell victim to the Red Scare after the Communist victory in China in 1949. Its activities ceased in the 1950s and dissolved.[2] The PPWA reorganized under a new name, the Pan-Pacific and South East Asia Women's Association (PPSEAWA), in 1955. The PPSEAWA holds Consultative Status in Category II of the United Nations (UN) Economic and Social Council (ECOSOC) and is represented at the UN, the UN Economic and Social Commission for Asia and the Pacific (ESCAP), the UN Children's Fund (UNICEF), and the UN Educational, Scientific and Cultural Organization (UNESCO).[3]

Queen Lili'uokalani did not live to see the Hawaiian Kingdom restored, but her faith in the founding principles of the United States and her brave decision not to fight the unlawful overthrow of her monarchy avoided bloodshed. People nurtured and interacted in her beloved land are becoming a force in correcting the past injustices experienced by various groups of people worldwide. For example, women with diverse feminist schemes incorporated themselves into the local, national, and international bureaucracy and politics to be a force in policymaking for their causes. Their efforts supported various intergovernmental efforts for equality and justice worldwide. Eleanor Roosevelt successfully led the UN to proclaim the Universal Declaration of Human Rights in 1948. In 1953, the UN adopted the Convention on the Political Rights of Women, pressing for women's equal rights to vote, hold public office, and exercise all public functions. Four years later, the UN Convention on the Nationality of Married Women that proclaimed women's equal right to retain or change nationality went into force. In 1957, the International Labour Organization (ILO) adopted the Indigenous and Tribal Population Convention (No. 107) for the protection and integration of Indigenous and Tribal populations in independent countries. Furthermore, the 1989 ILO's Indigenous and Tribal Peoples Convention (No. 169) was established for the protection of Indigenous and Tribal peoples' rights and the respect of their social and cultural identity.[4] These international developments added pressure on Democrat President Bill Clinton to sign the "Apology Resolution," officially known as U.S. Public Law 103-150 (107 Stat. 1510) in 1993. The resolution acknowledges that "the overthrow of the Hawaiian Kingdom occurred with the active participation of agents and citizens of the United States" and that "the Native Hawaiian people never directly relinquished to the United States their claims to their inherent sovereignty as a people over their national lands, either through the Kingdom of Hawaii or through a plebiscite or referendum."[5] Furthermore, the lasting effects of Hawai'i's maternalists' efforts with a strong emphasis on quality education for all were exemplified in nationally and internationally prominent Hawai'i-educated individuals—such as Democrat Patsy Matsu Takemoto Mink (1927–2002), the first woman of color U.S. Congresswoman (in office, 1965–1977 and 1990–2002); Haunani-Kay Trask (1949–2021), poet and educator who vocalized Indigenous peoples' demand for justice from Hawai'i; Barack Obama, who became the first African-American U.S. President; and Jennifer Doudna, one of the first U.S. woman scientists sharing the Nobel Prize.

W. E. B. Du Bois's vision for the "unity of the world" by the exploited and the oppressed to undo past injustices slowly proves its validity. Nonetheless, without shared historical memories, the shifting power relationship can also cause new social divides, contentions, and conflicts. With accelerating globalization and networking in the quest for wealth and power today, imperialism "lives not for itself, but as part of the strain and stress of the world," as Du Bois predicted and Kaplan confirmed.[6] We urgently need more dialogues and exchanges among peoples with diverse backgrounds to build common ground for mutual understanding and reconciliation.

Acknowledgments

After approximately a quarter century of obsession, this book is finally published. It was conceived in 1998 when I visited the late Yuji Ichioka at his office. There, he mentioned a conference organized by the late Sharon Ann Minichiello in Honolulu. I was intrigued by the idea of visiting Hawai'i. I wrote a proposal for a paper on the Pan-Pacific Women's Association (PPWA) about which I had developed an interest.

Since then, I have received much inspiration, encouragement, and assistance from distinguished and thoughtful individuals. I am indebted to the family members of two American citizens of Asian ancestry who actively participated in transnational and international women's solidarity-building efforts in the early twentieth century. First are Lillian Noda Yajima (1920–2022) and Lenny S. Yajima, who shared clipping collections and memories of their mother and grandmother Alice Sae Noda (1894–1964) and told me about their own experiences growing up in Hawai'i. In addition, James David Adams Jr. and Carrol A. Yuke generously opened their family records on their grandmother Anna Fojin Kong Mei (1891–1958). I am also grateful to Pan-Pacific and South-East Asian Women's Association (PASEAWA) members in Chicago and Honolulu who allowed me access to interwar-year Pan-Pacific Women's Conference (PPWC) proceedings and explained the organization's recent activities.

I owe much research gratitude to librarians and archivists in the United States, the Netherlands, and Japan—Hawai'i State Archives, Hawaii Mission

Children's Society Library and Archives, University of Hawai'i Mānoa Library and Archives, Bishop Museum Library and Archives, Hawai'i State Library, KCAA Preschools of Hawai'i Archives, Japanese Cultural Center of Hawai'i, Makiki Christian Church Archives, Swarthmore College Library and Archives, Smith College Sophia Smith Collection, Huntington Library, University of California Libraries at Los Angeles, Irvine, and Riverside, U.S. Library of Congress, U.S. National Archives and Records Administration, International Institute of Social History Archives in Amsterdam, Japan Ministry of Foreign Affairs Diplomatic Archives, Japanese Emigration to Hawai'i Museum, Yu-Ai Labor Historical Museum, Ichikawa Fusae Center for Women and Governance Library, Japan YWCA Tokyo Office, Japan Women's University Library, Kobe College Library, Tokyo University Library, Kyoto Prefectural Library, Kyoto City Library, Konan University Library, Doshisha University Library, and Japan National Diet Library.

I wrote bit by bit whenever I had time and tried to tell a cohesive story, but I faced enormous challenges. I am fortunate to have received academic guidance and inspiration from superb thinkers. Conversations with Judy Tzu-Chan Wu, Karen Leong, Myla Vicenti Carpio, Liette Gidlow, Bonnie G. Smith, and Nova Robinson through writing projects pushed me through muddy waters. I also received warm encouragement and suggestions from Ellen C. DuBois, Valerie J. Matsumoto, Eileen Boris, Meda Chesney Lind, Yuki Terazawa, Jin-kyung Lee, Rui Kohiyama, Maso Oota, Rebecca Mead, and Sarah Griffith. Members of the North America Ethnicity Study Group (Hokubei esunishitī kenkyūkai) and Tanaka Kikuyo's Study Group listened to and commented on my presentations in Japanese at various stages of this project. I am also grateful for comments and suggestions from Judy Tzu-Chun Wu, Brian M. Hayashi, Lisa Materson, Donna M. Binkiewicz, Sarah Pripas-Kapit, Catherine Ceniza Choy, and Sarah Griffith, and Robert Sauté, who read the entire manuscript in progress. Noriko Ishii, Sherry Vatter, Elena K. Abbot, Brian Niiya, and Karen Umemoto read a portion of the manuscript in progress. Their consultations and encouragement sustained my spirit to keep working. At the final stage, Columbia University Press senior editor Stephen Wesley supported and facilitated my writing and publication. I could not bring my diverging stories into one coherent work without Columbia University Press's anonymous reviewers' constructive and thoughtful criticisms. My manuscript became legible through careful, patient, and responsible editing by Robert Sauté, Kalie Hyatt, and her editorial team.

I am also grateful to Mire Koikari, Meda Chesney Lind, Kathy Ferguson, and Aya Kimura of University of Hawai'i Mānoa's Women, Gender, and Sexuality Studies Department, who hosted my one-year sabbatical in Hawai'i; and Brian Hayashi and Elaine Frantz Parsons of the Kent State University History Department, who hosted my half-year sabbatical in Ohio. I had enjoyable and fruitful sabbatical time with support and care provided by Alison Uyeda, Jeff and Andrew Okamoto in Honolulu, Hawai'i, and Brian Hayashi, Yu-Mei Song, and Esther Hayashi in Kent, Ohio.

My research was made possible by Konan University faculty research and library funds and Japan Grants-in-Aid for Scientific Research (JPS *Kakenhi* grant numbers 18401027, 24510362, and 18K01055).

I thank my family, who endured over two decades of my obsession, for their support and patience. My late father Susumu Yasutake, my mother Fumiko Yasutake, and my late mother-in-law Kinuko "Kay" Arikawa, *Nisei* daughter from the Big Island, were always supportive and encouraging. My sister-in-law Constance Inouye helped me in doing research in Hawai'i. This book is indebted to my husband August Y. Arikawa, who read countless versions of the manuscript in progress. He edited my English and straightened my writing with his logical thinking throughout. I also owe a great deal to his computer wizardry. To him, who sustained my ups and downs in this long journey, I dedicate this book.

I am grateful to the respective publishers and journals for their generosity and permission, with which I adopted and developed materials from my past publications for this book.

Chapter 1, material from Rumi Yasutake, "Re-Franchising Women of Hawai'i, 1912–1920: The Politics of Gender, Sovereignty, Race, and Rank at the Crossroads of the Pacific," in *Gendering the Trans-Pacific World*, ed. Catherine Ceniza Choy and Judy Tzu-Chun Wu (Boston: Brill, 2017), 114–39; "Hawaiian Nationalism, American Patriotism, and Re-franchising Women in Post-Annexation Hawai'i, 1912–1920," *Konan daigaku kiyō bungakuhen* [*Journal of Konan University: Faculty of Letters*] 165 (March 2014): 119–26; and "Hawai no Amerikaka ni tomonau seijiteki yūkensha no danseika oyobi hakujinka, 1820–1898," *Konan daigaku kiyō bungakuhen* [*Journal of Konan University: Faculty of Letters*] 160 (March 2010): 103–12.

Chapter 2, material from Rumi Yasutake, "Women in Hawai'i and the Nineteenth Amendment," *Journal of Women's History* 32, no. 1 (Spring 2020): 32–40.

Chapter 3, material from Rumi Yasutake, "Nationality, Citizenship, and Post-Suffrage Movements in the Atlantic and the Pacific," *Konan daigaku sōgō kenkyūsho sōsho [Konan Institute Research Series]: Movements of Women Across Nations and Their Effects on Nation-States and International Relationships* 131 (2018): 87–106.

Chapters 4 and 5, material from Rumi Yasutake, "The Rise of Women's Internationalism in the Countries of the Asia-Pacific Region During the Interwar Years, from a Japanese Perspective," *Women's History Review* 20, no. 4 (September 2011): 521–32; and "The First Wave of International Women's Movements from a Japanese Perspective: Western Outreach and Japanese Women Activists During the Interwar Years," *Women's Studies International Forum* 32, no. 1 (2009): 13–20.

Abbreviations

AAUW	American Association of University Women
ABCFM	American Board of Commissioners for Foreign Missions
AFL	American Federation of Labor
AWSA	American Woman Suffrage Association
CCP	Chinese Communist Party
CND	Council of National Defense
CNP	Chinese Nationalist Party
DOH	Daughters of Hawai'i
	Aloha-DOH (in Hawai'i)
DPI	Department of Public Instruction (Territory of Hawai'i)
DSHW	Daughters and Sons of Hawaiian Warriors (Māmakakaua)
ERA	Equal Rights Amendment
FBI	Federal Bureau of Investigation
FCC	Federal Council of Churches of Christ in America
FKCAAHI	Free Kindergarten and Children's Aid Association of the Hawaiian Islands
HEA	Hawaiian Evangelical Association
HLWV	League of Women Voters of the Territory of Hawai'i

HSPA	Hawaiian Sugar Planters Association
ICW	International Council of Women
ICWW	International Congress of Working Women
IES	Imperial Education Society (Teikoku Kyōiku Kai) (Japan)
IFSCM	International Federation of Student Christian Movement
IFTU	International Federation of Trade Unions
IFUW	International Federation of University Women
IFWW	International Federation of Working Women
ILC	International Labour Conference
ILO	International Labour Organization
IPR	Institute of Pacific Relations
IWSA	International Woman Suffrage Alliance
IWW	Industrial Workers of the World
JBS	Japanese Benevolent Society (Nihonjin Jizenkai) (Hawai'i)
JCSWC	Joint Committee of the Shanghai Women's Clubs
JCSWO	Joint Committee of the Shanghai Women's Organizations (Shanghai Joint Committee)
JMoAC	Japan Ministry of Agriculture and Commerce
JMoE	Japan Ministry of Education
JMoFA	Japan Ministry of Foreign Affairs
JMoHA	Japan Ministry of Home Affairs
JSCWIO	Joint Standing Committee of the Women's International Organizations (Geneva)
JWCIR	Japan Women's Committee for International Relations (Kokusai Renraku Fujin Iinkai)
JWPA	Japan Women's Peace Association (Japan WILPF, Nihon Fujin Heiwa Kyōkai)
JWS	Japanese Women's Society (Nihonjin Fujinkai) (Hawai'i)
JWU	Japan Women's University
LCWIO	Liaison Committee of Women's International Organizations (Geneva)
LNA	League of Nations Association (Kokusai Renmei Kyōkai) (Japan)

LWV	League of Women Voters
NAWSA	National American Woman Suffrage Association
NCCC	National Christian Council in China
NCCCW	National Conference on the Cause and Cure of War
NCCIL	National Committee for Constructive Immigration Legislation
NCL	National Consumers' League
NFPSTA	National Federation of Primary School Teachers' Association (Zenkoku Shōgakkō Rengō Jokyōinkai) (Japan)
NLWV	National League of Women Voters
NWF	National Women's Federation (Zenkoku Fujin Dōmei) (Japan)
NWP	National Woman's Party
NWS	New Women's Society (Shin Fujin Kyōkai) (Japan)
NWSA	National Woman Suffrage Association
PAU	Pan-American Union
PPA	Pan-Pacific Association (China)
PPCERRR	Pan Pacific Conference on Education, Rehabilitation, Reclamation, and Recreation
PPSEAWA	Pan-Pacific and South East Asia Women's Association
PPU	Pan-Pacific Union
PPWA	Pan-Pacific Women's Association
PPWC	Pan-Pacific Women's Conference
PTA	National Congress of Mothers and Parent-Teacher Association
SACJA	Society of American Citizens of Japanese Ancestry
SCM	Student Christian Movement
SMC	Shanghai Municipal Council
TFWO	Tokyo Federation of Women's Organizations (Tokyo Fujin Rengōkai)
TWCC	Tokyo Woman's Christian College
UN	United Nations
UWWC	United War Work Campaign
WBMI-Chicago	Woman's Board of Missions of the Interior (Chicago)

WBMPI-Honolulu	Woman's Board of Missions for the Pacific Islands (Honolulu)
WCTU	Woman's Christian Temperance Union
WESAH	Women's Equal Suffrage Association of Hawaiʻi
WILPF	Women's International League for Peace and Freedom
WJCC	Women's Joint Congressional Committee
WRAC	Women's Republican Auxiliary Club
WSAH	Women's Suffrage Association of Hawaiʻi
WSCF	World Student Christian Federation
WSL	Women's Suffrage League (Fujin Sanseiken Kakutoku Kisei Dōmeikai, later renamed Fusen Kakutoku Dōmei) (Japan)
WTUL	Women's Trade Union League
YMCA	Young Men's Christian Association
YWCA	Young Women's Christian Association

Notes

Introduction

1. Jane Addams, "Reflections on the First Pan-Pacific Women's Conference," *Women of the Pacific: Being a Record of the Proceedings of the Second Pan-Pacific Women's Conference* [hereafter *Women of the Pacific*] *Which Was Held in Honolulu from the 19th to the 22nd of August 1930, Under the Auspices of the Pan-Pacific Union* (Honolulu, HI: Pan-Pacific Union, 1933), ix–x.
2. In this book, the term "Native Hawaiian" refers both to full-blood (Hawaiian) and mixed-blood (part-Hawaiian) people who identified themselves as Hawaiians. Some scholars advocate using "Kanaka Maori," which displaces the blood-based definition. Still, this term also accompanies complicated debates over sovereignty, indigenous rights, and cultural autonomy. According to the State of Hawai'i Office of Native Hawaiian Affairs' definition, "native Hawaiian" with a lowercase "n" refers to individuals with 50 percent or more Hawaiian blood; "Native Hawaiian" with a capital "N" refers to all persons of Hawaiian ancestry regardless of blood quantum. "Racial-Ethnic Identification," in *OHA Contents 2021: Appendix Data Book*, August 20, 2023, http://www.ohadatabook.com/go_appendix.21.html.
3. Andrew William Lind, *Hawaii's People* (Honolulu: University of Hawai'i Press, 1955), 27. For discussions on Asian roles in U.S. colonial rule in Hawai'i, see Candace Fujikane and Jonathan Y. Okamura, eds., *Asian Settler Colonialism: From Local Governance to the Habits of Everyday Life in Hawai'i* (Honolulu: University of Hawai'i Press, 2008).

4. Barbara Del Piano, *Nā Lani Kaumaka/Daughters of Hawai'i: A Century of Historic Preservation* (Honolulu: Daughters of Hawaii, 2005), 111–16; United States National Park Service, "Hulihee Palace," in NP Gallery Digital Asset Management System, August 19, 2023, https://npgallery.nps.gov/NRHP/GetAsset/NRHP/73000653_text.
5. J. Patricia Morgan Swenson, "Swanzy, Julie Judd," in *Notable Women of Hawaii*, ed. Barbara Bennett Peterson (Honolulu: University of Hawai'i Press, 1984), 361–64; Tom Coffman, *Nation Within: The Story of America's Annexation of the Nation of Hawai'i* (Kāne'ohe, HI: Epicenter, 1998), 283.
6. Roger G. Rose, Sheila Conant, and Eric P. Kjellgren, "Hawaiian Standing Kāhili in the Bishop Museum: An Ethnological and Biological Analysis," *Journal of the Polynesian Society* 102, no. 3 (1993): 273–304.
7. Del Piano, *Nā Lani Kaumaka*, 111–16.
8. Gary Y. Okihiro, *Common Ground: Reimagining American History* (Princeton, NJ: Princeton University Press, 2001), xii.
9. "List of Delegates According to Countries," *Women of the Pacific* (1928), 278–80; "A Glimpse of the Past," *Women of the Pacific* (1949), 14–15.
10. Mrs. Francis M. Swanzy, "Greetings," *Women of the Pacific* (1928), 8.
11. Patricia Grimshaw, *Paths of Duty: American Missionary Wives in Nineteenth-Century Hawaii* (Honolulu: University of Hawai'i Press, 1989); Davianna Pōmaika'i McGregor, "Constructed Images of Native Hawaiian Women," in *Asian/Pacific Islander American Women: A Historical Anthology*, ed. Shirley Hune and Gail M. Nomura (New York: New York University Press, 2003), 25–32.
12. Paul F. Hooper, *Elusive Destiny: The Internationalist Movement in Modern Hawaii* (Honolulu: University of Hawai'i Press, 1980), 65–136; Brian Hayashi, "From Race to Nation: The Institute of Pacific Relations, Asian Americans, and George Blakeslee, from 1908 to 1929," *Japanese Journal of American Studies* 23 (2012): 51–71.
13. Linda K. Kerber, *Women of the Republic: Intellect and Ideology in Revolutionary America* (Chapel Hill: University of North Carolina Press, 1980); Mary Beth Norton, *Liberty's Daughters: The Revolutionary Experience of American Women, 1750–1800* (Ithaca, NY: Cornell University Press, 1996).
14. Grimshaw, *Paths of Duty*.
15. Robyn Muncy, *Creating a Female Dominion in American Reform, 1890–1935* (New York: Oxford University Press, 1991); Molly Ladd-Taylor, *Mother-Work: Women, Child Welfare, and the State, 1890–1930* (Urbana: University of Illinois Press, 1994); Kathleen A. Laughlin, *Women's Work and Public Policy: A History of the Women's Bureau, U.S. Department of Labor, 1945–1970* (Boston: Northeastern University Press, 2000); Ian R. Tyrrell, *Reforming the World: The Creation of America's Moral Empire* (Princeton, NJ: Princeton University Press, 2010); Cathleen

C. Cahill, *Federal Fathers and Mothers* (Chapel Hill: University of North Carolina Press, 2011); Margaret D. Jacobs, *White Mother to a Dark Race: Settler Colonialism, Maternalism, and the Removal of Indigenous Children in the American West and Australia, 1880–1940* (Lincoln: University of Nebraska Press, 2009).

16. Manfred B. Steger, *Globalization: A Very Short Introduction* (Oxford: Oxford University Press, 2020), 1–37; Sebastian Conrad, *What Is Global History?* (Princeton, NJ: Princeton University Press, 2017); Kathy E. Ferguson and Monique Mironesco, eds., *Gender and Globalization in Asia and the Pacific: Method Practice Theory* (Honolulu: University of Hawai'i Press, 2008), 1–12.

17. Amy Kaplan, *The Anarchy of Empire in the Making of U.S. Culture* (Cambridge, MA: Harvard University Press, 2002), 12–22, 178–212.

18. W. E. B. Du Bois, *Darkwater: Voices from Within the Veil* (New York: Washington Square Press, 1920), cited in Kaplan, *The Anarchy of Empire in the Making of U.S. Culture*, 210.

19. Kaplan, *The Anarchy of Empire in the Making of U.S. Culture*, 12–22, 178–212.

20. Robert Bickers and Christian Henriot, eds., *New Frontiers: Imperialism's New Communities in East Asia, 1842–1953* (Manchester: Manchester University Press, 2000); Isabella Jackson, *Shaping Modern Shanghai: Colonialism in China's Global City* (Cambridge: Cambridge University Press, 2017); Joseph M. Henning, *Outposts of Civilization: Race, Religion, and the Formative Years of American-Japanese Relations* (New York: New York University Press, 2000).

21. Sarah Marie Griffith, *The Fight for Asian American Civil Rights: Liberal Protestant Activism, 1900–1950* (Urbana: University of Illinois Press, 2018); David A. Hollinger, *Protestant Abroad: How Missionaries Tried to Change the World but Changed America* (Princeton, NJ: Princeton University Press, 2017); Hayashi, "From Race to Nation," 51–71.

22. Shirley Hune and Gail M. Nomura, eds., *Asian/Pacific Islander American Women: A Historical Anthology* (New York: New York University Press, 2003); Ferguson and Mironesco, *Gender and Globalization in Asia and the Pacific*; Catherine Ceniza Choy and Judy Tzu-Chun Wu, eds., *Gendering the Trans-Pacific World* (Boston: Brill, 2017).

23. Paul F. Hooper, "Feminism in the Pacific: The Pan-Pacific and South Asia Women's Association," *Pacific Historian* 20, no. 4 (1976): 367–77.

24. Angela Woollacott, "Inventing Commonwealth and Pan-Pacific Feminisms: Australian Women's Internationalist Activism in the 1920s–30s," in *Feminisms and Internationalism*, ed. Mrinalini Sinha, Donna Guy, and Angela Woollacott (Oxford: Blackwell, 1999), 81–104.

25. Fiona Paisley, *Glamour in the Pacific: Cultural Internationalism and Race Politics in the Women's Pan-Pacific* (Honolulu: University of Hawai'i Press, 2009); Fiona Paisley, "Cultivating Modernity: Culture and Internationalism in Australian Feminism's Pacific Age," *Journal of Women's History* 14, no. 3 (2002): 105–32.

26. Dorothy Sue Cobble, *For the Many: American Feminists and the Global Fight for Democratic Equality* (Princeton, NJ: Princeton University Press, 2021), 134–36.
27. Margaret H. McFadden, *Golden Cables of Sympathy: The Transatlantic Sources of Nineteenth-Century Feminism* (Louisville: Kentucky University Press, 1999); Leila J. Rupp, *Worlds of Women: The Making of an International Women's Movement* (Princeton, NJ: Princeton University Press, 1997); Ellen Carol DuBois, *Feminism and Suffrage: The Emergence of an Independent Women's Movement in America, 1848–1869* (Ithaca, NY: Cornell University Press, 1978); Lisa G. Materson, *For the Freedom of Her Race: Black Women and Electoral Politics in Illinois, 1877–1932* (Chapel Hill: University of North Carolina Press, 2009); Rebecca J. Mead, *How the Vote Was Won: Woman Suffrage in the Western United States, 1868–1914* (New York: New York University Press, 2004); Allison L. Sneider, *Suffragists in an Imperial Age: U.S. Expansion and the Woman Question, 1870–1929* (New York: Oxford University Press, 2008).
28. Kwok Pui-Lan, *Chinese Women and Christianity, 1860–1927* (Atlanta, GA: Scholars Press, 1992); Rumi Yasutake, *Transnational Women's Activism: The United States, Japan, and Japanese Immigrant Communities in California, 1859–1920* (New York: New York University Press, 2004); Noriko Kawamura Ishii, *American Women Missionaries at Kobe College, 1873–1909* (New York: Routledge, 2004); Motoe Sasaki, *Redemption and Revolution: American and Chinese New Women in the Early Twentieth Century* (Ithaca, NY: Cornell University Press, 2016); Barbara Reeves-Ellington, Kathryn Kish Sklar, and Connie Anne Shemo, eds., *Competing Kingdoms: Women, Mission, Nation, and the American Protestant Empire, 1812–1960* (Durham, NC: Duke University Press, 2010); Dana L. Robert, ed., *Converting Colonialism: Visions and Realities in Mission History, 1706–1914* (Grand Rapids, MI: William B. Eerdmans, 2008).
29. Liette Gidlow, *The Big Vote: Gender, Consumer Culture, and the Politics of Exclusion, 1890s–1920s* (Baltimore, MD: Johns Hopkins University, 2004); Sneider, *Suffragists in an Imperial Age*; Jacqueline Van Voris, *Carrie Chapman Catt: A Public Life* (New York: Feminist Press, 1987).
30. Ladd-Taylor, *Mother-Work*; Laughlin, *Women's Work*; Cobble, *For the Many*.
31. Mona L. Siegel, *Peace on Our Terms: The Global Battle for Women's Rights After the First World War* (New York: Columbia University Press, 2020); Cobble, *For the Many*; Woollacott, "Inventing Commonwealth and Pan-Pacific Feminisms"; Marie Sandell, *The Rise of Women's Transnational Activism: Identity and Sisterhood Between the World Wars* (London: I. B. Tauris, 2015); Karen Garner, *Shaping a Global Women's Agenda: Women's NGOs and Global Governance, 1925–1985* (Manchester: Manchester University Press, 2010); Louise Edwards and Mina Roces, eds., *Women's Suffrage in Asia: Gender, Nationalism, and Democracy* (London: RoutledgeCurzon, 2004).

1. Women's Separate Sphere and White Settler Colonialism

1. Glen Grant, "Introduction," in Liliuokalani, *Hawaii's Story by Hawaii's Queen* (Honolulu, HI: Mutual, 1990), vii–xiii.
2. Wilcox had also led an insurrection in 1889 to oppose the "reform" administration and its constitution of 1887, which King Kalākaua had been forced to sign at bayonet point. A. Grove Day, *History Makers of Hawaii: A Biographical Dictionary* (Honolulu, HI: Mutual, 1984), 127–28.
3. Ben Hyams and E. Curtis Cluff Jr., *Centennial Memoirs of the Pacific Club in Honolulu, from 1851 to 1951* (Honolulu, HI: Pacific Club in Honolulu, 1951), 48–49; Clifford Putney, *Missionaries in Hawai'i: The Lives of Peter and Fanny Gulick, 1797–1883* (Amherst: University of Massachusetts Press, 2010), 98–99.
4. Liliuokalani, *Hawaii's Story by Hawaii's Queen*, 273–77.
5. Liliuokalani, *Hawaii's Story by Hawaii's Queen*, 275–76.
6. Kathleen M. Brown, "Brave New Worlds: Women's and Gender History," *William and Mary Quarterly* 50, no. 2 (April 1993): 317–18.
7. Elizabeth Kieszkowski, ed., *Nā Hale Hō'ike'ike o Nā Mikanele* (Honolulu, HI: Mission Houses Museum, 2001), 1–14, 43–44.
8. Nancy F. Cott, *The Bonds of Womanhood: "Woman's Sphere" in New England, 1780–1835* (New Haven, CT: Yale University Press, 1977); Patricia Grimshaw, *Paths of Duty: American Missionary Wives in Nineteenth-Century Hawaii* (Honolulu: University of Hawai'i Press, 1989); Judith R. Gething, "Christianity and Coverture: Impact on the Legal Status of Women in Hawaii, 1820–1920," *Hawaiian Journal of History* 11 (1977): 188–220. See also Dana L. Robert, *American Women in Mission: A Social History of Their Thought and Practice* (Macon, GA: Mercer University Press, 1996).
9. For the history of Hawai'i from a kingdom to statehood, see Jonathan Kay Kamakawiwoʻole Osorio, *Dismembering Lāhui: A History of the Hawaiian Nation to 1887* (Honolulu: University of Hawai'i Press, 2002); Noenoe K. Silva, *Aloha Betrayed: Native Hawaiian Resistance to American Colonialism* (Durham, NC: Duke University Press, 2004); Ralph S. Kuykendall, *The Hawaiian Kingdom*, Vols. I–III (Honolulu: University of Hawai'i Press, 1938, 1953, 1967); Lawrence H. Fuchs, *Hawaii Pono "Hawaii the Excellent": An Ethnic and Political History* (Honolulu, HI: Bess, 1961); Gavan Daws, *Shoal of Time: A History of the Hawaiian Islands* (Honolulu: University of Hawai'i Press, 1968); Ralph S. Kuykendall and A. Grove Day, eds. *Hawaii: A History, from Polynesian Kingdom to American Statehood* (Englewood Cliffs, NJ: Prentice-Hall, 1976); Tom Coffman, *Nation Within: The Story of America's Annexation of the Nation of Hawai'i* (Kāneʻohe, HI: Epicenter,

1998). Sociohistorical and cultural overviews of Hawai'i are also provided by Japanese scholars such as Yujin Yaguchi and Yumiko Nakajima.
10. Gething, "Christianity and Coverture," 188–220; Patricia Grimshaw, "New England Missionary Wives, Hawaiian Women, and 'the Cult of True Womanhood,'" *Hawaiian Journal of History* 19 (1985): 71–100.
11. Silva, *Aloha Betrayed*, 93–94.
12. Davianna Pomaika'i McGregor, "Constructed Images of Native Hawaiian Women," in *Asian/Pacific Islander American Women: A Historical Anthology*, ed. Shirley Hune and Gail M. Nomura (New York: New York University Press, 2003), 31.
13. Gwenfread E. Allen, "Kaahumanu," in *Notable Women of Hawaii*, ed. Barbara Bennett Peterson (Honolulu: University of Hawai'i Press, 1984), 174–80; Kuykendall, *The Hawaiian Kingdom, Vol. I: 1778–1854*; F. Allan Hanson, "Female Pollution in Polynesia?," *Journal of the Polynesian Society* 91, no. 3 (1982): 335–83.
14. Silva, *Aloha Betrayed*, 27–35; McGregor, "Constructed Images of Native Hawaiian Women," 25–32.
15. Gething, "Christianity and Coverture," 188–93. Between 1819 and 1864, four women and two men of high ranking served as *kuhina-nui*: Ka'ahumanu (1819–1932), Kīna'u (1832–1839), Kekāuluohi (1839–1845), Keoni Ana (1845–1855), Victoria Kamāmalu (1855–1863), and Mataio Kekuānao'a (1863–1864). One of the men, Keoni Ana, was appointed to the position because Victoria Kamāmalu, Kīnau's daughter and the designated successor, was still a minor. The other was Kīnau's husband Mataio Kekuānao'a, who was appointed to the position by his son, Kamehameha V. State of Hawai'i Department of Accounting and General Services, "Centennial Exhibit," March 14, 2014, http://ags.hawaii.gov/archives/centennial-exhibit/kuhina-nui-1819-1864/.
16. Cott, *The Bonds of Womanhood*; Gething, "Christianity and Coverture," 188–93; Ellen Carol DuBois and Lynn Dumenil, *Through Women's Eyes: An American History with Documents* (Boston: Bedford/St. Martin's, 2009), 70–81.
17. Gerda Lerner, "The Lady and the Mill Girl: Changes in the Status of Women in the Age of Jackson," *Midcontinent American Studies Journal* 10, no. 1 (Spring 1969): 5–14; Gething, "Christianity and Coverture," 188–219.
18. Grimshaw, "New England Missionary Wives," 78.
19. Laura Fish Judd, *Honolulu: Sketches of Life: Social, Political, and Religious, in the Hawaiian Islands from 1828 to 1861* (New York: Anson D. F. Randolph, 1880), 36–58; Barbara Peterson, "Judd, Laura Fish," in *Notable Women of Hawaii*, 170–74.
20. Allen, "Kaahumanu," 174–80.
21. Linda K. Menton, "Cooke, Juliette Montague," in *Notable Women of Hawaii*, 83–86; Peterson, "Judd, Laura Fish," 170–74.

22. Linda K. Menton, "Christian and 'Civilized' Education: The Hawaiian Chiefs' Children's School, 1839–50," *History of Education Quarterly* 32 (Summer, 1992): 213–42; Mary A. Richards, *The Hawaiian Chiefs' Children's School, 1839–1850* (Tokyo: Charles E. Tuttle, 1970), 357–67.
23. Judd, *Honolulu*, 57, 127–28.
24. Irene was a daughter of John Papa 'Ī'ī who assisted the Cookes at the Royal School and became an attendant to Kamehameha III. David T. Brown, "Ii, Irene," in *Notable Women of Hawaii*, 156.
25. Osorio, *Dismembering Lāhui*, 13; Gething, "Christianity and Coverture," 195–97; Grimshaw, "New England Missionary Wives," 81–87.
26. McGregor, "Constructed Images of Native Hawaiian Women," 28–30; Osorio, *Dismembering Lāhui*, 9–13.
27. Robert, *American Women in Mission*, 69–70. Reverand William Richards began serving in the kingdom government in the late 1830s, followed by Dr. Gerrit P. Judd and Reverand Richard Armstrong in the 1840s.
28. "The 1839 Constitution" and "The 1840 Constitution," in Kamehameha Schools, "Ulukau: The Hawaiian Electronic Library," December 20, 2022, https://hooilina.org/cgi-bin/journal?e=p-0journal--00-0-0-004-Document---0-1--1en-50---20-docoptions-seaits+also+doodoorch-issue---001-0110escapewin&a=p&p=frameset&cl=&d=HASH0166acfd8ec6df2fa38fd161.5.1.1.
29. Osorio, *Dismembering Lāhui*, 24–30.
30. Gething, "Christianity and Coverture," 193, 197–98, 210. Under the 1840 constitution, the *kuhina-nui*'s approval was required before the "important business of the Kingdom" could be transacted; the king and the *kuhina-nui* had veto power over each other's acts. She was to be a special counselor to the king, and laws passed by the legislature had to be approved by both the king and the *kuhina-nui* before becoming law. Furthermore, the *kuhina-nui* was ex officio a member of the House of Nobles and the Supreme Court. See also Silva, *Aloha Betrayed*, 44; Osorio, *Dismembering Lāhui*, 27.
31. Benjamin O. Wist, *A Century of Public Education in Hawai'i* (Honolulu: Hawaiian Educational Review, 1940), 2.
32. Gething, "Christianity and Coverture," 201, 210; Hon. W. Frear, Associate-Justice of the Supreme Court, "The Evolution of the Hawaiian Judiciary," *Papers of the Hawaiian Historical Society* 7 (June 29, 1894), 9–10.
33. Gething, "Christianity and Coverture," 202–206.
34. Kuykendall, *The Hawaiian Kingdom, Vol. I: 1778–1854*, 287–98. The king personally managed Crown Lands until a court decision in 1864 and a statute passed in 1865 so that the lands could be kept intact for future monarchs. Jon M. Van Dyke, *Who Owns the Crown Lands of Hawai'i?* (Honolulu: University of Hawai'i Press, 2007).
35. Osorio, *Dismembering Lāhui*, 63–65.

36. McGregor, "Constructed Images of Native Hawaiian Women," 32.
37. Silva, *Aloha Betrayed*, 44; Osorio, *Dismembering Lāhui*, 67–73.
38. McGregor, "Constructed Images of Native Hawaiian Women," 31; Kuykendall and Day, *Hawaii*, 113.
39. *The Folio* (November 16, 1855), cited in Helen G. Chapin and David W. Forbes, "The Folio of 1855—A Plea for Women's Rights," *Hawaiian Journal of History* 19 (1985): 125.
40. Chapin and Forbes, "The Folio of 1855," 122–33. As for the case on the U.S. mainland, see Ellen Carol DuBois, *Feminism and Suffrage: The Emergence of an Independent Women's Movement in America, 1848–1869* (Ithaca, NY: Cornell University Press, 1978).
41. Clarence E. Glick, *Sojourners and Settlers: Chinese Migrants in Hawaiʻi* (Honolulu: University of Hawaiʻi Press, 1980), 1–4.
42. By 1909, over half of the privately owned land in Hawaiʻi fell into the hands of white corporations. Fuchs, *Hawaii Pono*, 14–24, 252.
43. Fuchs, *Hawaii Pono*, 14–24.
44. For example, Samuel M. Castle, an ABCFM financial agent who procured and distributed missionary supplies, joined other Western and Chinese merchants in exploring business opportunities in the kingdom. Castle was soon joined by Amos Starr Cooke, a former ABCFM missionary who had run the Royal School with his wife but recently lost his position when the school closed. Their business venture resulted in the incorporation of the mercantile house in 1851.
45. Glick, *Sojourners and Settlers*, 1–22.
46. Fuchs, *Hawaii Pono*, 24–25; Evelyn Nakano Glenn, "Race, Labor, and Citizenship in Hawaiʻi," in *American Dreaming, Global Realities: Rethinking U.S. Immigration History*, ed. Donna R. Gabaccia and Vicki L. Ruíz (Urbana: University of Illinois Press, 2006), 284–93; Ronald T. Takaki, *Pau Hana: Plantation Life and Labor in Hawaii, 1835–1920* (Honolulu: University of Hawaiʻi Press, 1983), 92–98.
47. Carol Silva, "The Sandwich Islands Mission," in *Nā Hale Hōʻikeʻike o Nā Mikanele*, ed. Kieszkowski, 1–8; "Evangelical Association of Congregational Christian Churches," *Honolulu Star-Bulletin*, August 13, 1962.
48. Linda A. Grzywacz, "Hawaiian Mission Children's Society," in *Nā Hale Hōʻikeʻike o Nā Mikanele*, ed. Kieszkowski, 10–14. In this organization, women and men had equal say. Chapin and Forbes, "The Folio of 1855," 124.
49. Ryo Yoshida, "Hawaian bood no shoki nihonjin imindendo, 1885–1887," *Kirisutokyō shakai mondai kenkyū*, no. 30 (1982): 132; Wayne Patterson, *The Ilse: First-Generation Korean Immigrants in Hawaiʻi, 1903–1973* (Honolulu: University of Hawaiʻi Press, 2000), 1–10.
50. Glenn, "Race, Labor, and Citizenship in Hawaiʻi," 290–91; Silva, *Aloha Betrayed*, 51–54.

51. For example, Henry Whitney, Samuel Damon, and Sanford Dole opposed the system of contract labor; Samuel N. Castle, one of the largest sugar producers of the islands, did not. Osorio, *Dismembering Lāhui*, 176; Chapin and Forbes, "The Folio of 1855," 125.
52. Glenn, "Race, Labor, and Citizenship in Hawai'i," 290–91.
53. Mary A. Richards, *The Historical Background of the Woman's Board of Missions for the Pacific Islands* [hereafter WBMPI] (Honolulu, HI: WBMPI, 1931), 5–15; Mary T. Hyde, "President Address: A Review of this Board's Work for Twenty-One Years," *Annual Report of the WBMPI* [hereafter *WBMPI Annual Report*] *21st Annual Meeting* (1892), 51–55. Both archived at the Hawai'i Mission Children's Society Library [hereafter HMCS Library]. Also see, Robert, *American Women in Mission*, 128–30.
54. Hyde, "President Address," 51–55.
55. Yoshida, "Hawaian bood no shoki nihonjin imindendo," 132–46.
56. Hyde, "President Address," 51–55.
57. Liliuokalani, *Hawaii's Story by Hawaii's Queen*, 367.
58. Alfons L. Korn and Barbara Peterson, "Emma," in *Notable Women of Hawaii*, 118–22.
59. Richard A. Greer, "Bishop, Bernice Pauahi," in *Notable Women of Hawaii*, 43–46.
60. Osorio, *Dismembering Lāhui*, 147–50.
61. Osorio, *Dismembering Lāhui*, 150.
62. Osorio, *Dismembering Lāhui*, 150–56, 166–73.
63. Silva, *Aloha Betrayed*, 88–122.
64. Osorio, *Dismembering Lāhui*, 231.
65. Coffman, *Nation Within*, 65–66; Kuykendall, *The Hawaiian Kingdom, Vol. III, 1874–1893*, 156.
66. Osorio, *Dismembering Lāhui*, 159–92.
67. Mary S. Whitney, "The President's Address," *Annual Report of the Woman's Christian Temperance Union of the Hawaiian Islands* [hereafter *Hawai'i WCTU Annual Report*], 1886–1887 (1887): 42–44; Mary S. Whitney, "A Brief History of Early Temperance Effort in the Hawaiian Islands" (1903): 22–26. HMCS Library.
68. Kuykendall, *The Hawaiian Kingdom, Vol. III, 1874–1893*, 257.
69. Frances E. Willard, *Glimpses of Fifty Years: The Autobiography of an American Woman* (Chicago: Woman's Temperance Publication Association, 1889); Ruth Bordin, *Woman and Temperance: The Quest for Power and Liberty, 1873–1900* (Philadelphia: Temple University Press, 1981).
70. Ian R. Tyrrell, *Woman's World / Woman's Empire: The Woman's Christian Temperance Union in International Perspective, 1880–1930* (Chapel Hill: University of North Carolina Press, 1991); Rumi Yasutake, *Transnational Women's Activism: The United States, Japan, and Japanese Immigrant Communities in California, 1859–1920* (New York: New York University Press, 2004).

71. "Mrs. Whitney Landed in Memorial Service for Her Good Work," *Honolulu Star-Bulletin*, February 9, 1925, 15.
72. Whitney, "A Brief History of Early Temperance Effort in the Hawaiian Islands," 26.
73. Patricia Grimshaw, "Settler Anxieties, Indigenous Peoples, and Women's Suffrage in the Colonies of Australia, New Zealand, and Hawai'i, 1888 to 1902," *Pacific Historical Review* 69, no. 4 (2000): 568.
74. Mrs. J. M. Whitney, "President's Address," *Hawai'i WCTU Annual Report, 1885–1886* (1887).
75. For example, the monarch's executive power was stripped and transferred to the legislature, and his every decision needed the approval of the cabinet; the House of Nobles was no longer subject to the king's appointment but by election, and his power to dismiss his cabinet was transferred to the legislature. Silva, *Aloha Betrayed*, 122.
76. Osorio, *Dismembering Lāhui*, 238–49; Ernest K. Wakukawa, *A History of the Japanese People in Hawai'i* (Honolulu, HI: Toyō shoin, 1938), 70–71; Roger J. Bell, *Last Among Equals: Hawaiian Statehood and American Politics* (Honolulu: University of Hawai'i Press, 1984), 25; Kuykendall, *The Hawaiian Kingdom, Vol. III, 1874–1893*, 406–407.
77. M. A. H. Green, "Report of Recording Secretary," *Hawai'i WCTU Annual Report*, 1886–1887 (1887): 7, partially cited in Grimshaw, "Settler Anxieties, Indigenous Peoples, and Women's Suffrage," 569.
78. Gething, "Christianity and Coverture," 211.
79. Native Hawaiians had formed the Hui Kalai'aina (Hawaiian Political Association) in 1888. Others joined the white-led organization called the Mechanics' and Workingmen's Political Protective Union. Members of the two associations formed the National Reform Party in 1890 to oppose the Reform Party, which was responsible for the enactment of the Bayonet Constitution of 1887. Silva, *Aloha Betrayed*, 125–45.
80. Kuykendall and Day, *Hawaii*, 171–73.
81. Marilyn Stassen-Mclaughlin, "Unlucky Star: Princess Ka'iulani," *Hawaiian Journal of History* 33 (1999): 21–54.
82. *Hawaii's Last Queen*, prod. Vivian Ducat, 56 min., PBS, 2006, DVD.
83. Silva, *Aloha Betrayed*, 123–30; *Hawaii's Last Queen*.
84. Neil Thomas Proto, *The Rights of My People: Liliuokalani's Enduring Battle with the United States, 1893–1917* (New York: Algora, 2009), 9.
85. *Hawaii's Last Queen*; Stassen-Mclaughlin, "Unlucky Star," 21–54.
86. Silva, *Aloha Betrayed*, 129–35; Gwenfread E. Allen, "Kawananakoa, Abigail Wahiikaa-huula Campbell," in *Notable Women of Hawaii*, 209; "Female Patriots: Original Officers Drew Out," *Honolulu Advertiser*, April 18, 1893, 5.
87. "President's Address on Hawaiian Work by Mrs. C. M. Hyde," *WBMPI Annual Report* (1893): 43–44.

88. Louise Michele Newman, *White Women's Rights: The Racial Origins of Feminism in the United States* (New York: Oxford University Press, 1999), 8–10.
89. Liliuokalani, *Hawaii's Story by Hawaii's Queen*, 188.
90. Silva, *Aloha Betrayed*, 136–38.
91. The other two members were Mrs. W. W. Hall and Mrs. Wm. Hopper. *Hawai'i WCTU Annual Report* (1893–1894): 1–11.
92. Mary T. Hyde, "President's Address: Woman's Influence in the Uplifting of a Race," *WBMPI Annual Report* (1894), 48.
93. According to an English-language newspaper, former Queen Lili'uokalani was against woman suffrage. "Liliuokalani Opposed to Female Suffrage," *Pacific Commercial Advertiser*, February 18, 1910.
94. As for local white WCTU members' suffrage demands, see Grimshaw, "Settler Anxieties, Indigenous Peoples, and Women's Suffrage," 569–72; "Women Meet: They Are Still Canvassing the Suffrage Question," *Hawaiian Gazette*, June 1, 1894; *Mary Whitney, Scrapbook, 1894–1898*, Newspaper Clipping. HMCS Library.
95. "Constitutional Convention Records, 1894 Stenographic Record of Proceedings [hereafter Constitutional Convention Records, 1894 Proceedings]: 9th, 10th Days," 340, 344, 355–61. Hawai'i State Archives [hereafter HSA].
96. "Constitutional Convention Records, 1894 Proceedings: 11th Day," 414.
97. *Hawai'i WCTU Annual Report* (1893–1894): 10–11.
98. Grimshaw, "Settler Anxieties, Indigenous Peoples, and Women's Suffrage," 569–72. Attendants included Mmes. J. M. Whitney, W. F. Frear, W. W. Hall, O. H. Gulick, Widdifield, S. A. McWayne, R. J. Greene, Wm. Hopper, Peter High, F. C. Lowrey, Edwards Moore, E. W. Jordan, and Misses Castle, Cornwell, and Chamberlain. "They Won the Committee, a Delegation of Women Appears in the Convention Hall: Favorable Report Will Be Made," *Hawaiian Gazette*, June 22, 1894, 6. *Mary Whitney Scrap Book*, Newspaper Clipping.
99. "Constitutional Convention Box, File Petitions for Women's Suffrage," HSA.
100. "They Won the Committee, a Delegation of Women Appears in the Convention Hall."
101. "Constitutional Convention Records, 1894 Proceedings: 17th, 18th Days," 696–98.
102. "Constitutional Convention Records, 1894 Proceedings: 17th, 18th Days," 699.
103. "Constitutional Convention Records, 1894 Proceedings: 17th, 18th Days," 696–725.
104. "Constitutional Convention Records, 1894 Proceedings: 17th, 18th Days," 696–725. Article 74 also prohibited the foreign-born from voting if they had become naturalized before 1893 and if they came from a country without a naturalization treaty with Hawaii, which excluded most Asians, mostly Chinese and some Japanese subjects of the kingdom, from the electorate. John

M. Van Dyke, "Hawai'i's Constitutions—1839 to 1894," *ScholarSpace* (University of Hawai'i at Mānoa), July 20, 2022, https://scholarspace.manoa.hawaii.edu/server/api/core/bitstreams/3e4a28b3-28b3-4ae6-925c-8cdebc71e982/content.

105. Silva, *Aloha Betrayed*, 136–37.
106. *Constitution of the Republic of Hawai'i and Laws Passed by the Executive and Advisory Councils of the Republic* (Honolulu, HI: Robert Grieve, 1895), 80, 102–104.
107. "President Address," *Hawai'i WCTU Annual Report* (1893–1894): 1–11, cited in Grimshaw, "Settler Anxieties, Indigenous Peoples, and Women's Suffrage," 571.
108. Liliuokalani, *Hawaii's Story by Hawaii's Queen*, 279–80.
109. Day, *A Biographical Dictionary*, 58; May Day Lo, "121 Churches to Join in Friendship Sunday, May 19," *Honolulu Star-Bulletin*, May 11, 1940, 7.
110. Liliuokalani, *Hawaii's Story by Hawaii's Queen*, 279–80.
111. Liliuokalani, *Hawaii's Story by Hawaii's Queen*, 289, 295.
112. Proto, *The Rights of My People*, 1–2; Van Dyke, *Who Owns the Crown Lands of Hawaii?* After the overthrow, the formerly divided Crown and Government Lands were joined together to be called "Crown Lands," which fell under the hands of the provisional government and the republic. After the annexation in 1898, they were managed as a public trust by the United States.
113. Van Dyke, *Who Owns the Crown Lands of Hawaii?*, 305–40.
114. Silva, *Aloha Betrayed*, 145–59.
115. Coffman, *Nation Within*, 283.
116. Barbara Del Piano, *Nā Lani Kaumaka/Daughters of Hawai'i: A Century of Historic Preservation* (Honolulu: Daughters of Hawaii, 2005), 145–50; Proto, *The Rights of My People*, 23, 96.
117. Silva, *Aloha Betrayed*, 151, 160–61.

2. The Politics of Woman Suffrage in the U.S. Territory of Hawai'i

1. Liliuokalani, *Hawaii's Story by Hawaii's Queen* (Honolulu, HI: Mutual, 1990), 372–73.
2. Allison L. Sneider, *Suffragists in an Imperial Age: U.S. Expansion and the Woman Question, 1870–1929* (New York: Oxford University Press, 2008), 87–116.
3. Liliuokalani, *Hawaii's Story by Hawaii's Queen*, 111–15; Patricia Grimshaw, *Paths of Duty: American Missionary Wives in Nineteenth-Century Hawaii* (Honolulu: University of Hawai'i Press, 1989); Patricia Grimshaw, "Settler Anxieties, Indigenous Peoples, and Women's Suffrage in the Colonies of Australia, New Zealand, and Hawai'i, 1888 to 1902," *Pacific Historical Review* 69, no. 4 (2000): 567–72.

4. Sneider, *Suffragists in an Imperial Age*, 87–114.
5. They were Anna H. Shaw (vice president), Rachel Foster Avery (corresponding secretary), Alice Stone Blackwell (recording secretary), Harriet Taylor Upton (treasurer), Laura Clay (auditor), Catharine Gouger Waugh McCulloch, and Carrie Chapman Catt.
6. "On Behalf of Hawaiian Women," *Woman's Journal* 11 (February 1899): 1–3. Also, see Sneider, *Suffragists in an Imperial Age*, 106–107.
7. Sneider, *Suffragists in an Imperial Age*, 6.
8. Ellen Carol DuBois, *Feminism and Suffrage: The Emergence of an Independent Women's Movement in America, 1848–1869* (Ithaca, NY: Cornell University Press, 1978), 31–40.
9. Sneider, *Suffragists in an Imperial Age*, 5–7, 88–116; Louise Michele Newman, *White Women's Rights: The Racial Origins of Feminism in the United States* (New York: Oxford University Press, 1999); Aileen S. Kraditor, *The Ideas of the Woman Suffrage Movement, 1890–1920* (New York: Columbia University Press, 1965); Ellen Carol DuBois, *Harriot Stanton Blatch and the Winning of Woman Suffrage* (New Haven, CT: Yale University Press, 1997); Rebecca J. Mead, *How the Vote Was Won: Woman Suffrage in the Western United States, 1868–1914* (New York: New York University Press, 2004); Jean H. Baker, ed., *Votes for Women: The Struggle for Suffrage Revisited* (Oxford: Oxford University Press, 2002); Lisa G. Materson, *For the Freedom of Her Race: Black Women and Electoral Politics in Illinois, 1877–1932* (Chapel Hill: University of North Carolina Press, 2009).
10. Ida Husted Harper and Susan B. Anthony, eds., *The History of Woman Suffrage 4, 1883–1900* (Indianapolis, IN: Hollenbeck, 1902), 346. Partially cited in Sneider, *Suffragists in an Imperial Age*, 106–107.
11. Sneider, *Suffragist in an Imperial Age*, 104–14; Harper and Anthony, *The History of Woman Suffrage 4*, 346–48.
12. In 1900, the population of Hawai'i was 25.7 percent Native Hawaiians (19.3 percent Hawaiians and 6.4 percent part-Hawaiians), 17.3 percent Caucasian (11.9 percent Portuguese and 5.4 percent other Caucasian), and 56.3 percent Asian (16.7 percent Chinese and 39.6 Japanese). Andrew William Lind, *Hawaii's People* (Honolulu: University of Hawai'i Press, 1955), 27.
13. Lauren L. Basson, "Fit for Annexation but Unfit to Vote? Debating Hawaiian Suffrage Qualifications at the Turn of the Twentieth Century," *Social Science History* 29, no. 4 (Winter 2005): 575–98.
14. Hawaiian Kingdom Weblog, "An Act to Provide a Government for the Territory of Hawaii," October 22, 2022, https://www.hawaiiankingdom.org/us-organic-act-1900.shtml.
15. Lawrence H. Fuchs, *Hawaii Pono "Hawaii the Excellent": An Ethnic and Political History* (Honolulu, HI: Bess, 1961), 161; Donna M. Binkiewicz, *Between the Sea and Sky: The Saga of My Portuguese American Family in Upcountry Maui, 1881–1941* (Independently Published, 2021), 87–88.

16. Fuchs, *Hawaii Pono*, 152–81.
17. Fuchs, *Hawaii Pono*, 152–81. The Republican dominance in the elected legislature continued until the election in 1946.
18. Fuchs, *Hawaii Pono*, 152–81.
19. Davianna Pomaikaʻi McGregor, "Constructed Images of Native Hawaiian Women," in *Asian/Pacific Islander American Women: A Historical Anthology*, ed. Shirley Hune and Gail M. Nomura (New York: New York University Press, 2003), 31–32.
20. "The founding seven" of the DOH were Emma Louise Smith Dillingham, Cornelia Hall Jones, Ann Elizabeth Alexander Dickey, Lucinda Maria Clark Severance, Sarah Eliza Coan Waters, Anna Matilda Paris, and Ellen Eliza Armstrong Weaver. Barbara Del Piano, *Nā Lani Kaumaka/Daughters of Hawaiʻi: A Century of Historic Preservation* (Honolulu: Daughters of Hawaii, 2005), 1–9.
21. The restriction changed from the original 1860 to 1890, to 1860, to 1870, and to 1880, where it remained as of 2005. Del Piano, *Nā Lani Kaumaka*, 16.
22. Irene Haʻalou Kahalelaukoa ʻĪʻī Brown-Holloway was a granddaughter of High Chief John Papa ʻĪʻī, a trusted councilor of Kamehameha I and an early Christian convert. After his death, one-year-old Irene was raised by Rev. and Mrs. C. M. Hyde, an ABCFM missionary couple through a *hānai* (Hawaii's adoption practice). David T. Brown, "Ii, Irene," in *Notable Women of Hawaii*, ed. Barbara Bennett Peterson (Honolulu: University of Hawaiʻi Press, 1984), 156–57.
23. Del Piano, *Nā Lani Kaumaka*, 11–17, 36; Eileen Root, "Kalanianaole, Princess Elizabeth Kahanu Kaleiwohi-Kaauwai," in *Notable Women of Hawaii*, 186–89.
24. Del Piano, *Nā Lani Kaumaka*, 15, 72. Beckley-Nākuina was a daughter of chiefess Kailikapuolono and an American Harvard-educated scholar, civil engineer, and sugar planter. E. Shan Correa, "Nakuina, Emma Kaili Metcalf Beckley" in *Notable Women of Hawaii*, 279–82. Elizabeth Lahilahi Rogers Webb had served as companion and lady-in-waiting during the deposed queen's later years. *An International Encyclopedia of Biography, 1940–41* (Honolulu, HI: Honolulu Star-Bulletin, 1941), 746–47.
25. Neil Thomas Proto, *The Rights of My People: Liliuokalani's Enduring Battle with the United States, 1893–1917* (New York: Algora, 2009), 23, 96, 102; Del Piano, *Nā Lani Kaumaka*, 145–47; "Hawaiians Mourn," *The Independent* (Honolulu, HI), February 7, 1899.
26. A. Grove Day, *History Makers of Hawaii: A Biographical Dictionary* (Honolulu, HI: Mutual, 1984), 37.
27. J. Patricia Morgan Swenson, "Swanzy, Julie Judd," in *Notable Women of Hawaii*, 361–64; Edwin P. Hoyt, *Davies: The Inside Story of a British-American Family in the Pacific and Its Business Enterprises* (Honolulu, HI: Topgallant, 1983), 191–92.
28. Swenson, "Swanzy, Julie Judd," in *Notable Women of Hawaii*; Del Piano, *Nā Lani Kaumaka*, 150–53; George F. M. Nellist, ed., *Women of Hawaii* (Honolulu, HI: E. A. Langton-Boyle, 1929), 261–63.

29. Del Piano, *Nā Lani Kaumaka*, 12–15, 31–37.
30. Del Piano, *Nā Lani Kaumaka*, 36. Pratt was a lineal descendant of Kamehamaha I.
31. In December 1910, Prince Kūhiō called Hawaiian women who had deep knowledge of ancient Hawai'i, including Leihulu Kapena Keohokalole, Puea Blaisdell, and Maluhi Rets, to discuss the organization of a society that would perpetuate the story of old Hawai'i.
32. UH Morgue by Subject Microfiche, "Daughters and Sons of Hawaiian Warriors," December 10, 1921 (University of Hawai'i at Mānoa, Hamilton Library).
33. Eleanor H. Williamson, "Taylor, Emma Ahuena Davison," in *Notable Women of Hawaii*, 369–73.
34. "Suffrage Live Question at Meeting: Ballot for Women Voted Down at Co-Operative League Session," *Pacific-Commercial Advertiser*, May 27, 1913, 1.
35. Bob Krauss, *Johnny Wilson: First Hawaiian Democrat* (Honolulu: University of Hawai'i Press, 1994), 115; "Democrats Taking Up Suffrage," *Evening Bulletin*, June 10, 1912, 1; "Wahines Demand the Ballot Argue for All 'Their Rights,'" *Pacific Commercial Advertiser*, June 11, 1912; "Woman's Suffrage Luau Is Changed," *Honolulu Star-Bulletin*, August 29, 1912, 5.
36. "Makawao Union Church Ladies Give Bazaar," *Honolulu Star-Bulletin*, October 18, 1912, 11.
37. Ida Husted Harper and Susan B. Anthony, eds., *The History of Woman Suffrage VI, 1900–1920* (New York: J. J. Little & Ives, 1922), 716.
38. *The Papers of Carrie Chapman Catt* (Washington, DC: Manuscript Division, Library of Congress, 1976), reel 1, 40, 42; "Mrs. Chapman Catt Speaks to Hawaii Audience on Suffrage," *Honolulu Star-Bulletin*, October 29, 1912, 5.
39. The other woman at the dock was Mrs. Sharpe, possibly Lilian Sharpe. "Noted Suffragist to Speak Here Tonight," *Honolulu Star-Bulletin*, October 28, 1912; *The Papers of Carrie Chapman Catt*, reel 1, 40. In the newspaper article, the Dowsett-headed organization was referred to as "the National Women's Equal Suffrage Association of Hawai'i."
40. She was born to a high chief mother and a German planter and politician father who opposed the U.S. annexation and married a businessman of English ancestry. The wedding of Wilhelmina K. Widemann and John M. Dowsett was held at St. Andrew's Cathedral in 1888, attended by King Kalakaua and his sister Princess Liliuokalani. "The Ceremony Takes Place at St. Andrew's Cathedral Before a Large Assemblage," *Pacific Commercial Advertiser*, May 1, 1888.
41. Grimshaw, "Settler Anxieties, Indigenous Peoples, and Women's Suffrage."
42. "Noted Suffragist to Speak Here Tonight."
43. "Noted Suffragist to Speak Here Tonight."
44. "Mrs. Chapman Catt Speaks to Hawaii Audience on Suffrage."
45. *The Papers of Carrie Chapman Catt*, reel 1, 43.
46. *The Papers of Carrie Chapman Catt*, reel 1, 42.

47. At the time of Catt's visit in Hawai'i in 1912, the WESAH had only twenty-two active members, four life members, and two annual members. "Mrs. Catt to Help Hawaii," *Honolulu Star-Bulletin*, October 30, 1912, 5.
48. Ida Husted Harper and Susan B. Anthony, eds., *The History of Woman Suffrage V, 1900-1920* (Salem, NH: Ayer, 1985), 381–82.
49. "Woman Suffrage in Non-Partisan Sense," *Commercial Advertiser Second Section*, October 31, 1912, 9. Nawahī's biographical information was retrieved from Women of the West Museum, "Emma 'Aima Nawahī (1854–1934)," December 21, 2013, http:/theautry.org/explore/exhibits/suffrage/nawahi_full.html.
50. "Woman Suffrage in Non-Partisan Sense."
51. "Suffrage Organization Grows Rapidly: Women Work Together," *Honolulu Star-Bulletin*, November 14, 1912, 5.
52. Asians composed 56.4 percent of the population in Hawai'i in 1910. Among them were Chinese (11.3 percent), Japanese (41.5 percent), Korean (2.4 percent), and Filipino (1.2 percent). Other substantial ethnic groups were Hawaiian (13.6 percent), part-Hawaiian (6.5 percent), Portuguese (11.6 percent), and other Caucasian (7.7 percent). Lind, *Hawaii's People*, 27.
53. Ralph S. Kuykendall and Lorin Tarr Gill, *Hawaii in the World War* (Honolulu, HI: Honolulu Historical Commission, 1928), 91–170, 298–306, 419–20.
54. Kuykendall and Gill, *Hawaii in the World War*, 91–124, 215–38. Alfred Lowrey Castle and Beatrice Castle were the descendants of Samuel Northrup Castle (1808–1894), an ABCFM missionary and a founder of Castle & Cooke, one of the Big Five.
55. The United War Work Campaign was carried out by the YMCA, the YWCA, the American Library Association, the War Camp Community Service, the National Catholic War Council (Knights of Columbus), the Jewish Welfare Board, and the Salvation Army. "Women in the Progressive Era: National Women's History Museum," September 11, 2011, www.nwhm.org/online-exhibits/progressiveera/worldwarI.html; Mary Sophia Stevens Sims, *The Natural History of a Social Institution: The Young Women's Christian Association* (New York: Woman's Press, 1936), 61–64; Richard Roberts, *Florence Simms: A Biography* (New York: Woman's Press, 1926), 209–20.
56. The CND's Women's Committee had twelve divisions, including Women in Industry, Child Welfare, Liberty Loan, and Home and Foreign Relief.
57. *Report of the Women's Committee Council of National Defense: Covering a Year's Activities up to April 21, 1918* (Washington, DC: Government Printing Office, 1918); William J. Breen, *Uncle Sam at Home: Civilian Mobilization, Wartime Federalism, and the Council of National Defense, 1917–1919* (Westport, CT: Greenwood, 1984), 115–36.
58. Kuykendall and Gill, *Hawaii in the World War*, 419–20; *The Women's Committee Council of National Defense Organization Charts, May, 1917–1918* (Washington, DC: Government Printing Office, 1918).

59. *The Women's Committee Council of National Defense Organization Charts.*
60. Kuykendall and Gill, *Hawaii in the World War*, 149–50; "Emma Ahuena Davison Taylor," January 2, 2013, http://www.findagrave.com/cgi-bin/fg.cgi?page=gr&GRid=36125975.
61. Binkiewicz, *Between the Sea and Sky*, 117–48.
62. Alice Park, "Tells of Women's Fight for Ballot," *Pacific Commercial Advertiser*, March 3, 1915, 3; "Moving Towards Woman Suffrage," in *Alice Park Papers Scrapbooks*, book 1, 108. Huntington Library, San Marino, CA.
63. *Journal of the House of Representatives of the Eighth Legislature of the Territory of Hawaii, Regular Session 1915* (Honolulu, HI: Hawaiian Gazette, 1915), 457, 1019, 1043; "Resolutions Adopted," *Pacific Commercial Advertiser*, April 23, 1915, 3.
64. Harper and Anthony, *The History of Woman Suffrage VI*, 716–19; "Benjamin F. Pitman," *New York Times*, July 3, 1918, 13.
65. Harper and Anthony, *The History of Woman Suffrage VI*, 717.
66. Harper and Anthony, *The History of Woman Suffrage VI*, 717–18.
67. House Committee on Woman Suffrage, *Woman Suffrage in Hawaii*, 65th Cong., 2nd sess., 1918, H. Rept. 536.
68. Harper and Anthony, *The History of Woman Suffrage VI*, 718–19.
69. McCarthy was a strong advocate of attaining statehood, and territorial delegate Prince Kūhiō introduced the first statehood bill in U.S. Congress. "Statehood Urged by McCarthy for Hawaii," *Maui News*, February 21, 1919, 3.
70. "Bill to Raise Maui Salaries Is Introduced," *Maui News*, March 7, 1919, 2; "Women Win Out in Senate," *Maui News*, March 7, 1919, 3; "Senate Puts Crimp in Suffrage," *Maui News*, March 7, 1919, 3; "Baldwin Opposed to Rushing Suffrage Bill," *Maui News*, March 7, 1919, 3.
71. "Women Win Out in Senate"; "Hawaiian Women Join with Haoles to Work for Vote," *Honolulu Star-Bulletin*, March 5, 1919, 1.
72. According to Dowsett, the women's suffrage association that she and her friends formed in 1912 was "abandoned, but another one started and continued until [their] war activities forced [them] to drop it." Dowsett revived the "Equal Suffrage Association," most possibly her WESAH in Honolulu, for the regeneration of the movement. See "Suffrage Meeting to Be Held at Mrs. J. M. Dowsett's," *Honolulu Star-Bulletin*, January 24, 1920, 12.
73. "Hawaiian Women Join with Haoles to Work for Vote."
74. "Women Win Out in Senate."
75. *Constitution of the Republic of Hawai'i and Laws Passed by the Executive and Advisory Councils of the Republic* (Honolulu, HI: Robert Grieve, Steam Book and Job Printer, 1895), 80, 102–104.
76. "Orientals Born Here Soon Vote," *Maui News*, July 30, 1920, 6. There were also the so-called 1.5 generation, who presumably were foreign born but arrived in the islands at a young age and had gained citizenship under the tradition

of monarchical or oligarchic paternalism/maternalism. Roberta Chang and Wayne Patterson, *The Koreans in Hawai'i: A Pictorial History, 1903–2003* (Honolulu: University of Hawai'i Press, 2003), 123.

77. "Women Ask Vote and Right to Use It at Municipal Elections," *Honolulu Star-Bulletin*, March 7, 1919.
78. "Suffrage Plebiscite Is Sought," *Honolulu Star-Bulletin*, March 11, 1919, 1–2.
79. "Vote on Measure Deferred," *Honolulu Star-Bulletin*, March 24, 1919, 1.
80. Among the notable speakers at the meeting were Dowsett, MacMillan, Lahilahi Webb, Emilie K. W. Macfarlane, Princess Kalaniana'ole, and Margaret Knepper. "Mrs. Atcherley" was also present at the meeting; she was most likely Mary Ha'aheo Kinimaka Atcherley (1874–1933), who later ran for office in 1920 and 1922 after women were granted voting rights but when their right to hold office was still being debated. Mrs. Kamanoulu, Mrs. Mignonette Miller, Mrs. Clara Miller, and Mrs. Elizabeth Robinson also spoke at the meeting. "Women Stage Suffrage Meet at A'ala Park," *Honolulu Star-Bulletin*, March 25, 1919, 10.
81. For example, see "Compromise on Suffrage Meets with Opposition," *Honolulu Star-Bulletin*, March 25, 1919; "City Hall Is Much Excited Over Suffrage," *Honolulu Star-Bulletin*, March 25, 1919; "Plebiscite Favored by Solons," March 26, 1919; "Vote on Suffrage Ends in Deadlock," *Honolulu Star-Bulletin*, March 26, 1919, 2; "Suffrage Bill Due to Come up Again in House," *Honolulu Star-Bulletin*, March 31, 1919; "Action on Suffrage Delayed," *Honolulu Star-Bulletin*, April 1, 1919; "Political Steam Roller Defeats Suffrage Bill," *Honolulu Star-Bulletin*, April 2, 1919, 4.
82. "Ask Congress for Suffrage," *Honolulu Star-Bulletin*, April 3, 1919; "Women Form Clubs to Get Into Politics," *Honolulu Star-Bulletin*, April 23, 1919.
83. "Women Divided on Election to Decide Suffrage: Some Favor Plebiscite at June Vote, Others Want It Next November," *Honolulu Star-Bulletin*, April 18, 1919.
84. "Women Are Losing Suffrage Interest; Divided on Policy," *Honolulu Star-Bulletin*, April 17, 1919.
85. Harper and Anthony, *The History of Woman Suffrage VI*, 719.
86. Roger J. Bell, *Last Among Equals: Hawaiian Statehood and American Politics* (Honolulu: University of Hawai'i Press, 1984), 45.
87. "Hastening Japanese Control," *Hawaiian Gazette*, September 18, 1917, 4.
88. Harper and Anthony, *The History of Woman Suffrage VI*, 717.
89. "Honolulu Women Not Sure About Suffrage," *Maui News*, February 14, 1919, 5.
90. "Park Travel (manuscript)," *Alice Park Papers Scrapbooks*, book 1, clippings 21: 11.
91. Basson, "Fit for Annexation but Unfit to Vote?," 575–98.
92. Krauss, *Johnny Wilson*, 172–73; "Mrs. Atcherley Still American She Asserts," *Honolulu Star-Bulletin*, September 3, 1920, 3; "Maui Woman First to Seek Candidacy: Mrs. Helen K. Snifften Sends Papers," *Maui News*, September 3,

1920, 1; "Nomination Papers of Women Accepted," *Maui News*, September 10, 1920, 7.
93. "Picture: Hawaiian Women on Deck Early to Sign Up," *Honolulu Star-Bulletin*, August 30, 1920, 7; "Rush of Women on Their Initial Registration Day," *Honolulu Advertiser*, August 31, 1920.
94. Krauss, *Johnny Wilson*, 172–73; "Hawaiian Women on Hand Early to Qualify as Voters," *Honolulu Star-Bulletin*, August 30, 1920, 1.
95. "Many Woman Voters Registered Yesterday," *Nippu Jiji*, August 31, 1920; Barbara Peterson, "Noda, Alice Sae Teshima," in *Notable Women of Hawaii*, 288–91. Alice Sae Noda's husband, Steere Gikaku Noda (1892–1986), was born in Hawai'i, worked as a police court interpreter, and later became a politician affiliated with the Democratic Party. He was elected to the territorial house of representatives in 1948 and to the state senate in 1959. The Nodas became cultural mediators and advocates for Japanese immigrant communities locally and Hawai'i nationally and internationally.
96. "Women at Fault Mayor's Opinion: Says There Are Plenty of Clerks but Few New Voters Are Registering," *Honolulu Star-Bulletin*, September 3, 1920, 1, 3.
97. "Women and Registration," *Honolulu Star-Bulletin*, September 2, 1920, 6. The managing editor of the English-language newspaper the *Honolulu Star-Bulletin* at the time was Wallace Rider Farrington, who, appointed by Republican presidents, would serve as the territorial governor for two terms from 1921 to 1929.
98. "Women Want More Deputies to Aid in Registration," *Pacific Commercial Advertiser Second Section*, September 3, 1920, 1–2; "To Aid Women Politically," *Pacific Commercial Advertiser Second Section*, September 3, 1920, 1. Among women who spoke at the mass meeting were Native Hawaiian women such as DOH member Lahilahi Webb and Alice Kahokuoluna, who would soon become the first woman ordained by the Hawaiian Evangelical Association; white settler women who had married into the prominent families of missionary heritage, such as Louise Olga Gaylord Dillingham, daughter of a prominent Chicago banker and the wife of missionary grandson planter-businessman Walter F. Dillingham, who was a brother of former DOH regent Mary E. Dillingham, and Lilian Kimball Wilder, a Massachusetts native married to missionary great-grandson Gerrit Parmele Wilder, a nephew of former DOH regent Julie Judd Swanzy; white settler activists such as Marguerite K. Ashford, who would soon become the first woman admitted to the Hawai'i territorial bar; and Honolulu YWCA president Harriet Cousens Andrews, a former high school teacher in New York married to Cornell professor Arthur Lynn Andrews who took a position on the faculty of the University of Hawai'i.
99. "Women Want More Deputies to Aid in Registration."
100. "Suit to Determine Right of Women to Seek Office Advised," *Maui News*, October 8, 1920, 8.

101. "All Women Urged to Attend Meeting," *Maui News*, May 30, 1919, 1, 3; "Large Membership in Suffrage Club," *Maui News*, June 6, 1919. For her husband H. A. Baldwin, see Day, *History Makers of Hawaii*, 7–8.
102. Frances B. Cameron and Barbara B. Lyons, "Baldwin, Ethel Frances Smith," in *Notable Women of Hawaii*, 19–22. Accordingly, she had contributed to the passage by the territorial legislature in 1919 of a bill that established a Board of Child Welfare and Old Age Pensions in each county.
103. "Maui Woman's Club Opens Its Year with Fine Attendance of Members," *Maui News*, October 8, 1920, 1; "Boys' Industrial School Criticized: Maui Women Advised to Used Their Votes to Secure Improvement in Care of Young Delinquents by the Territory," *Maui News*, October 8, 1920, 2; "Candidates Tell Women Voters Where They Stand on Questions Propounded," *Maui News*, October 15, 1920, 1.
104. "Big Vote by Women Features Election," *Honolulu Star-Bulletin*, October 2, 1920, 1–2; "Women Play Great Part," *Maui News*, March 28, 1922, 4; "Women Vote Heavily," *Maui News*, March 28, 1922, 1.
105. "Women May Run for Office But Rest Doubtful," *Maui News*, February 10, 1922, 1.
106. "Princess Kalanianaole Urged to Be Candidate for Hawaii's Delegate," *Honolulu Advertiser*, February 8, 1922, 1–2; Eileen Root, "Kalanianaole, Princess Elizabeth Kahanu Kaleiwohi-Kaanwai," in *Notable Women of Hawaii*, 186–89.
107. "Correction Offered," *Maui News*, February 21, 1922, 8.
108. Gwenfread E. Allen, "Kawananakoa, Abigail Wahi'ika'ahu'ula Campbell" in *Notable Women of Hawaii*, 209–11.
109. "Mary Atcherly Sought Candidacy But Gave Up Democratic Ticket 1922," *Honolulu Advertiser*, January 28, 1922, 1; Alice Stone, "Do Women Like Politics?—Ask Hawaii," *Woman Citizen*, July 15, 1922, 11, 16.
110. "Girl Who Worked for Harding Visits Hawaii," *Honolulu Star-Bulletin*, February 9, 1922, 10.
111. "Republicans Hold Rallies This Evening," *Honolulu Advertiser*, March 6, 1922, 1.
112. "Republican Auxiliary Club," *Honolulu Star-Bulletin*, March 6, 1922, 12; "Hawaiian Women's Republican Auxiliary Club," *Honolulu Star-Bulletin*, March 9, 1922; "Republican Auxiliary Manoa," *Honolulu Star-Bulletin*, March 18, 1922, 3; "G.O.P. Women Launch Two Precinct Clubs," *Honolulu Star-Bulletin*, February 28, 1922, 10.
113. Louise M. Young and Ralph A. Young, *In the Public Interest: The League of Women Voters, 1920–1970* (New York: Greenwood, 1989), 49.
114. "To Aid Women Politically."
115. "Letter from Mrs. George Gellhorn, Vice-Chairman to Mrs. Roy Noggle, March 1, 1921," League of Women Voters Papers II-1, Library of Congress Manuscript Division.

116. Edith Stone, "Voters League Is Formed by Hawaii Women," *Honolulu Star-Bulletin*, February 17, 1922, 1–2.
117. "Women of Maui Organize to Do Important Work," *Maui News*, March 17, 1922, 1.
118. As for the "lie," see "Democratic Candidate Fails in Discrediting Record of Baldwin," *Maui News*, March 10, 1922, 1.
119. Edith Stone, "Women's League to Take Active Part in Politics," *Honolulu Star-Bulletin*, March 21, 1922, 2; "Minutes of Organization Meeting, March 20, 1922" and "Minutes of Regular Monthly Meeting, April 27, 1922," in *League of Women Voters in Hawai'i Papers* [hereafter *HLWV Papers*], book 1. Hawai'i State Archives Manuscript Collection (HSAMC)-M356, Honolulu, HI.
120. "Minutes of Special Meeting of Executive Committee, April 6, 1922," "Minutes of Second Annual Meeting, May 8, 1924," in *HLWV Papers*, book 1.
121. Stone, "Do Women Like Politics?—Ask Hawaii," 11. Also see, "News Notes Around Town: A General Meeting of the Hawaiian Women's Republican Auxiliary Clubs," *Honolulu Advertiser*, March 22, 1922, 7.
122. Materson, *For the Freedom of Her Race*, 33–39.
123. Stone, "Do Women Like Politics?—Ask Hawaii," 16
124. "Landslide for Baldwin in All of Territory," *Honolulu Star-Bulletin*, March 26, 1922.
125. Stone, "Do Women Like Politics?—Ask Hawaii," 11, 16.
126. "Bill Giving Women Right to Hold Office Is Passed by Senate," *Honolulu Star-Bulletin*, September 1, 1922, 3; "No Disqualification of Sex," *Honolulu Star-Bulletin*, September 21, 1922, 6; "Hawaii Women Now Have Right to Hold Office," *Honolulu Star-Bulletin*, September 21, 1922, 2, 6; "Three Women Eligible for Hawaii House," *Honolulu Star-Bulletin*, September 22, 1922, 1.
127. "Minutes of First Meeting of Board of Administrative Control, September 12, 1922," "Minutes of Special Meeting of Board of Administrative Control, December 27, 1922," *HLWV Papers*, book 1.
128. "Amended Constitution," *HLWV Papers*, book 1.
129. Harriet Cousens Andrews, who assumed the HLWV presidency, was active in the women's society of the Central Union Church and also entrusted with leadership roles of other women's organizations in Honolulu, such as the Honolulu YWCA and the Women's Faculty Club of the University of Hawai'i. Nellist, *Women of Hawaii*, 12–13.
130. "Minutes of Organization Meeting, March 20, 1922," *HLWV Papers*, book 1.
131. "Women Urged as Candidates for the House," *Honolulu Star-Bulletin*, September 2, 1922, 1; "Mrs. J. M. Dowsett Says She Will Not Run in Campaign," *Honolulu Star-Bulletin*, September 4, 1922, 1.
132. "Minutes of First Meeting of Board of Administrative Control, September 12, 1922," "Special Meeting of Board of Administrative Control, December 27, 1922," *HLWV Papers*, book 1.

133. The HLWV's early leadership of culturally hybrid Euro-American and Native Hawaiian women, however, gradually came into the hands of newly arrived women from the U.S. mainland, some of whom married into missionary descendant families. It disbanded in May 1936. "Women Disband Voters League," *Honolulu Star-Bulletin*, May 15, 1936; Laura Lister Marques to Mrs. Chas. F. Weeber, May 21, 1936, *HLWV Papers*, book 4.
134. Catherine Kekoa Enomoto, "Keliʻinoi, Rosalie Enos Lyons," in *Notable Women of Hawaii*, 214–16; "Women Wielding Power: Pioneer Female State Legislators," August 14, 2013, http://www.nwhm.org/online-exhibits/legislators/Hawaii.html.

3. Territorial Motherhood's Double-Edged Sword: Women's Networks and Unequal Sisterhoods

1. Harriet Castle Coleman, "The Hope of the World Lies in the Children," *Annual Report of the Woman's Board of Missions for the Pacific Islands* (1895), 70–75.
2. Coleman, "The Hope of the World Lies in the Children."
3. Charlotte P. Dodge, *A History of the Free Kindergarten and Children's Aid Association of the Hawaiian Islands, 1895–1945* (Honolulu, HI: Mercantile Print, 1945), 3 [hereafter *A History of the FKCAAHI*]; A. Grove Day, *History Makers of Hawaii: A Biographical Dictionary* (Honolulu, HI: Mutual, 1984), 30–31. Rev. Frank W. Damon was a son of Hawaii's pioneer missionary Samuel C. Damon, and his wife Mary R. Happer Damon was a Presbyterian missionary daughter who herself had worked as a missionary in Guangzhou (Canton), China.
4. Dodge, *A History of the FKCAAHI*, 3–4; *Constitution, By-laws and Charter of the Free Kindergarten and Children's Aid Association of the Hawaiian Islands, with the List of Officers, Committees, Contributors and the Reports of Financial Secretary and a Treasurer* (Honolulu, HI: Robert Grieve, Steam Book and Job Printer, 1895) [hereafter, *Constitution, By-laws and Charter of the FKCAAHI*]; Margaret M. L. Catton, *Social Service in Hawaii* (Palo Alto, CA: Pacific Book, 1959), 23–25; Alfred L. Castle, "Harriet Castle and the Beginnings of Progressive Kindergarten Education in Hawaiʻi 1894–1900," *Hawaiian Journal of History* 23 (1989): 119–36.
5. Davianna Pomaikaʻi McGregor, "Constructed Images of Native Hawaiian Women," in *Asian/Pacific Islander American Women: A Historical Anthology*, ed. Shirley Hune and Gail M. Nomura (New York: New York University Press, 2003), 32.
6. Ann Taylor Allen, "Children Between Public and Private Worlds: The Kindergarten and Public Policy in Germany, 1840–Present," and Barbara Beatty, "'The Letter Killeth': Americanization and Multicultural Education in Kindergartens in the United States, 1856–1920," in *Kindergartens and Cultures: The Global*

Diffusion of an Idea, ed. Roberta Wollons (New Haven, CT: Yale University Press, 2000), 16–58.

7. Nina C. Vandewalker, *The Kindergarten in American Education* (New York: Macmillan, 1908), 76–128.

8. Congregationalists were involved in kindergarten missionary work in Asia, Africa, and elsewhere. Beatty, "'The Letter Killeth,'" 52.

9. Beatty, "'The Letter Killeth'"; Vandewalker, *The Kindergarten in American Education*.

10. Molly Ladd-Taylor, *Mother-Work: Women, Child Welfare, and the State, 1890–1930* (Urbana: University of Illinois Press, 1994), 8, 46–47.

11. John Dewey, "My Pedagogic Creed," *School Journal* 54, no. 3 (January 16, 1897): 77–80.

12. Ann Taylor Allen, Barbara Beatty, and Roberta Wollons, "How Did the Kindergarten Movement Provide Women with Opportunities for Professional Development and Social Activism in the United States and Internationally?," in *Women and Social Movement in the United States, 1600–2000* 16, no. 1 (March 2012), August 3, 2014, http:/asp6new.alexanderstreet.com/was2/was2.object.details.apsx?; Chicago Historical Society, "Kindergarten Movement," in *The Encyclopedia of Chicago*, August 5, 2014, http:/www.encyclopedia.chicagohistory.org/pages/691.html.

13. The National Congress of Mothers was formed in 1897 and changed its name to the National Congress of Mothers and Parent-Teacher Associations in 1908 and to the National Congress of Parents and Teachers in 1924. In 1908, the annual PTA meeting passed a resolution calling for kindergartens in public schools. Ladd-Taylor, *Mother-Work*, 1–14, 53.

14. Castle, "Harriet Castle and the Beginnings of Progressive Kindergarten Education in Hawaii 1894–1900," 119–36; Rosalind Rosenberg, *Beyond Separate Spheres: Intellectual Roots of Modern Feminism* (New Haven, CT: Yale University Press, 1982), 65–66.

15. Lawrence succeeded Hannah Eastman, who was hired from the Golden Gate Kindergarten Association in San Francisco. Dodge, *A History of the FKCAAHI*, 5.

16. Charlene Haddock Seigfried, "Introduction," in Jane Addams, *Democracy and Social Ethics* (Urbana: University of Illinois Press, 2002), ix–xxxviii.

17. "Address of Mrs. W. I. Thomas of Chicago," *Calendar of the Free Kindergarten and Children's Aid Association of the Hawaiian Islands* (1913), 68–76 [hereafter *Calendar of FKCAAHI*].

18. With the inauguration of the Hawaiian Republic in 1894, the Central Union Church in Honolulu built the Palama Chapel in a residential section of middle- and upper-class Native Hawaiians to serve as the venue for entertainment and Christian education, including a kindergarten. After a 1900 disinfection fire to contain bubonic plague burned the Chinatown section, the Palama

Chapel provided asylum to refugees, mostly Chinese and Japanese. In 1906, the Hawaiian Evangelical Association (HEA) converted the chapel into the Palama Settlement. While men's and women's voluntarism supported the settlement, the male-headed HEA, working with the Territorial Board of Health, managed the settlement. Warren S. Nishimoto, "The Progressive Era and Hawai'i: The Early History of Palama Settlement, 1896–1929," *Hawaiian Journal of History* 34 (2000): 169–84.

19. Ronald T. Takaki, *Pau Hana: Plantation Life and Labor in Hawaii, 1835–1920* (Honolulu: University of Hawai'i Press, 1983), 60–75, 92–98.
20. *Constitution, By-laws and Charter of the FKCAAHI*, 14; Dodge, *A History of the FKCAAHI*, 3–4.
21. *Calendar of the FKCAAHI* (1897), 26–28; Dodge, *A History of the FKCAAHI*, 4.
22. *Calendar of the FKCAAHI* (1899), 17.
23. Sucheng Chan, *Asian Americans: An Interpretative History* (Boston: Twayne, 1991), 92.
24. Andrew William Lind, *Hawaii's People* (Honolulu: University of Hawai'i Press, 1967), 27, 72.
25. Dodge, *A History of the FKCAAHI*, 13; *Calendar of the FKCAAHI* (1898), 20–21.
26. The Associate Charities of Hawai'i was established in 1899 with Sanford B. Dole as its first president. The United Welfare Fund was established in 1919. Frank C. Atherton served as its first president. Catton, *Social Service in Hawaii*, 32–61; Dodge, *A History of the FKCAAHI*, 9, 11.
27. *Constitution, By-laws and Charter of the FKCAAHI*, 8, 26–33.
28. Dodge, *A History of the FKCAAHI*, 9–12.
29. Dodge, *A History of the FKCAAHI*, 9–12, 20–23.
30. Catton, *Social Service in Hawaii*, 29–31.
31. Dodge, *A History of the FKCAAHI*, 20–23; Catton, *Social Service in Hawaii*, 23–32. During World War II, the FKCAAHI pressed for "daycare" for children under the compulsory school age so that their mothers could engage in war-support endeavors. In 1943, two years after the death of Julie Judd Swanzy, the territorial government passed a bill to fund twelve public kindergartens for two years, which was signed by Ingram Stainback (1883–1961), a Democratic governor from 1942 to 1951.
32. Maureen A. Flanagan, "Gender and Urban Political Reform: The City Club and the Woman's City Club of Chicago in the Progressive Era," *American Historical Review* 95, no. 4 (1990): 1032–50.
33. Robyn Muncy, *Creating a Female Dominion in American Reform, 1890–1935* (New York: Oxford University Press, 1991).
34. Mary Sophia Stevens Sims, *The National History of a Social Institution: The Young Women's Christian Association* (New York: Woman's Press, 1936), 18–52, 150–51.

35. Dorothea Browder, "A 'Christian Solution of the Labor Situation': How Working Women Reshaped the YWCA's Religious Mission and Politics," *Journal of Women's History* 19, no. 2 (2007): 85–110; Bruce P. Bottorff, "Continuity and Change: A History of the YWCA of Honolulu, 1900–1945" (PhD diss., University of Hawai'i, 1999), 200–203; Grace H. Wilson, *The Religious and Educational Philosophy of the Young Women's Christian Association* (New York: Teachers College, Columbia University, 1933), 85; Nancy Marie Robertson, *Christian Sisterhood, Race Relations, and the YWCA, 1906–46* (Urbana: University of Illinois Press, 2007), 78.

36. Many International Institutes ultimately left the Christian YWCA umbrella in the 1930s to merge into a national organization—the National Institute of Immigrant Welfare. Raymond A. Mohl, "Cultural Pluralism in Immigrant Education: The YWCA's International Institute, 1910–1940," in *Men and Women Adrift: The YMCA and the YWCA in the City*, ed. Nina Mjagkij and Margaret Spratt (New York: New York University Press, 1997), 111–37; Milton M. Gordon, *Assimilation in American Life: The Role of Race, Religion, and National Origins* (New York: Oxford University Press, 1964), 154; Celeste DeRoche, "How Wide the Circle of We: Cultural Pluralism and American Identity, 1910–1954" (PhD diss., University of Maine, 2000), 15, 64.

37. Among the Honolulu YWCA founders were Emma Smith Dillingham and her daughter Mary Dillingham Frear and Mary Tenney Castle and her daughter Harriet Castle Coleman. It drew most of its members from the Central Union Church in Honolulu. In 1906, the Honolulu YWCA became a charter member of the newly established National YWCA. Bottorff, "Continuity and Change," 1–16, 44–50, 79–80, 114.

38. The founding of the San Francisco Japanese YWCA was led by Yonako Abiko (1880–1944), a younger sister of Ume(ko) Tsuda, the founder of Tsuda College in Japan, and the wife of Kyutaro Abiko, the owner of a Japanese newspaper in San Francisco. Yonako Abiko, "Zaibei nihonjin kirisutokyō joshi seinenkai sōritsu no shidai," *Meiji no joshi* 9, no. 9 (1912): 17–19; Eriko Yamamoto, "Mainoritī josei no rentai: Nikkei Amerikajin joseishi ni miru tabunkashugi to komyunitī katsudō," in *Kita Amerika shakai o nagamete: Josei-jiku to esunisitī-jiku no kōsaten*, ed. Kikuyo Tanaka and Mariko Takagi-Kitayama (Nishinomiya, Japan: Kwansei gakuin daigaku shuppankai, 2004), 187–92.

39. Bottorff, "Continuity and Change," 73–77; "International Institute," in *International Institute Papers* [hereafter *II Papers*], box 3; Hawai'i State Archives Manuscript Collection [hereafter HSAMC]-M450. Hawai'i State Archives, Honolulu, HI.

40. Ralph S. Kuykendall and Lorin Tarr Gill, *Hawaii in the World War* (Honolulu, HI: Honolulu Historical Commission, 1928), 269–85; Bottorff, "Continuity and Change," 83–107; Sims, *The Natural History of a Social Institution*, 61–64; Richard Roberts, *Florence Simms: A Biography* (New York: Woman's Press, 1926), 209–20.

41. The United War Work Campaign was carried out by the YMCA, the YWCA, the American Library Association, the War Camp Community Service, the National Catholic War Council (Knights of Columbus), the Jewish Welfare Board, and the Salvation Army. "Women in the Progressive Era-National Women's History Museum," September 11, 2011, http://www.nwhm.org/online-exhibits/progressiveera/worldwarI.html. For example, Mary Dillingham Frear, Honolulu YWCA president (in office, 1914–1919), also became a vice chair of the Hawaiian branch of the CND Women's Committee.
42. Bottorff, "Community and Change," 83–107. As for the politics of *Nisei* fun-loving girls' networking, friendship, and social movements, see Valerie J. Matsumoto, *City Girls: The Nisei Social World in Los Angeles, 1920–1950* (New York: Oxford University Press, 2014).
43. Bruce P. Bottorff, "Immigrant Assimilation at the International Institute of Honolulu, 1916–1937," *Journal of Inquiry and Research*, no. 108 (September 2018): 69–85; Anne Soon Choi, "'Hawai'i Has Been My America': Generation, Gender, and Korean Immigrant Experience in Hawai'i Before World War II," *American Studies* 45, no. 3 (Fall 2004): 139–55.
44. Jan Doolittle Wilson, *The Women's Joint Congressional Committee and the Politics of Maternalism, 1920–30* (Urbana: University of Illinois Press, 2007), 38–49; J. Stanley Lemons, *The Woman Citizen: Social Feminism in the 1920s* (Urbana: University of Illinois Press, 1973), 25–32.
45. Mary Anderson and Mary N. Winslow, *Woman at Work: The Autobiography of Mary Anderson as Told to Mary N. Winslow* (Minneapolis: University of Minnesota Press, 1951), 96–97.
46. Wilson, *The Women's Joint Congressional Committee and the Politics of Maternalism, 1920–30*, 1–7, 175. WJCC's original ten charter member organizations were the League of Women Voters, the Women's Christian Temperance Union, the National Consumers' Leagues, the General Federation of Women's Clubs, the Women's Trade Union League, National Council of Women, National Federation of Business and Professional Women's Clubs, Association of Collegiate Alumnae, American Home Economics Association, and National Congress of Mothers and Parent-Teacher Association.
47. Robertson, *Christian Sisterhood, Race Relations, and the YWCA*, 79.
48. Ladd-Taylor, *Mother-Work*, 96–97; Muncy, *Creating a Female Dominion in American Reform*, xvi–xvii, 150; Wilson, *The Women's Joint Congressional Committee and the Politics of Maternalism*, 1–7, 171–74.
49. Frances Lawrence, "The Kindergarten Situation in Hawaii," *Childhood Education* 1, no. 1 (September 1924): 21–28; Kuykendall and Gill, *Hawaii in the World War*, 348.
50. Whang Ha Soo was a graduate of college in Athens, Georgia, and the first Korean social worker in Hawai'i. Her family was active in the Korean National Association, and her brothers were ordained Methodist ministers.

51. Bruce P. Bottorff, "Immigrant Assimilation at the International Institute of Honolulu, 1916–1937," *Kansai Gaikokugo Daigaku Kenkyū Ronshū* 108 (2018–2019): 69–85; "International Institute," *II Papers*, box 3. As for the role of bilingual first-generation immigrant women in Christian women's civilizing efforts, Anne Soon Choi discussed the case of Esther (Po Pae) Park, who assumed the position of Honolulu YWCA's Korean nationality secretary in 1922. See Choi, "'Hawai'i Has Been My America.'"
52. "Many Woman Voters Registered Yesterday," *Nippu Jiji*, August 31, 1920.
53. Barbara Peterson, "Noda, Alice Sae Teshima," in *Notable Women of Hawaii*, ed. Barbara Bennett Peterson (Honolulu: University of Hawai'i Press, 1984), 288–91; "Y.W.C.A. Notes," *Honolulu Star-Bulletin*, November 6, 1922, 7; Information provided by Mrs. Lillian Noda Yajima, daughter of Alice Sae Teshima Noda.
54. Dr. Ellen Stadtmuller, "Social Hygiene," in Pan-Pacific Women's Conference, *Women of the Pacific: Being a Record of the Proceedings of the First Pan-Pacific Women's Conference Which Was Held in Honolulu from the 9th to the 19th of August 1928, Under the Auspices of the Pan-Pacific Union* (Honolulu, HI: Pan-Pacific Union, 1928), 166.
55. Susan L. Smith, *Japanese American Midwives: Culture, Community, and Health Politics, 1880–1950* (Urbana: University of Illinois Press, 2005), 105.
56. Dr. Vivia B. Appleton (Mrs. Vivia Bell) started her higher education at Rockford College and transferred to Cornell University for a BA and went on to Johns Hopkins University for an MD. After various medical studies and projects in London, Berlin, Paris, New York, and San Francisco, she participated in American Red Cross war relief efforts during World War I. Then she went to China for the Council on Health Education and served as an advisory secretary for the National YWCA's work in China in 1921–1922. Smith, *Japanese American Midwives*, 122, 126, 232, note 77. Vivia B. Appleton, *A Doctor's Letters from China, Fifty Years Ago* (Honolulu, HI: Self-published, 1976), vii–ix; Boyd, *Emissaries*, 288.
57. Rosie K. Chang, "Smyth, Mabel Leilani," in *Notable Women of Hawaii*, 347–50. Smyth was from Kona. After completing her high school degree in Honolulu, she joined the Raths, who directed Palama Settlement in Honolulu, on their trip to the U.S. mainland as a nursemaid for their children and enrolled in the Springfield Hospital Training School for Nurses in Massachusetts. After returning to Hawai'i, she temporarily worked as director of the Hawaiian Humane Society and later became the head nurse of Palama Settlement. During 1921 and 1922, she took courses in public health at Simmons College in Boston and became the first director of the newly created Department of Public Health Nursing.
58. Dodge, *A History of the FKCAAHI*, 41–43.
59. Laura Ruby, ed., *Mo'ili'ili: The Life of a Community* (Honolulu, HI: Mo'ili'ili Community Center, 2005), 173.

60. Bottorff, "Continuity and Change," 130–62, 193–222.
61. Boyd, *Emissaries*, 77–83.
62. Roberts, *Florence Simms*, 241; Wilson, *The Religious and Educational Philosophy*, 86; Robertson, *Christian Sisterhood, Race Relations, and the YWCA*, 77–78, 79; Browder, "A 'Christian Solution of the Labor Situation.'"
63. Bruce P. Bottorff, "Forging American Womanhood: The Acculturation of Second-Generation Immigrant Girls in Honolulu, 1917–1938," *Japanese Journal of American Studies* 31 (2020): 75–86; *The International Woman Suffrage News* 20, no. 3 (December 1925): ii.
64. Wilcox was the second elected female territorial legislator and the first female territorial senator from Kaua'i. Judith Dean Gething Hughes, *Women and Children First: The Life and Times of Elsie Wilcox of Kaua'i* (Honolulu: University of Hawai'i Press, 1996).
65. Hughes, *Women and Children First*, 77.
66. For example, see Patsy Sumie Saiki, *Early Japanese Immigrants in Hawaii* (Honolulu: Japanese Cultural Center of Hawaii, 1993), 57–60.
67. Muncy, *Creating a Female Dominion in American Reform*.
68. Gary Y. Okihiro, *Cane Fires: The Anti-Japanese Movement in Hawaii, 1865–1945* (Philadelphia: Temple University Press, 1991), 19–23.
69. Patsy Sumie Saiki, *Japanese Women in Hawaii: The First 100 Years* (Honolulu, HI: Kisaku, 1985), 17–25; Tomoko Katsumura, "Honoruru mushō yōchien nihonjinbu ni okeru shodai shunin hobo Ozawa Itoko no kōken," *Seibo hishōten joshi tankidaigaku kiyō*, no. 29 (2003): 122–33; Yasutaro Soga, *Gojyūnenkan no Hawai kaiko* (Honolulu, HI: Gojūnenkan no Hawai kaiko kankōkai, 1953), 107–11.
70. Sophia Arabella Irwin received her higher education in her father's hometown of Philadelphia, took courses on early education at Columbia University, and received additional training in Froebelian and Montessori methods in Germany and Italy. In 1916, she established a Christian kindergarten and the Gyokusei Training School for Kindergarten (now the Irwin School), a school to train kindergarten teachers, in Tokyo. Denki hensan iinkai, *Kōya ni mizu wa wakite: Bera Aruwuin no shōgai* (Tokyo: Aruwuin Gakuen, 1980).
71. Nagako Sugimori, "Fujin heiwa kyōkai no kessei to katsudō no tenkai," in *Nijusseiki niokeru joseino heiwaundō*, ed. Kuni Nakajima and Nagako Sugimori (Tokyo: Domesu shuppan, 2006), 63–85; "Marian Osterhoust, Physiologist, Dead," *Special to the New York Times*, May 12, 1973, January 8, 2017, http:/www.nytimes.com/1973/05/12/archives/marian-osterhout-physiologist-dead.html?_r=0.
72. *Constitution, By-laws and Charter of the FKCAAHI*, 27; "Honolulu: Free Kindergarten Training School (List of Graduates)" in Dodge, *A History of the FKCAAHI*; *Calendar of the FKCAAHI* (1896), 19; (1897), 29.

73. Hawai nihonjin iminshi kankō iinkai, ed., *Hawai nihonjin iminshi* (Honolulu, HI: Hawai nikkeijin rengō kyōkai, 1964), 296–97, 330; Ernest K. Wakukawa, *A History of the Japanese People in Hawaii* (Honolulu, HI: Toyō shoin, 1938), 114.
74. "Tokyo kirisutokyō joshi seinenkai rekishi gairyaku," *Chi-no shio* 38 (February 1931), 1; "Kokorokara keifukusuru Imanishi Itoko fujin," *Joshi seinankai* 22, no. 3 (March 1925): 24–28.
75. Alan Takeo Moriyama, *Imingaisha: Japanese Emigration Companies and Hawaii, 1894–1908* (Honolulu: University of Hawai'i Press, 1985); Ronald Kotani, *The Japanese in Hawaii: A Century of Struggle* (Honolulu: Hawaii Hochi, 1985), 21–29; Hawai nihonjin iminshi kankō iinkai, *Hawai nihonjin iminshi*, 118–20.
76. Irwin first arrived in Japan as an employee of the Pacific Mail Steamship Company in 1866 and established close relationships with Japanese businessmen and government officers. Irwin had assisted them in building a Japanese trading and marine transport business. Hideo Matsunaga, *Hawai kanyaku imin no chichi R. W. Aauin* (Tokyo: Kodansha Business Partners, 2011); Kotani, *The Japanese in Hawaii*, 9–20; Okihiro, *Cane Fires*, 23–29.
77. For cruel treatment, see Erika Hori, *Hawai nikkeijin no rekishiteki hensen: Amerika kara yomigaeru "eiyu" Goto Katsu* (Tokyo: Sairyūsha, 2021).
78. Kotani, *The Japanese in Hawaii*, 91–116.
79. Iga Mori was educated at the Naval Medical College in Japan and Cooper Medical College in California. Michael M. Okihiro, "Japanese Doctors in Hawai'i," *Hawaiian Journal of History* 36 (2002): 108; Moriyama, *Imingaisha*, 94.
80. *Calendar of the FKCAAHI* (1898), 12.
81. WBMI-Chicago founded three schools in Kobe, Japan: a boarding school called Kobe Home in 1875 that later became Kobe College, a women's Bible training school in 1888 that later became a female theological seminary, and a kindergarten and kindergarten-teacher training school in 1889. Jane Addams and her Hull House supporters were linked to this network. Addams was listed as a board member of the Kobe College Corporation (KCC), established in 1920 to raise funds for the campus expansion. Kobe jogakuin, *Kobe jogakuin hyakunenshi, Kakuron* (Nishinomiya, Japan: Kobe jogakuin, 1981), 261, 288–91, 696–704; Mary Lynn McCree Bryan et al., eds., *The Jane Addams Papers 1868–1935* (Ann Arbor, MI: University Microfilm International, 1984), reel 42, 17, 22.
82. *Calendar of the FKCAAHI* (1897), 29, 30; Vandewalker, *The Kindergarten in American Education*, 96–102.
83. ABCFM missionary woman A. L. Howe came to Japan in 1887 at the request of the Japanese Women's Society of Kobe Church to provide kindergarten education to their children, and Fuji briefly worked as a teacher of her kindergarten. Fuji then moved to Hiroshima to assist a Methodist missionary woman

N. B. Gaines in building a kindergarten teachers' training school. Noriko Kawamura Ishii, *American Women Missionaries at Kobe College, 1873–1909* (New York: Routledge, 2004), 153–55; Kobe jogakuin, *Kobe jogakuin hyakunenshi*, 206, 224–25; Monbushō, *Yōchien kyōiku hyakunenshi* (Tokyo: Hikarinokuni, 1979), 43, 169–70.

84. Ishii, *American Women Missionaries at Kobe College*, 12–13, 153–55; Yumi Nagai, "Koga Fuji no Amerika ryūgaku to yōchien kyōiku jissen," *Nihon no kyōiku shigaku* 60 (2017): 32–44. The first continuing kindergarten in Japan was built in Tokyo in 1876 by the government, whose efforts were modeled after German kindergartens. It was attached to Tokyo Female Teachers' School, and its founding days were under the male management of Mr. Nobuzo Seki (1843–1879), a former Buddhist monk who studied in England, assisted by its head teacher Klara Ziedermann Matsuno (1853–1941), a German graduate of a Froebelian teacher training school in Germany and wife of a Japanese government official. Monbushō, *Yōchien kyōiku hyakunenshi*, 53–54.

85. *Calendar of the FKCAAHI* (1896), 19; Esther Atsuko Mitsunaga, "So, Yeiko Mizobe," in *Notable Women of Hawaii*, 350–52.

86. Her husband Toshisuke Kishimoto had come to Hawai'i as a member of the 1885 first group of the *kanyakuimin* contract-laborers and ran a Japanese inn after the maturity of his term. Soga, *Gojūnenkan no Hawaii kaiko*, 142; Personal Information Database as of January 6, 2011. Museum of Japanese Emigration to Hawaii, Oshima, Yamaguchi Prefecture, Japan.

87. For the experiences of the indentured daughters, see Toyoko Yamazaki and Karen F. Colligan-Taylor, *Sandakan Brothel No. 8: Journey into the History of Lower-class Japanese Women* (New York: Routledge, 1998); Patricia E. Tsurumi, *Factory Girls: Women in the Thread Mills of Meiji Japan* (Princeton, NJ: Princeton University Press, 1990), 174–90. For the missionary ideals of "Christian Home" and women's moral authority, see Peggy Pascoe, *Relations of Rescue: The Search for Female Moral Authority in the American West, 1874–1939* (New York: Oxford University Press, 1990), 34–40, 146–173; Rui Kohiyama, *Amerika fujin senkyōshi: rainichi no haikei to sono eikyō* (Tokyo: Tokyo Daigaku shuppankai, 1992), 252–62.

88. Nihon kirisutokyō fujin kyōfūkai, ed., *Nihon kirisutokyō fujin kyōfūkai hyakunenshi* (Tokyo: Domesu shuppan, 1986), 62–81.

89. Joan Hori, "Japanese Prostitution in Hawaii During the Immigration Period," *Hawaiian Journal of History* 15 (1981): 113–24; Kelli Yoshie Nakamura, "Yeiko Mizobe So and the Japanese Women's Home for Abused Picture Brides (1895–1905)," *Amerasia Journal* 36, no. 1 (2010): 1–32; Special Correspondence, "At the Cross Roads of the Pacific—in Hawaii," *Union Signal*, January 22, 1927, 7.

90. Nippu Jiji Editorial Board, ed., *Hawai dohō hatten kaikoshi* (Honolulu, HI: Nippu Jiji, 1921), 178–79; Yukiko Kimura, *Issei: Japanese Immigrants in Hawaii* (Honolulu: University of Hawai'i Press, 1992), 199–200.

4. Elusive Collaboration for Anglophone Hegemony: Maternalists, Liberals, and Internationalists

1. The conference gathered education specialists from various "countries" in the Pacific—e.g., Hawai'i, the U.S. mainland, Australia, Canada, China, Japan, Java, India, Korea, New Zealand, the Philippines, Portugal, Russia, and Siam. Pan-Pacific Union, *First Pan-Pacific Educational Conference, Honolulu, August 11–24, 1921, Program and Proceedings* (Honolulu, HI: 1921), 13–16 [hereafter PPU, *First Pan-Pacific Educational Conference, Program and Proceedings*].
2. Alexander Hume Ford, "The Opportunity of Educators," in PPU, *First Pan-Pacific Educational Conference, Program and Proceedings*, 26–27.
3. PPU, *First Pan-Pacific Educational Conference, Program and Proceedings*, 3–6, 24–27.
4. "Review of Early Plans of the Pan-Pacific Women's Conference," *Pan-Pacific Union Bulletin* new series [hereafter *PPU Bulletin* ns], no. 101 (June 1928): 7.
5. For a comprehensive study of the PPU, see Paul F. Hooper, *Elusive Destiny: The Internationalist Movement in Modern Hawaii* (Honolulu: University of Hawai'i Press, 1980), 65–104.
6. The IPR convened six international conferences before the outbreak of World War II. The first two conferences were in Honolulu in 1925 and 1927; the third in Kyoto, Japan, in 1929; the fourth in Hangzhou/Shanghai, China, in 1932; the fifth in Banff, Canada, in 1933; and the sixth at Yosemite in the United States in 1936. Michio Yamaoka, *"Taihiyō mondai chōsakai"kenkyū* (Tokyo: Ryūkei shosha, 1997); Nobuo Katagiri, *Taiheiyō mondai chōsakai no kenkyū: Senkanki nihon IPR no katsudō o chūshinto shite* (Tokyo: Keiō gijyuku daigaku shuppankai, 2003).
7. Hooper, *Elusive Destiny*, 105–36; John N. Thomas, *The Institute of Pacific Relations: Asian Scholars and American Politics* (Seattle: University of Washington Press, 1974); Tomoko Akami, *Internationalizing the Pacific: The United States, Japan and the Institute of Pacific Relations in War and Peace, 1919–1945* (New York: Routledge, 2002); Paul F. Hooper, ed., *Remembering the Institute of Pacific Relations: The Memoirs of William L. Holland* (Tokyo: Ryukei Shōsha, 1995). As for its relationship to Protestantism, see David A. Hollinger, *Protestants Abroad: How Missionaries Tried to Change the World but Changed America* (Princeton, NJ: Princeton University Press, 2017); Sarah Marie Griffith, *The Fight for Asian American Civil Rights: Liberal Protestant Activism, 1900–1950* (Urbana: University of Illinois Press, 2018).
8. As for the PPWA, see Fiona Paisley, *Glamour in the Pacific: Cultural Internationalism and Race Politics in the Women's Pan-Pacific* (Honolulu: University of Hawai'i Press, 2009); Paul F. Hooper, "Feminism in the Pacific: The Pan-Pacific and Southeast Asia Women's Association," *Pacific Historian* 20, no. 4 (1976): 367–77.

9. Bob Krauss, *Johnny Wilson: First Hawaiian Democrat* (Honolulu: University of Hawai'i Press, 1994), 167.
10. Eileen Tamura, *Americanization, Acculturation, and Ethnic Identity: The Nisei Generation in Hawaii* (Urbana: University of Illinois Press, 1994), 60; Ronald T. Takaki, *Pau Hana: Plantation Life and Labor in Hawaii, 1835–1920* (Honolulu: University of Hawai'i Press, 1983), 117–19.
11. Ford spent the 1890s in urban Chicago, engaging in an ecumenical and experimental religious movement, transcending religious "prejudice" in its social reform, and "rescuing" projects. He worked with Rev. John Rusk in the militant social reform/charity efforts supported by citizen voluntarism. "The Genesis of the Pan-Pacific Union: Being Some Reminiscences of Alexander Hume Ford, Director of the Pan-Pacific Union [hereafter, The Genesis of the PPU], First Installment," *Mid-Pacific Magazine* 30, no. 3 (September 1925): 270–78. For Alexander Hume Ford, see Hooper, *Elusive Destiny*, 65–104, and Valerie Noble, *Hawaiian Prophet: Alexander Hume Ford: A Biography* (New York: Exposition, 1980). On John Rusk and his Church Militant, see David Burns, *The Life and Death of the Radical Historical Jesus* (New York: Oxford University Press, 2013), 45–46.
12. Hooper, *Elusive Destiny*, 65–104; Barbara Del Piano, *Outrigger Canoe Club: The First One Hundred Years 1908–2008* (Honolulu, HI: Outrigger Canoe Club, 2008), 4–6; "The Genesis of the PPU, First Installment," 265–80.
13. In 1914, Ford traveled across the Pacific to Siberia, Russia, inland China, Java, Korea, and Japan, promoting the movement. His efforts, for example, resulted in the formation of a Pan-Pacific Club in Kobe, Japan, by March 1918. "Japan and Pan-Pacific Effort," *Mid-Pacific Magazine* 15, no. 3 (March 1918): 217.
14. Among the founding officers were First Vice President Frank Cooke Atherton (1877–1945), missionary grandson and vice president and later CEO of Castle & Cooke Co.; Second Vice President Chung Kun Ai (aka, Zhong Yu, 1865–1961), one of the first successful businessmen of Chinese ancestry active in church and philanthropic work and an ardent supporter of Chinese nationalist movements; and Recording Secretary Joaquim M. Camara, a long-time military officer and lawyer of Portuguese ancestry. Among the trustees were Arthur Kenzaburo Ozawa, brother of Ito(ko) Ozawa Imanishi, who became the first lawyer of Japanese ancestry and the president of the Japanese American Citizenship Association in Hawai'i; Dr. Syngman Rhee, Korean educator and nationalist leader who had received a doctorate from Princeton University and would later become the first president of the Republic of Korea; Rev. C. C. Ramirez, Christian leader of the Filipino communities in Hawai'i; George H. Vicars, successful businessman on the Big Island of Hawai'i who was originally from New Zealand; along with the local white businessmen and/or politicians of missionary heritage such as William R. Castle of O'ahu, Frank F. Baldwin of

Maui, and George N. Wilcox of Kauaʻi. "Pan-Pacific Union and Its Activities," *Mid-Pacific Magazine* 14, no. 3 (September 1917): 217–19.
15. "The Genesis of the PPU, First Installment," 265, 267.
16. Erez Manela, "Imagining Woodrow Wilson in Asia: Dreams of East-West Harmony and the Revolt Against Empire in 1919," *American Historical Review* 11, no. 5 (December 2006): 1327–51.
17. Japan sought the lion's share of the waning European control during the Great War in Europe and made the so-called Twenty-One Demands to China in 1915. The government in Beijing, under duress, accepted sixteen of them.
18. Gary Y. Okihiro, *Cane Fires: The Anti-Japanese Movement in Hawaii, 1865–1945* (Philadelphia: Temple University Press, 1991), 102–28; Roberta Chang and Wayne Patterson, *The Koreans in Hawaiʻi: A Pictorial History, 1903–2003* (Honolulu: University of Hawaiʻi Press, 2003), 100–116; Clarence E. Glick, *Sojourners and Settlers: Chinese Migrants in Hawaiʻi* (Honolulu: University of Hawaiʻi Press, 1980), 269–309; Melinda Tria Kerkvliet, "Interpreting Pablo Manlapit," *Social Process in Hawaii* 37 (1996): 1–25.
19. "Aims and Objects of the Pan Pacific Union," *PPU Bulletin* ns, no. 10 (August 1920): 2.
20. In Chicago, Ford once worked for the *Chicago Daily News Record*, where William E. Curtiss was one of his colleagues. Curtiss was an early advocate of the regional international cooperation that later developed into the Pan-American Union (PAU). Hooper, *Elusive Destiny*, 65–104.
21. For Sydney L. Gulick, see Sandra C. Taylor, *Advocate of Understanding: Sidney Gulick and the Search for Peace with Japan* (Kent, OH: Kent State University Press, 1984); Izumi Hirobe, *Japanese Pride, American Prejudice: Modifying the Exclusion Clause of the 1924 Immigration Act* (Stanford, CA: Stanford University Press, 2001); Son-Thierry Ly and Patrick Weil, "The Antiracist Origin of the Quota System," *Social Research* 77, no. 1 (Spring 2010): 45–78.
22. At its founding in 1908, the FCC issued the "Social Creed of the Churches," declaring its support for such issues as the abolition of child labor, reduction in working hours, and a living wage. In 1912, the creed included workers' right to collective bargaining. John A. Hutchison, *We Are Not Divided: A Critical and Historical Study of the Federal Council* (New York: Round Table, 1941), 46–47, 102; Presbyterian Historical Society, *Guide to the Federal Council of the Churches of Christ in America Records, 1894–1952*, 1–2, June 20, 2022, https://www.history.pcusa.org/collections/research-tools/guides-archival-collections/ncc-rg-18.
23. Taylor, *Advocate of Understanding*, 124, 153–54.
24. "The Genesis of the PPU, First Installment," 279–80; "The Genesis of the PPU, Second Installment," *Mid-Pacific Magazine* 30, no. 4 (October 1925): 379.
25. "The Genesis of the PPU, Sixth Installment," *Mid-Pacific Magazine* 31, no. 2 (February 1926): 109; Hooper, *Elusive Destiny*, 65–104.

26. Noble, *Hawaiian Prophet*, 43–69, 249.
27. Alexander Hume Ford, "Hawaii, the Radiating Center of Pan Pacific Civilization," in *The World's Moral Problems: Addresses at the Third World's Christian Citizenship Conference Held in Pittsburgh, PA, USA. November 9–16, 1919* (Pittsburgh, PA: National Reform Association, 1920), 1–8, 400–406, June 20, 2022, https://onlinebooks.library.upenn.edu/webbin/book/lookupid?key=ha008417224.
28. Gulick also gave a paper titled "The Next Step in Immigration Legislation." *The World's Moral Problems*, 152–59, 166–70.
29. Taylor, *Advocate of Understanding*, 124–48; Alexander H. Ford, "Pan-Pacific Propaganda in the United States," in *PPU Bulletin* ns, no. 6 (April 1920): 7–9.
30. Hooper, *Elusive Destiny*, 79–88; "The Genesis of the PPU, First Installment," 267–69.
31. For example, in Shanghai, the Pan-Pacific Association of China gathered three hundred members to entertain the congressional party. In Japan, where a Pan-Pacific Club was already in existence in Kobe, Ford's effort created the Pan-Pacific Association of Japan in Tokyo in 1920, electing Prince Iyesato Tokugawa, chair of the House of Peers, as its president. Additional new branches were also formed in Beijing and Seoul through Ford's facilitation. "Report of the Secretary," *PPU Bulletin* ns, no. 16 (February 1921): 13–16.
32. *PPU Bulletin* ns, no. 18 (April 1921): 1. Other names of dignitaries that appeared on the list include New Zealand prime ministers William Hughes and W. F. Massey; Japan's prime minister Takashi Hara; and Chinese Hsu Shih-chang, Li Yuan-Hung, and Tsao Kun, who served the president of the Republic of China in Beijing after the death of Yuan Shikai.
33. Hooper, *Elusive Destiny*, 88–94. The Pan-Pacific Science Congress became known as the Pan-Pacific Science Association and is still active today.
34. Barbara Del Piano, *Nā Lani Kaumaka/Daughters of Hawai'i: A Century of Historic Preservation* (Honolulu: Daughters of Hawaii, 2005), xv.
35. J. Patricia Morgan Swenson, "Swanzy, Julie Judd," in *Notable Women of Hawaii*, ed. Barbara Bennett Peterson (Honolulu: University of Hawai'i Press, 1984), 361–64.
36. "The Genesis of the PPU, Fifth Installment," *Mid-Pacific Magazine* 31, no. 1 (January 1926): 14–15.
37. "The Genesis of the PPU, Second Installment," 373–74.
38. Swenson, "Swanzy, Julie Judd"; Charlotte P. Dodge, *A History of the Free Kindergarten and Children's Aid Association of the Hawaiian Islands, 1895–1945* [hereafter *A History of the FKCAAHI*] (Honolulu, HI: Mercantile Print, 1945), 46.
39. "The Passing of America's Only Queen—Liliuokalani of Hawaii," *Mid-Pacific Magazine* 15, no. 2 (February 1918): 127; Noble, *Hawaiian Prophet*, 82. For analysis of the pageants and carnivals initiated by Ford, see Lori Pierce, "The Whites Have Created Modern Honolulu: Ethnicity, Racial Stratification, and

the Discourse of Aloha," in *Racial Thinking in the United States: Uncompleted Independence*, ed. Paul Spickard and G. Reginald Daniel (Notre Dame, IN: University of Notre Dame Press, 2004), 124–54.

40. Okihiro, *Cane Fires*, 102–28; William J. Breen, *Uncle Sam at Home: Civilian Mobilization, Wartime Federalism, and the Council of National Defense, 1917–1919* (Westport, CT: Greenwood, 1984), 159–75.
41. Hooper, *Elusive Destiny*, 82; Breen, *Uncle Sam at Home*, 164–65.
42. "The Pan-Pacific Union Elects Woodrow Wilson as Its Honorary President, Secretary Franklin K. Lane Bears the Message," *Mid-Pacific Magazine* 16, no. 3 (September 1918): 216–21.
43. Cited in Ralph S. Kuykendall and Lorin Tarr Gill, *Hawaii in the World War* (Honolulu, HI: Honolulu Historical Commission, 1928), 415.
44. "A Pan-Pacific Declaration of Independence," *Mid-Pacific Magazine* 16, no. 4 (October 1918): 317; Hooper, *Elusive Destiny*, 82. On the same day, there was another event to assure the local multiracial and multinational population's loyalty to the United States and the unity of peoples in the Pacific for the Allied Powers under the leadership of the United States. See, for example, "Celebration to Be Cementing of Closer Bonds," *Honolulu Advertiser*, July 4, 1918, 7.
45. Andrew William Lind, *Hawaii's People* (Honolulu: University of Hawai'i Press, 1967), 72.
46. Hawaiian Kingdom Weblog, "An Act to Provide a Government for the Territory of Hawaii," August 8, 2023, https://www.hawaiiankingdom.org/us-organic-act-1900.shtml.
47. Takaki, *Pau Hana*, 117–19; Paul F. Nahoa Lucas, "*E Ola Mau Kākou I Ka 'Ōleo Makuahine*: Hawaiian Language Policy and the Courts," *Hawaiian Journal of History* 34 (2000): 1–28; Tracie Ku'uipo Losch and Momi Kamahele, eds., *Hawai'i: Center of the Pacific* (Acton, MA: Copley Custom Textbooks, 2008), 119–29.
48. Takaki, *Pau Hana*, 92–93; Meyer Weinberg, *Asian-American Education: Historical Background and Current Realities* (New York: Routledge, 1997), 47–48; Yukuji Okita, *Hawai nikkei imin no kyōikushi* (Tokyo: Minerva shobō, 1997).
49. Vaughan MacCaughey, "Education in Hawaii," in PPU, *First Pan-Pacific Educational Conference, Program and Proceedings*, 91–92; Lucas, "*E Ola Mau Kākou I Ka 'Ōleo Makuahine*," 1–28; Weinberg, *Asian-American Education*, 47–48.
50. Tamura, *Americanization, Acculturation, and Ethnic Identity*, 107–12.
51. For example, Julie Judd Swanzy's father, Charles Hastings Judd accompanied King Kalakaua on his world tour in 1881, which led to the contract between the Japanese and Hawaiian governments to import of Japanese laborers. Her husband, Francis Mills Swanzy, whom she married in 1884, served as the director of sugar giant Theo H. Davies. He also played an important role in bringing foreign laborers to the islands. George F. M. Nellist, ed., *The Story of Hawaii*

and Its Builders (Honolulu, HI: Honolulu Star-Bulletin, 1925), 133–35; Edwin P. Hoyt, *Davies: The Inside Story of a British-American Family in the Pacific and Its Business Enterprises* (Honolulu, HI: Topgallant, 1983), 191–92.

52. Okihiro, *Cane Fires*, 134–38; Noriko Asato, *Teaching Mikadoism: The Attack on Japanese Language Schools in Hawaii, California, and Washington, 1919–1927* (Honolulu: University of Hawai'i Press, 2006), 24.
53. MacCaughey also served as the head of the territorial department of natural sciences. He was a committed member of the Hawaiian Evangelical Association (HEA) and Central Union Church in Honolulu, serving as chairman of the Religious Education Committee of the church. Marquis Who's Who, *Who Was Who in America*, Vol. 3 (Chicago: Marquis Who's Who, 1963), 540, cited in Asato, *Teaching Mikadoism*, 27, 129 note 48.
54. MacCaughey's wife served as the chair of the FKCAAHI's standing committee for affiliated kindergartens and playgrounds in 1920. *Calendar of the Free Kindergarten and Children's Aid Association of the Hawaiian Islands* (1919–1920), 21 [hereafter *Calendar of the FKCAAHI*].
55. Vaughan MacCaughey, "Hawaii's Public Schools and the Pan-Pacific Idea," *Mid-Pacific Magazine* 17, no. 6 (June 1919): 569.
56. The commission's other members were W. W. Kemp, Education Department chairman of the University of California; Park R. Kolbe, president of Municipal University in Akron, Ohio; and George R. Twiss, professor of secondary education at Ohio State University and state high school inspector. Asato, *Teaching Mikadoism*, 28–29.
57. Department of the Interior Bureau of Education, *A Survey of Education in Hawaii* (Washington, DC: Government Printing Office, 1920), 43, 142–43 [hereafter, DI Bureau of Education, *A Survey of Education in Hawaii*].
58. Okihiro, *Cane Fires*, 134–36; DI Bureau of Education, *A Survey of Education in Hawaii*, 134–39.
59. A. Grove Day, *History Makers of Hawaii: A Biographical Dictionary* (Honolulu, HI: Mutual, 1984), 58–59.
60. "Daughters of Hawaii," in "Hawai'i Newspaper Morgue," compiled by University of Hawai'i at Manoa Hamilton Library. Other original officers were Mrs. Abbie Cordelia Alexander, vice regent; Miss Susanne Patch, secretary; Miss Flora Wilfong Girvin, treasurer; and Miss Agnes E. Judd (daughter of the regent), registrar. "History of the Aloha Chapter DAR Is Given," *Honolulu Star-Bulletin*, April 10, 1937; Hazel H. Bond, "Aloha Chapter of DAR Is Observing 50th Birthday," *Honolulu Advertiser*, March 2, 1947.
61. Simon Wendt, "Defenders of Patriotism or Mothers of Fascism? The Daughters of the American Revolution, Antiradicalism, and Un-Americanism in the Interwar Period," *Journal of American Studies* 47, no. 4 (2013): 943–69.

62. DI Bureau of Education, *A Survey of Education in Hawaii*, 37, 47–48, 70–75.
63. DI Bureau of Education, *A Survey of Education in Hawaii*, 6; "The Immigration Problem: Japanese in Hawaii," *Woman Citizen* 5, no. 31 (1921): 842–43.
64. DI Bureau of Education, *A Survey of Education in Hawaii*, 139–42; Tamura, *Americanization, Acculturation, and Ethnic Identity*, 110.
65. DI Bureau of Education, *A Survey of Education in Hawaii*, 42–44.
66. DI Bureau of Education, *A Survey of Education in Hawaii*, 143.
67. DI Bureau of Education, *A Survey of Education in Hawaii*, 5.
68. Dodge, *A History of the FKCAAHI*, 20.
69. For example, to fight against the exclusionist forces, Japan's capitalist giant Shibusawa established the Japanese-American Relations Committee (*Nichibei Kankei Iinkai*) in the Tokyo Chamber of Commerce in 1916 to match the efforts of Hawaii's missionary grandson and sugar-business giant Wallace M. Alexander who had organized the Japanese Relations Committee in the San Francisco Chamber of Commerce in 1905. Nobuo Katagiri, *Minkan kōryū no pionia: Shibusawa eiichi no kokumin gaikō* (Tokyo: Fujiwara shoten, 2013), 39–127. Hawaiʻi's planter paternalists of missionary heritage expected the Japanese consul and his collaborator Japanese internationalists to be capable of mediating between the white planters/managers and Japanese plantation workers. See, for example, "F. C. Atherton to Viscount Shibusawa, February 1922," *Documents on Japanese Foreign Policy, Honpō imin kankei zakken: Hawai no bu*, 3-8-2-X-285-7, Diplomatic Archives of the Ministry of Foreign Affairs of Japan [hereafter MoFA Diplomatic Archives], Tokyo, Japan.
70. Hawai nihonjin iminshi kankō iinkai, ed., *Hawai nihonjin iminshi* (Honolulu, HI: Hawai nikkeijin rengō kyōkai, 1964), 232–33; Tomoe Moriya, *Amerika bukkyō no tanjo* (Tokyo: Gendai shiryō shuppan, 2001), 150–51.
71. Okita, *Hawai nihon nikkei imin no kyōikushi*, 61–62, 205–11; Hawai nihonjin iminshi kankō iinkai, *Hawai nihonjin iminshi*, 232–33.
72. *Calendar of the FKCAAHI* (1920–1921): 37; (1921–1922): 19; Nippu Jiji Editorial Board, ed., *Hawai dōhō hatten kaikoshi* (Honolulu, HI: Nippu Jiji, 1921), 178–79.
73. Evelyn Nakano Glenn, *Unequal Freedom: How Race and Gender Shaped American Citizenship and Labor* (Cambridge, MA: Harvard University Press, 2002), 197, 223–24.
74. Okihiro, *Cane Fires*, 65–81; Edward D. Beechert, *Working in Hawaii: A Labor History* (Honolulu: University of Hawaiʻi Press, 1985); Hawai nihonjin iminshi kankō iinkai, *Hawai nihonjin iminshi*, 275–80; Roland Kotani, *The Japanese in Hawaii: A Century of Struggle* (Honolulu: Hawaii Hochi, 1985), 46–48.
75. Glenn, *Unequal Freedom*, 216–18, 226.
76. Okihiro, *Cane Fire*, 137–38; Hawai nihonjin iminshi kankō iinkai, *Hawai nihonjin iminshi*, 236–39; Asato, *Teaching Mikadoism*, 41.

77. "Governor Signs Schools Measure: Effective July 1," *Honolulu Star-Bulletin*, November 24, 1920; "Act 30 (S.B. 32)," *Honolulu Advertiser*, December 3, 1920, 11.
78. "Consul General Yada Urges Language Law to Japanese Teachers," *Pacific Commercial Advertiser*, December 22, 1920, 5.
79. "Foreign Language Test Results Will Be Known Next Week," *Honolulu Advertiser*, July 9, 1921, 7.
80. "Alien Language Schools Curbed and Scope Limited by Joint Committee Act," *Honolulu Star-Bulletin*, July 29, 1922, 1–2; Hawai nihonjin iminshi kankō iinkai, *Hawai nihonjin iminshi*, 240.
81. Although the program and proceedings noted that the conference was called by the "U.S. Department of Education," it was before the Bureau of Education became a department. The bureau was part of the Department of the Interior.
82. PPU, *First Pan-Pacific Educational Conference, Program and Proceedings*, 4.
83. "Activities of Pan-Pacific Union," U.S. Military Intelligence Reports: Surveillance of Radicals in the United States, 1917–1941; File Series 10110: Bureau of Investigation Bulletins of Radical Activities, 1920–1921; Record Group 165. Records of the War Department General and Special Staffs, Records of Military Intelligence Division, National Archives, College Park, Maryland. Folder 002371-018-0866 dated October 1, 1921 to October 31, 1921; *Japanese Affairs: Japanese Aggression Liable to Result in War*, 9, July 7, 2018, https://congressional.proquest.com/histvault?q=002371-018-0886.
84. Teiji Kenjo, Akiko Iimori, and Jun Inoue, eds., *Kiitsu kyōkai no chōsen to Shibusawa Eiichi* (Kyoto, Japan: Minerva shobō, 2018); Katagiri, *Minkan kōryū no pionia*, 39–127.
85. "The Educational System in Korea," PPU, *First Pan-Pacific Educational Conference, Program and Proceedings*, 101–106.
86. "What This Conference Has Meant to Me," PPU, *First Pan-Pacific Educational Conference, Program and Proceedings*, 238–39.
87. Asato, *Teaching Mikadoism*, 27–28, 63–64; Tamura, *Americanization, Acculturation, and Ethnic Identity*, 127, 158, 204; Benjamin O. Wist, *A Century of Public Education in Hawaiʻi* (Honolulu: Hawaii Educational Review, 1940), 156.
88. MacCaughey, "Education in Hawaii," in PPU, *First Pan-Pacific Educational Conference, Program and Proceedings*, 89–94.
89. MacCaughey, "Education in Hawaii," in PPU, *First Pan-Pacific Educational Conference, Program and Proceedings*, 89–94.
90. PPU, *First Pan-Pacific Educational Conference, Program and Proceedings*, 13–16.
91. Frances Lawrence, "The Kindergarten in Hawaii," in PPU, *First Pan-Pacific Educational Conference, Program and Proceedings*, 168–72.
92. Julia Wade Abbott, "The Kindergarten," in PPU, *First Pan-Pacific Educational Conference, Program and Proceedings*, 158–62.
93. Barbara Greenwood, "The International Kindergarten Union," in PPU, *First Pan-Pacific Educational Conference, Program and Proceedings*, 164–68.

94. Frances Lawrence, "Kindergartens in Hawaii's Public Schools," *Hawaii Educational Review* (January 1921): 133, 156.
95. "Alien Language Schools Curbed and Scope Limited by Joint Committee Act." At the time, a DPA-appointed joint committee consisting of local white and Japanese members endeavored to revise textbooks to be more suitable for future citizens of the United States. Ernest K. Wakukawa, *A History of the Japanese People in Hawaii* (Honolulu, HI: Toyō shoin, 1938), 265–90; Hawai nihonjin iminshi kankō iinkai, *Hawai nihonjin iminshi*, 237–40.
96. Hawai nihonjin iminshi kankō iinkai, *Hawai nihonjin iminshi*, 223–59; "Language School Progress," *The Friend* (August 1922): 173; Okihiro, *Cane Fires*, 137–38.
97. "Alien Language Schools Curbed and Scope Limited by Joint Committee Act."
98. MacCaughey, "Education in Hawaii," in PPU, *First Pan-Pacific Educational Conference, Program and Proceedings*, 92.
99. Sucheng Chan, *Asian Americans: An Interpretative History* (Boston: Twayne, 1991), 86; *Calendar of the FKCAAHI* (1921–1922): 19.
100. MacCaughey, "Education in Hawaii," in PPU, *First Pan-Pacific Educational Conference, Program and Proceedings*, 92.
101. For example, see Milton Murayama, *All I Asking for Is My Body* (San Francisco: Supa, 1975); Momoko Iko, *Gold Watch*, film (Lloyd Richards dir., KCET Drama, first aired on November 11, 1976), UCLA Film and Television Archive.
102. "Hawaii Japanese Send $38,861,175 Home," *Honolulu Star-Bulletin*, November 10, 1922, 1.
103. "The Genesis of the Pan-Pacific Union: Sixth Installment," 114–15; "Abate Opposition to Language School Reform, Press Comment Indicates," "Friction Due to Not Enough Publicity," *Honolulu Advertiser*, August 18, 1922, 1.
104. "Japanese Bow to Changes in School System," *Honolulu Advertiser*, August 18, 1922, 2; Tamura, *Americanization, Acculturation, and Ethnic Identity*, 150–51.
105. PPU, *First Pan-Pacific Educational Conference, Program and Proceedings*, 6; "The Genesis of the Pan-Pacific Union: Sixth Installment," 115.
106. He claimed that a majority of Japanese members had approved the recommendations made by American members because "the territorial Republican Party, American Legion, and influential citizens were marshaled" to pass the new regulations. Pointing out that the American Legion had pushed for abolishing all foreign-language schools, Soga asserted that the opposition to DPI policy would further damage the interests of Hawai'i's Japanese communities. "Protest on Language School Change Brings Reply: Up to Japanese," *Honolulu Advertiser*, August 19, 1922, 1–2.
107. Wakukawa, *A History of the Japanese People in Hawaii*, 281–88; "Alien Schools Must Follow New System," *Honolulu Star-Bulletin*, August 26, 1922, 2; Hawai nihonjin iminshi kankō iinkai, *Hawai nihonjin iminshi*, 240–46.

108. Dodge, *A History of the FKCAAHI*, 37; Swenson, "Swanzy, Julie Judd," in *Notable Women of Hawaii*.
109. "Plan to Establish Kindergarten for Every 1,000 Pupils in Hawai'i," *Honolulu Advertiser*, December 17, 1922, 36.
110. Frances Lawrence, "The Kindergarten and Children's Aid Association," *Hawaii Educational Review* (November 1922): 7.
111. "From Mrs. M. Yamada to Mr. V. MacCaughey, 8 January 1923," Hawai'i State Archive Manuscript Collection (SAMC)-316 *Foreign Language School File*, Program File, Public Instruction Superintendent 1922–1926. Hawai'i State Archive, Honolulu, HI.
112. Okihiro, *Cane Fires*, 154–55; Tamura, *Americanization, Acculturation, and Ethnic Identity*, 150–51; Wakukawa, *A History of the Japanese People in Hawaii*, 331–32.
113. The *Farrington v. Tokushige* decision also nullified similar foreign-language school laws in California. Asato, *Teaching Mikadoism*, 102–106. For its longtime effect, see Ralph Thomas Kam, "Language and Loyalty: Americanism and the Regulation of Foreign Language Schools in Hawai'i," *Hawaiian Journal of History* 40 (2006): 131–47.
114. "Women Given Pledges of Aid by Candidates" in "Minutes of Special Meeting of the League of Women Voters of the Territory of Hawai'i (HLWV), September 25, 1922," in *League of Women Voters in Hawaii Papers* [hereafter *HLWV Papers*], book 1. Hawai'i State Archives Manuscript Collection (HSAMC)-M356, Honolulu, HI.
115. "Minutes of First Meeting of Board of Administrative Control of HLWV, September 12, 1922," in *HLWV Papers*, book 1. At the time, HLWV's board members included Gertrude D. Bunker—the wife of Dr. Frank F. Bunker who had led the 1919 Federal Survey Commission and who was then serving as the PPU's executive secretary—and Julie Judd Swanzy chaired its legislative committee.
116. Dr. Harada, "Dual Citizenship," Minutes of Executive Committee Meeting of HLWV, November 18, 1922, in *HLWV Papers*, book 1.
117. Yuji Ichioka, *The Issei: The World of the First Generation Japanese Immigrants, 1885–1924* (New York: Free Press, 1988), 153–56; Japanese American National Museum [hereafter JANM] and Brian Niiya, eds., *Encyclopedia of Japanese American History* (New York: Checkmark, 2001), 111–12.
118. Dr. Harada, "Dual Citizenship"; Ichioka, *Issei*, 196–210; Hawai nihonjin iminshi kankō iinkai, *Hawai nihonjin iminshi*, 339–41; Mitsuhiro Sakaguchi, "Nijyūkokusekimondai to Hawai no nikkei Amerikajin," *Atarashii rekishigaku no tameni* 207 (1992): 13–25; Mitsuhiro Sakaguchi, "Zaibeinihonjin no 'nijyū kokuseki mondai' kaiketsu undō: Taiheiyō engan nihonjinkai kyōgikai no torikumi o chūshin ni," *Hisutoria* 145 (1993): 82–102.
119. JANM and Niiya, *Encyclopedia of Japanese American History*, 111–12. Similar laws were also established in Washington State and Texas.
120. Taylor, *Advocate of Understanding*, 130.

121. Ichioka, *Issei*, 210–26; Chan, *Asian Americans*, 93–94; JANM and Niiya, *Encyclopedia of Japanese American History*, 331–32.
122. For example, U.S. ambassador to Japan Roland S. Morris called attention to the diplomatic importance of *Nisei* sons' dual nationality in 1920. Toshihiro Minohara, *Kariforunia-shū no hainichi undō to nichi-bei kankei: Imin mondai o meguru nichi-bei masatsu, 1906–1921* (Tokyo: Yūhikaku, 2006), 149.
123. DI Bureau of Education, *A Survey of Education in Hawaii*, 18–19, 83, 95.
124. Asato, *Teaching Mikadoism*, 17.
125. Sakaguchi, "Nijyūkokusekimondai to Hawai no nikkei Amerikajin," 17.
126. "Japanese-Americans Urged to Ignore Tokio's Summons to Serve in Nippon's Army," *Honolulu Star-Bulletin*, September 11, 1920, 1; "American Citizens of Japanese Blood Form New Society," *Pacific Commercial Advertiser*, October 12, 1920, 6; Mitsuhiro Sakaguchi, *Nihonjin Amerika iminshi* (Tokyo: Fuji shuppan, 2001), 280–300; Sakaguchi, "Nijyūkokusekimondai to Hawai no nikkei Amerikajin," 17.
127. JANM and Niiya, *Encyclopedia of Japanese American History*, 413; "Over 800 Immigrant Japanese and Nisei Served in the US Army During World War I," Japanese American National Museum, *Discover Nikkei*, July 8, 2019, http://www.discovernikkei.org/en/journal/2019/6/3/wwi-veterans/.
128. "The Genesis of the Pan-Pacific Union: Sixth Installment," 109–16.
129. "Minutes of First Meeting of Board of Administrative Control of HLWV, 12 September 1922," in *HLWV Papers*, book 1.
130. Also among those consulted were S. C. Huber and H. W. Vaughan who served as U.S. district attorney. For Tasuku Harada, see Masao Ota, "Harada Tasuku to Hawai daigaku," *Kirisutokyō shakai mondai kenkyu* 46 (1998): 179–229.
131. Dr. Harada, "Dual Citizenship."
132. "Minutes of Special Meeting of Board of Administrative Control of HLWV, 27 December 1922," in *HLWV Papers*, book 1; "Letter from HLWV President Harriet C. Andrews to Baron Togo, 27 December 1922," in *HLWV Papers*, book 1; Sakaguchi, "Nijyūkokusekimondai to Hawai no nikkei Amerikajin," 20.
133. Sakaguchi, *Nihonjin Amerika iminshi*, 290–300; Sakaguchi, "Nijyūkokusekimondai to Hawai no nikkei Amerikajin," 12–16.
134. "Minutes of Executive Committee Meeting of HLWV, 9 October 1924," in *HLWV Papers*, book 1. For Kurokawa, see Colbert N. Kurokawa, "Japanese Young People in Hawaii and Their Duties," *Mid-Pacific Magazine* 19, no. 1 (January 1920): 67–70. For the Nuuanu Branch YMCA and Japanese immigrant community in Honolulu, see Ryo Yoshida, "1920 nendai Honolulu kirisutokyō seinenkai no jinshu kyōiku: Nuanu shibu YMCA o chūshin ni," in *Kindai yōroppa no tankyū 3: Kyōkai* (Kyoto, Japan: Minerva shobō, 2000), 339–84.

135. The Expatriation Act of 1907 made any female U.S. citizen married to an alien man assume her husband's nationality, while an alien immigrant woman who was eligible for naturalization and who married a U.S. citizen man automatically became a U.S. citizen.
136. Candice Lewis Bredbenner, *A Nationality of Her Own: Women, Marriage, and the Law of Citizenship* (Berkeley: University of California Press, 1998), 1–14, 45–112.
137. Chan, *Asian Americans*, 106; Glenn, *Unequal Freedom*, 25–26.
138. "Letter from Grace Love to Mrs. Robert Speer, June 15, 1921"; "Letter from Mrs. Walter G. Barnwell to Mrs. John French, June 17, 1921," reel 170 in YWCA of the USA Records, Record Group 11, Microfilmed Headquarters Files, Local Association Files, Hawaii. Sophia Smith Collection, Smith College Special Collection, Northampton, Massachusetts.
139. *First Pan-Pacific Educational Conference, Program and Proceedings*, 4, 6, 22–23.
140. "Aloha Committee," "Women's Auxiliary of the Pan-Pacific Union," *PPU Bulletin* ns, no. 28 (February 1922): 13–14.
141. "Cooperation Between All Voters Is Urged," *Daily Nippu Jiji*, September 19, 1923.
142. "Dr. Bunker Resigns Pan-Pacific Union," *Daily Nippu Jiji*, December 1, 1923.
143. "Review of Early Plans of the Pan-Pacific Women's Conference."
144. "The Pan-Pacific Women's Conference, 1928," *PPU Bulletin* ns, no. 62 (December 1924): 15.
145. "The Pan-Pacific Women's Conference," *PPU Bulletin* ns, no. 68 (September 1925): 12–14.
146. "Officers of the Conference," *Women of the Pacific: Being a Record of the Proceedings of the First Pan-Pacific Women's Conference* [hereafter *Women of the Pacific*] (1928), inside front cover. Harriet Cousens Andrews was a Chicagoan born to New Englander parents and came to Hawai'i in 1910, accompanying her husband Arthur Lynn Andrews, who became the first dean of the University of Hawai'i College of Arts and Sciences in 1920. She headed multiple women's civic organizations, including the HLWV and the Honolulu YWCA. "Harriet Cousens Andrews," in *Women of Hawaii*, ed. George F. M. Nellist (Honolulu, HI: E. A. Langton-Boyle, 1929), 13.
147. "Pan-Pacific Women's Club Organizes," *PPU Bulletin* ns, no. 84 (February 1927): 9.
148. "Agenda-Committee of Pan-Pacific Women's Conference, Jan. 20, 1925," in *The Jane Addams Papers 1868–1935*, ed. Mary Lynn McCree Bryan et al. (Ann Arbor, MI: University Microfilm International, 1984), reel 42, 907–908. University of California Los Angeles Library Microfilm Collection. Los Angeles, CA.
149. "The Pan-Pacific Women's Conference," *PPU Bulletin* ns, no. 68 (September 1925): 12.
150. "Pan-Pacific Women's Club Organizes."

151. Satterthwaite was born in Yardley, Pennsylvania. George F. M. Nellist, ed., *Pan-Pacific Who's Who: An International Reference Work, 1940–41* (Honolulu, HI: Honolulu Star-Bulletin, 1941); "Pacific Yearly Meeting of the Religious Society of Friends," *Friends Bulletin* 32, no. 5 (February 1964): 4, January 21, 2010, https://archive.org/stream/friendsbulletinp325unse_2/friendsbulletin p325unse_2_djvu.txt.
152. "A Pan-Pacific Women's Conference," *PPU Bulletin* ns, no. 77 (June 1926): 3.
153. "Review of Early Plans of the Pan-Pacific Women's Conference."
154. "Pan-Pacific Women's Conference, 1928," *PPU Bulletin* ns, no. 102 (July 1928): 5.
155. "Pan-Pacific Women's Conference," *PPU Bulletin* ns, no. 64 (May 1925): 11.
156. Convened in Honolulu right after the discriminatory 1924 U.S. immigration law establishing the "Asiatic barred zone," the IPR's first conference focused on race, and its subsequent meetings focused on urgent political and international issues.

5. Forming the Delegation to the 1928 Pan-Pacific Women's Conference: United States, Hawai'i, Japan, and China

1. Angela Woollacott, "Inventing Commonwealth and Pan-Pacific Feminisms: Australian Women's Internationalist Activism in the 1920s–30s," in *Feminisms and Internationalisms*, ed. Mrinalini Shinha, Donna Guy, and Angela Wollacott (Oxford: Blackwell, 1999), 81–104; Leila J. Rupp, *Worlds of Women: The Making of an International Women's Movement* (Princeton, NJ: Princeton University Press, 1997), 13–48; Marie Sandell, *The Rise of Women's Transnational Activism: Identity and Sisterhood Between the World Wars* (London: I. B. Tauris, 2015), 34–79.
2. These women's efforts became a force in forming and/or operating intergovernmental and international commissions and committees, e.g., the League's Advisory Committee in Traffic of Women and Children, the Child Welfare Committee, the Women's Consultative Committee on Nationality, and the Peace and Disarmament Committee. Rupp, *Worlds of Women*, 37–42; Susan Zimmermann, "Liaison Committees of International Women's Organizations and the Changing Landscape of Women's Internationalism, 1920 to 1945," in *Women and Social Movements, International, 1840 to Present*, ed. Kathryn Kish Sklar and Thomas Dublin (Alexandria, VA: Alexander Street, 2012); Karen Garner, *Shaping a Global Women's Agenda: Women's NGOs and Global Governance, 1925–1985* (Manchester: Manchester University Press, 2010), 23–24; Joëlle Droux, "A League of Its Own? The League of Nations' Child Welfare Committee (1919–1936) and International Monitoring of Child Welfare Policies," in *League of Nation's Work on Social Issues: Visions, Endeavours and Experiments*, ed.

United Nations (Herndon, VA: United Nations, 2016), 89–103; Carol Miller, "'Geneva—The Key to Equality': Inter-War Feminists and the League of Nations," *Women's History Review* 3, no. 2 (1994): 219–45.
3. Rupp, *Worlds of Women*, 37–44; Garner, *Shaping a Global Women's Agenda*, 25–26, 31–34.
4. The act prohibited interstate commerce of goods produced by child labor. Molly Ladd-Taylor, *Mother-Work: Women, Child Welfare, and the State, 1890–1930* (Urbana: University of Illinois Press, 1994), 91–98.
5. Ladd-Taylor, *Mother-Work*, 91–98.
6. Jan Doolittle Wilson, *The Women's Joint Congressional Committee and the Politics of Maternalism, 1920–30* (Urbana: University of Illinois Press, 2007), 133–74.
7. For example, see the case of Grace Abbott who served as the director of the U.S. Children's Bureau between 1921 and 1931. John Sorensen, ed., *A Sister's Memories: The Life and Work of Grace Abbott from the Writings of Her Sister, Edith Abbott* (Chicago: University of Chicago Press, 2015); Droux, "A League of Its Own?," 89–103.
8. Richard Roberts, *Florence Simms: A Biography* (New York: Woman's Press, 1926), 229–30; Karen Garner, *Precious Fire: Maud Russell and the Chinese Revolution* (Amherst: University of Massachusetts Press, 2003), 39.
9. Dana L. Robert, *American Women in Mission: A Social History of Their Thought and Practice. The Modern Mission Era, 1792–1992* (Macon, GA: Mercer University Press, 1996), 302–16; Peggy Pascoe, *Relations of Rescue: The Search for Female Moral Authority in the American West, 1874–1939* (New York: Oxford University Press, 1990), 177–207.
10. See, for example, Connie A. Shemo, *The Chinese Medical Ministries of Kang Cheng and Shi Meiyu, 1872–1937* (Bethlehem, PA: Lehigh University Press, 2011), 137, 142–143.
11. Yau Tsit Law (aka, Agnes Lou Youjie) attended Mount Holyoke College and received a BA in 1915 and a BS from Teachers' College at Columbia University in 1916. Dong Wang, *Managing God's Higher Learning: U.S.-China Cultural Encounter and Canton Christian College (Lingnan University), 1888–1952* (Lanham, MD: Lexington Books, 2007), 109. At Mount Holyoke, Law served as the president of the Chinese Students' Monthly, while Ting Me Iung Ting, who later led the Chinese delegation to the first PPWC, served as treasurer.
12. "The Pan-Pacific Women's Conference," *Pan-Pacific Union Bulletin* new series [hereafter *PPU Bulletin* ns], no. 68 (September 1925): 12–14; "Who's Who at the Institute of Pacific Relations," in *Takagi Hasshaku bunko: Taihaiyō mondai chōsakai kankei shiryō* (Takagi Hasshaku Collection, IPR materials), file 2. Tokyo University Special Collection, Tokyo, Japan [hereafter TH Collection: IPR].
13. J. Stanley Lemons, *The Woman Citizen: Social Feminism in the 1920s* (Urbana: University of Illinois Press, 1973), vii–xiii, 181–208; Wilson, *The Women's Joint Congressional Committee and the Politics of Maternalism*; Christine Bolt, *Sisterhood*

Questioned? Race, Class, and Internationalism in the American and British Women's Movements, c. 1880s–1970s (London: Routledge, 2004), 51–75.

14. For Latin American women's internationalism through the PAU, see Katherine M. Marino, *Feminism for the Americas: The Making of an International Human Rights Movement* (Chapel Hill: University of North Carolina Press, 2019).

15. Paul F. Hooper, *Elusive Destiny: The Internationalist Movement in Modern Hawaii* (Honolulu: University of Hawai'i Press, 1980), 79–88.

16. Special Correspondence, "At the Cross Roads of the Pacific—in Hawaii," *Union Signal*, January 22, 1927, 7.

17. "List of Names of Women Likely to Be Interested and Helpful If the W.I.L. Holds a Conference in Hawaii: Given to Catherine Marshal at the Maison International by Mrs. W. D. Westervelt, Sept. 16, 1926," in *Women's International League and Freedom Papers, 1915–1978* [hereafter *WILPF Papers* 1915–1978], reel 105, 1230–33. University of California Riverside Library Microfilm Collection. Riverside, CA.

18. "Who's Who at the Institute of Pacific Relations," in *TH Collection: IPR*, file 2; "Minutes, June 7, 1927," in *League of Women Voters in Hawaii Papers* [hereafter *HLWV Papers*], book 2; Hawai'i State Archives Manuscript Collection (HSAMC)-M356; "Pan-Pacific Women's Conference, July 1928, Honolulu," *PPU Bulletin* ns, no. 92 (September 1927): 3; Sorensen, ed., *A Sister's Memories*, 797–98; Garner, *Precious Fire*, 73–74.

19. Eleanor M. Hinder, "Pacific Women: Personnel of the Pan-Pacific Women's Conference Honolulu, August 9–19, 1928," *Pacific Affairs* 1, no. 3 (1928): 9–12; "Minutes, June 7, 1927," in *HLWV Papers*, book 2.

20. The eleven member organizations were the American Association of University Women, the Council of Women for Home Missions, the Federation of Woman's Boards for Foreign Missions of North America, the General Federation of Women's Clubs, the National Board of the Young Women's Christian Associations, the National Council of Jewish Women, the National Federation of Business and Professional Women's Clubs, the National League of Women Voters, the National Woman's Christian Temperance Union, the National Women's Trade Union League, and the National Women's Conference of American Ethical Union. Ellen Carol DuBois, *Suffrage: Women's Long Battle for the Vote* (New York: Simon & Schuster, 2020), 286–87; Jacqueline Van Voris, *Carrie Chapman Catt: A Public Life* (New York: Feminist Press, 1987), 198–210; Mary Gray Peck, *Carrie Chapman Catt: A Biography* (New York: H. W. Wilson, 1944), 409–32.

21. Harriet Hyman Alonso, *Peace as a Women's Issue: A History of the U.S. Movement for World Peace and Women's Rights* (Syracuse, NY: Syracuse University Press, 1993), 85–124.

22. Carrie Chapman Catt, "Ideals and Aspirations of the United States," Institute of Pacific Relations Second Session-1927. *TH Collection: IPR*, file 13.

23. Catt, "Ideals and Aspirations of the United States."
24. "Minutes, June 13, 1927," in *HLWV Papers*, book 2.
25. Francis M. Swanzy, "Greetings," in Pan-Pacific Women's Conference, *Women of the Pacific: Being a Record of the Proceedings of the First Pan-Pacific Women's Conference* [hereafter *Women of the Pacific*] *Which Was Held in Honolulu from the 9th to the 19th of August 1928, Under the Auspices of the Pan-Pacific Union* (Honolulu, HI: Pan-Pacific Union, 1928), 8.
26. Elizabeth Green to Miss Muna Lee, July 1, 1931, 002613_047_0756. ProQuest ®History Vault, National Woman's Party Papers, Part I: 1913–1974, Series 1: Correspondence, Section A: 1877–1933.
27. Elizabeth Green, "'Pacific Affairs' Is Praised in New York," *Honolulu Star-Bulletin*, May 19, 1930, 15; Paul F. Hooper, ed., *Remembering the Institute of Pacific Relations: The Memoires of William L. Holland* (Tokyo: Ryūkei shyosha, 1995), 186; Kelbi Culwell, "Biographical Sketch of Elizabeth Green Kalb," in *Women and Social Movements in the United States, 1600–2000* (New York: Alexander Street, 2022), April 29, 2022, https:/documents.alexanderstreet.com/d/1008297925.
28. Mary Anderson and Mary N. Winslow, *Woman at Work: The Autobiography of Mary Anderson as Told to Mary N. Winslow* (Minneapolis: University of Minnesota Press, 1951), 197; A. Y. Satterthwaite, "The Pan-Pacific Women's Congress," *Mid-Pacific* 35, no. 2 (February 1928): 107–108.
29. By then, male European labor reformers had already established the IFTU. At the ICWW, the participating delegates reached a consensus on a variety of issues, e.g., pushing the ILO to have mandatory women representatives at its meetings, endorsing the eight-hour work day and forty-four-hour work week for all workers, opposing child labor under the age of sixteen, urging provision of maternity benefits, and calling for equal rights for all immigrants. Nonetheless, the delegates had to wait for the second ICWW conference at Athenée in Geneva, Switzerland, in 1921 to reach a compromise on the membership qualification, which required members to be either women representing trade unions recognized by the IFTU or working-class women from other unions that had the same "spirits, aims, and principles." This qualification requirement, in practice, excluded Christian and communist trade unions. Lara Vapnek, "The International Federation of Working Women," *Women and Social Movements, International, 1840 to Present*, August 22, 2012, http://wasi.alexanderstreet.com/help/view/the_international_federation_of_working_women.
30. The IFWW decided to be a woman-directed Women's Department of the IFTU in 1922, but the IFTU created only a male-directed women's committee, not a woman-directed women's department. Vapnek, "The International Federation of Working Women"; Carol Riegelman Lubin and Anne Winslow, *Social Justice for Women: The International Labor Organization and Women* (Durham, NC: Duke University Press, 1990), 9–42; Geert Van Goethem,

"An International Experiment of Women Workers: The International Federation of Working Women, 1919–1924," *Revue belge de philologie et d'histoire* 84, no. 4 (2006): 1025–47.

31. Anderson and Winslow, *Woman at Work*, 132. Anderson was a Swedish immigrant who had moved in her career from a house servant to a factory hand to an officer of the Chicago WTUL, the National WTUL, and the first director of the U.S. Federal Women's Bureau.

32. On Takako Tanaka's social feminism, see Sharon H. Nolte, *Liberalism in Modern Japan: Ishibashi Tanzan and His Teachers, 1905–1960* (Berkeley: University of California Press, 1987), 118–30; Dorothy Sue Cobble, "Japan and the 1919 ILO Debates Over Rights, Representation and Global Labour Standards," in *The ILO from Geneva to the Pacific Rim: West Meets East*, ed. Jill M. Jensen and Nelson Lichtenstein (New York: Palgrave Macmillan & ILO, 2016), 55–79; Mona L. Siegel, *Peace on Our Terms: The Global Battle for Women's Rights After the First World War* (New York: Columbia University Press, 2020), 220–29. Returning to Japan, Tanaka married a Waseda University philosophy professor, Tanaka Odo, who had studied with John Dewey at the University of Chicago and introduced Dewey's ideas of pragmatism to the German theory–dominant Japanese philosophers' circle of the time.

33. Kamada Eikichi (1857–1934) was then the president of Keio University and a member of the House of Peers.

34. Cobble, "Japan and the 1919 ILO Debates Over Rights, Representation and Global Labour Standards," 55–79.

35. As for Chinese women, Anderson wrote, "the Chinese women were free, they could say what they wanted and do what they wanted." Anderson and Winslow, *Woman at Work*, 125–29, 198–200.

36. Anderson and Winslow, *Woman at Work*, 197; Satterthwaite, "The Pan-Pacific Women's Congress."

37. University of California Calisphere, *Ellen Smith Stadtmuller, Pediatrics: San Francisco*, December 31, 2016, http:/texts.cdlib.org/view?docId=hb3199n7tr&doc.view=frames&chunk.id=div00013&toc.depth=1&toc.id=.

38. "List of Delegates According to Countries," *Women of the Pacific* (1928), 280; Eleanor Hinder, "The Pan-Pacific Women's Conference and American Trade Union Women," *Life and Labor Bulletin* 6, no. 9 (October 1928): 1–2.

39. Susan Zimmermann, "The Challenge of Multinational Empire for the International Women's Movement: The Habsburg Monarchy and the Development of Feminist Inter/National Politics," *Journal of Women's History* 17, no. 2 (2005): 87–117.

40. "Delegates to the Pan-Pacific Women's Conference," *PPU Bulletin*, no. 100 (May 1928): 12.

41. "Conference Delegations," *PPU Bulletin* ns, no. 102 (July 1928): 10–11.

42. Barbara Del Piano, *Nā Lani Kaumaka/Daughters of Hawai'i: A Century of Historic Preservation* (Honolulu: Daughters of Hawaii, 2005), 106–16.
43. "List of Delegates According to Countries," *Women of the Pacific* (1928), 278–79.
44. Irma Tam Soong, "Li, Tai Heong Kong," in *Notable Women of Hawaii*, ed. Barbara Bennett Peterson (Honolulu: University of Hawai'i Press, 1984), 236–39.
45. Dorothy Jim Luke, "Ellen Fook Len Leong, M.D.," in *Chinese Women Pioneers in Hawai'i*, ed. May Lee Chung and Dorothy Jim Luke (Honolulu, HI: Associated Chinese University Women, 2002), 9–11.
46. Barbara Bennett Peterson, "Noda, Alice Sae Teshima," in *Notable Women of Hawaii*, 288–91.
47. "Union Director Visits Orient," *PPU Bulletin* ns, no. 84 (February 1927): 8.
48. Carol Gluck, *Japan's Modern Myths: Ideology in the Late Meiji Period* (Princeton, NJ: Princeton University Press, 1985); Andrew Gordon, *Labor and Imperial Democracy in Prewar Japan* (Berkeley: University of California Press, 1991).
49. Vera C. Mackie, *Feminism in Modern Japan: Citizenship, Embodiment, and Sexuality* (Cambridge: Cambridge University Press, 2003), 1–98.
50. Shizuko Koyama, *Ryōsai kenbo to iu kihan* (Tokyo: Keisō shobō, 1991); Sunmi Park, "Teikoku no jokyōshitachi: Chōsen de oshieta jokyōshitachi," in *Teikoku to bunka: Sheikusupia kara Antonio Neguri made*, ed. Hideichi Eto (Yokohama, Japan: Shunpūsha, 2016), 333.
51. Noriko Kawamura Ishii, *American Women Missionaries at Kobe College, 1873–1909* (New York: Routledge, 2004), 1–17, 129–31; Rui Kohiyama, "Nitobe Inazo to kōtō naru okusamagata," *Tokyo joshi daigaku hikakubunka kenkyūsho kiyō*, no. 73 (2012): 1–21; George M. Oshiro, "Internationalist in Prewar Japan: Nitobe Inazo, 1862–1944" (PhD diss., University of British Columbia, 1985).
52. George M. Oshiro, "Mary P. E. Nitobe and Japan," *Quaker History* 86, no. 2 (Fall 1997): 1–15.
53. Yūko Takahashi, "A Japanese American Enterprise: Umeko Tsuda's Bryn Mawr Network and the Founding of Tsuda College," in *China's Christian Colleges: Cross-Cultural Connections, 1900–1950*, ed. Daniel H. Bays and Ellen Widmer (Stanford, CA: Stanford University Press, 2009), 271–86; Masako Iino, Kinuko Kameda, and Yūko Takahashi, eds., *Tsuda Umeko o sasaeta hitobito* (Tokyo: Yūhikaku, 2000); Yūko Takahashi, *Tsuda Umeko no shakaishi* (Machida, Japan: Tamagawa daigaku shuppan, 2002); Sally Ann Hastings, "Women Educators of the Meiji Era and the Making of Modern Japan," *International Journal of Social Education* 6, no. 1 (1991): 83–94; "Her Stories: Mary Harris Morris," Centre County Historical Society, February 19, 2017, https://centrehistory.org/her-stories/.
54. Rui Kohiyama, "No Nation Can Rise Higher Than Its Women: The Women's Ecumenical Missionary Movement and Tokyo Woman's Christian College," in *Competing Kingdoms: Women, Mission, Nation, and the American Protestant Empire,*

1812–1960, ed. Barbara Reeves-Ellington, Kathryn Kish Sklar, and Connie Anne Shemo (Durham, NC: Duke University Press, 2010), 218–39.

55. Takako Aoki, *Ima o ikiru Naruse Jinzō: Joshi kyōiku no paionia* (Tokyo: Kōdansha, 2001); Kuni Nakajima, *Naruse Jinzo* (Tokyo: Yoshikawa kōbunkan, 2002); Hastings, "Women Educators of the Meiji Era and the Making of Modern Japan," 83–94. Among the Kiitsu Kyōkai members during its founding days were Sidney Gulick, a descendant of Hawai'i's pioneer missionary couple, Clay MacCauley of the Tokyo Unitarian Church, Inazo Nitobe, and Eiichi Shibusawa. Sandra C. Taylor, *Advocate of Understanding: Sidney Gulick and the Search for Peace with Japan* (Kent, OH: Kent State University Press, 1984), 65; Teiji Kenjō, Akiko Iimori, and Jun Inoue, eds., *Kiitsu kyōkai no chōsen to Shibusawa Eiichi* (Kyoto, Japan: Minerva shobō, 2018), 2, 246; Kuni Nakajima, "Kiitsu kyōkai shokō 1 & 2," *Nihon joshidai kiyō bungakubu*, no. 36 (1986): 53–64; no. 37 (1987): 47–76.

56. Yoko Kobayashi, "Inoue Hide no Amerika ryūgaku taiken no imi," *Nihon joshi daigaku sogō kenkyusho Kiyō*, no. 5 (2002): 161–67.

57. Ishii, *American Women Missionaries at Kobe College, 1873–1909*, 153–55.

58. Both listed their names as founding members of the Tokyo YWCA and the Japan YWCA. Ito(ko) Ozawa Imanishi, a Hawai'i-born *Nisei* daughter married to a Japanese businessman, was also a founding member of the Tokyo YWCA. "Tokyo kirisutokyō joshi seinenkai rekishi gairyaku," *Chi-no shio* 38 (February 1931), 1.

59. Nihon YWCA 80-nenshi henshu iinkai, ed., *Mizu-o kaze-o hikari-o: Nihon YWCA 80 nenshi, 1905–1985* (Tokyo: kirisutokyō joshi seinenkai, 1987), 56–58.

60. Kazuto Oshio, "Fujin heiwa kyōkai e mukete: Nitobe Inazo fusai to Naruse Jinzo," in *Nijuseiki niokeru joseino heiwaundō*, ed. Kuni Nakajima and Nagako Sugimori (Tokyo: Domesu shuppan, 2006), 37–62; Nagako Sugimori, "Fujin heiwa kyōkai no kessei to katsudō no tenkai," in *Nijuseiki niokeru joseino heiwaundō*, ed. Nakajima and Sugimori, 65–85.

61. "Nenpyō," in *Nijuseiki niokeru joseino heiwaundō*, ed. Nakajima and Sugimori, 193–200. JWU professors, such as Hideko Inouye, Tano Jodai, and Tomi (Kora) Wada, remained active in the transnational WILPF's network and international peace work in general.

62. Masaru Ikei, "Nihon kokusai renmei kyōkai: Sono seiritsu to henshitsu," *Hōgaku kenkyū* 68, no. 2 (1995): 23–48. Eiichi Shibusawa served as the League of Nations Association's first president, and the House of Peers' chairman Prince Tokugawa Iyesato (1864–1940) served as its honorary president.

63. Yuji Yamazaki, "Dai-ichiji taisengo ni okeru kokusai kyōiku undō' no seiritsu to tenkai: Taisho-ki kyōiku kaizō undō no kusaishugiteki sokumen," *Kyōiku kenkyū*, no. 30 (1986): 71–97.

64. Margaret Prang, *A Heart at Leisure from Itself: Caroline Macdonald of Japan* (Vancouver: University of British Columbia Press, 1995), 98–102; Fusae Ichikawa, *Ichikawa Fusae jiden, Senzen-hen* (Tokyo: Shinjyuku shobō, 1999), 56–57.
65. Patricia E. Tsurumi, *Factory Girls: Women in the Thread Mills of Meiji Japan* (Princeton, NJ: Princeton University Press, 1990), 174–98; Wakizō Hosoi, *Jokō aishi* (Tokyo: Kaizōsha, 1925).
66. Vera C. Mackie, *Creating Socialist Women in Japan: Gender, Labour, and Activism, 1900–1937* (Cambridge: Cambridge University Press, 1997), 76; Janet Hunter, *Women and the Labour Market in Japan's Industrializing Economy: The Textile Industry Before the Pacific War* (London: Routledge, 2003), 89–143; Elyssa Faison, *Managing Women: Disciplining Labor in Modern Japan* (Berkeley: University of California Press, 2007), 22–26; Hosoi, *Jokō aishi*.
67. Kiyoaki Haga, *Suzuki Bunji no iru fūkei* (Akita, Japan: Mumyōsha, 2010), 9–46.
68. Yuji Ichioka, *The Issei: The World of the First Generation Japanese Immigrants, 1885–1924* (New York: Free Press, 1988), 128–45.
69. Mackie, *Creating Socialist Women in Japan*, 78–80; Yūko Suzuki, *Josei to rōdō kumiai* (Tokyo: Renga shōbō, 1991), 37–64.
70. Faison, *Managing Women*, 22–26; Mackie, *Creating Socialist Women in Japan*, 76.
71. The name was changed for the second time to Nihon Sōdōmei (Japan Federation of Labor) in 1921.
72. Ichikawa, *Ichikawa Fusae jiden, Senzen-hen*, 2–48.
73. Nolte, *Liberalism in Modern Japan*, 90–130; Ichikawa, *Ichikawa Fusae jiden, Senzen-hen*, 39–48; Cobble, "Japan and the 1919 ILO Debates Over Rights, Representation and Global Labour Standards," 55–79.
74. "Report of Charlotte H. Adams: Japan and China, April 1919-April 1920," 9, reel 59, no. 03–01 in *YWCA of the USA Records, Microfilmed Portion, Part 3, Series II Minutes and Reports Sub-series B: Communities and Departments* [hereafter *YWCA of USA Records Microfilmed, P3-SII-SsB*], Sophia Smith Collection, Smith College Special Collections, Northampton, Massachusetts.
75. Ernestine L. Friedmann, "Report on Japan Made to the Federation on Women's Boards of Missions Visited March 1920," reel 59, no. 03–20 in *YWCA of USA Records Microfilmed, P3-SII-SsB*.
76. Suzuki, *Josei to rōdō kumiai*, 70–91; Akiko Esashi, *Mezameyo josei tachi: Sekirankai no hitobito* (Tokyo: Ōtsuki shoten, 1980).
77. Katharine H. Hawes, "Report of Visit to Japan, March 7–July 16, 1919," 34, reel 59, no. 03–23; Blanche Best, "Kyoto, Japan, March, April, May, 1923," reel 59, no. 03–07; Carolyn E. Allen, "Business Women of Japan," *Woman's Press*, February 1925, 109–10, reel 59, no. 3–02, all in *YWCA of USA Records Microfilmed, P3-SII-SsB*. See also, Nihon YWCA 100 nenshi hensan iinkai, *Nihon YWCA 100 nenshi: Josei no jiritsu o motomete* (Tokyo: Nihon kirisutokyō joshi seinenkai, 2005), 24–25; Kahoru Nakamoto, "Senzen no Tokyo YWCA

yūshoku fujinbu ni yoru joshi seinen kyōiku," *Nihon Shakai Kyōikugakkai Kiyō* 49, no. 2 (June 2013): 33–42.

78. Sharon H. Nolte, *Liberalism in Modern Japan: Ishibashi Tanzan and His Teachers, 1905–1960* (Berkeley: University of California Press, 1987), 123–24; Ichikawa, *Ichikawa Fusae jiden, Senzen-hen*, 50–101. Hiratsuka and the NWS also demanded a prohibition on men carrying sexually transmissible diseases from marrying and sought to allow wives to divorce such men. Mackie, *Creating Socialist Women in Japan*, 45–71.

79. Ichikawa's eldest brother had worked in the San Francisco Bay Area as a schoolboy, a student working part-time as a house servant, and her younger sister cultivated her life as a "picture bride" in Seattle. Ichikawa, *Ichikawa Fusae jiden, Senzen-hen*, 10, 104.

80. Ichikawa, *Ichikawa Fusae jiden, Senzen-hen*, 57.

81. Nihon kirisutokyō fujin kyōfūkai, ed., *Nihon kirisutokyō fujin kyōfūkai hyakunenshi* (Tokyo: Domesu shuppan, 1986), 218–25; Rumi Yasutake, *Transnational Women's Activism: The United States, Japan, and Japanese Immigrant Communities in California, 1859–1920* (New York: New York University Press, 2004), 95–103.

82. Nihon kirisutokyō fujin kyōfūkai, *Nihon kirisutokyō fujin kyōfūkai hyakunenshi*, 390–94; Manako Ogawa, "The 'White Ribbon League of Nations' Meets Japan: The Trans-Pacific Activism of the Woman's Christian Temperance Union, 1906–1930," *Diplomatic History* 31, no. 1 (January 2007): 35–37.

83. Tsuneko Gauntlett, *Nanajū nana nen no omoide* (Tokyo: Uemura shoten, 1949), 98–124; Nihon kirisutokyō fujin kyōfūkai, *Nihon kirisutokyō fujin kyōfūkai hyakunenshi*, 512–20.

84. Ichikawa, *Ichikawa Fusae jiden, Senzen-hen*, 57.

85. Prang, *A Heart at Leisure from Itself*, 163–80, 201–19.

86. Sally Ann Hastings, *Neighborhood and Nation in Tokyo, 1905–1937* (Pittsburgh, PA: University of Pittsburgh Press, 1995), 54, 58; Nihon kirisutokyō fujin kyōfūkai, *Nihon kirisutokyō fujin kyōfūkai hyakunenshi*, 385–86.

87. Nihon YWCA 80-nenshi henshu iinkai, *Mizu-o kaze-o hikari-o*, 120–21.

88. Charles Beard—historian, one-time Columbia University professor, and a founder of the New School for Social Research in New York—closely worked with progressive colleagues such as John Dewey and Luther Halsey Gulick (1892–1993), a born-in-Japan son of Sidney L. Gulick and political scientist specializing in public administration. Arguably, the Gulicks' extensive connection to Japanese liberal internationalists, such as Inazo Nitobe and Shimpei Goto, brought the Beards to Japan. Yasuo Endo, "Beard fusai to 1920 nendai no Nihon," in *Gendai Amerika zō no saikōchiku*, ed. Nagayo Honma, Shunsuke Kamei, and Kenzaburō Shinkawa (Tokyo: Tokyo University Press, 1990), 141–57; Chikako Uemura, *Mary Beard to joseishi: Nihon josei no majikara o hakkutsu shita beirekishika* (Tokyo: Fujiwara shoten, 2019), 58–100.

89. Shinpei Goto was a German-educated doctor, bureaucrat, politician, and educator who filled government posts and Upper House membership. Goto served as Tokyo mayor, the Minister of Home Affairs, and the Minister of Foreign Affairs. He was known for contributing to Japan's colonial rule in Taiwan, where he headed the colonial government's civil affairs department and recruited Inazo Ninobe to take charge of agricultural and forestry policies.
90. Mackie, *Feminism in Modern Japan*, 48; Miyako Orii and Josei no Rekishi Kenkyūkai, eds., *Onnatachi ga tachiagatta: Kantō daishinsai to Tokyo fujin rengō kai* (Tokyo: Domesu shuppan, 2017), 10–46.
91. Kozo Kagawa, "Naimushō shakaikyōiku no secchi ni tsuite," *Hyōron: Shakai kagaku*, no. 22 (1983): 1–34.
92. Prang, *A Heart at Leisure from Itself*, 204–19; Orii and Josei no Rekishi Kenkyukai, *Onnatachi ga tachiagatta*, 10–46.
93. Faison, *Managing Women*, 24–25; Mackie, *Creating Socialist Women in Japan*, 76.
94. Uemura, *Mary Beard to joseishi*, 58–100; Orii and Josei no Rekishi Kenkyukai, *Onnatachi ga tachiagatta*, 10–46.
95. Barbara Molony, "Women's Rights, Feminism, and Suffrage in Japan, 1870–1925," *Pacific Historical Review* 69, no. 4 (2000): 639–61; Barbara Molony, "Citizenship and Suffrage in Interwar Years," in *Women's Suffrage in Asia: Gender, Nationalism, and Democracy*, ed. Louise Edwards and Mina Roces (London: Routledge Curzon, 2004), 127–51; Yukiko Matsukawa and Kaoru Tachi, "Women's Suffrage and Gender Politics in Japan," in *Suffrage and Beyond: International Feminist Perspectives*, ed. Caroline Daley and Melanie Nolan (New York: New York University Press, 1994), 171–83; Nihon kirisutokyō fujin kyōfūkai, *Nihon kirisutokyō fujin kyōfūkai hyakunenshi*, 513–50.
96. Kikue Ide, "Japan's New Woman: Legal and Political Relationships of Women of Japan Today: An Interpretation," *Pacific Affairs* 1, no. 4 (1928): 1–11.
97. Ichikawa Fusae, "Shiyatoru-nite: beikoku-yori," *Josei domei*, no. 12 (January 1922); Ichikawa, *Ichikawa Fusae jiden, Senzen-hen*, 104–23; Kazuko Sugawara, *Ichikawa Fusae to fujin sanseiken kakutoku undō: Mosaku to kattō no rekishi* (Tokyo: Seori shobō, 2002), 94–107.
98. Fusae Ichikawa, "Amerika no jochutachi wa gekkyu hyakuen ijo," *Yomiuri Shinbun*, October 22, 1921.
99. Ichikawa, *Ichikawa Fusae jiden, Senzen-hen*, 123–34. Taka Kato was trained from 1913 to 1915 at the Milwaukee YWCA in Wisconsin and the National Training School in New York. Nihon YWCA 80-nenshi henshu iinkai, *Mizu-o kaze-o hikari-o*, 72–73; Teruko Ishikawa, "Nihon YWCA no kokusai shugi, nashonarizumu, jendā: Kato Taka no keiken to gensetsu o tegakari to shite," in *Nihon kindai kokka no seiritsu to jendā*, ed. Mikito Ujiie, Yuki Sakurai, Masayuki Tanimoto, and Hiroko Nagano (Tokyo: Kashiwa shobō, 2003), 256–92.

100. For Shoda, see Ichikawa Fusae Kinenkai, ed., *Fujin sansei kankeishi shiryō, 1918–1946* [hereafter *FSKSM* (Woman Suffrage History Related Materials)] (Tokyo: Nihon tosho sentā, 2005), microfilm, reel 58, 1041. Shoda studied at a high school in Ithaca, New York, and Cornell University for a master's degree in sociology while working as a typist. For Akamatsu, see Suzuki, *Josei to rōdō kumia*, 112–16.
101. Ichikawa, *Ichikawa Fusae jiden, senzenhen*, 131–200, 621.
102. Nihon YWCA 80-nenshi henshu iinkai, *Mizu-o kaze-o hikari-o*, 120–29.
103. Ian R. Tyrrell, *Reforming the World: The Creation of America's Moral Empire* (Princeton, NJ: Princeton University Press, 2010), 25, 196, 242–43; Noriko Ishii, "Kirisutokyō seinen undō to josei: Bankoku kirisutokyō gakusei renmei no sōseiki no katudō kara," in *Hokubei kenkyū nyūmon 2: Nashonaru to mukiau*, ed. Sophia University Institute of America and Canada Studies (Tokyo: Sophia University Press, 2019), 61–85.
104. Reiko Mitsui, ed., *Gendai fujin undōshi nenpyō* (Tokyo: Sanichi shobō, 1978), 121; Nihon YWCA 100 nenshi hensan iinkai, *Nihon YWCA 100 nenshi*, 10, 23; "Senmon gakkō ni okeru seito no sayoku undō," in *Nihon josei undō shiryōshūsei 3: Shisō, seiji III*, ed. Yuko Suzuki (Tokyo: Fuji shuppan, 1997), 156–71.
105. "Kaisetsu," in *Nihon josei undō shiryōshūsei 5: Seikatsu, rōdō II*, ed. Yuko Suzuki (Tokyo: Fuji shuppan, 1993), 23–24.
106. "Pacific Women's Parley in Hawaii," *Japan Times and Mail*, June 24, 1927.
107. Kobayashi, "Inoue Hide no Amerika ryūgaku taiken no imi," 161–67.
108. *FSKSM*, reel 58, 1032–55. For Yayoi Yoshioka, see Shizuoka Prefecture, City of Kakegawa, Yayoi Yoshioka Website, 1–4, March 17, 2016, https://www.city.kakegawa.shizuoka.jp/gyosei/docs/8014.html. Also among this Tokyo women leaders group was the Japanese delegate Sumi Oye, a mission school graduate and alumna of Tokyo Women's Higher Normal School who had studied home economics at a Polytechnic as well as social hygiene at Bedford College in London on government funding. Oye established the Tokyo Home Economics School in 1923. Takeko Otawa, another JWU alumna and an ethics teacher at the JWU-attached high school, was also in the group. For Sumi Oye, see "Tokyo Kasei Gakuin: Soritsusha Oe Sumi," August 16, 2013, https://www.kasei-gakuin.ac.jp/houjin/houjin/founder.
109. In Japan, a Pan-Pacific Club was formed in Kobe by the Japan Tourist Bureau staff in March 1918. "Japan and Pan-Pacific Effort," *Mid-Pacific Magazine* 15, no. 3 (March 1918): 217.
110. Kyo Kiuchi, "Kyōiku ichiro," in Kyo Kiuch, *Denki sōsho 65: Kyōiku ichiro / Han taihiyō fujin kaigi ni resshite* (Tokyo: Ōzorasha, 1989), 133–46.
111. Sawayanagi started his career as a JMoE bureaucrat and rose in his official career, serving as a principal of a middle school and a high school. He went on to be a president of Tohoku and Kyoto Imperial Universities, the vice minister

of Education, and the IES president. As an elite bureaucrat and educator, he developed connections with U.S. and Japanese liberal internationalists, such as Sidney Gulick, Inazo Nitobe, and Eiichi Shibusawa. Mark E. Lincicome, "Nationalism, Imperialism, and the International Education Movement in Early Twentieth-Century Japan," *Journal of Asian Studies* 58, no. 2 (May 1999): 338–60. Kazuomi Sakai, "Sawayanagi Masataro no ajia shugi," in *Kiitsu kyōkai no chōsen to Shibusawa Eiichi*, ed. Kenjo, Iimori, and Inoue, 127–42.

112. Kiuchi, "Kyōiku ichiro," 133–37; *FSKSM*, reel 58, 1032–33; *Women of the Pacific* (1928), 278–80. The first PPWC's official records listed Kiuchi and two other members as delegates, and another three as associate delegates.

113. *Fusen* 2, no. 5 (July 1, 1928): 6. *FSKSM*, reel 58, 1032–42. The first PPWC's proceedings listed eighteen names for the Japanese delegation.

114. Ichikawa, *Ichikawa Fusae jiden, senzenhen*, 192–94; *Fusen* 2, no. 5 (July 1, 1928): 9.

115. Zenkoku fujin dōmei, "Han-taiheiyō fujin kaigi ni kansuru hantai seimeisho," in *Nihon josei undō shirō shūsei 5: seikatu, rōdō II*, 73.

116. *FSKSM*, reel 58, 1032–55; *Women of the Pacific* (1928), 278–80.

117. "Union Director Visit Orient," *PPU Bulletin* ns, no. 84 (February 1927): 8; "Shanghai and the Pan-Pacific Women's Conference," *PPU Bulletin* ns, no. 86 (April 1927): 4–5.

118. The member organizations were American Association of University Women, American Women's Club of Shanghai, Inc., Associacao das Senhoras Portuguezas, British Women's Association, Chinese Women's Suffrage Association, Danube Countries Women's Association, Foreign YWCA, German Women's Club, Japanese WCTU, Netherlands Ladies Club, Shanghai Women's Club, and Shanghai Chinese YWCA. "The Joint Committee of Shanghai Women's Organizations: Participation of Women in Government in European and Pacific Countries: A Contribution to the Pan-Pacific Women's Conference, August 9–19, 1928," in *JA Papers*, reel 36, 735–37, 755–57. University of California Irvine Library Microfilm Collection. Irvine, CA.

119. Emily Honig, *Sisters and Strangers: Women in the Shanghai Cotton Mills, 1919–1949* (Stanford, CA: Stanford University Press, 1986), 9–40.

120. Isabella Jackson, *Shaping Modern Shanghai: Colonialism in China's Global City* (Cambridge: Cambridge University Press, 2017), 1–21.

121. Pui-Lan Kwok, *Chinese Women and Christianity, 1860–1927*, American Academy of Religion Academy Series, no. 75 (Atlanta, GA: Scholars Press, 1992), 120–32; Teruko Ishikawa, "Shanhai no YWCA: Sono soshiki to hito no nettowāku," in *Shanhai: Jūsosuru nettowāku*, ed. Nihon Shanhaishi kenkyūkai (Tokyo: Kyūko shoin, 2000), 257–84.

122. Kazuko Ono, *Chinese Women in a Century of Revolution, 1850–1950*, ed. Joshua A. Fogel (Stanford, CA: Stanford University Press, 1988), 54–92.

123. Peck, *Carrie Chapman Catt*, 196–204.

124. Louise Edwards, "Women's Suffrage in China: Changing Scholarly Conventions," in *Globalizing Feminisms, 1789–1945*, ed. Karen Offen (New York: Routledge, 2010), 275–85; Ono, *Chinese Women in a Century of Revolution*, 93–111.
125. Motoe Sasaki, *Redemption and Revolution: American and Chinese New Women in the Early Twentieth Century* (Ithaca, NY: Cornell University Press, 2016), 15–110.
126. Yuki Terazawa, *Knowledge, Power, and Women's Reproductive Health in Japan, 1690–1945* (New York: Palgrave Macmillan, 2018), 133–36, 180–81; Hiro Fujimoto, *Igaku to kirisutokyō: Nihon ni okeru Amerika Purotesutanto no iryō senkyō* (Tokyo: Hosei digaku shuppankai, 2021), 3–51; Michio Takaya, *Hebon* (Tokyo: Yoshikawa kōbunkan, 1986).
127. Ruth Rogaski, *Hygienic Modernity: Meanings of Health and Disease in Treaty-Port China* (Berkeley: University of California Press, 2004); Shemo, *The Chinese Medical Ministries of Kang Cheng and Shi Meiyu, 1872–1937*.
128. Carl W. Rufus, "Twenty-Five Years of the Barbour Scholarship," *Michigan Alumnus Quarterly Review* 49, no. 11 (1942): 14–26; "Legacy of Levi Barbour," August 22, 2020, https:/rackham.umich.edu/rackham-life/diversity-equity-and-inclusion/barbour-scholars/history/.
129. Jackson, *Shaping Modern Shanghai*, 203–38; Honig, *Sisters and Strangers*, 9–40.
130. Honig, *Sisters and Strangers*, 9–40; Ono, *Chinese Women in a Century of Revolution*, 112–39; Jackson, *Shaping Modern Shanghai*, 203–204.
131. Irene Harrison, *Agatha Harrison: An Impression by Her Sister* (London: Allen & Unwin, 1956), 23–45.
132. "The Joint Committee of Shanghai Women's Organizations," 33–45, in *Jane Addams Papers*, reel 36, 755–56; Frances Wheelhouse, *Eleanor Mary Hinder: An Australian Woman's Social Welfare Work in China Between the Wars* (Sydney, Australia: Wentworth, 1978), 17.
133. Elizabeth Littell-Lamb, "Caught in the Crossfire: Women's Internationalism and the YWCA Child Labor Campaign in Shanghai, 1921–1925," *Frontiers: A Journal of Women Studies* 32, no. 3 (2011): 134–66; Garner, *Precious Fire*, 96–97.
134. She was born as Fo-Jin Kong (Hezhen Gong) and also known as Mrs. H. C. Mei/Mrs. Mei Hua-chuan or rendered as Jiang Hezhen or Mei Jiang Hezhen. Kwok, *Chinese Women and Christianity*, 90, 222; "Contemporaneous Chinese Leaders," *Chinese Recorder* 58 (September 1927): 576–77.
135. Betty Mei Yuke, "My Talk at Senior Center," in Mei Family Papers owned by Dr. James David Adams Jr. and Diane Mei Lin Mark. For M. C. Mei, see "H. C. Mei (Mei Hua-chuan)," in *Who's Who in China; Biographies of Chinese Leaders* (Shanghai, China: Weekly Review, 1936), 314; "Notes on Contributors," *Chinese Recorder* 48 (March 1917): 141. For Anna Kong Mei, see "Mrs. Mei Hua-chuan," in *Who's Who in China*, 315; "Contemporaneous Chinese Leaders"; Diane Mei Lin Mark, *Seasons of Light: The History of Chinese Christian Churches in Hawaii* (Honolulu: Chinese Christian Association of Hawaii, 1989), 215.

136. Anna Kong Mei joined the National Committee of the China YWCA in 1916 and served as its chair from 1922 to 1929. For World YWCA's indigenization efforts, see Elizabeth Littell-Lamb, "Localizing the Global: The YWCA Movement in China, 1899 to 1939," in *Women and Transnational Activism in Historical Perspective*, ed. Kimberly Jensen and Erika Kuhlman (St. Louis, MO: Republic of Letters, 2010), 63–87.
137. Littell-Lamb, "Caught in the Crossfire," 134–66; Harrison, *Agatha Harrison*, 43–45.
138. Littell-Lamb, "Caught in the Crossfire," 134–66; Wheelhouse, *Eleanor Mary Hinder*, 14–18.
139. Littell-Lamb, "Caught in the Crossfire," 134–66; Wheelhouse, *Eleanor Mary Hinder*, 14–18.
140. "The Joint Committee of Shanghai Women's Organizations," 735–37, 755–57; Wheelhouse, *Eleanor Mary Hinder*, 15–21.
141. Alexandra Epstein, "International Feminism and Empire-Building Between the Wars: The Case of Viola Smith," *Women's History Review* 17, no. 5 (2008): 699–719; Heather Barker, "Smith, Addie Viola," *Australian Dictionary of Biography*, August 20, 2017, http:/adb.anu.edu.au/biography/smith-addie-viola-11717; Sarah Paddle, "'For the China of the Future': Western Feminists, Colonization and International Citizenship in China in the Inter-War Years," *Australian Feminist Studies* 16, no. 36 (2001): 325–41.
142. Hinder graduated from Sydney University in 1913. Paddle, "'For the China of the Future,' Western Feminists"; Wheelhouse, *Eleanor Mary Hinder*, 1–11, 19; Fiona Paisley, *Glamour in the Pacific: Cultural Internationalism and Race Politics in the Women's Pan-Pacific* (Honolulu: University of Hawai'i Press, 2009), 34.
143. "For International Friendship," *Chinese Recorder* 56 (December 1925): 841; Nihon YWCA 80-nenshi henshu iinkai, *Mizu-o, kaze-o, hikari-o*, 112–13. For Helen Kim, see J. Manning Potts, ed., *Grace Sufficient: The Story of Helen Kim by Herself* (Nashville, TN: Upper Room, 1964).
144. Karen Garner, "Redefining Institutional Identity: The YWCA Challenge to Extraterritoriality in China, 1925–1930," *Women's History Review* 10, no. 3 (2001): 409–40.
145. "Christian Women and Chinese Aspirations," *Chinese Recorder* 58 (July 1927): 470–71.
146. Garner, *Precious Fire*, 67–93; Ono, *Chinese Women in a Century of Revolution*, 129–39.
147. Honig, *Sisters and Strangers*, 94–131.
148. Mrs. H. C. Mei, "Making the Home Christian," *Chinese Recorder* 53 (July 1922): 472–76.
149. Littell-Lamb, "Caught in the Crossfire," 141.
150. Garner, *Precious Fire*, 91.

151. "Union Director Visits Orient," 8.
152. "Shanghai and the Pan-Pacific Women's Conference," 4–5.
153. Mrs. Chindon Yui Tang was an alumna of Teacher's College, Columbia University. *PPU Bulletin* ns, no. 103 (August 1928), 15.
154. For Shu-ching Ting, see Elizabeth Littell-Lamb, "Ding Shujing: The YWCA Pathway for China's 'New Women,'" in *Salt and Light: Lives of Faith That Shaped Modern China*, ed. Carol Lee Hamrin (Eugene, OR: Pickwick, 2009), 79–97.
155. "Officers of the Conference," *Women of the Pacific* (1928), inside front cover.
156. Epstein, "International Feminism and Empire Building Between the Wars," 713–14.
157. *Women of the Pacific* (1928), 71–76, 278.

6. Pan-Pacific Women's Voices and Global Feminism

1. Alexander Hume Ford, "Greetings from the Pan-Pacific Union," *Women of the Pacific: Being a Record of the Proceedings of the First Pan-Pacific Women's Conference* [hereafter *Women of the Pacific*] *Which Was Held in Honolulu from the 9th to the 19th of August 1928, Under the Auspices of the Pan-Pacific Union* (Honolulu, HI: Pan-Pacific Union, 1928), 11–12.
2. *Women of the Pacific* (1928), 276–77, inside front cover.
3. Eleanor M. Hinder, *Women in the Pacific: A Contribution to the Pan-Pacific Women's Conference, Honolulu, August 9–19, 1928* (Shanghai, China: n.p., 1928), 1–9, stored at University of Hawai'i at Mānoa Library Hawaiian and Pacific Collection.
4. Francis M. Swanzy, "Greetings," *Women of the Pacific* (1928), 8.
5. Hinder, *Women in the Pacific*, 1–9.
6. *Women of the Pacific* (1928), 274–75.
7. Mary Anderson and Mary N. Winslow, *Woman at Work: The Autobiography of Mary Anderson as Told to Mary N. Winslow* (Minneapolis: University of Minnesota Press, 1951), 197–201.
8. Anderson and Winslow, *Woman at Work*, 197–201.
9. Yoshi Shoda, "Japanese Women in Industry," *Women of the Pacific* (1928), 78–83.
10. Anderson and Winslow, *Woman at Work*, 197–201.
11. Bae-tsung Kyong, "China's Industrial Women," *Women of the Pacific* (1928), 71–76.
12. *Women of the Pacific* (1928), 267–73.
13. Eleanor M. Hinder, "The Pan-Pacific Women's Conference and American Trade Union Women," *Life and Labor Bulletin* 6, no. 9 (October 1928): 1–2.
14. Elizabeth Green, "The Pacific and the International Labour Conference," *Pacific Affairs* 3, no. 9 (1930): 849.
15. Fusae Ichikawa, "Han-taiheiyō fujinkaigi oyobi beikoku shisatsu hōkoku," *Fusen* 3, no. 1 (January 1, 1929): 5. After the first PPWC, Ichikawa extended

her trip to the U.S. mainland to have the firsthand experience of U.S. women's political and social movements.

16. Barbara Molony, "Activism Among Women in the Taishō Cotton Textile Industry," in *Recreating Japanese Women, 1600–1945*, ed. Gail Lee Bernstein (Berkeley: University of California Press, 1991), 217–38; Elyssa Faison, *Managing Women: Disciplining Labor in Modern Japan* (Berkeley: University of California Press, 2007), 91–106.

17. Faison, *Managing Women*, 22–27; Vera C. Mackie, *Feminism in Modern Japan: Citizenship, Embodiment, and Sexuality* (Cambridge: Cambridge University Press, 2003), 76.

18. *Women of the Pacific* (1928), 176–78; Fusae Ichikawa, *Ichikawa Fusae jiden, Senzen-hen* (Tokyo: Shinjyuku shobō, 1999), 195; Ichikawa, "Han-taiheiyō fujinkaigi oyobi beikoku shisatsu hōkōku," 5.

19. Kikue Ide, "Japan's New Woman: Legal and Political Relationships of Women of Japan Today: An Interpretation," *Pacific Affairs* 1, no. 4 (1928): 1–11.

20. To the relief of Ichikawa and her cohort, the bill did not pass the House of Peers. Kazuko Sugawara, *Ichikawa Fusae to fujin sanseiken kakutoku undō: Mosaku to kattō no rekishi* (Tokyo: Seori shobō, 2002), 149–52.

21. Ichikawa, *Ichikawa Fusae jiden, Senzen-hen*, 196.

22. *Women of the Pacific* (1928), 176–78.

23. Foreign Affairs Minister to League of Nations Codification Conference Japanese delegates, March 14, 1930, *Documents on Japanese Foreign Policy, Kokuai hōten hensan kaigi ni kansuru fujin no kibō ni kansuru ken*, B-9-2-0-2. Ministry of Foreign Affairs (MoFA) Diplomatic Archives, Tokyo, Japan. Cited in Rikiya Takahashi, "1930 nen Hāgu kokusai hōten hensankaigi ni okeru 'tsuma no kokuseki' mondai to nihon: 'kokusaihō no shinpo to 'teikoku no rieki," *Kokusai Seiji* 188 (March 2017): 15–29; Ichikawa Fusae Kinenkai, ed., *Fujin sansei kankeishi shiryō, 1918–1946* [hereafter *FSKSM* (Woman Suffrage History Related Materials)] (Tokyo: Nihon tosho sentā, 2005), microfilm, reel 2, 1310–11; Fusae Ichikawa, "Fujin no kokuseki mondai," *Nihon kokumin, bekkan* 1, no. 1 (May 1932): 43–56.

24. *Women of the Pacific* (1928), 42, 84. As for the case of IPR conferences, Korea, unlike the case of the Philippines, sent delegates only to the first two IPR conferences held in 1925 and 1927 due to Japan's opposition. Tomoko Akami, *Internationalizing the Pacific: The United States, Japan and the Institute of Pacific Relations in War and Peace, 1919–1945* (London: Routledge, 2002), 98–101.

25. Fusa Ishikawa, "Tendencies of the New Educational Movement Japan," *Women of the Pacific* (1928), 43–45; Helen F. Kim, "Korean Women and Education," *Women of the Pacific* (1928), 42.

26. Kyo Kiuchi, "Han taihiyō fujin kaigi ni resshite," in Kyo Kiruch, *Denki sōsho 65: Kyōiku ichiro/Han taihiyō fujin kaigi ni resshite* (Tokyo: Ōzorasha, 1989), 88–100.

27. *Women of the Pacific* (1928), 274–77.

28. Gwenfread E. Allen, "Women Close Pacific Meet Dramatically: Invitation to Convene in Shanghai Causes Discussion," August 22, 1928 [newspaper name unknown], in *Jane Addams Papers*, reel 42, 920. University of California Los Angeles Library Microfilm Collection, Los Angeles, CA [hereafter UCLA-MC].
29. Me-Iung Ting attended the McTyeire School for Girls, founded by the American Southern Methodist Mission in Shanghai in 1890. The school was also known as the Chinese Western Girls' Academy, and among its alumnae were the Soong sisters, Ai-ling (Mrs. Hsiang-Hsi Kung), Ching-ling (Madame Sun Yat-sen), and Mei-ling (Madame Chiang Kai-shek). "McTyeire School for Girls—Early American Education in Shanghai," *AMCHAM Shanghai*, April 1, 2015, July 1, 2022, https://www.amcham-shanghai.org/en/article/mctyeire-school-girls-early-american-education-shanghai.
30. "To Boldly Go," Mount Holyoke College Alumnae Association website, September 5, 2016, https:/alumnae.mtholyoke.edu/blog/to-boldly-go/; Stacey Bieler, *"Patriots" or "Traitors"? A History of American-Educated Chinese Students* (New York: Routledge, 2009); Carl W. Rufus, "Twenty-Five Years of the Barbour Scholarships," *Michigan Alumnus Quarterly Review* 49, no. 11 (1942): 14–26.
31. Ruth Rogaski, *Hygienic Modernity: Meanings of Health and Disease in Treaty-Port China* (Berkeley: University of California Press, 2004), 187–88; Connie A. Shemo, *The Chinese Medical Ministries of Kang Cheng and Shi Meiyu, 1872–1937: On a Cross-Cultural Frontier of Gender, Race, and Nation* (Bethlehem, PA: Lehigh University Press, 2011).
32. *Women of the Pacific* (1928), 274–77.
33. *Women of the Pacific* (1928), 274–77; Eleanor Hinder to Jane Addams, September 14, 1928, in *Jane Addams Papers*, reel 20, 257. UCLA-MC.
34. Lawrence H. Fuchs, *Hawaii Pono "Hawaii the Excellent": An Ethnic and Political History* (Honolulu, HI: Bess, 1961), 152–53.
35. Ford to Addams, November 9, 1928, *Jane Addams Papers*, reel 20, 493–94; Eleanor Hinder to Jane Addams, December 6, 1928, *Jane Addams Papers*, reel 20, 599. UCLA-MC
36. For the subsequent work by Hinder in the Shanghai International Settlement as the only woman director in the SMC and its relationship to the transnational women's community and Chinese nationalism, see Sarah Paddle, "'For the China of the Future': Western Feminists, Colonization and International Citizenship in China in the Inter-War Years," *Australian Feminist Studies* 16, no. 36 (2001): 325–41; Isabella Jackson, *Shaping Modern Shanghai: Colonialism in China's Global City* (Cambridge: Cambridge University Press, 2017), 105–112.
37. "Report of the Joint Standing Committee of Women's International Organizations," April 23, 1929, 3, Liaison Committee of Women's International Organizations Archives in Amsterdam, folder 1. International Institute of Social History, Amsterdam, the Netherlands.

38. Its first presidency was assumed by Matsu Tsuji, who had served as the deputy president of Tsuda College from 1919 to 1925 and was then the chair of the National Committee of the Japan YWCA. Tsune(ko) Gauntlett, active in the Japan WCTU and the JWPA, became JWCIR's vice president. Fusae Ichikawa, the president of Japan's Woman Suffrage League (WSA), served as its secretary. *FSKSM*, reel 3, 1424, 1452, reel 52, 111–12; "Fujin dantai kokusai renraku iinkai," *Joshi seinenkai* 30, no. 6 (June 1933): 28–29. The JWCIR changed its name to the Standing Committee of Women's Organizations of Japan (JSCWIO; *Nihon Fujin Dantai Kokusai Renraku Iinkai*) in 1933.
39. The list of JWCIR/JSCWIO member organizations included the names of Japan's branch organizations of the World YWCA, the World WCTU, and the WILPF, along with the suffrage group, the WSA, and other Tokyo-headquartered organizations of professionals, such as primary school teachers, doctors, and writers. In some years, the list also included organizations of women Buddhists, socialists, and midwives. *FSKSM*, reel 2, reel 3, reel 51, reel 52.
40. See *Documents on Japanese Foreign Policy, Han-haiheiyō fujin kaigi kankei ikken* B-10-10-0-2. MoFA Diplomatic Archives.
41. "Dai nikai Taiheiyō Fujin kaigi nihon daihyō senshutsu ni tsuite," reel 51, 199.
42. For example, the JWCIR passed a resolution disqualifying Kaneko Kitamura—a journalist, suffragist, and aviator who had attended the first PPWC as an "associate visitor"—as the Japanese woman representative to the Eleventh IWSA to be held in Berlin in June 1929. It notified the IWSA's secretary Emilie Gourd. Japanese delegates to the First PPWC were critical of Kitamura's fun-loving attitude in Honolulu. From Japan Women's Committee for International Relations to Mrs. Emilie Gourd, May 20, 1929, in *FSKSM*, reel 51, 275.
43. *FSKSM*, reel 20, 734–40; reel 51, 322–26.
44. Fusae Ichikawa, *Ichikawa Fusae shū*, vols. 1 and 2 (Tokyo: Nihon tosho sentā, 1994).
45. The eleven "countries" included Australia, Canada, China, Hawaii, India, Japan, Mexico, New Zealand, Philippine Islands, Samoa, and the United States. "List of Delegates According to Countries," *Women of the Pacific* (1930), 390–92; "The Y.W.C.A. at the Pan-Pacific Women's Conference," *World's Y.W.C.A. Supplement to the International Women's News* 25, no. 3 (September 1930): 51–52.
46. *Pan-Pacific Union Bulletin* new series [hereafter *PPU Bulletin* ns], no. 126 (August 1930): cover page.
47. *Women of the Pacific* (1930), 3–6.
48. Satterthwaite to Mrs. Thomas Carter, February 12, 1930, *FSKSM*, reel 51, 280.
49. Ann Kraus Meeropol, "A Practical Visionary: Mary Emma Woolley and the Education of Women" (PhD diss., University of Massachusetts, 1992); Lillian Faderman, *To Believe in Women: What Lesbians Have Done for America —A History* (Boston: Houghton Mifflin, 1999), 217–36.

50. "Three Problems for American Women, Dr. Woolley Believes," *Honolulu Star-Bulletin*, July 25, 1927, 11.
51. Presumably, Woolley became occupied with U.S. congressional debate in including a woman to the U.S. delegation to the 1932 League of Nations Disarmament Conference in Geneva, as she became one of the very few female delegates at the conference. Harriet Hyman Alonso, *Peace as a Women's Issue: A History of the U.S. Movement for World Peace and Women's Rights* (Syracuse, NY: Syracuse University Press, 1993), 121.
52. Japanese American National Museum and Brian Niiya, eds., *Encyclopedia of Japanese American History* (New York: Checkmark, 2001), 162.
53. *First Pan-Pacific Conference on Education, Rehabilitation, Reclamation and Recreation: Report of Proceedings* (Washington, DC: U.S. Government Printing Office, 1927), 141–51.
54. "P.T.A. Reunites Families, Is View of Jane Addams," *Honolulu Advertiser*, August 15, 1928.
55. *Women of the Pacific* (1930), i, 6–9; William W. Cutler III, *Parents and Schools: The 150-Year Struggle for Control in American Education* (Chicago: University of Chicago Press, 2000), 1–14; Harry Overstreet and Bonaro Overstreet, *Where Children Come First: A Study of the P.T.A. Idea* (Chicago: National Congress of Parents and Teachers, 1949), 199–201.
56. Molly Ladd-Taylor, *Mother-Work: Women, Child Welfare, and the State, 1890–1930* (Urbana: University of Illinois Press, 1994), 8, 53.
57. Cutler, *Parents and Schools*, 42–126.
58. "Noted Women Who Will Attend August Conference," *Honolulu Star-Bulletin*, July 26, 1930, 6.
59. As for other sections, the Health Section was codirected by Australian Ethel E. Osborne and Dr. March R. Jones, Research Associate of Queens Hospital in Honolulu. The Social Service Section was directed by New Zealander Jean Begg, an expert on health and welfare who engaged in YWCA work in India, *Women of the Pacific* (1930), iv–v, 817; Fiona Paisley, *Glamour in the Pacific: Cultural Internationalism and Race Politics in the Women's Pan-Pacific* (Honolulu: University of Hawai'i Press, 2009), 32, 35.
60. *Women of the Pacific* (1930), 83–102, 231–75.
61. *Women of the Pacific* (1930), 390. Zen Way Koh received her D.P.D. from Yale in 1926 and held important positions in private- and government-funded medical schools, bureaus, and hospitals. Rufus, "Twenty-Five Years of the Barbour Scholarship," 22. For Ah Chin Loo Lam, see George F. M. Nellist, ed., *Men of Hawaii: A Biographical Record of Men of Substantial Achievement in the Hawaiian Islands*, vol. IV (Honolulu, HI: Honolulu Star-Bulletin 1930), 295–96. As for Fitch, see Karen J. Leong, *The China Mystique: Pearl S. Buck,*

Anna May Wong, Mayling Soong, and the Transformation of American Orientalism (Berkeley: University of California Press, 2005), 121–23.

62. Sadakata received medical training at the University of Michigan and other medical institutions in the United States. Saito studied nursing and social hygiene for more than ten years in the United States. *Michigan Alumnus* 32, no. 1 (October 10, 1925): 486.
63. St. Luke International Hospital was founded by U.S. Episcopal missionary doctor Rudolf Bolling Teusler in 1902 to address the weaknesses of Japan's upper-class-oriented modern medical care system and the lack of interest and fitness in the realm of public health. It received funding from the Japanese aristocracy and government and Japanese and American philanthropists, including Eiichi Shibusawa and the Carnegie Endowment for International Peace. Garrett L. Washington, "St. Luke's Hospital and the Modernization of Japan, 1874–1928," *Health and History* 15, no. 2 (2013): 5–28; St. Luke's International University, "History," July 20, 2022, https:/university.luke.ac.jp/english/university_information/history.html; Hiro Fujimoto, *Igaku to kirisutokyō: Nihon ni okeru Amerika Purotestanto no iryō senkyō* (Tokyo: Hosei University Press, 2021), 201–33.
64. Toshiko Tsutsumi, "Kimura Yukiko to YWCA—Kokusai jin no tanjō," *Jiroscconsultus*, no. 22 (January 2013): 78–81.
65. Hawai nihonjin iminshi kankō iinkai, ed., *Hawai nihonjin iminshi* (Honolulu, HI: Hawai nikkeijin rengō kyōkai, 1964), 252–53.
66. *Women of the Pacific* (1930), 391–92.
67. *Women of the Pacific* (1930), 49–50; "S. Korean President, UH Leaders Honor 'Women Patriots,' Korean Immigrants," *University of Hawai'i News*, September 23, 2021, July 4, 2022, https://www.hawaii.edu/news/2021/09/23/south-korean-president-visits-uh/.
68. J. Stanley Lemons, *The Woman Citizen: Social Feminism in the 1920s* (Urbana: University of Illinois Press, 1973), 63–68; Candice Lewis Bredbenner, *A Nationality of Her Own: Women, Marriage, and the Law of Citizenship* (Berkeley: University of California Press, 1998), 80–194; Ellen C. DuBois, "Storming the Hague: The 1930 Campaign for Independent Nationality for Women Regardless of Marital Status," *Tijdschrift voor Gender Studies* 16, no. 4 (2013): 18–29.
69. Anna Brennan, "Nationality of Married Women," *Mid-Pacific Magazine* 40, no. 2 (August 1930): 113–16.
70. Ruth L. T. Yap, "The Legal Status of Chinese Women in China and Hawaii," *Mid-Pacific Magazine* 40, no. 2 (August 1930): 121–25.
71. *Women of the Pacific* (1928), vii.
72. Bredbenner, *A Nationality of Her Own*, 166–71.
73. Martha Mabie Gardner, *The Qualities of a Citizen: Women, Immigration, and Citizenship, 1870–1965* (Princeton, NJ: Princeton University Press, 2005), 140–56. The amendment required residency in the United States on July 2, 1932.

74. A. Y. Satterthwaite to Emily Green Balch, September 30, 1930; Eleanor M. Barr, ed., *Women's International League for Peace and Freedom, US Section, 1919–1959*, reel 54, 283–84.
75. "M. M. Scott Is Dead: Noted as an Educator," *Honolulu Star-Bulletin*, May 3, 1922, 1, 11.
76. Emma Wold, "Women and Nationality: Towards Equality in Citizenship Laws," *Pacific Affairs* 4, no. 6 (1931): 511–15; Manley O. Hudson, "The First Conference for the Codification of International Law," *American Journal of International Law* 24, no. 2 (1930): 367–69, February 12, 2023, http:/www.jstor.org/stable/2189414.
77. California LWV member Mrs. J. L. Criswell presented a paper on "Women on City Planning," *Women of the Pacific* (1930), 146.
78. *Women of the Pacific* (1930), vii, 127–37. Fiona Paisley, "Citizens of Their World: Australian Feminism and Indigenous Rights in the International Context, 1920s and 1930s," *Feminist Review* 58, no. 1 (February 1998): 66–84.
79. "On Juries in Hawaii," *Woman's Journal* 14, no. 12 (1929): 29.
80. "Minutes," in *League of Women Voters in Hawaii Papers* [hereafter *HLWV Papers*], books 1–3; Hawai'i State Archives Manuscript Collection (HSAMC)-M356, Honolulu, HI; Catherine Kekoa Enomoto, "Keli'inoi, Rosaline Enos Lyons," in *Notable Women of Hawaii*, ed. Barbara Bennett Peterson (Honolulu: University of Hawai'i Press, 1984), 214–16.
81. Alice Parsons (Mrs. Edgerton), "At the Pan-Pacific," *Woman's Journal* 15, no. 11 (1930): 28.
82. Parsons (Mrs. Edgerton), "At the Pan-Pacific."
83. Angela Woollacott, "Inventing Commonwealth and Pan-Pacific Feminisms: Australian Women's Internationalist Activism in the 1920s–30s," in *Feminisms and Internationalisms*, ed. Mrinalini Shinha, Donna Guy, and Angela Wollacott (Oxford: Blackwell, 1999), 81–104.
84. Georgina Sweet, "History of the Pan-Pacific Women's Association," *Women of the Pacific* (1930), 7.
85. *Women of the Pacific* (1930), 394–95.
86. *Hawai Hochi*, August 21, 1930, and September 6, 1930; *Women of the Pacific* (1930), 394–95.
87. *Hawai Hochi*, September 6, 1930; *Women of the Pacific* (1930), 394–95.
88. Paul F. Hooper, *Elusive Destiny: The Internationalist Movement in Modern Hawaii* (Honolulu: University of Hawai'i Press, 1980), 100–104.
89. *International Woman Suffrage News* 26, no. 2 (November 1931): 3.
90. Nihon kirisutokyō fujin kyōfūkai, ed., *Nihon kirisutokyō fujin kyōfūkai hyakunenshi* (Tokyo: Domesu shuppan, 1986), 623–30; Ochimi Kubushiro, "Shanhai Nankin homon to nisshi no shourai," *Fujin shinpō* 407 (February 1932): 9; Reiko Suetsugu, *Nijyu seiki Chūgoku joseishi* (Tokyo: Aoki shoten, 2009), 243–45.

91. Nihon kirisutokyō fujin kyōfūkai, *Nihon kirisutokyō fujin kyōfūkai hyakunen-shi*, 589–93; Tsuneko Gauntlett, *Nanajyū nana nen no omoide* (Tokyo: Uemura shoten, 1949), 132–40.
92. Michi Kawai and Ochimi Kubushiro, *Japanese Women Speak: A Message from the Christian Women of Japan to the Christian Women of America* (Boston: Central Committee on the United Study of Foreign Missions, 1934), 168–69. As for wartime WCTU activism in the 1930s, see, for example, Manako Ogawa, "Estranged Sisterhood: The Wartime Trans-Pacific Dialogue of the World's Woman's Christian Temperance Union, 1931–1945," *Japanese Journal of American Studies* 18 (2007): 163–85.
93. American peace advocates met the same criticism domestically. So did Korean Christians, such as Helen Kim, who yielded to the Japanese authority to protect the students of the Ewha Women's College she headed. Insook Kwon, "Feminists Navigating the Shoals of Nationalism and Collaboration: The Post-Colonial Korean Debate Over How to Remember Kim Hwallan," *Frontiers: A Journal of Women Studies* 27, no. 1 (2006): 39–66.
94. Karen Garner, *Precious Fire: Maud Russell and the Chinese Revolution* (Amherst: University of Massachusetts Press, 2003), 139–42; Emily Honig, "Christianity, Feminism, and Communism: The Life and Times of Deng Yuzhi," in *Christianity in China: From the Eighteenth Century to the Present*, ed. Daniel H. Bays (Stanford, CA: Stanford University Press, 1996), 243–62.
95. Pui-Lan Kwok, *Chinese Women and Christianity, 1860–1927* (Atlanta, GA: Scholars Press, 1992), 126–32.
96. Garner, *Precious Fire*, 139–42.
97. Garner, *Precious Fire*, 142–44.
98. Leong, *The China Mystique*, 120–23.
99. "Minutes, May 1929–June 1932," in *HLWV Papers*, book 3. Hawai'i State Archives Manuscript Collection (HSAMC)-M356. Hawai'i Honolulu, HI.
100. David E. Stannard, *Honor Killing: Race, Rape, and Clarence Darrow's Spectacular Last Case* (New York: Penguin, 2005); *The Massie Affair*, DVD (prod. and dir. Mark Zwonitzer, 60 min., PBS, 2005).
101. "Newspaper Coverage of the Massie Affair," *PBS American Experience*, March 20, 2024, https://www.pbs.org/wgbh/americanexperience/features/island-murder-newspaper-coverage-massie-affair/.
102. Stannard, *Honor Killing*, 184–87; *The Massie Affair*.
103. Alice Parsons (Mrs. Edgerton), "At the Pan-Pacific," *Woman's Journal* 15, no. 11 (1930): 28.
104. "Radiogram from Belle Sherwin to Gertrude Damon"; "Women Press for Jury Duty," *Honolulu Star-Bulletin*, newspaper clipping in *HLWV Papers*, book 4; "Assistance Welcomed on Jury Effort," *Honolulu Advertiser*, February 3, 1932, 2.
105. "Minutes of Regular Monthly Meeting Minutes Postponed from October 27, November 3, 1932," in *HLWV Papers*, book 4.

106. "Women Protest Against Change in Hawaii Government: A Resolution Presented by the Efficiency in Government Committee and Adopted Unanimously on December 6, 1932," in *HLWV Papers*, book 4.
107. Cited in Stannard, *Honor Killing*, 391–92.
108. For example, the Massie Affair made the islands' people reflect on the Myles Fukunaga case in 1928, in which a nineteen-year-old Japanese American was sentenced to death for kidnapping and killing the ten-year-old son of a white banker whose rent collectors repeatedly distressed his mother. Although the Japanese community collected a thousand petitions pleading for commutation of the death sentence to life imprisonment, Governor Judd turned a deaf ear, and Fukunaga was executed on November 19, 1929.
109. Stannard, *Honor Killing*, 388–418; Fuchs, *Hawaii Pono*, 182–205.
110. "The Special Meeting of the Executive Board Minutes, October 27, 1932," in *HLWV Papers*, book 4. After Straub's protest and subsequent resignation in December 1932, which were covered by local newspapers, the HLWV began to lose membership and ceased its activity. After a period of inactivity, the HLWV officially decided to disband on May 14, 1936. "Women Disband Voters League," *Honolulu Star-Bulletin*, May 15, 1936.
111. The Korean delegation was composed of Mary C. Kim (Mary C. Kim Joh, 1904–2005), a Barbour scholar who was then teaching music at her alma mater, Ewha Woman's College; and Nodie Kimhaikim, principal of the Korean Christian Institute in Honolulu, Hawai'i. "List of Delegates by Countries," *Women of the Pacific* (1934), 68–70.
112. Gauntlett, *Nanajyu nana nen no omoide*, 142–45.
113. Gauntlett, *Nanajyu nana nen no omoide*, 146–47.
114. Ting not only served as the General Secretary of the Chinese YWCA and World YWCA Executive Council vice president, but she also sat on the Executive Council of the Child Welfare Association and the Executive Committee of the National Christian Council. She was a board member of various schools and colleges, including the McTyeire Girls' School, Jinling College, and the People's Welfare Committee of the Greater Shanghai Municipality.
115. Elizabeth Littell-Lamb, "Ding Shujing: The YWCA Pathway for China's 'New Women,'" in *Salt and Light: Lives of Faith That Shaped Modern China*, ed. Carol Lee Hamrin (Eugene, OR: Pickwick, 2009), 95.
116. Garner, *Precious Fire*, 152.
117. Gauntlett, *Nanajū nana nen no omoide*, 147; Tsuneko Gauntlett, "Dai 46 kai taikai ni atarite," *Fujin shinpō* (May 1937): 8–11; "Shina o kataru," *Joseitenbō* 15, no. 1 (January 1937): 8–13.
118. "Dr. Hua Chuen Mei, May 20, 1925," in Mei Family File owned by Dr. James David Adams Jr.

119. "From Anna Kong Mei to Miss Satterthwaite, July 4, 1937," in Pan-Pacific Union Papers, box 3-308, University of Hawai'i at Mānoa Library Special Collections, Honolulu, Hawai'i.
120. Gauntlett, *Nanajū nana nen no omoide*, 148–51; Tsuneko Gauntlett, "Daiyonkai han taihiyō fujinkaigi e shusseki shite," *Fujin heiwa kyōkai kaihō* 20 (December 1937): 2.
121. Ruth Crow, *A Tribute to Doris McRae 1893 to 1988: A Life Dedicated to Peace and Social Justice*, in VU Research Repository, 7, December 31, 2016, http://vuir.vu.edu.au/16168/.
122. Paisley, *Glamour in the Pacific*, 206–17; Fiona Paisley, "From Nation of Islam to Goodwill Tourist: African-American Women at Pan-Pacific and South East Asia Women's Conferences, 1937 and 1955," *Women's Studies International Forum* 32, no. 1 (2009): 21–28.
123. *Women of the Pacific* (1937), 61.
124. Paisley, *Glamour in the Pacific*, 206–11; Paisley, "From Nation of Islam to Goodwill Tourist," 21–28.
125. "A Pro-American Appeals for Better Understanding: Strong Through Education for Universal Equality Without Race or Color Prejudice," *Vancouver News Herald*, July 23, 1937, 3. Cited partially in Paisley, *Glamour in the Pacific*, 208–209.
126. *Women of the Pacific* (1937), 61–64.
127. Sweet, "History of the Pan-Pacific Women's Association," 6–12.
128. *Women of the Pacific* (1937), 11.

Epilogue

1. Amy Kaplan, *The Anarchy of Empire in the Making of U.S. Culture* (Cambridge, MA: Harvard University Press, 2002), 171–212.
2. Paul F. Hooper, *Elusive Destiny: The Internationalist Movement in Modern Hawaii* (Honolulu: University of Hawai'i Press, 1980), 65–136.
3. Nihon Han-Taihaiyō Tonan Ajia Fujin Kyōkai, *Han-Taiheiyō Tōnan Ajia Fujin Kyōkai rokujyū-nen shi* (Tokyo: Domesu shuppan, 1993), 32–35; PPSEAWA International, July 20, 2022, https://www.ppseawa.org/.
4. For women's achievements at intergovernmental organizations including the League of Nations, the ILO, and the UN, see Nitza Berkovitch, *From Motherhood to Citizenship: Women's Rights and International Organizations* (Baltimore, MD: Johns Hopkins University Press, 1999). For Indigenous peoples' rights, see International Labour Organization, "Conventions and Recommendations," August 20, 2023, https://www.ilo.org/global/standards/introduction-to-international-labour-standards/conventions-and-recommendations/lang—en/index.htm.
5. Pete Pichaske, "U.S. Acknowledges Wrong in 1893 Hawaii Overthrow," *Honolulu Star-Bulletin*, November 23, 1993, 1.
6. Kaplan, *The Anarchy of Empire in the Making of U.S. Culture*, 212.

Selected Bibliography

Manuscripts and Collections

Bishop Museum Library and Archives, Honolulu, HI, USA
    Francis Mills Swanzy Papers
Hawaiian Mission Children's Society Library and Archives, Honolulu, HI, USA
    Woman's Christian Temperance Union of Hawaiian Islands Records
    Woman's Board of Missions Pacific Islands Records
Hawai'i State Archives, Honolulu, HI, USA
    Foreign Language School Files
    International Institute Files
    League of Women Voters Hawaiian Islands Files
    Republic of Hawaii Constitutional Convention Records (1894)
Huntington Library, San Marino, CA, USA
    Alice Park Papers
Library of Congress, Washington, DC, USA
    Carrie Chapman Catt Papers (microfilm)
    Chronicling America (digitalized newspaper collection)
    League of Women Voters Papers II
Tokyo University Library and Archives, Tokyo, Japan
    Takagi Yasaka Collection, *Taihaiyō mondai chōsakai kankei shiryō* [IPR materials]
Ichikawa Fusae Center for Women and Governance, Tokyo, Japan
    Fujin sansei kankeishi shiryō [Woman Suffrage History–related materials] (microfilm)
Japan Ministry of Foreign Affairs Diplomatic Archives, Tokyo, Japan

Han-Taiheiyō fujin kaigi kankei [Pan-Pacific Women's Conferences–related materials]

Kokuai hōten hensan kaigi kakei [International Codification Conference–related materials]

National Archives and Records Administration, College Park, MD, USA

Military Intelligence Division Records

Swarthmore College Library and Archives, Swarthmore, PA, USA

Peace Collection, Jane Addams Papers (microfilm and manuscripts)

Barr, Eleanor M. "Women's International League for Peace and Freedom, US Section, 1919–1959" (microfilm)

Smith College Special Archives, Northampton, MA, USA

Sophia Smith Collection, YWCA of the USA Records (microfilm)

University of Hawai'i Mānoa Hamilton Library, Collections and Archives, Honolulu, HI, USA

Bob Krauss Research Index

Pan-Pacific Union Records

Hawaii Newspaper Morgue (microfiche)

International Institute of Social History Archives, Amsterdam, the Netherlands

Liaison Committee of Women's International Organizations/Joint Standing Committee of the Women's International Organizations Records

Other

McCree Bryan, Mary Lynn, et al., eds. *The Jane Addams Papers 1868–1935*. Ann Arbor, MI: University Microfilm International, 1984. (microfilm)

Periodicals

English

Calendar
Chinese Recorder
Evening Bulletin (Hawai'i)
Friend
Hawaii Hochi
Hawaii Tribune-Herald
Hawaiian Gazette
Honolulu Star-Bulletin
Independent
Japan Times and Mail
Jus Suffragii
Life and Labor Bulletin

Maui News
Michigan Alumnus
Mid-Pacific Magazine
New York Daily News
New York Times
Nippu Jiji
Pacific Commercial Advertiser (Honolulu Advertiser)
Pan-Pacific Union Bulletin
Vancouver News Herald
Woman Citizen
Woman's Journal

Japanese

Chi-no shio
Fujin heiwa kyōkai kaihō,
Fujin shinpō
Fusen
Hawaii Hōchi
Josei dōmei
Joshi seinan kai
Katei shūhō
Megumi
Nippū Jiji
Yomiuri shimbun

Government Documents

Hawaii Legislature House of Representatives. *Journal of the House of Representatives of the Eighth Legislature of the Territory of Hawaii, Regular Session 1915.* Honolulu, HI: Hawaiian Gazette, 1915.

U.S. Committee on Public Information. *The Women's Committee of the Council of National Defense Organization Charts.* n.p., 1918.

U.S. Congress. *Woman Suffrage in Hawaii: Hearings Before the Committee on Woman Suffrage, House of Representatives, Sixty-Fifth Congress, Second Session, on S. 2380 and H. R. 4665.* Washington, DC: Government Printing Office, 1918.

U.S. Department of Interior. *A Survey of Education in Hawaii.* Washington, DC: Government Printing Office, 1920.

———. *First Pan Pacific Conference on Education, Rehabilitation, Reclamation and Recreation: Called by the President of the United States of America in Conformity with a Joint Resolution of the Senate and House of Representatives of the United States and Held Under the Auspices of the Department of the Interior at Honolulu, Hawaii, April 11 to 16, 1927: Report of the Proceedings.* Washington, DC: Government Printing Office, 1927.

Conference Proceedings and Annual Reports

Annual Report of the Woman's Christian Temperance Union of the Hawaiian Islands
Annual Report of the Woman's Board of Missions for the Pacific Islands
First Pan-Pacific Educational Conference, Honolulu, August 11–24, 1921, Program and Proceedings
First Pan Pacific Conference on Education, Rehabilitation, Reclamation and Recreation, April 11–16, 1927, Report of the Proceedings
Women of the Pacific: Being a Record of the Proceedings of the Pan-Pacific Women's Conference (1928, 1930, 1934, 1937, 1949)

Books, Articles, and Theses

Abbott, Edith, and John Sorensen. *A Sister's Memories: The Life and Work of Grace Abbott from the Writings of Her Sister, Edith Abbott.* Chicago: University of Chicago Press, 2015.

Addams, Jane, and Charlene Haddock Seigfried. *Democracy and Social Ethics.* Urbana: University of Illinois Press, 2002.

Akami, Tomoko. *Internationalizing the Pacific: The United States, Japan and the Institute of Pacific Relations in War and Peace, 1919–1945.* London: Routledge, 2002.

Akiyama, Tsune. *Han Taiheiyō Tōnan Ajia fujin kyōkai rokujūnenshi.* Tokyo: Domesu shuppan, 1993.

Allen, Ann Taylor, Barbara Beatty, and Roberta Wollons. "How Did the Kindergarten Movement Provide Women with Opportunities for Professional Development and Social Activism in the United States and Internationally?" In *Women and Social Movement in the United States.* August 3, 2014. http://asp6new.alexanderstreet.com/was2/was2.object.details.apsx?.

Alonso, Harriet Hyman. *Peace as a Women's Issue: A History of the U.S. Movement for World Peace and Women's Rights.* Syracuse, NY: Syracuse University Press, 1993.

Anderson, Mary. *Woman at Work: The Autobiography of Mary Anderson as Told to Mary N. Winslow.* Minneapolis: University of Minnesota Press, 1951.

Aoki, Takako. *Ima o ikiru Naruse Jinzō: Joshi kyōiku no paionia.* Tokyo: Kōdansha, 2001.

Appleton, Vivia B. *A Doctor's Letters from China, Fifty Years Ago.* Honolulu, HI: Self-published, 1976.

Asato, Noriko. *Teaching Mikadoism: The Attack on Japanese Language Schools in Hawaii, California, and Washington, 1919–1927.* Honolulu: University of Hawai'i Press, 2006.

Austin, Allan W. *From Concentration Camp to Campus: Japanese American Students and World War II.* Urbana: University of Illinois Press, 2004.

Baker, Jean H., ed. *Votes for Women: The Struggle for Suffrage Revisited.* Oxford: Oxford University Press, 2002.

Basson, Lauren L. "Fit for Annexation but Unfit to Vote? Debating Hawaiian Suffrage Qualifications at the Turn of the Twentieth Century." *Social Science History* 29, no. 4 (January 2005): 575–98.

Bays, Daniel H., ed. *Christianity in China: From the Eighteenth Century to the Present.* Stanford, CA: Stanford University Press, 1996.

Bays, Daniel H., and Ellen Widmer. *China's Christian Colleges: Cross-Cultural Connections, 1900–1950.* Stanford, CA: Stanford University Press, 2009.

Beechert, Edward D. *Working in Hawaii: A Labor History.* Honolulu: University of Hawai'i Press, 1985.

Bell, Roger J. *Last Among Equals: Hawaiian Statehood and American Politics.* Honolulu: University of Hawai'i Press, 1984.

Berkovitch, Nitza. *From Motherhood to Citizenship: Women's Rights and International Organizations.* Baltimore, MD: Johns Hopkins University Press, 1999.

Bernstein, Gail Lee, ed. *Recreating Japanese Women, 1600–1945.* Berkeley: University of California Press, 1991.

Bickers, Robert, and Christian Henriot, eds. *New Frontiers: Imperialism's New Communities in East Asia, 1842–1953.* Manchester: Manchester University Press, 2000.

Bieler, Stacey. *"Patriots" or "Traitors"? A History of American-Educated Chinese Students.* New York: Routledge, 2009.

Binkiewicz, Donna M. *Between the Sea and Sky: The Saga of My Portuguese American Family in Upcountry Maui, 1881–1941.* Independently Published, 2021.

Bolt, Christine. *Sisterhood Questioned? Race, Class, and Internationalism in the American and British Women's Movements, c. 1880s–1970s.* London: Routledge, 2004.

Bordin, Ruth. *Woman and Temperance: The Quest for Power and Liberty, 1873–1900.* Philadelphia: Temple University Press, 1981.

Boris, Eileen. *Making the Woman Worker: Precarious Labor and the Fight for Global Standards, 1919–2019.* New York: Oxford University Press, 2019.

Bottorff, Bruce P. "Continuity and Change: A History of the YWCA of Honolulu, 1900–1945." PhD diss., University of Hawai'i, 1999.

———. "Forging American Womanhood: The Acculturation of Second-Generation Immigrant Girls in Honolulu, 1917–1938." *Japanese Journal of American Studies* 31 (2020): 65–86.

———. "Foundations of Influence: YWCA of Honolulu Structures and the Assertion of Moral Authority, 1900–1927." *Hawaiian Journal of History* 52, no. 1 (2018): 117–42.

———. "Immigrant Assimilation at the International Institute of Honolulu, 1916–1937." *Kansai Gaikokugo Daigaku Kenkyū Ronshū* 108 (2018–2019): 69–85.

Boyd, Nancy. *Emissaries: The Overseas Work of the American YWCA, 1895–1970.* New York: Woman's Press, 1986.

Bredbenner, Candice Lewis. *A Nationality of Her Own: Women, Marriage, and the Law of Citizenship.* Berkeley: University of California Press, 1998.

Breen, William J. *Uncle Sam at Home: Civilian Mobilization, Wartime Federalism, and the Council of National Defense, 1917–1919.* Westport, CT: Greenwood, 1984.

Browder, Dorothea. "A 'Christian Solution of the Labor Situation': How Working Women Reshaped the YWCA's Religious Mission and Politics." *Journal of Women's History* 19, no. 2 (2007): 85–110.

Brown, Kathleen M. "Brave New Worlds: Women's and Gender History." *William and Mary Quarterly* 50, no. 2 (April 1993): 311–28.

Burns, David. *The Life and Death of the Radical Historical Jesus.* New York: Oxford University Press, 2013.

Cahill, Cathleen C. *Federal Fathers and Mothers.* Chapel Hill: University of North Carolina Press, 2011.

Castle, Alfred L. "Harriet Castle and the Beginnings of Progressive Kindergarten Education in Hawai'i 1894–1900." *Hawaiian Journal of History* 23 (1989): 119–36.

Catton, Margaret M. L. *Social Service in Hawaii.* Palo Alto, CA: Pacific Book, 1959.

Chan, Sucheng. *Asian Americans: An Interpretative History.* Boston: Twayne, 1991.

Chang, Roberta, and Wayne Patterson. *The Koreans in Hawai'i: A Pictorial History, 1903–2003.* Honolulu: University of Hawai'i Press, 2003.

Chapin, Helen G., and David W. Forbes. "The Folio of 1855—A Plea for Women's Rights." *Hawaiian Journal of History* 19 (1985).

Choi, Anne Soon. "'Hawaii Has Been My America': Generation, Gender, and Korean Immigrant Experience in Hawai'i Before World War II." *American Studies* 45, no. 3 (2004): 139–55.

Choy, Catherine Ceniza, and Judy Tzu-Chun Wu, eds. *Gendering the Trans-Pacific World.* Leiden, the Netherlands: Brill, 2017.

Chung, May Lee, Dorothy Jim Luke, and Associated Chinese University Women, eds. *Chinese Women Pioneers in Hawaii: A Collection of Stories.* Honolulu, HI: Associated Chinese University Women, 2002.

Cobble, Dorothy Sue. *For the Many: American Feminists and the Global Fight for Democratic Equality.* Princeton, NJ: Princeton University Press, 2021.

Coffman, Tom. *Nation Within: The Story of America's Annexation of the Nation of Hawai'i.* Kāne'ohe, HI: Epicenter, 1998.

Conrad, Sebastian. *What Is Global History?* Princeton, NJ: Princeton University Press, 2017.

Cott, Nancy F. *The Bonds of Womanhood: "Woman's Sphere" in New England, 1780–1835*. New Haven, CT: Yale University Press, 1977.

Culwell, Kelbi. "Biographical Sketch of Elizabeth Green Kalb." In *Women and Social Movements in the United States, 1600–2000*. New York: Alexander Street, 2022. April 29, 2022. https://documents.alexanderstreet.com/d/1008297925.

Cutler III, William W. *Parents and Schools: The 150-Year Struggle for Control in American Education*. Chicago: University of Chicago Press, 2000.

Daley, Caroline, and Melanie Nolan, eds. *Suffrage and Beyond: International Feminist Perspectives*. New York: New York University Press, 1994.

Daws, Gavan. *Shoal of Time: A History of the Hawaiian Islands*. Honolulu: University of Hawai'i Press, 1968.

Day, A. Grove. *History Makers of Hawaii: A Biographical Dictionary*. Honolulu, HI: Mutual, 1984.

Del Piano, Barbara. *Outrigger Canoe Club: The First One Hundred Years 1908–2008*. Honolulu, HI: Outrigger Canoe Club, 2008.

———. *Nā Lani Kaumaka/Daughters of Hawai'i: A Century of Historic Preservation*. Honolulu: Daughters of Hawaii, 2005.

Denki hensan iinkai. *Kōya ni mizu wa wakite: Bera Aruwuin no shōgai*. Tokyo: Tokyo Aruwuin Gakuen, 1980.

DeRoche, Celeste. "How Wide the Circle of We: Cultural Pluralism and American Identity, 1910–1954." PhD diss., University of Maine, 2000.

Dewey, John. "My Pedagogic Creed." *School Journal* 54, no. 3 (January 16, 1897): 77–80.

Dodge, Charlotte P. *A History of the Free Kindergarten and Children's Aid Association of the Hawaiian Islands, 1895–1945*. Honolulu, HI: Mercantile Print, 1945.

Droux, Joëlle. "A League of Its Own? The League of Nations' Child Welfare Committee (1919–1936) and International Monitoring of Child Welfare Policies." In *League of Nation's Work on Social Issues: Visions, Endeavours and Experiments*, ed. United Nations. Herndon, VA: United Nations, 2016.

Du Bois, W. E. B. *Darkwater: Voices from Within the Veil*. New York: Washington Square Press, 1920.

DuBois, Ellen Carol. *Feminism and Suffrage: The Emergence of an Independent Women's Movement in America, 1848–1869*. Ithaca, NY: Cornell University Press, 1978.

———. *Harriot Stanton Blatch and the Winning of Woman Suffrage*. New Haven, CT: Yale University Press, 1997.

———. *Suffrage: Women's Long Battle for the Vote*. New York: Simon & Schuster, 2020.

DuBois, Ellen Carol, and Lynn Dumenil. *Through Women's Eyes: An American History with Documents*. Boston: Bedford/St. Martin's, 2009.

Edwards, Louise, and Mina Roces, eds. *Women's Suffrage in Asia: Gender, Nationalism, and Democracy*. London: RoutledgeCurzon, 2004.

Epstein, Alexandra. "International Feminism and Empire-Building Between the Wars: The Case of Viola Smith." *Women's History Review* 17, no. 5 (2008): 699–719.

Epstein, Barbara Leslie. *The Politics of Domesticity: Women, Evangelism and Temperance in Nineteenth Century America.* Middletown, CT: Wesleyan University Press, 1981.

Esashi, Akiko. *Mezameyo josei tachi: Sekirankai no hitobito.* Tokyo: Ōtsuki shoten, 1980.

Faderman, Lillian. *To Believe in Women: What Lesbians Have Done for America—A History.* Boston: Houghton Mifflin, 1999.

Faison, Elyssa. *Managing Women: Disciplining Labor in Modern Japan.* Berkeley: University of California Press, 2007.

Ferguson, Kathy E., and Monique Mironesco, eds. *Gender and Globalization in Asia and the Pacific: Method Practice Theory.* Honolulu: University of Hawai'i Press, 2008.

Flanagan, Maureen A. "Gender and Urban Political Reform: The City Club and the Woman's City Club of Chicago in the Progressive Era." *American Historical Review* 95, no. 4 (1990): 1032–50.

Free Kindergarten and Children's Aid Association of the Hawaiian Islands. *Constitution, By-laws and Charter of the Free Kindergarten and Children's Aid Association of the Hawaiian Islands, with the List of Officers, Committees, Contributors and the Reports of Financial Secretary and a Treasurer.* Honolulu, HI: Robert Grieve, Steam Book and Job Printer, 1895.

Fuchs, Lawrence H. *Hawaii Pono "Hawaii the Excellent": An Ethnic and Political History.* Honolulu, HI: Bess, 1961.

Fujikane, Candace, and Jonathan Y. Okamura, eds. *Asian Settler Colonialism: From Local Governance to the Habits of Everyday Life in Hawai'i.* Honolulu: University of Hawai'i Press, 2008.

Fujimoto, Hiro. *Igaku to kirisutokyō: Nihon ni okeru Amerika Purotesutanto no iryō senkyō.* Tokyo: Hosei daigaku shuppankyoku, 2021.

Gabaccia, Donna R., and Vicki L. Ruíz, eds. *American Dreaming, Global Realities: Rethinking U.S. Immigration History.* Urbana: University of Illinois Press, 2006.

Gardner, Martha Mabie. *The Qualities of a Citizen: Women, Immigration, and Citizenship, 1870–1965.* Princeton, NJ: Princeton University Press, 2005.

Garner, Karen. *Precious Fire: Maud Russell and the Chinese Revolution.* Amherst: University of Massachusetts Press, 2003.

———. "Redefining Institutional Identity: The YWCA Challenge to Extraterritoriality in China, 1925–1930." *Women's History Review* 10, no. 3 (2001): 409–40.

———. *Shaping a Global Women's Agenda: Women's NGOs and Global Governance, 1925–1985.* Manchester: Manchester University Press, 2010.

Gauntlett, Tsuneko. *Nanajyū nana nen no omoide.* Tokyo: Uemura shoten, 1949.

Gething, Judith R. "Christianity and Coverture: Impact on the Legal Status of Women in Hawaii, 1820–1920." *Hawaiian Journal of History* 11 (1977): 188–220.

Glenn, Evelyn Nakano. *Unequal Freedom: How Race and Gender Shaped American Citizenship and Labor.* Cambridge, MA: Harvard University Press, 2002.

Glick, Clarence E. *Sojourners and Settlers: Chinese Migrants in Hawai'i.* Honolulu: University of Hawai'i Press, 1980.

Gluck, Carol. *Japan's Modern Myths: Ideology in the Late Meiji Period.* Princeton, NJ: Princeton University Press, 1985.

Gordon, Andrew. *Labor and Imperial Democracy in Prewar Japan.* Berkeley: University of California Press, 1991.

Gordon, Milton M. *Assimilation in American Life: The Role of Race, Religion, and National Origins.* New York: Oxford University Press, 1964.

Green, Elizabeth. "The Pacific and the International Labour Conference." *Pacific Affairs* 3, no. 9 (1930): 845–53.

Green, Mary E. "Report of Work Among Hawaiian." *Annual Report of the Woman's Christian Temperance Union of the Hawaiian Islands.* 1885.

Griffith, Sarah Marie. *The Fight for Asian American Civil Rights: Liberal Protestant Activism, 1900–1950.* Urbana: University of Illinois Press, 2018.

Grimshaw, Patricia. "New England Missionary Wives, Hawaiian Women, and 'the Cult of True Womanhood.'" *Hawaiian Journal of History* 19 (1985): 71–100.

———. *Paths of Duty: American Missionary Wives in Nineteenth-Century Hawaii.* Honolulu: University of Hawai'i Press, 1989.

———. "Settler Anxieties, Indigenous Peoples, and Women's Suffrage in the Colonies of Australia, New Zealand, and Hawai'i, 1888 to 1902." *Pacific Historical Review* 69, no. 4 (2000): 553–72.

Haga, Kiyoaki. *Suzuki Bunji no iru fūkei.* Akita, Japan: Mumyōsha, 2010.

Hamrin, Carol Lee, and Stacey Bieler, eds. *Salt and Light: Lives of Faith That Shaped Modern China.* Eugene, OR: Pickwick, 2009.

Hanson, F. Allan. "Female Pollution in Polynesia?" *Journal of the Polynesian Society* 91, no. 3 (1982): 335–81.

Harper, Ida Husted, and Susan B. Anthony, eds. *The History of Woman Suffrage 4, 1883–1900.* Indianapolis, IN: Hollenbeck, 1902.

———, eds. *The History of Woman Suffrage V, 1900–1920.* Salem, NH: Ayer, 1985.

———, eds. *The History of Woman Suffrage VI, 1900–1920.* New York: J. J. Little & Ives, 1922.

Harrison, Irene. *Agatha Harrison: An Impression by Her Sister.* London: Allen & Unwin, 1956.

Hastings, Sally Ann. *Neighborhood and Nation in Tokyo, 1905–1937.* Pittsburgh, PA: University of Pittsburgh Press, 1995.

———. "Women Educators of the Meiji Era and the Making of Modern Japan." *International Journal of Social Education* 6, no. 1 (1991): 83–94.

Hawai nihonjin iminshi kankō iinkai, ed. *Hawai nihonjin iminshi.* Honolulu, HI: Hawai nikkeijin rengō kyōkai, 1964.

Hayashi, Brian. "From Race to Nation: The Institute of Pacific Relations, Asian Americans, and George Blakeslee, from 1908 to 1929." *Japanese Journal of American Studies* 23 (2012): 51–71.

Henning, Joseph M. *Outposts of Civilization: Race, Religion, and the Formative Years of American-Japanese Relations.* New York: New York University Press, 2000.

Henry, Alice. *Women and the Labor Movement.* New York: Arno, 1971.

Hinder, Eleanor M. "Pacific Women: Personnel of the Pan-Pacific Women's Conference Honolulu, August 9–19, 1928." *Pacific Affairs* 1, no. 3 (1928): 9–12.

———. *Women in the Pacific: A Contribution to the Pan-Pacific Women's Conference, Honolulu, August 9–19, 1928.* Shanghai, China: n.p., 1928.

Hirobe, Izumi. *Japanese Pride, American Prejudice: Modifying the Exclusion Clause of the 1924 Immigration Act.* Stanford, CA: Stanford University Press, 2001.

Holland, William L., and Paul F. Hooper. *Remembering the Institute of Pacific Relations: The Memoirs of William L. Holland.* Tokyo: Ryūkei Shōsha, 1995.

Hollinger, David A. *Protestants Abroad: How Missionaries Tried to Change the World but Changed America.* Princeton, NJ: Princeton University Press, 2017.

Honig, Emily. *Sisters and Strangers: Women in the Shanghai Cotton Mills, 1919–1949.* Stanford, CA: Stanford University Press, 1986.

Honma, Nagayo, Shunsuke Kamei, and Kenzaburō Shinkawa, eds. *Gendai Amerika zō no saikōchiku: Seiji to bunka no gendaishi.* Tokyo: Tokyo Daigaku shuppankai, 1990.

Hooper, Paul F. *Elusive Destiny: The Internationalist Movement in Modern Hawaii.* Honolulu: University of Hawai'i Press, 1980.

———. "Feminism in the Pacific: The Pan-Pacific and Southeast Asia Women's Association." *Pacific Historian* 20, no. 4 (1976): 367.

———, ed. *Remembering the Institute of Pacific Relations: The Memoires of William L. Holland.* Tokyo: Ryūkei shyosha, 1995.

Hori, Erika. *Hawai nikkeijin no rekishiteki hensen: Amerika kara yomigaeru "eiyu" Goto Katsu.* Tokyo: Sairyūsha, 2021.

Hori, Joan. "Japanese Prostitution in Hawaii During the Immigration Period." *Hawaiian Journal of History* 15 (1981): 113–24.

Hosoi, Wakizō. *Jokō aishi.* Tokyo: Kaizōsha, 1925.

Hoyt, Edwin P. *Davies: The Inside Story of a British-American Family in the Pacific and Its Business Enterprises.* Honolulu, HI: Topgallant, 1983.

Hudson, Manley O. "The First Conference for the Codification of International Law." *American Journal of International Law* 24, no. 2 (1930): 367–69.

Hughes, Judith Dean Gething. *Women and Children First: The Life and Times of Elsie Wilcox of Kaua'i.* Honolulu: University of Hawai'i Press, 1996.

Hune, Shirley, and Gail M. Nomura, eds. *Asian/Pacific Islander American Women: A Historical Anthology.* New York: New York University Press, 2003.

Hunter, Janet. *Women and the Labour Market in Japan's Industrializing Economy: The Textile Industry Before the Pacific War.* London: Routledge, 2003.

Hutchison, John A. *We Are Not Divided: A Critical and Historical Study of the Federal Council.* New York: Round Table, 1941.

Hyams, Ben, and E. Curtis Cluff Jr. *Centennial Memoirs of the Pacific Club in Honolulu, from 1851 to 1951.* Honolulu, HI: Pacific Club in Honolulu, 1951.

Ichikawa, Fusae. "Fujin sanseiken undō no fujinundō ni okeru chii." *Fujin kōron* 10, no. 3 (March 1925).

——. *Ichikawa Fusae jiden, Senzen-hen*. Tokyo: Shinjyuku shobō, 1999.

——. *Ichikawa Fusae shū*. Vols. 1 and 2. Tokyo: Nihon tosho sentā, 1994.

Ichioka, Yuji. *The Issei: The World of the First Generation Japanese Immigrants, 1885–1924*. New York: Free Press, 1988.

Ide, Kikue. "Japan's New Woman: Legal and Political Relationships of Women of Japan Today: An Interpretation." *Pacific Affairs* 1, no. 4 (1928): 1–11.

Iida, Kōjirō. *Honoruru nikkeijin no rekishi chiri*. Kyoto, Japan: Nakanishiya shuppan, 2013.

Iino, Masako, Kinuko Kameda, and Yūko Takahashi, eds. *Tsuda Umeko o sasaeta hitobito*. Tokyo: Yūhikaku, 2000.

Ikei, Masaru. "Nihon kokusai renmei kyōkai: Sono seiritsu to henshitsu." *Hōgaku kenkyū* 68, no. 2 (1995): 23–48.

Ishii, Noriko. "Kirisutokyō seinen undō to josei: Bankoku kirisutokyō gakusei renmei no sōseiki no katudō kara." In *Hokubei kenkyū nyūmon 2: Nashonaru to mukiau*, ed. Sophia University Institute of America and Canada Studies. Tokyo: Sophia University Press, 2019.

Ishii, Noriko Kawamura. *American Women Missionaries at Kobe College, 1873–1909. New Dimensions of Gender*. New York: Routledge, 2004.

Ishikawa, Teruko. "Shanhai no YWCA: Sono soshiki to hito no nettowāku." In *Shanhai: Jūsosuru nettowaku*, ed. Nihon Shanhaishi kenkyūkai. Tokyo: Kyūko shoin, 2000.

Jackson, Isabella. *Shaping Modern Shanghai: Colonialism in China's Global City*. Cambridge: Cambridge University Press, 2017.

Jacobs, Margaret D. *White Mother to a Dark Race: Settler Colonialism, Maternalism, and the Removal of Indigenous Children in the American West and Australia, 1880–1940*. Lincoln: University of Nebraska Press, 2009.

Japanese American National Museum and Brian Niiya, eds. *Encyclopedia of Japanese American History*. New York: Checkmark, 2001.

Jensen, Jill M., and Nelson Lichtenstein, eds. *The ILO from Geneva to the Pacific Rim: West Meets East*. New York: Palgrave Macmillan & ILO, 2016.

Jolly, Margaret. *Family and Gender in the Pacific: Domestic Contradictions and the Colonial Impact*. New York: Cambridge University Press, 1989.

Judd, Laura Fish. *Honolulu: Sketches of Life: Social, Political, and Religious, in the Hawaiian Islands from 1828–1861, With a Supplementary Sketch of Events to the Present Time*. New York: Anson D. F. Randolph, 1880.

Kagawa, Kozo. "Naimushō shakaikyōiku no secchi ni tsuite." *Hyōron: Shakai kagaku*, no. 22 (1983): 1–34.

Kam, Ralph Thomas. "Language and Loyalty: Americanism and the Regulation of Foreign Language Schools in Hawai'i." *Hawaiian Journal of History* 40 (2006): 131–47.

Kame'eleihiwa, Lilikalā. *Native Land and Foreign Desires: Pehea Lā E Pono Ai? How Shall We Live in Harmony*. Honolulu, HI: Bishop Museum, 1992.

Kaplan, Amy. *The Anarchy of Empire in the Making of U.S. Culture*. Cambridge, MA: Harvard University Press, 2002.

Katagiri, Nobuo. *Minkan kōryū no paionia: Shibusawa eiichi no kokumin gaikō*. Tokyo: Fujiwara shoten, 2013.

——. *Taiheiyō mondai chōsakai no kenkyū: Senkanki nihon IPR no katsudō o chūshin to shite*. Tokyo: Keiō gijuku daigaku shuppankai, 2003.

Katsumura, Tomoko. "Honoruru mushō yōchien nihonjinbu ni okeru shodai shunin hobo Ozawa Itoko no kōken." *Seibo hishōten joshi tankidaigaku kiyō*, no. 29 (2003): 122–33.

——. "Yōji kyōikushi kenkyū–Mushō yōchien undō 1: Honolulu no nihonjin yōchien to Koga Fuji no hatashita yakuwari." *Shōin higashi tankidaigaku kenkyūronshū*, no. 9 (2006): 45–52.

Kawai, Michi, and Ochimi Kubushiro. *Japanese Women Speak: A Message from the Christian Women of Japan to the Christian Women of America*. Boston: Central Committee on the United Study of Foreign Missions, 1934.

Kenjō, Teiji, Akiko Iimori, and Jun Inoue, eds. *Kiitsu kyōkai no chōsen to Shibusawa Eiichi: Gurōbaru jidai no "fuhen" o mezashite*. Kyoto, Japan: Minerva shobō, 2018.

Kerber, Linda K. *Women of the Republic: Intellect and Ideology in Revolutionary America*. Chapel Hill: University of North Carolina Press, 1980.

Kerkvliet, Melinda Tria. "Interpreting Pablo Manlapit." *Social Process in Hawaii* 37 (1996): 1–25.

Kieszkowski, Elizabeth, ed. *Nā Hale Hō'ike'ike o Nā Mikanele*. Honolulu, HI: Mission Houses Museum, 2001.

Kim, Hwal-lan. *Grace Sufficient: The Story of Helen Kim*. Nashville, TN: Upper Room, 1964.

Kimura, Keiko. *Kawai Michi no shōgai*. Tokyo: Iwanami shoten, 2002.

Kiuchi, Kyo. *Kyōiku Ichiro: Han taiheiyō fujin kaigi ni resshite: Denki Kiuchi Kyo*. Tokyo: Ōzorasha, 1989.

Kobayashi, Yoko. "Inoue Hide no Amerika ryūgaku taiken no imi." *Nihon joshi daigaku sogō kenkyusho Kiyō*, no. 5 (November 2011): 151–93.

Kōbe Jogakuin, ed. *Kōbe jogakuin hyakunenshi*. Kobe: Kobe Jogakuin, 1976.

Kohiyama, Rui. *Amerika fujin senkyōshi: rainichi no haikei to sono eikyō*. Tokyo: Tokyo Daigaku shuppankai, 1992.

——. "No Nation Can Rise Higher Than Its Women: The Women's Ecumenical Missionary Movement and Tokyo Woman's Christian College." In *Competing Kingdoms: Women, Mission, Nation, and the American Protestant Empire, 1812–1960*, ed. Barbara Reeves-Ellington, Kathryn Kish Sklar, and Connie Anne Shemo. Durham, NC: Duke University Press, 2010.

———. "Nitobe Inazo to kōtō naru okusamagata." *Tokyo joshi daigaku hikakubunka kenkyūsho kiyō*, no. 73 (2012): 1–21.
Kotani, Roland. *The Japanese in Hawaii: A Century of Struggle*. Honolulu, HI: Hawaii Hochi, 1985.
Koyama, Shizuko. *Ryōsai kenbo to iu kihan*. Tokyo: Keisō shobō, 1991.
Kraditor, Aileen S. *The Ideas of the Woman Suffrage Movement, 1890–1920*. New York: Columbia University Press, 1965.
Krauss, Bob. *Johnny Wilson: First Hawaiian Democrat*. Honolulu: University of Hawai'i Press, 1994.
Kuykendall, Ralph S. *The Hawaiian Kingdom, Vol. I: Foundation and Transformation, 1778–1854*. Honolulu: University of Hawai'i Press, 1938.
———. *The Hawaiian Kingdom, Vol. II: Twenty Critical Years, 1854–1874*. Honolulu: University of Hawai'i Press, 1953.
———. *The Hawaiian Kingdom, Vol. III: The Kalakaua Dynasty, 1874–1893*. Honolulu: University of Hawai'i Press, 1967.
Kuykendall, Ralph S., and A. Grove Day, eds. *Hawaii: A History, from Polynesian Kingdom to American Statehood*. Englewood Cliffs, NJ: Prentice-Hall, 1976.
Kuykendall, Ralph S., and Lorin Tarr Gill. *Hawaii in the World War*. Honolulu, HI: Honolulu Historical Commission, 1928.
Kwok, Pui-Lan. *Chinese Women and Christianity, 1860–1927*. American Academy of Religion Academy Series, no. 75. Atlanta, GA: Scholars Press, 1992.
Kwon, Insook. "Feminists Navigating the Shoals of Nationalism and Collaboration: The Post-Colonial Korean Debate Over How to Remember Kim Hwallan." *Frontiers: A Journal of Women Studies* 27, no. 1 (2006): 39–66.
Ladd-Taylor, Molly. *Mother-Work: Women, Child Welfare, and the State, 1890–1930*. Women in American History. Urbana: University of Illinois Press, 1994.
Laughlin, Kathleen A. *Women's Work and Public Policy: A History of the Women's Bureau, U.S. Department of Labor, 1945–1970*. Boston: Northeastern University Press, 2000.
Lawrence, Frances. "Kindergartens in Hawaii's Public Schools." *Hawaii Educational Review* (January 1921).
———. "The Kindergarten Situation in Hawaii." *Childhood Education* 1, no. 1 (September 1924): 21–28.
Lemons, J. Stanley. *The Woman Citizen: Social Feminism in the 1920s*. Urbana: University of Illinois Press, 1973.
Leong, Karen J. *The China Mystique: Pearl S. Buck, Anna May Wong, Mayling Soong, and the Transformation of American Orientalism*. Berkeley: University of California Press, 2005.
Lerner, Gerda. "The Lady and the Mill Girl: Changes in the Status of Women in the Age of Jackson." *Midcontinent American Studies Journal* 10, no. 1 (Spring 1969): 5–14.

Liliuokalani. *Hawaii's Story by Hawaii's Queen.* Honolulu, HI: Mutual, 1990.

Lincicome, Mark E. "Nationalism, Imperialism, and the International Education Movement in Early Twentieth-Century Japan." *Journal of Asian Studies* 58, no. 2 (May 1999): 338–60.

Lind, Andrew William. *Hawaii's People.* 3rd ed. Honolulu: University of Hawai'i Press, 1967.

Littell-Lamb, Elizabeth. "Caught in the Crossfire: Women's Internationalism and the YWCA Child Labor Campaign in Shanghai, 1921–1925." *Frontiers: A Journal of Women Studies* 32, no. 3 (2011): 134–66.

———. "Ding Shujing: The YWCA Pathway for China's 'New Women.'" In *Salt and Light: Lives of Faith That Shaped Modern China*, ed. Carol Lee Hamrin. Eugene, OR: Pickwick, 2009.

———. "Localizing the Global: The YWCA Movement in China, 1899 to 1939." In *Women and Transnational Activism in Historical Perspective*, ed. Kimberly Jensen and Erika Kuhlman. St. Louis, MO: Republic of Letters, 2010.

Losch, Tracie Ku'uipo, and Momi Kamahele, eds. *Hawai'i: Center of the Pacific-Readings for Hawaiian Studies 107.* Acton, MA: Copley Custom Textbooks, 2008.

Lubin, Carol Riegelman, and Anne Winslow. *Social Justice for Women: The International Labor Organization and Women.* Durham, NC: Duke University Press, 1990.

Lucas, Paul F. Nahoa. "*E Ola Mau Kākou I Ka 'Ōleo Makuahine*: Hawaiian Language Policy and the Courts." *Hawaiian Journal of History* 34 (2000): 1–28.

Ly, Son-Thierry, and Patrick Weil. "The Antiracist Origin of the Quota System." *Social Research* 77, no. 1 (Spring 2010): 45–78.

MacCaughey, Vaughan. "Hawaii's Public Schools and the Pan-Pacific Idea." *Hawaii Educational Review* 7 (n.d.).

Mackie, Vera C. *Creating Socialist Women in Japan: Gender, Labour, and Activism, 1900–1937.* Cambridge: Cambridge University Press, 1997.

———. *Feminism in Modern Japan: Citizenship, Embodiment, and Sexuality.* Contemporary Japanese Society. Cambridge: Cambridge University Press, 2003.

Marino, Katherine M. *Feminism for the Americas: The Making of an International Human Rights Movement.* Chapel Hill: University of North Carolina Press, 2019.

Mark, Diane Mei Lin. *Seasons of Light: The History of Chinese Christian Churches in Hawaii.* Honolulu: Chinese Christian Association of Hawaii, 1989.

Materson, Lisa G. *For the Freedom of Her Race: Black Women and Electoral Politics in Illinois, 1877–1932.* Chapel Hill: University of North Carolina Press, 2009.

Matsumoto, Valerie J. *City Girls: The Nisei Social World in Los Angeles, 1920–1950.* New York: Oxford University Press, 2014.

Matsunaga, Hideo. *Hawai kanyaku imin no chichi R. W. Aauin.* Tokyo: Kodansha Business Partners, 2011.

McFadden, Margaret H. *Golden Cables of Sympathy: The Transatlantic Sources of Nineteenth-Century Feminism.* Louisville: Kentucky University Press, 1999.

Mead, Rebecca J. *How the Vote Was Won: Woman Suffrage in the Western United States, 1868–1914*. New York: New York University Press, 2004.

Meeropol, Ann Karus. "A Practical Visionary: Mary Emma Woolley and the Education of Women." PhD diss., University of Massachusetts, 1992.

Miller, Carol. "'Geneva—The Key to Equality': Inter-War Feminists and the League of Nations." *Women's History Review* 3, no. 2 (1994): 219–45.

Minohara, Toshihiro. *Kariforunia-shū no hainichi undō to nichi-bei kankei: Imin mondai o meguru nichi-bei masatsu, 1906–1921*. Tokyo: Yūhikaku, 2006.

Mitsui, Reiko, ed. *Gendai fujin undōshi nenpyō*. Tokyo: Sanichi shobō, 1978.

Mjagkij, Nina, and Margaret Spratt, eds. *Men and Women Adrift: The YMCA and the YWCA in the City*. New York: New York University Press, 1997.

Molony, Barbara. "Citizenship and Suffrage in Interwar Years." In *Women's Suffrage in Asia: Gender, Nationalism, and Democracy*, ed. Louise Edwards and Mina Roces. London: RoutledgeCurzon, 2004.

———. "Women's Rights, Feminism, and Suffragism in Japan, 1870–1925." *Pacific Historical Review* 69, no. 4 (2000): 639–61.

Monbushō. *Yōchien kyōiku hyakunenshi*. Tokyo: Hikarinokuni, 1979.

Moriya, Tomoe. *Amerika bukkyō no tanjō*. Tokyo: Gendai shiryō shuppan, 2001.

Moriyama, Alan Takeo. *Imingaisha: Japanese Emigration Companies and Hawaii, 1894–1908*. Honolulu: University of Hawai'i Press, 1985.

Muncy, Robyn. *Creating a Female Dominion in American Reform, 1890–1935*. New York: Oxford University Press, 1991.

Murayama, Milton. *All I Asking for Is My Body*. San Francisco: Supa, 1975.

Nakajima, Kuni. "Kiitsu kyōkai shokō 1 & 2." *Nihon joshidai kiyō bungakubu*, nos. 36 and 37 (1986, 1987).

———. *Naruse Jinzo*. Tokyo: Yoshikawa kōbunkan, 2002.

Nakamoto, Kahoru. "Senzen Tokyo YWCA yūshoku fujinbu ni yoru joshi seinen kyōiku." *Nihon Shakai Kyōikugakkai Kiyō* 49, no. 2 (June 2013): 33–42.

Nellist, George F. M., ed. *Men of Hawaii: An Historical Outline of Hawaii with Biographical Sketches of Its Men of Substantial Achievement in the Hawaiian Islands*. Honolulu, HI: Honolulu Star-Bulletin, 1930.

———, ed. *Pan-Pacific Who's Who: An International Reference Work, 1940–41*. Honolulu, HI: Honolulu Star-Bulletin, 1941.

———, ed. *The Story of Hawaii and Its Builders*. Honolulu, HI: Honolulu Star-Bulletin, 1925.

———, ed. *Women of Hawaii*. Honolulu, HI: E. A. Langton-Boyle, 1929.

Newman, Louise Michele. *White Women's Rights: The Racial Origins of Feminism in the United States*. New York: Oxford University Press, 1999.

Nihon kirisutokyō fujin kyōfukai, ed. *Nihon kirisutokyō fujin kyōfūkai hyakunenshi*. Tokyo: Domesu shuppan, 1986.

Nihon YWCA, ed. *Mizu o kaze o hikari o: Nihon YWCA 80-nen 1905–1985*. Tokyo: Nihon YWCA, 1987.

Nihon YWCA 100 nenshi hensan iinkai. *Nihon YWCA 100 nenshi: Josei no jiritsu o motomete*. Tokyo: Nihon kirisutokyō joshi seinenkai, 2005.

Nippu Jiji Editorial Board, ed. *Hawai dōhō hatten kaikoshi*. Honolulu, HI: Nippu Jiji, 1921.

Nishimoto, Warren S. "The Progressive Era and Hawai'i: The Early History of Palama Settlement, 1896–1929." *Hawaiian Journal of History* 34 (2000): 169–84.

Noble, Valerie. *Hawaiian Prophet: Alexander Hume Ford: A Biography*. New York: Exposition, 1980.

Nolte, Sharon H. *Liberalism in Modern Japan: Ishibashi Tanzan and His Teachers, 1905–1960*. Berkeley: University of California Press, 1987.

Norton, Mary Beth. *Liberty's Daughters: The Revolutionary Experience of American Women, 1750–1800*. Ithaca, NY: Cornell University Press, 1996.

Ogawa, Manako. "Estranged Sisterhood: The Wartime Trans-Pacific Dialogue of the World's Woman's Christian Temperance Union, 1931–1945," *Japanese Journal of American Studies* 18 (2007): 163–85.

Okihiro, Gary Y. *Cane Fires: The Anti-Japanese Movement in Hawaii, 1865–1945*. Philadelphia: Temple University Press, 1991.

———. *Common Ground: Reimagining American History*. Princeton, NJ: Princeton University Press, 2001.

Okihiro, Michael M. "Japanese Doctors in Hawai'i." *Hawaiian Journal of History* 36 (2002): 14.

Okita, Yukuji. *Hawai nikkei imin no kyōikushi: Nichi-bei bunka, sono deai to sōkoku*. Tokyo: Minerva shobō, 1997.

Ono, Kazuko. *Chinese Women in a Century of Revolution, 1850–1950*, ed. Joshua A. Fogel. Stanford, CA: Stanford University Press, 1988.

Orii, Miyako, and Josei no Rekishi Kenkyūkai, eds. *Onnatachi ga tachiagatta: Kanto daishinsai to Tokyo fujin rengō kai*. Tokyo: Domesu shuppan, 2017.

Oshio, Kazuto. "Fujin heiwa kyōkai e mukete: Nitobe Inazo fusai to Naruse Jinzo." In *Nijusseiki niokeru joseino heiwaundō*, ed. Kuni Nakajima and Nagako Sugimori. Tokyo: Domesu shuppan, 2006.

Oshiro, George M. "Internationalist in Prewar Japan: Nitobe Inazo, 1862–1944." PhD diss., University of British Columbia, 1985.

———. "Mary P. E. Nitobe and Japan." *Quaker History* 86, no. 2 (Fall 1997): 1–15.

Osorio, Jonathan Kay Kamakawiwoʻole. *Dismembering Lāhui: A History of the Hawaiian Nation to 1887*. Honolulu: University of Hawai'i Press, 2002.

Ota, Masao. "Harada Tasuko to Hawai Daigaku." *Kirisutokyō shakai mondai kenkyū* 46 (1998).

Overstreet, Harry, and Bonaro Overstreet. *Where Children Come First: A Study of the P.T.A. Idea*. Chicago: National Congress of Parents and Teachers, 1949.

Paddle, Sarah. "'For the China of the Future': Western Feminists, Colonization and International Citizenship in China in the Inter-War Years." *Australian Feminist Studies* 16, no. 36 (2001): 325–41.

Paisley, Fiona. "Citizens of Their World: Australian Feminism and Indigenous Rights in the International Context, 1920s and 1930s." *Feminist Review* 58, no. 1 (February 1998): 66–84.

———. "Cultivating Modernity: Culture and Internationalism in Australian Feminism's Pacific Age." *Journal of Women's History* 14, no. 3 (2002): 105–32.

———. "From Nation of Islam to Goodwill Tourist: African-American Women at Pan-Pacific and South East Asia Women's Conferences, 1937 and 1955." *Women's Studies International Forum* 32, no. 1 (2009): 21–28.

———. *Glamour in the Pacific: Cultural Internationalism and Race Politics in the Women's Pan-Pacific*. Honolulu: University of Hawai'i Press, 2009.

Park, Sunmi. "Teikoku no jokyōshitachi: Chōsen de oshieta jokyōshitachi." In *Teikoku to bunka: Sheikusupia kara Antonio Neguri made*, ed. Hideichi Eto. Yokohama, Japan: Shunpūsha, 2016.

Parsons, Alice (Mrs. Edgerton). "At the Pan-Pacific." *Woman's Journal* 15, no. 11 (1930).

Pascoe, Peggy. *Relations of Rescue: The Search for Female Moral Authority in the American West, 1874–1939*. New York: Oxford University Press, 1990.

Peck, Mary Gray, and Carrie Chapman Catt. *Carrie Chapman Catt: A Biography*. New York: H. W. Wilson, 1944.

Peterson, Barbara Bennett. *Notable Women of Hawaii*. Honolulu: University of Hawai'i Press, 1984.

Pierce, Lori. "The Whites Have Created Modern Honolulu: Ethnicity, Racial Stratification, and the Discourse of Aloha." In *Racial Thinking in the United States: Uncompleted Independence*, ed. Paul Spickard and G. Reginald Daniel. Notre Dame, IN: University of Notre Dame Press, 2004.

Prang, Margaret. *A Heart at Leisure from Itself: Caroline Macdonald of Japan*. Vancouver: University of British Columbia Press, 1995.

Proto, Neil Thomas. *The Rights of My People: Liliuokalani's Enduring Battle with the United States, 1893–1917*. New York: Algora, 2009.

Putney, Clifford. *Missionaries in Hawai'i: The Lives of Peter and Fanny Gulick, 1797–1883*. Amherst: University of Massachusetts Press, 2010.

Reeves-Ellington, Barbara, Kathryn Kish Sklar, and Connie Anne Shemo, eds. *Competing Kingdoms: Women, Mission, Nation, and the American Protestant Empire, 1812–1960*. Durham, NC: Duke University Press, 2010.

Richards, Mary A. *The Hawaiian Chiefs' Children's School, 1839–1850: A Record Compiled from the Diary and Letters of Amos Starr Cooke and Juliette Montague Cooke*. Reprint. Tokyo: Charles E. Tuttle, 1970.

———. *The Historical Background of the Woman's Board of Missions for the Pacific Islands*. Honolulu, HI: The Woman's Board of Missions for the Pacific Islands, 1931.

Robert, Dana L. *American Women in Mission: A Social History of Their Thought and Practice. The Modern Mission Era, 1792–1992*. Macon, GA: Mercer University Press, 1996.

———, ed. *Converting Colonialism: Visions and Realities in Mission History, 1706–1914.* Grand Rapids, MI: William B. Eerdmans, 2008.

Roberts, Richard. *Florence Simms: A Biography.* New York: Woman's Press, 1926.

Robertson, Nancy Marie. *Christian Sisterhood, Race Relations, and the YWCA, 1906–46.* Urbana: University of Illinois Press, 2007.

Roces, Mina, and Louise P. Edwards, eds. *Women's Movements in Asia: Feminisms and Transnational Activism.* New York: Routledge, 2010.

Rogaski, Ruth. *Hygienic Modernity: Meanings of Health and Disease in Treaty-Port China.* Asia—Local Studies/Global Themes. Berkeley: University of California Press, 2004.

Rose, Roger G., Sheila Conant, and Eric P. Kjellgren. "Hawaiian Standing Kāhili in the Bishop Museum: An Ethnological and Biological Analysis." *Journal of the Polynesian Society* 102, no. 3 (1993): 273–304.

Rosenberg, Rosalind. *Beyond Separate Spheres: Intellectual Roots of Modern Feminism.* New Haven, CT: Yale University Press, 1982.

Ruby, Laura, ed. *Moʻiliʻili: The Life of a Community.* Honolulu, HI: Moʻiliʻili Community Center, 2005.

Rufus, Carl W. "Twenty-Five Years of the Barbour Scholarships." *Michigan Alumnus Quarterly Review* 49, no. 11 (1942): 14–26.

Rupp, Leila J. *Worlds of Women: The Making of an International Women's Movement.* Princeton, NJ: Princeton University Press, 1997.

Saiki, Patsy Sumie. *Early Japanese Immigrants in Hawaii.* Honolulu: Japanese Cultural Center of Hawaii, 1993.

———. *Japanese Women in Hawaii: The First 100 Years.* Honolulu, HI: Kisaku, 1985.

Sakaguchi, Mitsuhiro. *Nihonjin Amerika iminshi.* Tokyo: Fuji shuppan, 2001.

———. "Nijyūkokusekimondai to Hawai no nikkei Amerikajin." *Atarashii rekishigaku no tameni* 207 (1992): 13–25.

———. "Zaibeinihonjin no 'nijyū kokuseki mondai' kaiketsu undō: Taiheiyō engan nihonjinkai kyōgikai no torikumi o chūshin ni." *Hisutoria* 145 (1993): 82–102.

Sandell, Marie. *The Rise of Women's Transnational Activism: Identity and Sisterhood Between the World Wars.* London: I. B. Tauris, 2015.

Sasaki, Motoe. *Redemption and Revolution: American and Chinese New Women in the Early Twentieth Century.* Ithaca, NY: Cornell University Press, 2016.

Shemo, Connie A. *The Chinese Medical Ministries of Kang Cheng and Shi Meiyu, 1872–1937: On a Cross-Cultural Frontier of Gender, Race, and Nation.* Bethlehem, PA: Lehigh University Press, 2011.

Siegel, Mona L. *Peace on Our Terms: The Global Battle for Women's Rights After the First World War.* New York: Columbia University Press, 2020.

Silva, Noenoe K. *Aloha Betrayed: Native Hawaiian Resistance to American Colonialism.* Durham, NC: Duke University Press, 2004.

Sims, Mary Sophia Stevens. *The Natural History of a Social Institution: The Young Women's Christian Association*. New York: Woman's Press, 1936.

Sinha, Mrinalini, Donna Guy, and Angela Woollacott, eds. *Feminisms and Internationalisms*. Oxford: Blackwell, 1999.

Smith, Bonnie G., and Nova Robinson, eds. *The Routledge Global History of Feminism*. New York: Routledge, 2022.

Smith, Susan L. *Japanese American Midwives: Culture, Community, and Health Politics, 1880–1950*. Urbana: University of Illinois Press, 2005.

Sneider, Allison L. *Suffragists in an Imperial Age: U.S. Expansion and the Woman Question, 1870–1929*. New York: Oxford University Press, 2008.

Stannard, David E. *Honor Killing: Race, Rape, and Clarence Darrow's Spectacular Last Case*. New York: Penguin, 2005.

Stassen-Mclaughlin, Marilyn. "Unlucky Star—Princess Ka'iulani." *Hawaiian Journal of History* 33 (1999): 21–54.

Steger, Manfred B. *Globalization: A Very Short Introduction*. Oxford: Oxford University Press, 2020.

Suetsugu, Reiko. *Nijyu seiki Chūgoku joseishi*. Tokyo: Aoki shoten, 2009.

Sugawara, Kazuko. *Ichikawa Fusae to fujin sanseiken kakutoku undō: Mosaku to kattō no seijishi*. Yokohama, Japan: Seori shobō, 2002.

Sugimori, Nagako. "Fujin heiwa kyōkai no kessei to katsudō no tenkai." In *Nijusseiki niokeru joseino heiwaundō*, ed. Kuni Nakajima and Nagako Sugimori. Tokyo: Domesu shuppan, 2006.

Suzuki, Yūko. *Josei to rōdō kumiai*. Tokyo: Renga shobō shinsha, 1991.

———, ed. *Nihon josei undō shiryō shūsei*. Tokyo: Fuji shuppan, 1993.

Takagi, Mariko. *Nikkei Amerikajin no Nihon-kan: Tabunka shakai Hawai kara*. Kyoto, Japan: Tankōsha, 1992.

Takahashi, Yūko. *Tsuda Umeko no shakaishi*. Machida, Japan: Tamagawa daigaku shuppanbu, 2002.

Takaki, Ronald T. *Pau Hana: Plantation Life and Labor in Hawaii, 1835–1920*. Honolulu: University of Hawai'i Press, 1983.

Tamura, Eileen. *Americanization, Acculturation, and Ethnic Identity: The Nisei Generation in Hawaii*. Urbana: University of Illinois Press, 1994.

Taylor, Sandra C. *Advocate of Understanding: Sidney Gulick and the Search for Peace with Japan*. Kent, OH: Kent State University Press, 1984.

Terazawa, Yuki. *Knowledge, Power, and Women's Reproductive Health in Japan, 1690–1945*. New York: Palgrave Macmillan, 2018.

Thomas, John N. *The Institute of Pacific Relations: Asian Scholars and American Politics*. Seattle: University of Washington Press, 1974.

Tsurumi, Patricia E. *Factory Girls: Women in the Thread Mills of Meiji Japan*. Princeton, NJ: Princeton University Press, 1990.

Tsutsumi, Toshiko. "Kimura Yukiko to YWCA—Kokusai jin no tanjō." *Jirosconsultus*, no. 22 (January 2013): 78–81.

Tyrrell, Ian R. *Reforming the World: The Creation of America's Moral Empire*. America in the World. Princeton, NJ: Princeton University Press, 2010.

———. *Woman's World / Woman's Empire: The Woman's Christian Temperance Union in International Perspective, 1880–1930*. Chapel Hill: University of North Carolina Press, 1991.

Uemura, Chikako. *Meari Biādo to joseishi: Nihon josei no majikara o hakkutsu shita beirekishika*. Tokyo: Fujiwara shoten, 2019.

Ujiie, Mikito, ed. *Nihon kindai kokka no seiritsu to jendā*. Tokyo: Kashiwa shobō, 2003.

Van Dyke, Jon M. *Who Owns the Crown Lands of Hawaii?* Honolulu: University of Hawai'i Press, 2007.

Van Goethem, Geert. "An International Experiment of Women Workers: The International Federation of Working Women, 1919–1924." *Revue belge de philologie et d'histoire* 84, no. 4 (2006): 1025–47.

Van Voris, Jacqueline. *Carrie Chapman Catt: A Public Life*. New York: Feminist Press at the City University of New York, 1987.

Vandewalker, Nina C. *The Kindergarten in American Education*. New York: Macmillan, 1908.

Wakukawa, Ernest K. *A History of the Japanese People in Hawaii*. Honolulu, HI: Toyō shoin, 1938.

Wang, Dong. *Managing God's Higher Learning: U.S.-China Cultural Encounter and Canton Christian College (Lingnan University), 1888–1952*. Lanham, MD: Lexington Books, 2007.

Washington, Garrett L. "St. Luke's Hospital and the Modernization of Japan, 1874–1928." *Health and History* 15, no. 2 (2013): 5–28.

Weinberg, Meyer. *Asian-American Education: Historical Background and Current Realities*. New York: Routledge, 1997.

Wendt, Simon. "Defenders of Patriotism or Mothers of Fascism? The Daughters of the American Revolution, Antiradicalism, and Un-Americanism in the Interwar Period." *Journal of American Studies* 47, no. 4 (2013): 943–69.

Wheelhouse, Frances. *Eleanor Mary Hinder: An Australian Woman's Social Welfare Work in China Between the Wars*. Sydney, Australia: Wentworth, 1978.

Who's Who in China; Biographies of Chinese Leaders. Shanghai, China: Weekly Review, 1936.

Willard, Frances E. *Glimpses of Fifty Years: The Autobiography of an American Woman*. Chicago: Woman's Temperance Publication Association, 1889.

Wilson, Grace H. *The Religious and Educational Philosophy of the Young Women's Christian Association: A Historical Study of the Changing Religious and Social Emphases of the Association as They Relate to Changes in Its Educational Philosophy and to Observable Trends in Current Religious Thought, Educational Philosophy, and Social Situations*. New York: Teachers College, Columbia University, 1933.

Wilson, Jan Doolittle. *The Women's Joint Congressional Committee and the Politics of Maternalism, 1920–30*. Women in American History. Urbana: University of Illinois Press, 2007.

Wist, Benjamin O. *A Century of Public Education in Hawai'i*. Honolulu: Hawaiian Educational Review, 1940.

Wold, Emma. "Women and Nationality: Towards Equality in Citizenship Laws." *Pacific Affairs* 4, no. 6 (1931): 511–15.

Wollons, Roberta. *Kindergartens and Cultures: The Global Diffusion of an Idea*. New Haven, CT: Yale University Press, 2000.

Woollacott, Angela. "Inventing Commonwealth and Pan-Pacific Feminisms: Australian Women's Internationalist Activism in the 1920s–30s." In *Feminisms and Internationalisms*, ed. Mrinalini Shinha, Donna Guy, and Angela Wollacott. Oxford: Blackwell, 1999.

Wu, Judy Tzu-Chun, and Gwendolyn Mink. *Fierce and Fearless: Patsy Takemoto Mink, First Woman of Color in Congress*. New York: New York University Press, 2022.

Yamamoto, Eriko. "Mainoritī josei no rentai: Nikkei Amerikajin joseishi ni miru tabunnkashugi to komyunitī katsudō." In *Kita Amerika shakai o nagamete: Joseijiku to esunisitī-jiku no kōsaten*, ed. Kikuyo Tanaka and Mariko Takagi-Kitayama. Nishinomiya, Japan: Kwansei gakuin daigaku shuppankai, 2004.

Yamaoka, Michio, and Waseda Daigaku, eds. *Taiheiyō mondai chōsakai (IPR) to Sono gunzō*. Tokyo: Waseda Daigaku Ajia Taiheiyō kenkyū sentā, 2016.

Yamazaki, Yuji. "Dai-ichiji taisengo ni okeru kokusai kyōiku undō' no seiritsu to tenkai: Taisho-ki kyōiku kaizō undō no lokusaiteki sokumen." *Kyōiku kenkyū*, no. 30 (1986): 71–97.

Yasutake, Rumi. *Transnational Women's Activism: The United States, Japan, and Japanese Immigrant Communities in California, 1859–1920*. New York: New York University Press, 2004.

Yoshida, Ryo. "1920 nendai Honolulu kirisutokyō seinenkai no jinshu kyōiku: Nuanu shibu YMCA o chūshin ni." In *Kindai yōroppa no tankyū 3: Kyōkai*. Kyoto, Japan: Minerva shobō, 2000.

———. "Hawaian bood no shoki nihonjin imindendo, 1885–1887." *Kirisutokyō shakai mondai kenkyū*, no. 30 (1982).

Young, Louise M., and Ralph A. Young. *In the Public Interest: The League of Women Voters, 1920–1970*. New York: Greenwood, 1989.

Zimmermann, Susan. "Liaison Committees of International Women's Organizations and the Changing Landscape of Women's Internationalism, 1920 to 1945." In *Women and Social Movements, International, 1840 to Present*, ed. Kathryn Kish Sklar and Thomas Dublin. Alexandria, VA: Alexander Street, 2012.

———. "The Challenge of Multinational Empire for the International Women's Movement: The Habsburg Monarchy and the Development of Feminist Inter/National Politics." *Journal of Women's History* 17, no. 2 (2005): 87–117.

Video Recordings

Gold Watch. KCET Drama, November 11, 1976. UCLA Film and Television Archive.
Hawaii's Last Queen. DVD. PBS Video, 2006.
The Massie Affair. DVD. PBS Video, 2005.

Index

12-12-12 meetings, 111, 136

Aʻala Park suffrage meeting, 63
AAUW. *See* American Association of University Women
Abbott, Grace, 144, 147
Abbott, Julia W., 128–29
ABCFM. *See* American Board of Commissioners for Foreign Missions
Adams, Charlotte H., 159
Ad Club, 119
Addams, Jane, 1, 3–4, 8, 12, 81, 83, 89, 141, 144, 148, 150, 156, 177, 187–88
AFL. *See* American Federation of Labor
African Americans, 23, 45, 109, 202, 207
Aikoku Fujinkai. *See* Japan Patriotic Women's Association
Akamatsu, Tsuneko, 164
Akana, Akaiko, 63, 73
Alexander & Baldwin, 25
aliʻi, 16–17, 19–20, 22, 50, 52, 153
All-Asian Women's Conference, 186
Aloha-DAR. *See* Daughters of the American Revolution Aloha Chapter

American Association of University Women (AAUW), 128, 147, 172, 188, 192
American Board of Commissioners for Foreign Missions (ABCFM), 15–16, 20, 25–28, 32, 54, 79, 98, 101, 136
American Federation of Labor (AFL), 158
Americanism, 11, 107, 118, 125
Americanization, 20, 57, 92, 114–16, 119, 121, 127, 133, 136–37, 166, 188
American Legion, 136
American Peace Society of Japan, 158
American Seamen's Friend Society, 23
American Woman Suffrage Association (AWSA), 46
American Women's Club, 168, 171
American Women's Federated Mission Boards, 172
Anderson, Dame Adelaide, 172
Anderson, Mary, 93, 145, 150–52, 180–81, 189
Anderson, Rufus, 20
Andrews, Elsie, 203
Andrews, Harriet Cousens, 76, 153
Anesaki, Masaharu, 127

annexation of Hawai'i, 10, 16, 26, 29, 35–36, 41–45, 50–51, 56, 69, 85, 112, 117
Anthony, Susan B., 45–46
Apology Resolution of 1993, 207
Appleton, Vivia Belle, 95, 153, 243n56
Armstrong, William Nevins, 30
Asians in Hawai'i: with birthright U.S. citizenship, 11, 48, 63, 79, 106, 111, 121, 136, 200; and exclusionists, 102–103, 106, 111–12, 123–24, 134–35, 158, 192; women and girls, 56, 59, 62–64, 66, 68, 79–80, 90–92, 97–98, 107, 138, 153, 192
Associate Charities of Hawai'i, 86
Atcherley, Mary Ha'aheo Kinimaka, 67, 71, 75, 234n80
Atherton, Frank C., 84
Atherton, Juliette Montague Cooke, 84
Australasian (Australia/New Zealand), 116
Australia(n), 3, 112, 167, 173, 177, 181, 185, 190–91, 193–94, 201–202
AWSA. *See* American Woman Suffrage Association

Baghat Sing Thind v. United States (1923), 135
Baldwin, Ethel Frances Smith, 70, 76
Baldwin, Harry A., 62, 70–71, 73–75
Baldwin, Henry Perrine, 38–39, 62, 70
Barbour Scholarship, 170, 184, 190
Barnard College, 171
Barnwell, Mrs. Walter G., 139
Bayonet Constitution. *See* Constitution of the Kingdom of Hawai'i 1887
BCL. *See* British Commonwealth League
Beard, Charles, 162, 267n88
Beard, Mary Ritter, 162–63
Beiyang Women's Hospital (China), 176, 184
Bickerton, Richard F., 99
Big Five, 24–25, 42, 52, 131
Big Island (Hawai'i), 42, 52, 63, 133, 211

Bingham III, Hiram, 193
Bishop, Charles R., 19, 29
Black/Black people, 13, 46, 74, 122, 199, 204. *See also* African Americans
Blount, James H., 35
Bluestockings (Seito), 157
Bolshevik Revolution, 108, 144
Boston University, 182
Bremer, Edith Terry, 90
Brennan, Anna, 191
British Commonwealth League (BCL), 7
British Women's Association, 171
Brown, Raymond C., 69
Brown Lea, Charlotte A., 73
Bryn Mawr College, 155–56, 165
Buddhist Musashino Girls' Seminary, 190
Bunker, Frank F., 72, 119, 126, 140
Bunker, Gertrude D., 72–73, 140, 256n115

Cable Act of 1922, 137–38, 191–92; amendment of 1930, 191; amendment of 1931 and 1932, 192. *See also* nationality right
Campbell, Abigail Kuaihelani Maipinepine Bright, 35, 42, 56, 71
Carter, George R., 94
Carter, Helen Strong (Mrs. George R. Carter), 94
Castle, Alfred Lowrey, 57
Castle, Alice Beatrice, 57, 153
Castle, Helen. *See* Mead, Helen Castle
Castle, Henry, 83
Castle, Mary Tenney, 36, 79
Castle & Cooke, 25
Catt, Carrie Chapman, 8, 10, 46, 53–56, 58, 111, 144, 147–49, 161, 169, 188, 196
CCP. *See* Chinese Communist Party
Central Grammar School (Hawai'i), 117–18
Channon, Grace, 139, 153
Chen, T., 191
Chiang Kai-shek, 172, 175, 198

Chian Iji Hō. *See* Peace Preservation Law of 1925
Chian Keisatu Hō. *See* Police Security Law of 1900
Chicago Kindergarten College, 83
Chicago Normal School on funds, 156
Chiefs' Children's School. *See* Royal School
child labor, 144, 147, 172–73, 175–76, 181, 262n29
Child Labor Commission (Shanghai), 172–73, 198
Child Labor Tax Law of 1919 (U.S.), 144
Children's Bureau (U.S.), 92–94, 144, 147, 173
Chinese Communist Party (CCP), 173–75, 197–98, 202
Chinese Nationalist Party (CNP), 174–75, 197–98, 202
Chinese Women's Suffrage Association, 196
Christian Home, 102, 175
Christman, Elizabeth, 152, 180
Claxton, Philander P., 119
Cleveland, Grover, 35–36, 41
Clinton, Bill, 207
CND. *See* Council of National Defense
Coffin, Jo, 152, 180
Colby, Bainbridge, 64, 70
Coleman, Harriet Angeline Castle, 60, 78–79, 83
Columbia Teachers College, 156
Columbia University, 165, 171, 182
Committee of Twenty-One, 31–32
Constitutional Convention of the Republic of Hawai'i, 1894, 14, 36–39
Constitutional Convention (Republic of Hawai'i, Territory of Hawai'i), 14, 37–38
Constitution of the Kingdom of Hawai'i 1839, 21; 1840, 21; 1852, 23, 26; 1864, 23, 29; 1887, 14, 33–34
Constitution of the Republic of Hawai'i 1894, 38, 39–40, 47
Cook, James, 15, 24, 28
Cooke, Amos Starr, 19
Cooke, Constance M. Ternent, 193
Cooke, Juliette Montague, 19, 29
Coolidge, Calvin, 149, 188
Cornell University, 118, 164
Council of National Defense (CND), 57–58, 91, 115; Women's Committee, 91
Council of the Victorian League of Nations Union, 146
coverture, 15, 18, 21, 33
Coyle, Grace, 152
Croly, Herbert, 178
Crowdy, Dame Rachel, 186, 193–94
Crown Lands of Hawai'i, 41
Cullom, Shelby M., 47
cult of (true) womanhood, 10, 15, 18, 29, 44, 47, 54, 65, 87, 198, 206
Cynn, Heung-Wo, 126–27

Damon, Frank W., 79
Damon, Gertrude M., 200
Damon, Julia, 23–24
Damon, Mary R. Happer, 79
Damon, Samuel C., 23, 26
Damon, Samuel M., 38–39
DAR. *See* Daughters of the American Revolution (DAR)
Daughters and Sons of Hawaiian Warriors (DSHW), 53–54, 58, 60, 63, 73, 153
Daughters of Hawai'i (DOH), 2, 50–54, 60, 63, 73, 76–77, 105, 113, 153, 230n20
Daughters of the American Revolution (DAR), 120
Daughters of the American Revolution Aloha Chapter (Aloha-DAR), 119–20
Davies, Theophilus H., 42, 52
Davis, Isaac, 28
Deng, Cora (Deng Yuzhi), 197
denizenship, 22, 24
Dental Hygienists' Club, 94
Department of Public Instruction (DPI, Territory of Hawai'i), 87, 94, 107, 117–18, 120–21, 125–27, 129–34, 136, 138, 167, 255n106

Desha, Stephen L., 62–63
Dewey, John, 82–83
Dickenson, Kathleen, 71–73
Dillingham, Emma Louise Smith, 50, 54
Dingman, Mary A., 145, 147, 162, 171, 173
Djang, Siao-sung, 190
DOH. *See* Daughters of Hawai'i
Dole, Sanford B., 14, 36–37, 41, 47
Dominis, John Owen, 15
Doudna, Jennifer, 207
Dowsett, John McKibbin, 51
Dowsett, Wilhelmina Kekelaokalaninui Widemann, 51, 53–54, 56, 58–60, 62–64, 68, 72, 74, 76, 231n40
DPI. *See* Department of Public Instruction
DSHW. *See* Daughters and Sons of Hawaiian Warriors
dual citizenship (nationality), 134–38, 191
Du Bois, W. E. B., 5, 205, 207, 208

Economic and Social Commission for Asia and the Pacific (ESCAP), 206
Economic and Social Council (ECOSOC), 206
Edson, Katherine Philips, 152
Ely, Ella P., 176
Emma (Emma Kalanikaumaka'amano Kaleleonālani Na'ea, Queen), 19, 28–29
Equal Rights Amendment (ERA), 146, 188–89, 191, 198
Equal Rights Treaty (ERT), 146
ESCAP. *See* Economic and Social Commission for Asia and the Pacific
Esperanto, 183
Ewaliko, David K., 88
Ewa Plantation Company, 84
Ewha Women's University (Korea), 147, 182
extraterritorial rights, 154, 168, 174

Factory Law of 1911, 1916, 1923, 1929 (Japan), 158, 181
Fan, Gwan, 190
Farrington, Catherine McAlpine Crane, 153
Farrington, Wallace R., 71, 74, 88, 133, 136–37, 153, 165, 187
Farrington v. Tokushige (1927), 133, 188
FBI. *See* Federal Bureau of Investigation
FCC. *See* Federal Council of Churches of Christ in America
Federal Bureau of Investigation (FBI), 126
Federal Council of Churches of Christ in America (FCC), 105, 110–11; Social Creed of the Churches, 96
Federal Survey Commission in Hawai'i, 72, 119, 122, 126
Federal Survey Commission in Hawai'i Report (1920), 120–23, 135–36
Federation of Women's Boards of Foreign Missions, 160
female dominion, 5, 92, 97, 101
Fifteenth Amendment (U.S.), 46
Filipina/o, 25, 85, 94, 111, 116, 124, 153
Fitch, George Ashmore, 190
Fitch, Geraldine Townsend (Mrs. George Ashmore Fitch), 190, 198
FKCAAHI. *See* Free Kindergarten and Children's Aid Association of the Hawaiian Islands
Folio, 23
Fong, Chun (Ah Fong), 24
Ford, Alexander Hume, 104, 107–108, 110–13, 116, 118, 130–32, 136, 140–41, 153, 167–68, 173, 175, 177, 184–85, 187, 195, 206, 248n13, 249n20
foreign language school controversy, 12, 87, 117–19, 121, 124–25, 127, 130–34, 188; joint American-Japanese committee, 125, 130, 132
Foreign Missionary Association of Friends of Philadelphia, 155
Foreign Mission School in Connecticut, 15

Foreign Missions Conference of North America Educational Commission to China, 188
France, 30, 78, 109, 175
Frear, Mary Emma Dillingham, 36, 54, 56, 58, 63, 73, 76, 105, 128, 139
Frear, Walter Francis, 47, 55, 108, 116, 125
Free Kindergarten and Children's Aid Association of the Hawaiian Islands (FKCAAHI), 52, 79, 83–88, 93, 95, 99, 101, 103, 105, 107, 113, 118, 120, 122–23, 129, 134, 138, 153, 156
French Revolution, 80
Friedmann, Ernestine L., 160
Froebel, Friedrich, 80–82, 101
Froebel Association Training School (Chicago), 82–83
Fujin Sanseiken Kakutoku Kisei Dōmeikai (Fusen Kakutoku Dōmei). See Women's Suffrage League (WSL, Japan)
Fujita, Taki, 165, 182
Furuya, Yeiichi, 124

Gaines, N. B., 101
gannenmono, 98, 100
Gauntlett, (Constance) Tsune(ko) Yamada, 156, 161, 165, 194–96, 201–202, 276n38
Geneva, 3, 9, 12, 105, 143, 145, 156, 159, 161, 177–78, 185, 187
Gibson, Walter Murray, 30, 32
Gompers, Samuel, 150
Good Relations Clubs, 111
Goodykoontz, Bess, 189
Goto, Shimpei, 162
Great Awakening, 18
Great Kanto Earthquake of 1923, 162
Great Māhele (land division), 22
Green Kalb Hardy, Elizabeth, 147, 150, 182, 192
Green, M. A. H., 33
Greenwood, Barbara, 128–29
Gulick, Ann Eliza Clark, 101–102, 110–12
Gulick, Charles Thomas, 15

Gulick, Orramel H., 100, 110
Gulick, Sidney Lewis, 110–12, 158

Hall, Stanley, 82
hānai, 19–20, 28, 50
Hands-Around-the-Pacific, 108, 114
Harada, Saki, 153
Harada, Tasuku, 136, 141, 153
Harding, Warren G., 71, 75, 161
Harrison, Agatha, 171–72
Harrison, Benjamin, 35
Harvard University, 83
Hawaiian Education Association, 133
Hawaiian Evangelical Association (HEA), 26–27, 40, 100, 110, 120
Hawaiian Kingdom, 14, 16, 23, 34, 36, 40–41, 49, 51–52, 62, 66, 79, 99–100, 117, 206–207
Hawaiian Mission Children's Society, 26
Hawaiian Organic Act (1900), 45–48, 60, 62, 66, 70, 75–76, 85, 117, 193, 199
Hawaiian Patriotic League (Hui Hawai'i Aloha 'Aina), 35, 42, 51, 56
Hawaiian Pineapple Company, 14
Hawaiian Political Association (Hui Kalai'ana), 34, 42, 226n79
Hawaiian Sugar Planters' Association (HSPA), 48, 88, 124
Hawaii Hochi, 130, 132
Hawai'i Territorial Board of Health, 94–95, 153
Hayashi, Utako, 196
HEA. See Hawaiian Evangelical Association
Henry Street Settlement, 111
High Treason Incident (Japan), 154, 158
Hilo (Hawai'i), 42, 60
Hinder, Eleanor M., 173–74, 176–79, 181, 183–85, 272n142, 275n36
Hirano Midori (Saito), 190
Hiratsuka, Raicho, 157, 160–61, 267n78
Hirooka, Asako, 156
Hitt, Robert R., 47
HLWV. See League of Women Voters of the Territory of Hawai'i

INDEX [309]

Home Rule Party of Hawai'i, 48
Honolulu Central Union Church, 79, 90, 124
Honolulu Dental Hygiene School, 94
Honolulu Dental Infirmary, 94
Honolulu Kindergarten Training School, 99
Honolulu Korean Institute, 190
Hoover, Herbert, 193, 199
House of Nobles (Hawaiian Kingdom), 21, 23, 223n30, 226n75
House of Peers American-Japanese Relations Committee (Japan), 137, 165
House of Representatives: Hawaii, 21, 23, 37, 40; Japan, 182; U.S., 48, 71, 76
Houston, Victor S. K., 199–200
Howe, Annie Lyon, 101, 245n83
HSPA. *See* Hawaiian Sugar Planters' Association
Hui Hawai'i Aloha 'Aina. *See* Hawaiian Patriotic League
Hui Hawai'i Aloha 'Aina o Na Wahine. *See* Women's Hawaiian Patriotic League
Hui Kalai'aina. *See* Hawaiian Political Association
hula, 20, 30
Hulihe'e Palace, 1–2, 77, 152
Hull House, 5, 8, 81–82, 89–90, 150, 164
Hyde, Charles McEwen, 20
Hyde, Mary T. Knight, 20, 27, 37, 50, 79, 230n22

Iaukea, Curtis P., 124
Ichikawa, Fusae, 159–60, 163–65, 167, 181–83, 186, 274n20
Ichioka, Yuji, 158, 209
ICW. *See* International Council of Women
ICWW. *See* International Congress of Working Women
Ide, Kikue, 165, 182
IES. *See* Japan Imperial Education Society

IFTU. *See* International Federation of Trade Unions
IFUW. *See* International Federation of University Women
IFWW. *See* International Federation of Working Women
'Ī'ī, Irene Brown-Holloway, 20, 50, 223n24, 230n22
'Ī'ī, John Papa, 20
IKU. *See* International Kindergarten Union
ILC. *See* International Labour Conference
ILO. *See* International Labour Organization
Imanishi, Ito(ko) (Ozawa), 98–101
Imperial Constitution of 1890 (Japan), 154
Imperial Diet (Japan), 137, 158, 182
Imperial Education Society (IES, Japan), 166, 183
Indigenous rights, 193, 207
Industrial Workers of the World (IWW), 164
Inoue, Hideko, 156, 165
Institute of Pacific Relations (IPR), 11–12, 106, 109, 123, 141–42, 146, 148–50, 166, 178, 183, 186, 188, 190, 194, 206
Inter-American Commission of Women (Comisión Interamericana de Mujeres), 147
International Committee on Intellectual Cooperation (UNESCO predecessor), 156
International Congress of Working Women (ICWW), 150–51
International Council of Women (ICW), 178, 182, 186
International Federation of Trade Unions (IFTU), 150, 262n29, 262n30
International Federation of University Women (IFUW), 173
International Federation of Working Women (IFWW), 150

International Kindergarten Union (IKU), 128–29
International Labour Conference (ILC), 150–51, 159–60, 162, 173, 180
International Labour Organization (ILO), 9, 142, 145, 150–51, 159, 162, 164, 173, 207; Constitution, 150, 159; Indigenous and Tribal Peoples Convention of 1989, 207; Tokyo Office, 163–64; tri-patriotism, 151. *See also* International Labour Conference (ILC)
International Typographical Union in New York, 152
International Union of American Republics, 110
International Woman Suffrage Alliance (IWSA), 54, 147–48, 161, 178
'Iolani Palace, 30, 34, 113
'Iolani Unit, 59
IPR. *See* Institute of Pacific Relations
Irwin, Harry, 70
Irwin, Iki (Takechi), 99
Irwin, Robert Walker, 99–100, 245n74
Irwin, Sophia Arabella Bella, 99, 244n70
Ishikawa, Fusa, 183
Issei, 90, 103, 123–25, 131–33, 135–38
Ito, Noe, 162
IWSA. *See* International Woman Suffrage Alliance

Jacobs, Aletta, 156
Japanese Benevolent Society (JBS, Nihonjin Jizenkai, Hawai'i), 99
Japanese Women's Society (JWS, Nihonjin Fujinkai, Hawai'i), 103, 123
Japan International Education Association (Nihon Kokusai Kyōiku Kyōkai), 157
Japan League for the Realization of Women's Suffrage. *See* Women's Suffrage League (WSL, Japan)
Japan Ministry of Agriculture and Commerce, 158
Japan Ministry of Education (JMoE), 123, 154–55, 157, 162, 165–66, 183
Japan Ministry of Foreign Affairs (JMoFA), 182, 186
Japan Ministry of Home Affairs (JMoHA), 135, 137, 162, 166
Japan Nationality Law of 1916, 135–37; Revised Law of 1924, 135, 137
Japan Patriotic Women's Association, 163
Japan Special Higher Police [*Tokkō*], 154
Japan Women's Committee for International Relations (JWCIR, Kokusai Renraku Fujin Iinkai), 185–86, 276n38
Japan Women's Peace Association (JWPA, Nihon Fujin Heiwa Kyōkai), 99, 156, 165
Japan Women's University (JWU), 101, 155–57, 164, 167
Jim Crow, 45
Jinling College (China), 190
Joint Committee of the Shanghai Women's Club (JCSWC), 171–73, 176
Joint Committee of the Shanghai Women's Organizations (JCSWO), 168, 171, 173–77, 184, 202
Joint Standing Committee of the Women's International Organizations (JSCWIO, Geneva), 143, 159, 177, 185; Japan affiliate, 185
JSCWIO. *See* Joint Standing Committee of the Women's International Organizations
Judd, Agnes Hall Boyd, 120
Judd, Albert Francis, 20, 40, 120
Judd, Charles Hastings, 30, 51
Judd, (Emily) Catherine (Cutts), 2, 51
Judd, Gerrit Parmele, 18, 20, 51
Judd, Laura Fish, 2, 18–19, 30, 40, 51
Judd, Lawrence M., 187, 199
jury right, 21, 77, 134, 193, 199
jus sanguinis (right of blood), 134

jus soli (right of soil), 134–35
JWCIR. *See* Japan Women's Committee for International Relations
JWPA. *See* Japan Women's Peace Association
JWS. *See* Japanese Women's Society
JWU. *See* Japan Women's University

Kaʻahumanu, 17–18, 20, 51
Kaʻahumanu II. *See* Kīnaʻu, Elizabeth (Kaʻahumanu II)
Kagawa, Toyohiko, 164
kāhili, 3, 153
Kailua-Kona (Hawaiʻi), 1
Kaʻiulani (Princess), 30, 34–35, 42
Kalākaua (King), 2, 29–34, 49, 51–52, 99
Kalanianaʻole, Elizabeth Kahanu Kaleiwohi-Kaʻauwai (Princess), 50, 53, 59, 63, 71, 74, 76
Kalanianaʻole, Jonah Kūhiō (Prince), 14, 49, 50, 53, 59, 60–61, 64, 71, 73, 112
Kalanikaumakaʻamano Kaleleonālani Naʻea. *See* Emma (Queen)
Kalauokalani, David, 68–69
Kali, Sera, 53
Kalua, John William, 38
Kamada, Eikichi, 151, 263n33
Kamehameha, 1–2, 17–18, 28–29, 50, 71; I (the Great), 1, 17, 20, 53; II (Liholiho), 17, 39; III (Kauikeaouli), 17, 21–23, 27–28, 32, 50–52; IV (Alexander Iolani Liholiho), 19, 28–29; V (Lot), 29
kanyaku imin, 100
Kapiʻolani (Queen), 32, 49
Kaplan, Amy, 5, 205, 208
kapu, 17, 20, 39
Kato, Shizue, 163
Kato, Taka, 164, 268n99
Kauhane, John, 39
Kawai, Michi, 156–57, 163, 197
Kawaiahaʻo Church (Honolulu), 52
Kawānanakoa, Abigail (Princess), 58, 71, 200

Kawānanakoa, David (Prince), 49, 58, 71
Kawasaki, Shizuko, 190
Keating-Owen Act of 1916, 144
Keauhou (Hawaiʻi), 52
Keliʻinoi, Rosalie Enos Lyons, 76, 193
Keliʻinoi, Samuel, 76
Kellogg-Briand Peace Pact, 148, 196
Keōpūolani, 17, 20
Kiitsu Kyōkai (Association Concordia), 155, 265n55
Kim, Helen (Hwal-lan), 147, 174, 182–83
Kimura, Yukiko, 190
Kīnaʻu, Elizabeth (Kaʻahumanu II), 17–18, 20, 29, 51
Kinoʻole-o-Liliha, 60
Kishimoto, Tsuru Masuda, 90–91, 94–95, 98, 102, 153, 194
Kitamura, Kaneko, 167, 276n42
Kiuchi, Kyō, 165–66, 183, 270n112
Knepper, Margaret, 63
Kobe College, 102
Koga, Fuji, 98, 101, 156
Kokusai Renmei Kyōkai. *See* Japan League of Nations Association
Kokusai Renraku Fujin Iinkai. *See* Japan Women's Committee for International Relations
Korea, 3, 25, 109, 112, 126–27, 147, 154, 166, 174, 182–83
Korean, 90, 94, 109, 111, 116, 119, 124, 126–27, 162, 174, 183, 190–91, 201
Kuakini, John Adams, 1
Kubushiro, Ochimi, 161, 163–64, 197
kuhina-nui, 17, 21, 23, 50, 53
Kyōiku kōshu iinkai. *See* Teachers' Training Committee
Kyong, Bae-tsung, 176, 180

Ladies of the Protestant Mission, 23
Lam, Mrs. Fred K. (Ah Chin Loo Lam), 190
Lane, Franklin K., 112, 115–16, 119
Lathrop, Julia, 144, 173
Law, Yau Tsit, 146, 260n11
Lawrence, Frances, 83, 101, 123, 128–29, 133, 153

LCWIO. *See* Liaison Committee on Women's International Organizations
Lea, Charlotte A. Brown (Mrs. Charles M. Lea), 73
League of Nations, 112, 142–43, 145–47, 150, 155–56, 186, 193–94, 196–97, 201
League of Nations Association (Kokusai Renmei Kyōkai, Japan), 157
League of Women Voters (LWV), 72, 164; Pennsylvania, 73; San Francisco Central, 146
League of Women Voters of the Territory of Hawai'i (HLWV), 76, 113, 134, 136–38, 140, 149, 153, 192, 198–200; inception in 1922, 134; NLWV support, 193; disbandment, 200
Leavitt, Mary C., 31–32, 36, 102, 161
Lee, Shao Chang, 141
Leong, Ellen F. L., 153
Li, Tai Heong Kong, 153
Liaison Committee on Women's International Organizations (LCWIO, Geneva), 143
Ligot, Cayetano, 153
Ligot, Petra, 153
Lili'uokalani (Queen), 14–16, 19, 27, 30, 33–37, 40–43, 45, 47, 49, 51–52, 58, 78–79, 113–15, 153, 206
Lodge, Henry Cabot, 112
London Naval Conference, 196
London Naval Treaty, 196
London School of Economics, 171, 197
Love, Grace, 139
lū'au, 53
Lunalilo, William Charles, 29
LWV. *See* League of Women Voters
Lyons, Benjamin, 76

MacCaughey, Vaughan, 87–88, 107, 118–19, 125–28, 130–34, 136
MacCauley, Clay, 158, 265n55
Macdonald, Caroline, 156, 161–62, 164
Macfarlane, Emilie Kekauluohi Widemann, 35, 50–51, 53, 58, 63

Macfarlane, Fredrick Walter, 51
MacMillan, Louise, 63, 234n80
Maddux, Parker S., 146
Makino, Fred Kinzaburo, 132–33
Mamakakaua. *See* Daughters and Sons of Hawaiian Warriors (DSHW)
Manchukuo, 202
Manchuria, 196
Manlapit, Pablo, 124
Manning, Caroline, 152, 180
Mary Lambuth Girls' School (Japan), 165
Massie Affair, 12, 198–200; Grace Hubbard Fortescue, 199; Joseph Kahahawai, 199–200; Pinkerton Detective Agency, 199
Master Servant Act of 1850 (Hawai'i), 26
Maui Woman's Club, 70
Maui Women's Suffrage Association, 70
May Fourth movement (China), 169
May Thirtieth Incident (China), 173–74
McCarthy, Charles J., 61–62, 112
McGregor, Louise Aoe Wong, 67
McKinley, William, 41
McKinley High School (Honolulu), 63, 171, 192
McKinley Tariff Bill of 1890, 34
McNaughton, Violet, 204
McRae, Doris, 202
Mead, George Herbert, 83
Mead, Helen Castle, 83
Mei, Anna Fo-Jin Kong, 171–76, 182, 202, 271n134, 272n136
Mei, H. C., 171–72
Mekata, Itsuko, 156
Mekata, Tanetaro, 156
Meyer v. Nebraska (1923), 133
Mid-Pacific Magazine, 108, 112, 114–15, 118, 191
Mills College, 2, 51
Mink, Patsy Matsu Takemoto, 207
miscegenation, 16, 22
Mission Memorial Hall (Honolulu), 68, 73
Mitchell, Janet, 146
MoFA. *See* Japan Ministry of Foreign Affairs

Morgan, John T., 47
Morgan, Julia, 92
Morgan, Rosamond Swanzy, 73, 76, 149, 153
Mori, Iga, 100, 125
Morris, Mary H., 155
Mount Holyoke College, 147, 184, 187

Nākuina, Emma Kaili Metcalf Beckley, 50, 60, 230n24
Nanjing (China), 175, 190, 202
Nanjing Incident (1927, China), 175
Naruse, Jinzo, 155
National American Woman Suffrage Association (NAWSA), 45–46, 53–55, 58, 60–61, 72; "Hawaiian Appeal" to Congress, 45
National Christian Council (China), 172
National Committee for Constructive Immigration Legislation (NCCIL, U.S.), 111–12, 172, 174
National Committee on the Cause and Cure of War (NCCCW, U.S.), 148, 196, 203
National Congress of Mothers and Parent-Teacher Association (PTA, U.S.), 82–83, 93, 128, 144, 164, 187–89, 239n13
National Consumers' League (NCL, U.S.), 144
National Council of Women (U.S.), 152
National Council of Women of China, 196
National Education Association (U.S.), 83; Hawai'i chapter, 118
National Federation of Primary School Teachers' Association (NFPSTA, Japan), 166, 186
National Kindergarten Association (U.S.), 83
National League of Teachers' Associations (U.S.), 128
National League of Women Voters (NLWV), 12, 72, 74–76, 93, 138, 144, 146–47, 149, 152, 176, 188–89, 191–93, 199–200

National Woman's Party (NWP, U.S.), 12, 72, 138, 146–47, 150, 164, 182, 188, 191–92
National Woman Suffrage Association (NWSA, U.S.), 46
National Women's Federation (NWF, Japan), 167
National Women's Suffrage Association of Hawai'i. See Women's Suffrage Association of Hawai'i (WSAH)
National Women's Trade Union League (NWTUL, U.S.), 144, 150, 152, 180, 192
nationality right, 68, 137–38, 182, 191–92. See also Cable Act
Nāwahī, Emma ʻAima Aiʻi, 42, 56
Nāwahī, Joseph, 30, 35, 42
NAWSA. See National American Woman Suffrage Association
NCCCW. See National Committee on the Cause and Cure of War
NCCIL. See National Committee for Constructive Immigration Legislation
NCL. See National Consumers' League
Newlands Resolution of 1898, 42, 45
New Life Movement (China), 198
New Women's Society (NWS, Japan), 160–61
New York University, 171
New Zealand, 3, 13, 112, 140, 167, 174, 181, 190, 204
NFPSTA. See National Federation of Primary School Teachers' Association
Nihon Fujin Heiwa Kyōkai. See Japan Women's Peace Association
Nihonjin Fujinkai. See Japanese Women's Society (JWS)
Nihonjin Jizenkai. See Japanese Benevolent Society (JBS)
Nihon Kokusai Kyōiku Kyōkai. See Japan International Education Association
Nineteenth Amendment (U.S.), 10, 64, 70, 120, 137

Nippu Jiji, 130, 132, 201
Nisei, 64, 92, 98, 107, 116, 123, 127, 131, 133–38, 166, 190
Nitobe, Inazō, 155–57
Nitobe, Mary Patterson Elkinton, 155–56
NLWV. *See* National League of Women Voters
Noda, Alice Sae Teshima, 68, 94, 153
Noggle, Stella Payne, 72
Normal School (Territory of Hawai'i), 118; admission policy, 136
North America Educational Commission to China, 188
NWF. *See* National Women's Federation
NWP. *See* National Woman's Party
NWS. *See* New Women's Society
NWSA. *See* National Woman Suffrage Association
NWTUL. *See* National Women's Trade Union League

O'ahu Strike of 1920, 107, 124, 131
Obama, Barack, 207
Oberlin College, 83
Ogata, Setsu, 151
opium, 30, 31, 169, 193; wars, 168
Organization of American States (OAS). *See* Pan-American Union (PAU)
Osterhout, Marian (Irwin), 99
Outdoor Circle (Hawai'i), 65
Outrigger Canoe Club (Hawai'i), 108, 113; Women's Auxiliary, 113, 140
Ozawa, Ito. *See* Imanishi, Ito(ko) (Ozawa)
Ozawa, Kintaro, 99
Ozawa, Tomi, 99
Ozawa v. United States (1922), 135

Pacheco, Manuel C., 62
Pacific Affairs, 150, 182, 192
Pacific Commercial Advertiser, 69, 108
Palama Japanese Language School, 133
Palama Settlement, 95, 239n18
Palmer, Albert W., 73, 124

Pan-American Association for the Advancement of Women, 147
Pan-American Union (PAU), 110, 147
Pan-Pacific and South East Asia Women's Association (PPSEAWA), 206
Pan-Pacific Association (PPA), 184; China, 168, 173, 175–76, 184; Japan, 137, 165
Pan-Pacific Club, 108, 165
Pan-Pacific Conference on Education, Rehabilitation, Reclamation, and Recreation (PPCERRR), 188
Pan-Pacific Educational Conference (1921), 104, 106, 112, 125–29, 132, 136, 138–40
Pan-Pacific Food Conservation Conference, 140
Pan-Pacific Medical Conference (1929), 141
Pan-Pacific Science Congress (1920), 112
Pan-Pacific Union (PPU), 11, 22, 104–108, 125, 128, 139, 166, 168, 173, 183–84, 195, 206; inception and Pan–Pacific aspiration, 108–12, 114, 147, 248n14; and Americanization, 115, 116, 118, 123, 125, 131, 133–34, 136; and women, 12, 107, 113, 116, 139–42, 150–51, 177, 184–85, 187, 195, 201
Pan-Pacific Women's Association (PPWA), 3, 6–7, 9, 12–13, 106, 141, 179, 183–84, 194–95, 203, 206; bylaws, 183, 201; constitution, 194
Pan-Pacific Women's Club, 141
Pan-Pacific Women's Conference (PPWC): in general, 6–7, 12, 52, 141, 143, 150, 166, 169, 179, 183, 186, 193, 195, 204; 1928 first PPWC, 2–4, 12, 105–106, 140–41, 143, 146–50, 152–54, 165–67, 175–79; 1928 Government Section, 181–82; 1928 Industrial Section, 180–81; 1930 second PPWC, 3, 12, 179, 185–95; 1934 third PPWC, 3, 195, 201; 1937 fourth PPWC, 3, 13, 195, 201; 1938 antilynching campaign 203; fifth PPWC, 13, 204

Parent-Teacher Association. *See*
  National Congress of Mothers and
  Parent-Teacher Association (PTA)
Paris Peace Conference, 109, 111, 169
Park, Alice Locke, 60–61, 65
Park, Maud Wood, 61, 72, 76
Parker, Valeria H., 152
Parsons, Alice, 189, 193
Patriotic Women's Association (Aikoku
  Fujinkai, Japan), 163
PAU. *See* Pan-American Union
Pauahi, Bernice (Princess), 19, 29
Peabody, Elizabeth, 81
Peace Preservation Law of 1925 (Chian
  Iji Hō, Japan), 154
Pearl Harbor, 32–33, 198
Perkins, Frances, 93, 195
Peterson, Agnes, 189
Philippines, 3, 43, 109–10, 112, 124
pidgin, 11, 50, 66, 85, 92, 106–107,
  117–18, 120–21
Pierce v. Society of Sisters (1925), 133
Pilahiuilani, Mary Kaumana, 51
Pitman, Almira Hollander, 60–61, 65
Pitman, Benjamin F. Keolaokalani, 60
Police Security Law of 1900 (Chian
  Keisatsu Hō, Japan), 154, 160;
  Amendment of 1922, 161; Article
  Five, 160–61
PPA. *See* Pan-Pacific Association (PPA)
PPCERRR. *See* Pan-Pacific Conference
  on Education, Rehabilitation,
  Reclamation, and Recreation
PPSEAWA. *See* Pan-Pacific and South
  East Asia Women's Association
PPU. *See* Pan-Pacific Union (PPU)
PPWA. *See* Pan-Pacific Women's
  Association
PPWC. *See* Pan-Pacific Women's
  Conference
Pratt, Elizabeth Keka'aniau La'anui
  (Princess), 50, 52
Prince Kūhiō. *See* Kalaniana'ole, Jonah
  Kūhiō
property rights, 18, 21–23, 33, 77, 120,
  193

PTA. *See* National Congress of
  Mothers and Parent-Teacher
  Association (PTA)
Punahou School (Hawai'i), 2, 51
Putnam, Alice Harvey Whiting, 82

Raker, John E., 61
Red Cross, 57–58, 74, 91
Red Scare, 144, 206
Reeve, Margaretta Willis, 187–89, 194
republican motherhood, 4, 18
Republican Revolution of 1911
  (China), 169
Republic of Hawai'i, 14–15, 36, 39–41,
  47, 63, 79, 100, 120
Robins, Margaret Dreier, 150–51
Rockefeller Fund, 170, 174
Rockefeller University, 99
Rooke, Thomas Charles Byde, 28
Roosevelt, Eleanor, 207
Roosevelt, Franklin Delano, 195
Royal School, 19, 29, 34, 52
Russell, Maud, 147, 197
Russell, Nellie R. (Mrs. James Russell), 93
Russo-Japanese War, 154, 161

SACJA. *See* Society of American
  Citizens of Japanese Ancestry
Sadakata, Kameyo, 190, 278n62
Salisbury, Helen, 90–91
Satterthwaite, Ann Yardley, 141, 150–53,
  187, 201, 259n151
Sawayanagi, Masataro, 166, 183
Schoff, Hanna Kent, 189
Scott, Marion McCarrell, 192
Seneca Falls Convention, 23
separate sphere strategy, 4, 16, 18, 82, 84,
  89, 97, 140–41, 145, 150, 176, 178–79,
  184–85, 187, 195, 205–206
Shafroth, John F., 61
Shanghai International Mixed Court,
  168, 172, 174
Shanghai International Settlement, 143,
  168, 170–72, 176–78, 184–85
Shanghai Municipal Council (SMC),
  168, 171–74

Shaw, Anna Howard, 57, 61
Sheppard-Towner Maternity and
   Infancy Act of 1921, 92–94, 144
Sherrod, Pearl B. (Mrs. Pearl Takasaki),
   203–204
Shibusawa, Eiichi, 126–27, 151, 156,
   158–59, 166
Shimoda, Utako, 163
Shinrinkan (Friendly Neighborhood
   Hall, Japan), 161–62
Shoda, Yoshiko, 164, 167, 180, 269n100
Shojokai (Maiden Association, Japan),
   166
Simms, Florence, 89
Sino-Japanese War: First (1894–1895),
   154, 169–70; Second (1937–1945),
   202
Sixth Point Group (British), 186
Smith, Addie Viola, 173, 175–76, 184
Smyth, Mabel Leilani, 95, 243n57
Sniffen, Helen Makakoa, 67, 70
So, Yeiko (Mizobe), 98, 102–103
Society of American Citizens of
   Japanese Ancestry (SACJA), 136
Soga, Yasutaro, 132, 201
Sohn, Nodie Kimhaikim, 190
Soong, Mei-ling (Mrs. Chiang Kai-shek),
   172, 198, 275n29
Spanish-American War of 1898, 42, 45
Spanish flu pandemic of 1919, 124
Spreckels, Claus, 30
Stadtmuller, Ellen Smith, 152
St. Andrew's Cathedral Church
   (Honolulu), 28, 231n40
Stanford University, 151
Stanley, Louise, 152, 189
Stevens, John L., 34
St. John's University (Shanghai), 176
St. Luke's International Hospital
   (Tokyo), 99–100, 190, 278n63
Stone, Edith, 74–75
St. Peter's Episcopal Church
   (Honolulu), 171
Strangers' Friend Society (Hawai'i), 36
Straub, George, 192
Straub, Gertrude Scott, 192–93, 200

Student Christian Movement, 165, 170
Student Volunteer Movement for
   Foreign Missions (SVM), 105,
   170–71
suffrage: China, 169, 196; Hawai'i to
   1898, 10, 22–23, 36–40; Hawai'i
   from 1898 to 1920, 10, 48, 51,
   53–57, 59–66, 117; Hawai'i after
   1920, 10, 66–67, 69–71, 73–76, 117,
   147; Hawai'i WCTU's suffrage
   committee, 36–38, 40; Hawai'i
   settler anxiety, 38, 44; international,
   8, 143, 147, 178, 181; Japan, 154, 161,
   163–65, 182; U.S. mainland, 8, 18, 23,
   31, 36, 44–46, 55, 58, 60–61, 64, 72,
   75, 148, 188
Sun Yat Sen, 109
Suzuki, Bunji, 158
SVM. *See* Student Volunteer Movement
   for Foreign Missions (SVM)
Swanzy, Francis Mills, 51–52
Swanzy, Julie Judd, 1–3, 8, 30, 51–52, 73,
   76, 87, 105, 113, 118, 120, 128, 133,
   139–40, 149, 153, 178, 187, 194, 201
Sweet, Georgina, 194, 201, 204

Taiwan, 154–55
Tanaka, Takako (Takanishi), 151,
   159–60
Tang, Mrs. Chindon Yui, 176, 273n153
Taylor, Emma Ahuena Davison,
   53, 58, 60, 73
Teachers' Training Committee (Kyōiku
   kōshu iinkai, Japan), 125
Teikoku kyōiku kai. *See* Imperial
   Education Society (IES, Japan),
   166, 183
territorial motherhood, 4, 11, 79–80, 85,
   92–93, 99, 103, 107, 118, 152
Teusler, Rudolf Bolling, 190, 278n63
TFWO. *See* Tokyo Federation of
   Women's Organizations
Thomas, Harriet Park, 83–84
Thomas, William I., 83
Thurston, Lorrin A., 33–34, 69–70, 108
Tianjin (China), 169, 176, 184

Ting, Me-Iung (Ding, Maoying), 176, 184, 194, 260n11, 275n29
Ting, Shu-ching, 201–202
Togo, Yasushi, 137
Tokugawa, Iyesato, 165
Tokyo Federation of Women's Organizations (TFWO, Japan), 162–63, 165–66
Tokyo Imperial University, 158
Tokyo Rengō Fujinkai. *See* Tokyo Federation of Women's Organizations
Tokyo Unitarian Church, 158–59
Tokyo University, 127
Tokyo Woman's Christian College (TWCC), 155
Tokyo Women's Medical College, 163, 165
Topping, Helen, 90
Toyota v. United States (1925), 136
Trask, Haunani-Kay, 207
Treaty of Versailles, 109
Tsing-Hua University (China), 191
Tsuda, Umeko, 155–57, 241n38
Tsuda Women's College, 99, 155–56, 163–65
TWCC. *See* Tokyo Woman's Christian College

unequal treaty, 154, 168, 170
UNESCO (UN Educational, Scientific and Cultural Organization), 156, 206
UNICEF (UN Children's Fund), 206
United States v. Wong Kim Ark (1898), 85
United War Work Campaign (UWWC), 57–58, 91
United Welfare Fund, 86, 131
Universal Declaration of Human Rights (1948), 207
University of California, 128
University of Chicago, 82–83, 101, 151
University of Hawai'i, 118, 136, 141, 191
University of Michigan, 170, 184, 190
University of Southern California, 126
U.S. 1924 Immigration Act, 191

U.S.-Hawai'i reciprocity treaty (1857, 1887), 29, 32–34
U.S. Congress, 34, 43–48, 60–61, 64, 71, 75, 93, 138, 144, 149, 192–93, 199–200
U.S. Department of the Interior Bureau of Education, 83, 114–15, 118–19
U.S. Food Administration, 58
U.S. Supreme Court, 85, 133, 135–36, 144, 188

Vancouver (Canada), 3, 13, 195, 202, 204
Vancouver News Herald, 203
Vasco Núñez de Balboa, 114
Vaughn, Horace, 136
Victoria (British Queen), 23, 28, 33, 35

Wald, Lillian D., 111
Washington Naval Conference, 161, 169
WBMI-Chicago. *See* Woman's Board of Missions of the Interior
WBMPI-Honolulu. *See* Woman's Board of Missions for the Pacific Islands
WCTU. *See* Woman's Christian Temperance Union
Webb, Elizabeth Lahilahi, 50, 63, 76, 153
WESAH. *See* Women's Equal Suffrage Association of Hawai'i
Westervelt, Caroline Dickinson Castle (Mrs. W. D. Westervelt), 147
Whang, Ha(i) Soo (Hwang Hae-su), 94, 153, 244n50
Whitney, Catherine, 23–24
Whitney, Henry, 26
Whitney, John Morgan, 32
Whitney, Mary Sophronia Rice, 32, 36, 38, 40
Widemann, Hermann A., 42, 51
Wilcox, Elsie Hart, 14, 96–97, 244n64
Wilcox, Robert William, 14, 34, 40, 48–49
Willard, Frances E., 31
WILPF. *See* Women's International League for Peace and Freedom
Wilson, John H., 68

Wilson, Woodrow, 57, 61, 109, 111–12, 115–16, 148
WJCC. *See* Women's Joint Congressional Committee
Wold, Emma, 192
Woman's Board of Missions of the Interior (WBMI-Chicago), 27, 101–102, 245n81
Woman's Board of Missions for the Pacific Islands (WBMPI-Honolulu), 26–27, 32, 36–37, 78–79, 99; Free Kindergarten Department, 78
Woman's Christian Temperance Union, 31–32, 36, 81, 93, 98, 102, 144, 147, 164, 192; China WCTU, 196; Hawai'i WCTU, 32–33, 36–38, 40, 147; Japan WCTU, 102–103, 156, 161–65, 196–97; National WCTU, 147, 192; Territory of Hawai'i WCTU, 103, 147; Woman Suffrage Committee (Hawai'i), 36; World WCTU, 31, 103, 147, 157, 161, 169
Woman's Peace Party, 58, 148
Woman Suffrage Association of Hawai'i (WSAH), 53–55, 73
Women's Bureau (U.S.), 92–93, 145, 150, 152, 180, 189
Women's Congress at the Hague (1915), 156
Women's Equal Suffrage Association of Hawai'i (WESAH), 53–54, 74, 233n72
Women's Hawaiian Patriotic League [Hui Hawai'i Aloha 'Aina o Na Wahine], 35, 42, 51, 56
Women's International League for Peace and Freedom (WILPF), 99, 144, 147, 156–57, 178, 192; Japan WILPF, 156, 165
Women's Joint Congressional Committee (WJCC), 93, 144, 146
Women's Labor Commission (Japan), 164
Women's Republican Auxiliary Club (WRAC), 73–74
Women's Suffrage Association of Hawai'i (WSAH), 53–55, 73

Women's Suffrage League (WSL, Japan), 53, 163, 182
Women's Trade Union League (WTUL), 93
Woolley, Mary Emma, 147, 149, 187–88, 277n51
World Christian Citizenship Conference, 112
World Commission on Immigration, 112
World Parliament of Religions (1893), 105
World Student Christian Federation (WSCF), 105, 165
World War I, 9–11, 44, 57, 87, 89, 91–94, 105–11, 113–15, 124, 126, 135–36, 142, 144, 148, 152, 154, 161, 169, 171
World War II, 3, 12–13, 166, 195, 204
WRAC. *See* Women's Republican Auxiliary Club
WSAH. *See* Women's Suffrage Association of Hawai'i (WSAH)
WSCF. *See* World Student Christian Federation
WSL. *See* Women's Suffrage League
WTUL. *See* Women's Trade Union League

Xiang, Jingyu, 175

Yada, Chiyoko, 123, 125, 167
Yada, Chonosuke, 124–25, 127, 135
Yajima, Kajiko, 161
Yale University, 141
Yamada, Mrs. M. of Pepeekeo Japanese Language School, 133
Yamada, Waka, 167
Yamaguchi, Toshiko, 190
Yamakawa, Kikue, 163, 167
Yamasaki, Keiichi, 132
Yap, Ruth L. T., 191
YMCA. *See* Young Men's Christian Association
Yorihito, (Japanese Prince), 30
Yosano, Akiko, 167
Yoshioka, Yayoi, 163, 165
Young, Grace Kama'iku'i, 28
Young, John, 28

Young Men's Christian Association, 57, 90, 96, 105–109, 112, 125–26, 137, 139, 164, 170–72, 174–75, 186, 190; pan-Pacific conferences, 106, 139

Young Women's Christian Association, 57, 81, 89, 91, 93, 96, 98, 105, 139, 144–46, 160–61, 164, 170, 174–75, 178; Australian YWCA, 194; Blue Triangle Houses (U.S.), 91; Champéry Switzerland meeting (World), 145; China YWCA, 147, 172, 174–75, 196–97, 202; Honolulu YWCA, 58, 79, 90–92, 94, 96, 102, 138–40, 153, 194; Hostess Houses (U.S.), 91; immigrant work and expanding national networks, 90; industrial work (U.S.), 89, 96; industrial work (World), 145, 162; International Institute (Honolulu), 92, 95–96, 102–103, 153; International Institute (U.S.), 80, 89–90, 94; Japan YWCA, 156–57, 160–62, 164–65, 167, 174, 186, 201–202; Kaua'i YWCA, 96; Korea YWCA, 147, 174; Melbourne YWCA, 146; National YWCA (U.S.), 89–96, 139, 152–53, 159, 192; Training School (U.S.), 164; Pacific Coast Field (U.S.), 90, 139; Pan-Pacific YWCA Conference, 139; Patriotic League/Girl's Reserve (Honolulu), 91; San Francisco Japanese YWCA, 90; Shanghai Chinese YWCA, 171, 174, 176; Tokyo YWCA, 99, 156, 164; Traveler's Aid, 91; World YWCA, 145, 147, 156, 162, 164, 169, 171–74, 185, 187, 197

Yūaikai (Friendly Society, 1912–1919), 158–59; Sōdōmei-Yūaikai (Dai-Nihon Rōdō Sōdōmei-Yūaikai, 1919–1921), 159–61; Sōdōmei (Nihon Rōdō Sōdōmei, 1921–1940), 164

YWCA. *See* Young Women's Christian Association

Zenkoku Fujin Dōmei. *See* National Women's Federation (NWF, Japan)
Zen, Way Koh (Zung Wei Koh), 190, 277n61

GPSR Authorized Representative: Easy Access System Europe, Mustamäe tee 50, 10621 Tallinn, Estonia, gpsr.requests@easproject.com

www.ingramcontent.com/pod-product-compliance
Lightning Source LLC
Chambersburg PA
CBHW022032290426
44109CB00014B/840